OLD LANDMARKS AND HISTORIC PERSONAGES OF BOSTON

BOOKS BY SAMUEL ADAMS DRAKE

A BOOK OF NEW ENGLAND LEGENDS AND FOLK LORE

HISTORIC MANSIONS AND HIGHWAYS AROUND BOSTON

OLD LANDMARKS AND HISTORIC PERSONAGES OF BOSTON

Boston in 1830, from City Point, Windmill Point in Foreground.

OLD LANDMARKS AND HISTORIC PERSONAGES OF BOSTON

by SAMUEL ADAMS DRAKE

"I love everything that's old: old friends, old times, old manners, old books, old wines."—GOLDSMITH

REVISED EDITION

with Numerous Illustrations

CHARLES E. TUTTLE COMPANY
Rutland, Vermont

Representatives
Continental Europe: BOXERBOOKS, INC., *Zurich*
British Isles: PRENTICE-HALL INTERNATIONAL, INC., *London*
Australasia: BOOK WISE (AUSTRALIA) PTY. LTD.
104-108 Sussex Street, Sydney 2000

Published by the Charles E. Tuttle Company, Inc.
of Rutland, Vermont & Tokyo, Japan
with editorial offices at Suido 1-chome, 2–6
Bunkyo-ku, Tokyo, Japan

Library of Congress Catalog Card No. 70-157258

International Standard Book No. 0-8048-0993-3

First edition published 1872
Revised edition published 1906
by Little, Brown, and Company, Boston
First Tuttle edition published 1971
Fourth printing, 1986

PRINTED IN JAPAN

TABLE OF CONTENTS

CHAPTER II.

FROM THE ORANGE-TREE TO THE OLD BRICK.

CHAPTER III.

FROM THE OLD STATE HOUSE TO BOSTON PIER.

CHAPTER IV.

BRATTLE SQUARE AND THE TOWN DOCK.

CHAPTER V.

FROM BOSTON STONE TO THE NORTH BATTERY.

CHAPTER VI.

A VISIT TO THE OLD SHIPYARDS.

CHAPTER VII.

COPP'S HILL AND THE VICINITY.

CHAPTER VIII.

THE OLD SOUTH AND PROVINCE HOUSE.

CHAPTER IX.

FROM THE OLD SOUTH ROUND FORT HILL.

CHAPTER X.

A TOUR ROUND THE COMMON.

CHAPTER XI.

A TOUR ROUND THE COMMON CONTINUED.

CHAPTER XII.

VALLEY ACRE, THE BOWLING GREEN, AND WEST BOSTON.

CHAPTER XIII.

FROM CHURCH GREEN TO LIBERTY TREE.

CHAPTER XIV.

LIBERTY TREE AND THE NEIGHBORHOOD.

CHAPTER XV.

THE NECK AND THE FORTIFICATIONS.

LIST OF ILLUSTRATIONS

FULL-PAGE ILLUSTRATIONS

ILLUSTRATIONS IN THE TEXT

PUBLISHER'S FOREWORD TO THE NEW EDITION

NO other city in America has as many historically famous landmarks as Boston, which is known variously as the Hub and the Athens of America. The same can be said about historic personages, names which strike stirring and nostalgic chords in the memory—for example, Standish, Otis, Webster, Faneuil, Revere, Mather, Beecher, Coffin, and Emerson.

This monumental work, originally published almost one hundred years ago and revised in 1900, lists hundreds of famous persons and places, giving posterity an imperishable record. Samuel Adams Drake probably knew Boston and vicinity better than any other social historian of his or any time. Thus he wrote with an accuracy and authority little short of amazing. His books—really labors of love—required decades of diligent and demanding research and preparation—evident in the end products, which were received with the wide acclaim befitting work of this stature.

He painted his word pictures on an unusually wide canvas, as will be seen in the biographical sketch below, but New England always claimed his greatest attention. It was in this general arena that the colonial stripling suddenly sprang erect, a David planting a blow full on the front of Old England, the insular Goliath—a blow that made the giant reel with the shock. It was here that the people of the "Old Thirteen" first acted together as one nation, and here the separate streams of their existence united into one mighty flood: America.

Samuel Adams Drake was born in Boston on December 20, 1833. His father, Samuel Gardner Drake, established in that city in 1828 one of the first antiquarian bookstores in the United States. A large portion of his stock consisted of books relating to the early history of this country. His brother, Francis Samuel Drake, a writer prominent in literary circles, influenced young Samuel in delving into early New England legend and folk lore.

Upon finishing his education in the public schools of Boston, young Samuel became interested in newspaper work and decided to make journalism his career. In 1858 he went to Kansas (his brother had an antiquarian bookshop in Leavenworth) as telegraphic agent of the New York Associated Press. Later he became a regular correspondent of the *St. Louis Republican* and the *Louisville Journal* and for a while edited the *Leavenworth Times*. His first work published under his own name was a pamphlet entitled *Hints to Emigrants to Pike's Peak*.

Soon after the outbreak of the Civil War, the Kansas State Militia was organized. Drake became adjutant general of the Northern Division and late in 1861 was captain of militia in the Union Army. He rose to the rank of brigadier general of the militia in 1863, and in 1864 he commanded the post at Paola, Kansas, during Price's invasion of Missouri.

Upon retirement from military service in 1871, Drake returned to Massachusetts and resumed work in the literary field. In 1872 he published the present work, *Old Landmarks and Historic Personages of Boston* and, in 1873, *Historic Mansions and Highways Around Boston* (now available in the Tut Book series). *Nooks and Corners of the New England Coast* and *Bunker Hill* were published in 1875.

Drake's later publications include *Around the Hub*, 1881; *Heart of the White Mountains*, 1881; *A Book of New England Legends and Folk Lore* (now available in the Tut Book series), 1884; *Our Great Benefactors*, 1885; *The Making of New England*, 1886; *The Making of the Great West*, 1887; *Burgoyne's Invasion*, 1889; *The Taking of Louisburg*, 1891; *The Pine Tree Coast*, 1891; *The Battle of Gettysburg*, 1892; *The Making of Virginia*, 1893; *Our Colonial Homes*, 1894; *The Campaign of Trenton*, 1895; *The Watch Fires of '76*, 1895; *On Plymouth Rock*, 1898; *The Myths and Fables of Today*, 1900; and *The Young Vigilantes*, 1904.

Possessed of a remarkable memory, Drake delighted in constructively criticizing the efforts of many contemporary self-styled historians, whom he classified as "textbook hacks." He lived a full life, enjoying the fruits of his labor and glorying in the progress of the American people. He died at Kennebunkport, Maine, in his seventy-second year, beloved by New Englanders, Southerners, and Westerners alike and enshrined in the hearts of the "proper Bostonians," who took great pleasure in reading his literary efforts pertaining to the early history of New England.

BETWEEN OURSELVES.

"Boast, Harry, that you are a true-born child, and that you are a true Bostonian." — *Colonel Jackson to General Knox in* 1777.

MORE perhaps than the natives of any American city Bostonians have the feeling of "inhabitiveness and adhesiveness" abnormally developed. In whatever part of the world you may meet with him you can tell a Bostonian a mile off. But aside from the peculiar charm surrounding one's birthplace, common to all men, the Bostonian knows that his own is pre-eminently the historic city of America, and he feels that no small part of its world-wide renown has descended to him as his peculiar inheritance.

That is all very well. But it is one thing to be proud of our history and to boast of it on all occasions, and quite another to remain indifferent to the threatened spoliation of what we lay claim to as our inalienable inheritance, our birthright. I mean the really historic buildings of Boston and what they stand for. This book is my appeal to the historical conscience. It is only at the price of perpetual vigilance that a few of these old edifices, known throughout the whole world, remain on their foundations at this hour.

Boston would be a barren place indeed without its Faneuil Hall, its Old State House, Old South and Old

North. It is to be hoped that we shall not soon repeat the inexcusable folly of the Hancock House.

The frequent and capricious changing of street names is another rock of danger, besides being a source of endless confusion and annoyance to historians and property-owners alike. Mr. Lowell said truly that "we change our names as often as we can, to the great detriment of all historical association."

Boston to-day is hardly more like the Boston of fifty years ago than a new growth resembles that which has replaced the original forest, after fire has swept over it. It then had a good deal of the "Indian-summer atmosphere of the past." What it will be like fifty years hence no man can say. In a hundred, of the old city perhaps not one stone will remain upon another. In truth, such surprising physical transformation as has been brought about, even within the last thirty years, by the Great Fire, the levelling of Fort Hill, the filling up of the Back Bay, the extension of Washington Street, and the improvements incident to the building of the great railway stations and Subway, strongly emphasizes the fact that in the very nature of things, nothing is, nothing can be permanent save the written record. Like every great city Boston is forever out-growing its old garments, and must be patched and pieced accordingly.

But it is in the heart of the old city that we remark the greatest havoc. Scores of old buildings, rich in historical association, have given place to modern structures. Of a dozen ancient churches, not one now remains on its original site. The last remnants too of their congregations have silently emigrated to that newer region, where boys were wont to sail their boats in summer, and fishermen to catch smelts in winter. Moreover, a new generation has come upon the stage to whom the old conditions are unknown and hard to realize.

To re-establish these conditions by present landmarks, so that it may continue to be a faithful guide to what is best worth seeing, as well as what is most worth remembering, in older Boston, a careful and thorough revision of OLD LANDMARKS has been made and many new features introduced. No pains have been spared to make it a work of permanent value and interest. And as it was originally undertaken as a labor of love, so now, in its revised form, the book again is sent forth, in the spirit of the motto with which this Preface begins, with a hearty greeting to all true Bostonians and to all others, wherever born, who shall derive from the story of a great Past hope and inspiration for a still greater Future.

AUGUST, 1900.

INTRODUCTION.

Myles Standish. — William Blackstone. — Shawmut. — Settlement by Winthrop's Company. — Trimountain. — Boston. — Physical Features. — Area. — Settlement by Indians. — Character of first Buildings. — First Location of the Settlers. — Geographical Divisions. — Wood and Water. — Dress. — Manners and Customs. — Slavery. — Curious old Laws. — Government of the Town. — Allotment of Lands. — Intolerance of the Times. — The Pulpit a Means of Intelligence. — Accounts by various Writers. — Town Records. — General Growth and Progress. — Population. — Wards. — Paving the Streets. — Lighting the Streets. — Supply of Water. — Enlargement of Boston. — Communication with Mainland. — Ferries. — Bridges. — Coaches, public and private. — Railways.

AN old Boston divine says, "It would be no unprofitable thing for you to pass over the several streets and call to mind who lived here so many years ago." We learn from the poet Gay how to prepare for our rambles through the town: —

> "How to walk clean by day, and safe by night;
> How jostling crowds with prudence to decline,
> When to assert the wall and when resign."

To see or not to see is the problem presented to him who walks the streets of town or village. What to one is a heap of ruins or a blank wall may to another become the abode of the greatest of our ancestors or the key to a remote period. A mound of earth becomes a battlement; a graveyard, a collection of scattered pages whereon we read the history of the times.

Facts are proverbially dry, and we shall trouble the reader as little as possible with musty records or tedious chronology;

but before we set out to explore and reconstruct, a brief glance at the material progress of Boston seems desirable.

For a hundred years Boston must be considered as little more than a sea-shore village, straggling up its thicket-grown hillsides. The Indian camp-fire, the axe of Blackstone, the mattock and spade of Winthrop's band, — each have their story and their lesson. We shall pass each period in rapid review.

Whether Myles Standish, "broad in the shoulders, deep-chested, with muscles and sinews of iron," was the first white man who stood on the beach of the peninsula is a matter merely of conjecture. Certain it is that in 1621 this redoubtable Puritan soldier, with ten companions, sailed from Plymouth and landed somewhere in what is now Boston Bay. They crossed the bay, "which is very large, and hath at least fifty islands in it"; and, after exploring the shores, decided "that better harbors for shipping there cannot be than here." They landed, hobnobbed with Obbatinewat, lord of the soil, feasted upon lobsters and boiled codfish, and departed, leaving no visible traces for us to pursue. This expedition was undertaken to secure the friendship of the "Massachusetts" Indians, — a result fully accomplished by Standish.

The Indians told the Englishmen that two large rivers flowed into the bay, of which, however, they saw but one. This circumstance, indefinite as it is, justifies the opinion that Standish's party landed at Shawmut, the Indian name for our peninsula. If they had landed at Charlestown and ascended the heights there, as is supposed by some writers, they could hardly have escaped seeing both the Mystic and Charles, while at Shawmut they would probably have seen only the latter river.

In William Blackstone, Episcopalian, we have the first white settler of the peninsula. The date of his settlement has been supposed to have been about 1626, although there is nothing conclusive on this point known to the writer. Here he was, however, in 1628, when we find him taxed by the Plymouth Colony twelve shillings, on account of the expenses incurred by the colony in the capture of Thomas Morton at Mount Wollaston.

The place where Blackstone located his dwelling has given rise to much controversy, but can be fixed with some degree of certainty. Like a sensible man, Blackstone chose the sunny southwest slope of Beacon Hill for his residence. The records show that in April, 1633, "it is agreed that William Blackstone shall have fifty acres set out for him near his house in Boston to enjoy forever." In the following year Blackstone sold the town all of his allotment except six acres, on part of which his house then stood; the sale also including all his right in and to the peninsula, — a right thus, in some form, recognized by Winthrop and his associates. The price paid for the whole peninsula of Boston was £ 30, assessed upon the inhabitants of the town, some paying six shillings, and some more, according to their circumstances and condition.

TRIMOUNTAIN.

The Charlestown records locate Blackstone as "dwelling on the other side of Charles River, alone, to a place by the Indians called Shawmut,* where he only had a cottage at a place not far off the place called Blackstone's Point"; this is also confirmed by Johnson, in his "Wonder Working Providence" printed in 1654. After the purchase by the town of Blackstone's forty-four acres, they laid out the "training field, which was ever since used for that purpose and the feeding of cattle." This was the origin of Boston Common. Two landmarks existed to fix the site of Blackstone's house, namely, the orchard planted by him, — the first in New England, — and his spring. The orchard is represented on the early maps; is mentioned in 1765 as still bearing fruit; and is named in the deeds of sub-

* Perhaps an abbreviation of "Mushauwomuk," as given in Grindal Rawson's "Confessions of Faith," printed in 1699. Probably meaning unclaimed land.

sequent possessors. The spring, which must have determined to some extent the location of the house, was probably near the junction of Beacon Street with Charles, although others existed in the neighborhood. The six acres which Mr. Blackstone reserved have been traced through Richard Pepys, an original possessor by a sufficiently clear connection,—supplied where broken by depositions,—to the Mount Vernon proprietors. Copley, the celebrated painter, was once an owner of Blackstone's six acres, which were bounded by the Common on the south and the river on the west.

Blackstone was as singular a character as can be found in the annals of Boston. He is supposed to have come over with Robert Gorges in 1623. But what induced him to withdraw to such a distance from the settlements remains a mystery. By a coincidence, his namesake, Sir William Blackstone, the great commentator of the laws of England, wrote at a later period the following lines:—

> "As by some tyrant's stern command,
> A wretch forsakes his native land,
> In foreign climes condemned to roam,
> An endless exile from his home."

The nature of Blackstone's claim to the peninsula is doubtful, though we have seen it recognized by Winthrop's company. Mather grumblingly alludes to it thus in his Magnalia: "There were also some godly Episcopalians; among whom has been reckoned Mr. Blackstone; who, by happening to sleep first in an old hovel upon a point of land there, laid claim to all the ground whereupon there now stands the Metropolis of the whole English America, until the inhabitants gave him satisfaction." This concedes only a squatter's title to Blackstone. He seems to have had a kind heart, capable of feeling for the sufferings of his fellow-men, for, hearing of the vicissitudes of Winthrop's infant settlement at Charlestown by disease and death, he invited them over to Shawmut in 1630. Water, the great desideratum of a settlement, was very scarce at Charlestown, and Blackstone "came and acquainted the Governor of an excellent spring there, withal inviting him and soliciting him thither." If seclusion was Blackstone's object, it gave way to his interest in the welfare of his fellow-colonists.

Upon Blackstone's advice the Charlestown settlers acted, and many removed to Shawmut by the end of August, 1630. In the first boat-load that went over was Anne Pollard, who lived to be nearly, if not quite, one hundred and five years old. She herself related, when more than one hundred years of age, that she "came over in one of the first ships that arrived in Charlestown; that in a day or two after her arrival, on account of the water there being bad, a number of the young people, including herself, took the ship's boat to cross over to Boston; that as the boat drew up towards the shore, she (being then a romping girl) declared she would be the first to land, and accordingly, before any one, jumped from the bow of the boat on to the beach." According to this statement, which is based upon good authority, Anne Pollard was the first white female that trod upon the soil of Boston. Hudson's Point, now the head of Charlestown bridge, but formerly the site of the old ferry, was probably the place where Anne first left the impress of her foot. Her portrait, at the age of one hundred and three years, is in the possession of the Massachusetts Historical Society, and her deposition, at the age of eighty-nine years, was used to substantiate the location of Blackstone's house. In it she says that Mr. Blackstone, after his removal from Boston, frequently resorted to her husband's house, and that she never heard any controversy about the land, between her husband, Pepys, or Blackstone, but that it was always reputed to belong to the latter.

Blackstone, in 1634, removed to Rehoboth, not liking, we may conclude, the close proximity of his Puritan neighbors, of whom he is reported to have said, that he left England because of his dislike to the Lords Bishops, but now he would not be under the Lords Brethren.

In 1659 Blackstone was married to Mary Stevenson of Boston, widow, by Governor Endicott. He died in 1675, a short time before the breaking out of King Philip's War, during which his plantation was ravaged by the Indians, and his dwelling destroyed, with his papers and books, — a circumstance that has prevented, perhaps, the veil being lifted that shrouds his early history. It is said no trace of his grave exists; but he left his name to a noble river, and the city which he founded perpetuates it by a public square and street.

The settlers at Charlestown called Shawmut Trimountain, not, says Shaw, on account of the three principal hills, — subsequently Copp's, Beacon, and Fort, — but from the three peaks of Beacon Hill, which was then considered quite a high mountain, and is so spoken of by Wood, one of the early writers about Boston; the reader will know that Beacon and its two outlying spurs of Cotton (Pemberton) and Mt. Vernon are meant.

On the 7th of September, 1630 (old style), at a court held in Charlestown, it was ordered that Trimountain be called Boston. Many of the settlers had already taken up their residence there, and "thither the frame of the governor's house was carried, and people began to build their houses against winter." Clinging to the old associations of their native land, the settlers named their new home for old Boston in Lincolnshire, England, whence a number of members of the company had emigrated. The name itself owes its origin to Botolph, a pious old Saxon of the seventh century, afterwards canonized as the tutelar saint of mariners, and shows an ingenuity of corruption for which England is famed. Reciprocal courtesies have been exchanged between English Boston and her namesake. The former presented her

ST. BOTOLPH'S, BOSTON, ENGLAND.

charter in a frame of the wood of old Saint Botolph's church, which hangs in our City Hall, while Edward Everett, in the name of the descendants and admirers of John Cotton, gave $ 2,000 for the restoration of a chapel in St. Botolph's, and the erection therein of a monument to the memory of that much venerated divine, who had been vicar of St. Botolph's and afterwards minister of the First Church of Christ in Boston, New England.

Boston had three striking topographical features. First, its peninsular character, united by a narrow isthmus to the main land ; next, its three hills, of which the most westerly (Beacon) was the highest, all washed at their base by the sea ; and lastly, corresponding to her hills, were three coves, of which the most easterly, enclosed by the headlands of Copp's and Fort Hill, became the Town Cove and Dock. Of the other coves, the one lying to the south of the Town Cove was embraced between the point of land near the foot of South Street, formerly known as Windmill Point, and the head of the bridge to South Boston ; this bight of water was the South Cove. A third inlet on the northwest of the peninsula, lying between the two points of land from which now extend bridges to Charlestown and East Cambridge, became subsequently the Mill Pond, by the building of a causeway on substantially the present line of Causeway Street. Only the most salient features are here given ; other interesting peculiarities will be alluded to in their places.

At high tides the sea swept across the narrow neck, and there is every reason to believe also covered the low ground now traversed by Blackstone Street. This would make, for the time being, two islands of Boston. The early names given to the streets on the water front described the sea-margin, as Fore (North) Beach, and Back (now Salem) Streets.

In process of time these distinctive characteristics have all changed. Boston can no longer be called a peninsula ; one of its summits, Fort Hill, has to-day no existence, while the others have been so shorn of their proportions and altitude as to present a very different view from any quarter of approach ; as for the three coves, they have been converted into *terra firma*.

The area of original Boston has been variously estimated. By Shaw, at 700 acres; Dr. Morse, the geographer, placed it in 1800 at 700 acres, admitting that some accounts fix it as high as 1,000 acres, while Dr. Shurtleff says less than 1,000 acres.

There is good authority, however, for computing the original peninsula at not more than 625 acres of firm ground. To this has been added, by the filling of the Mill Pond, 50 acres; the South Cove, 75 acres (up to 1837); and by the filling of the Town Cove or Dock, and the building of new streets on the water front, enough had been reclaimed by 1852 to amount to 600 acres, — nearly the original area. Since that time the Back Bay improvement, which covers 680 acres, and Atlantic Avenue, which follows the old Barricado line, have added as much more to the ancient territory, so that we may safely consider her original limits trebled, without reference to what has been acquired by annexation.

At the time of the English settlement hostilities existed between the Massachusetts and the eastern Indians; the natives, who seldom neglected to provide for retreat in case of defeat, chose rather to locate their villages farther inland, at Mystic and elsewhere.

INDIAN WIGWAM.

There is evidence, however, that Shawmut was either inhabited by the Indians at a very early period, or used as a place of sepulture by them. Dr. Mather related that three hundred skull-bones had been dug up on Cotton (Pemberton) Hill when he was a youth, and tradition long ascribed to this locality a sort of Golgotha. To support this view there was found in April 1733, says the New England Journal, a number of skulls and larger human bones by workmen digging in a garden near Dr. Cooper's house on Cotton Hill. These remains were considered, at the time, to be those of the natives. Boston has been thoroughly excavated without finding any further material to confirm this belief.

The character of the first buildings was extremely rude. They were of wood, with thatched roofs, and chimneys built of pieces of wood placed crosswise, the interstices and outside covered with clay. Such was the economy of the times, that Governor Winthrop reproved his deputy, in 1632, "that he did not well to bestow so much cost about wainscotting and adorning his house in the beginning of a plantation, both in regard of the public charges, and for example." The answer was, that it was for the warmth of his house, and the charge was little, being but clapboards nailed to the walls in the form of wainscot.*

It is comparatively recent that Boston began to be a city of brick and stone. A few solidly built structures were scattered here and there over a wide area; but the mass were of wood, in spite of some attempts made by the town to induce a safer and more durable style of architecture. A lady, entering Boston in 1795, remarks: "The ranges of wooden buildings all situated with one end towards the street, and the numerous chaises we met, drawn by one horse, the driver being placed on a low seat in front, appeared to me very singular." Another writer observes of the town in 1805: "The houses were most of them wood, seldom enlivened by paint, and closely resembling the old-fashioned, dark-looking edifices still to be seen in Newport, R. I." At this time there was but one brick house in the whole of Tremont Street, and it was not until 1793 that the first block of brick buildings was erected in what is now Franklin Street. In 1803 the inflammable character of the town was thus described by Winthrop Sargent:—

> "A pyre of shapeless structures crowds the spot,
> Where taste, and all but cheapness is forgot.
> One little spark the funeral pile may fire,
> And Boston, blazing, see itself expire."

* Winthrop's Journal, p. 88.

Winthrop's company located chiefly within the space comprised between what are now Milk, Bromfield, Tremont, and Hanover Streets and the water. Pemberton Hill was also a favorite locality, as we shall have occasion to note. The North End, by removals and accessions, soon became also settled; that portion of the town lying north of Union Street being thus designated, while all south of that boundary was called the South End. A third geographical division, embracing the district lying to the west and north of Beacon Hill, and west and south of the Mill Pond, was known as New Boston, and also as West Boston, and finally as the West End. These names have been retained, but the boundaries of all but the North End have been considered movable, and would be difficult to follow.

The first settlers found Boston thinly wooded, whatever its original condition may have been. The timber lay mainly along the Neck, with clumps of trees here and there. The great elm on the Common was doubtless one of native growth, and before the Revolution of 1776 there was another almost equally large near the corner of what is now West and Tremont Streets. Traditions exist of the Indians having planted on the peninsula, clearing away the wood, as is their custom, by burning. There are old houses now standing at the North End, the timbers of which, some of them a foot square, are said to have been cut near Copp's Hill.

Water was abundant and good. Besides the spring or springs near Blackstone's house, mention is made in the early records of the "great spring" in what is now Spring Lane. The latter was filled up, but people now living have seen it bubbling out of the ground after heavy spring rains. Opinions are divided as to which spring Blackstone had reference, when he invited the thirsty Charlestown company to Shawmut, but the fact of so many people having located by the site of the "great spring," and Isaac Johnson in the immediate vicinity, is convincing. Other springs existed, or were found in course of time on the Neck and elsewhere.

The settlement of Boston opens in the reign of Charles the

First, and the dress, as well as the manners and customs of the people bear the impress of that time, with the distinction, that the religious sentiments of the settlers entered largely into both questions. The short cloak, doublet, and silk stockings were worn by people of condition, but the colors were subdued and sober, and the rapier, which King Charles's gallants were so ready to draw, was not much worn abroad, except on state occasions. Some, like Winthrop, wore the stiff, plaited ruff, containing a furlong of linen, and making the modern beholder sympathize with the pillory the unfortunate head is placed in, while others wore the broad falling collar in which we always see the great Protector. High-crowned felt hats were worn out of doors, while the velvet skull-cap was the favorite headdress within.

CAVALIER.

Myles Standish, whom we single out as a type of the Puritan soldier of those days, is described by Longfellow as "clad in doublet and hose, with boots of Cordovan leather"; glancing complacently at his arms on the wall, "cutlass and corslet of steel, and his trusty sword of Damascus," with its curved point and Arabic inscription. The manner of wearing the hair became very early an apple of discord. Those of the straitest sect, and it may be of the straightest hair, cut their locks in the short fashion of the roundheads ; while others, to whom nature had, perhaps, been more lavish in this respect, wore their hair long. The wearing of veils by ladies when abroad was the subject of a crusade by Rev. John Cotton, though championed by Endicott.

In 1750 cocked-hats, wigs, and red cloaks were usually worn by gentlemen. Except among military men, boots were rarely seen. In winter, round coats were worn, made stiff with buckram, and coming down to the knees in front. Boys wore wigs and cocked-hats until about 1790. Powder was worn by gentlemen until after 1800.

The toilets of ladies were elaborate, especially the hair, which was arranged on crape cushions so as to stand up high. Sometimes ladies were dressed the day before a party, and slept in easy-chairs to keep their hair in condition. Hoops were indispensable in full dress until after 1790. The usual dinner hour was two o'clock. Drinking punch in the forenoon, in public houses, was the common practice. Wine was little used, convivial parties drinking punch or toddy.

The bearing of the townspeople in public was grave and austere. How could it be otherwise under the operation of such ordinances as the following. "No strangers were permitted to live within the town without giving bonds to save the town harmless from all damage and charge for entertaining them." "For galloping through the streets, except upon days of military exercise or any extraordinary case require," was two shillings fine. Football was prohibited in the streets. "No person shall take any tobacco publicly, under penalty of one shilling." "For entertaining foreigners," or receiving "inmates, servants, or journeymen coming for help in physic or surgery, without leave of the selectmen," was twenty shillings fine a week. The selectmen had authority, under the colony, to order parents to bind their children as apprentices, or put them out to service, and, if they refused, the town took the children from the charge of the parents.

Sobriety was strictly inculcated, though the sale of liquors was licensed. It is on record that, September 15, 1641, there was a training of twelve hundred men at Boston for two days, but no one was drunk, and no one swore. Officers were appointed, with long wands, to correct the inattentive or slumbering at church. To be absent from meeting was unlawful, while to speak ill of the minister was to incur severe punishment. An instance is mentioned of a man being fined for kissing his wife in his own grounds; and do not the following instructions to the watch smack strongly of Dogberry's famous charge? The number being eight, they are "to walk two by two together; a youth joined with an older and more sober person." "If after ten o'clock they see lights, to inquire if there be warrantable cause; and if they hear any noise or disorder, wisely to demand the reason; if they are dancing and singing vainly, to admonish them to cease; if they do not discontinue, after moderate admonition, then the constable to take their names and acquaint the authorities therewith." "If they find young men and maidens, not of known fidelity, walking after ten o'clock, modestly to demand the cause; and if they appear ill-minded, to watch them narrowly, command them to go to their lodgings, and if they refuse, then to secure them till morning."

Negro slavery appears in Boston as early as 1638, when at least three slaves were held by Maverick on Noddle's Island. In this year the ship Desire brought negroes here from the West Indies. In 1680, according to Judge Sewall, there were not above two hundred African slaves in the colony. An effort is on record in 1702 to put a stop to holding blacks as slaves, and to encourage the use of white servants, the representatives of the town being instructed to this purpose. Slavery seems, however, to have steadily increased in the colony, the traffic proving profitable, until at length it was as common to see negroes offered for sale in the public prints, as it ever was in the Southern colonies. In 1767 the town again moved, through its representatives for the abolition of slavery, to no effect. A Tory writer asserts that there were at this time two thousand slaves in Boston. During the troubles of 1768 the British officers were charged with inciting the slaves to insurrection, and blacks were held in servitude until after the Revolution.

But this was not all. It is but little known that white slavery was tolerated in the colony, and that the miserable dependents of feudal power were sold into servitude in England and transported to this country. Prisoners of war were thus disposed of under the great Cromwell, some of the captives of Dunbar having been shipped over seas to America. A shipload of Scotch prisoners was consigned 1651 to Thomas Kemble of Charlestown, the same who was afterwards a resident of Boston. They were generally sold for a specific term of service, and used chiefly as farm laborers. Many were sent to North Carolina, and indeed but few of the colonies were without them.

Among the early customs was that of the watchmen crying the time of night and giving an account of the weather as they went their rounds, a practice which prevailed for a hundred years. The British sentinels later gave the cry of "All 's well!" as they paced their beats. The ringing of the nine-o'clock bell was first ordered in 1649. The watchman's rattle was introduced about the time Boston became a city.

The government of the town was vested in nine selectmen, and is first found on the records, November, 1643; but not until November 29, 1645, is the official statement recorded that John Winthrop and nine others were chosen selectmen. This continued to be the form of government until the city was incorporated, Feburary 23, 1822. The first city government was organized on the first of May following, and John Phillips was the first, Josiah Quincy the second, and Harrison Gray Otis the third mayor. Steps were taken as early as 1708 to petition the General Court to have the town incorporated into a city or borough, and again in 1784, but without success.

In 1632 the Colonial legislature declared it to be "the fittest place for public meetings of any place in the Bay," since which time it has remained the capital of Massachusetts. Boston at first included within its government the islands of the harbor,—Muddy River (Brookline), Winnisimet (Chelsea), Mount Wollaston (Braintree), Randolph, and Quincy. She is now striving to recover portions of her ancient territory.

For a long time the allotment of lands was the principal business of the town officers. In the limits of the peninsula the rule was, "two acres to plant on, and for every able youth one acre within the neck and Noddle's Island" (East Boston). In 1635 it was agreed, "no new allotments should be granted unto any new-comer, but such as may be likely to be received members of the congregation." The town regulated the price of cattle, commodities, victuals, and the wages of laborers, and none other were to be given or taken.

The spirit of intolerance which the fathers of Boston exhibited towards the Quakers, Anabaptists, Episcopalians, and other sects illustrates their view of religious liberty. Well did Dryden say: —

> " Of all the tyrannies on human kind,
> The worst is that which persecutes the mind;
> Let us but weigh at what offence we strike,
> 'T is but because we cannot think alike;
> In punishing of this we overthrow
> The laws of nations, and of nature too."

It was an offence to harbor a Quaker; to attend a Quaker meeting was a fine of ten shillings, to preach, £5. When the Baptists first attempted to enter their meeting-house in Stillman Street, they found the doors nailed up, and when they proceeded to worship in the open air, they were arrested and imprisoned. No one could be found to sell land for an Episcopal church, nor could a place be had to hold services in until Andros obtained the Old South by forcible entry. The criminal law decreed banishment to such as broached or maintained "damnable heresies," by which was meant such as did not agree with the views of the congregation.

The excessive severity of the following deserves notice. "Any one denying the Scripture to be the word of God should pay not exceeding £50, and be severely whipped, not exceeding forty strokes, unless he publicly recants, in which case he shall not pay above £10, or be whipped in case he pay not the fine." The repetition of this offence was to be punished by banishment or death, as the court might determine. "'T is death for any child of sound understanding to curse or strike his parents, unless in his own defence."

There is a grim humor in the following decisions. In 1640 one Edward Palmer, for asking an excessive price for a pair of stocks, which he was hired to frame, had the privilege of sitting an hour in them himself. "Captain Stone is sentenced to pay £100, and prohibited coming within the patent without the governor's leave, upon pain of death, for calling Mr. Ludlow (a magistrate) a "*Justass*." We infer the punishment must have been inflicted more for the joke than the offence.

"Catherine, wife of William Cornish, was found suspicious of incontinency, and seriously admonished to take heed." "Sergeant Perkins ordered to carry forty turfs to the fort for being drunk."

According to Neal, the principal festival days were that of the annual election of magistrates at Boston, and Commencement at Cambridge. Business was then laid aside, and the people were as cheerful among their friends and neighbors as the English are at Christmas. He adds that:

"They have a greater veneration for the evening of Saturday than for that of the Lord's Day itself; so that all business is laid aside by sunset or six o'clock on Saturday night. The Sabbath itself is kept with great strictness; nobody being to be seen in the streets in time of Divine service, except the constables, who are appointed to search all public houses; but in the evening they allow themselves great liberty and freedom."

This custom has prevailed up to a comparatively late period.

In those days the pulpit took the lead in matters temporal as well as of theology. Public questions were discussed in the pulpit, and news from a distance, of moment to the colony, was disseminated through it; the first newspaper was not attempted in Boston until 1690, and then only a single number was published. The whole field was open to the preacher, who might either confine himself to doctrinal points or preach a crusade against the savages. The attire of the ladies, the fashion of the hair, the drinking of healths, afterwards abolished by law, were all within the jurisdiction of the teacher of the people; the constituted authorities might make the laws, but the minister expounded them. The official proclamations were then, as now, affixed to the meeting-house door, which thus stood to the community as a vehicle of public intelligence.

Many intelligent travellers, both English and French, have recorded their impressions of Boston. Wood, who is accounted the earliest of these writers, says: —

"This harbor is made by a great company of islands, whose high cliffs shoulder out the boisterous seas; yet may easily deceive any unskilful pilot, presenting many fair openings and broad sounds which afford too shallow water for ships, though navigable for boats and pinnaces. It is a safe and pleasant harbor within, having but one common and safe entrance, and that not very broad, there scarce being room for three ships to come in board and board at a time; but being once in, there is room for the anchorage of five hundred ships."

"Boston is two miles N. E. of Roxbury. *His* situation is very pleasant, being a peninsula hemmed in on the south side by the bay of Roxbury, and on the north side with Charles River, the marshes on the back side being not half a quarter of a mile over; so that a little fencing will secure their cattle from the wolves; it being a neck, and bare of wood, they are not troubled with these great annoyances, wolves, rattlesnakes, and mosquitoes. This neck of land is not above four miles in compass, in form almost square, having on the south side a great broad hill, whereon is planted a fort which can command any ship as she sails into the harbor.* On the north side is another hill equal in bigness, whereon stands a windmill.† To the northwest is a high mountain, with three little rising hills on the top of it, wherefore it is called the Tramount.‡ This town, although it be neither the greatest nor the richest, yet is the most noted and frequented, being the centre of the plantations where the monthly courts are kept."

John Josselyn arrived at Boston July, 1663. He says: —

"It is in longitude 315 degrees, and 42 degrees 30 minutes of north latitude. The buildings are handsome, joining one to the other as in London, with many large streets, most of them paved with pebble; in the high street, toward the Common, there are fair buildings, some of stone; the town is not divided into parishes, yet they have three fair meeting-houses."

Edward Johnson says: —

"The form of this town is like a heart, naturally situated for fortifications, having two hills on the frontier part thereof next the sea, the one well fortified on the superficies thereof, with store of great artillery well mounted. The other hath a very strong battery built of whole timber, and filled with earth; betwixt these two strong arms lies a cove or bay, on which the chief part of this town is built, overtopped with a third hill; all these, like overtopping towers, keep a constant watch to see the approach of foreign dangers, being furnished with a beacon and loud babbling guns to

* Fort Hill. † Copp's Hill. ‡ Beacon Hill.

give notice to all the sister towns. The chief edifice of this city-like town is crowded on the sea-banks, and wharfed out with great labor and cost; the buildings beautiful and large, some fairly set forth with brick, tile, stone, and slate, and orderly placed with seemly streets, whose continual enlargement presageth some sumptuous city."

M. l'Abbé Robin, who accompanied the army of Count Rochambeau, published a small work in 1781, in which a good description of Boston is given. Says M. l'Abbé: —

"The high, regular buildings, intermingled with steeples, appeared to us more like a long-established town of the Continent than a recent colony. A fine mole, or pier, projects into the harbor about two thousand feet, and shops and warehouses line its whole length. It communicates at right angles with the principal street of the town, which is long and wide, curving round towards the water; on this street are many fine houses of two and three stories. The appearance of the buildings seems strange to European eyes; being built entirely of wood, they have not the dull and heavy appearance which belongs to those of our continental cities; they are regular and well-lighted, with frames well joined, and the outside covered with slight, thinly planed boards, overlapping each other somewhat like the tiles upon our roofs. The exterior is painted generally of a grayish color, which gives an agreeable aspect to the view."

M. l'Abbé states that codfish was the principal article of commerce with the Bostonians; that they preferred Maderia, Malaga, or Oporto to French wines, but their ordinary beverage was rum, distilled from molasses. Some credit attaches to this statement, when we remember that Boston had half a dozen still-houses in 1722, and a score when the Abbé was writing. "Piety," continues the acute Frenchman, "is not the only motive which brings a crowd of ladies into their church. They show themselves there clothed in silk, and sometimes decked with superb feathers. Their hair is raised upon supports, in imitation of those worn by the French ladies some years since. They have less grace, less freedom, than the French ladies, but more dignity."

"Their shoon of velvet, and their muilis!
In kirk they are not content of stuilis,
Thc sermon when they sit to heir,
But carries cusheons like vain fulis;
And all for newfangleness of geir."

The Abbé, alluding to the strict observance of the Sabbath, naively says: "A countryman of mine, lodging at the same inn with me, took it into his head one Sunday to play a little upon his flute; but the neighborhood became so incensed that our landlord was obliged to acquaint him of their uneasiness." Another French writer remarked of Newport, which he thought Boston resembled, "This is the only place I ever visited where they build old houses." M. le Compte Segur and the Marquis Chastellux have written about Boston, but there is little to add to what is already given.

The first volume of the Town Records begins September, 1634, and the first entries are said to be in the handwriting of Governor Winthrop. An unknown number of leaves have been torn out or destroyed, and, as the first business of the town was the allotment of land to the inhabitants, the loss is irreparable, and has proved such to those who have had occasion to trace the titles of property. The need for prompt action, to preserve the invaluable town records from destruction, having become imperative, they have now been printed under the direction of the city authorities. Several later volumes of the records are missing, and for many years, while William Cooper was Town Clerk, no record exists of the births or deaths. A manuscript volume called the "Book of Possessions," is in the City Clerk's office, compiled, it is thought, as early as 1634, by order of the General Court. There are two hundred and forty-five names in this "Doomsday Book," as it has been termed, but all of them were not original settlers.

The general growth and progress of the New England metropolis has been steady and remarkable. The early settlers having built wholly of wood, were not long exempt from destructive fires. In 1654 occurred what was known as "the great fire," but its locality is not given. This was succeeded by another in 1676, at the North End, which consumed forty-five dwellings, the North Church, and several warehouses, within the space enclosed by Richmond, Hanover, and Clark Streets. After this fire a fire-engine was imported from England, but another great fire in 1678, near the Town Dock, destroyed eighty dwelling-houses and seventy warehouses, entailing a loss of £200,000.

With extraordinary energy these losses were repaired, and the townspeople, admonished by their disasters, built their houses with more regard to safety, — many building of stone and brick, — while more efficient means were obtained for controlling the devouring element. The town was divided into four quarters, patroled by a watch detailed from the foot-companies. Six hand-engines, four barrels of powder, and two crooks were assigned each quarter. This appears to have been the beginning of a fire department.

The first fire-engine made in Boston was built by David Wheeler, a blacksmith in Newbury, now Washington Street. It was tried at a fire August 21, 1765, and found to perform extremely well.

The data from which to estimate the population of the town in the first decade of its settlement is very meagre. In 1639 the Bay mustered a thousand soldiers in Boston, but they were of course drawn from all the towns. For the first seventy years after its settlement Boston did not probably contain over seven thousand people. In 1717 it was reckoned at only twelve thousand. A hundred years after the settlement it contained fifteen thousand, with seventeen hundred dwellings; in 1752 there were seventeen thousand five hundred, — a decrease of five hundred in the previous ten years, accounted for by the wars with the Indians and French, in which Boston sustained severe losses. In 1765 the number of people had fallen below sixteen thousand, with sixteen hundred and seventy-six houses. During the siege in 1775–76 the town was nearly depopulated, but few remaining who could get away. An enumeration made in July, 1775, before the last permission was given to leave the town, showed only six thousand five hundred and seventy-three inhabitants, the troops with their women and children numbering thirteen thousand six hundred. At the peace of 1783 there were only about twelve thousand inhabitants. By the first census of 1791 the number of people was a little over eighteen thousand, with two thousand three hundred and seventy-six houses.

From this period the increase has been steady and rapid. In 1800 there were twenty-five thousand; 1820, forty-three thousand; 1840, eighty-five thousand; 1860, one hundred and seventy-seven thousand, and in 1890, the latest census, four hundred and forty-six thousand.

The division of the town into eight wards is mentioned as early as the great fire of 1678–79. In 1715 these wards were named North, Fleet, Bridge, Creek, King's, Change, Pond, and South. In 1735 the number of wards was increased to twelve, corresponding with the number of companies in the Boston regiment, one of which was attached to each ward for service at fires. Besides the military there was also a civil division, an overseer of the poor, a fireward, a constable, and a scavenger, belonging to each ward. In 1792 the number of military wards was nine, the regiment having been reduced to that number of companies; the civil division continued to be twelve. The first four of these wards, and the greater part of the fifth, were in the North End; the seventh was at the West End; while the rest, with a part of the fifth, were in the South End, as it was then bounded. The present number is twenty-five, thrice the original number.

The paving of the public thoroughfares seems to have begun at a very early period. Josselyn, describing Boston in 1663, says most of the streets "are paved with pebble," meaning the smooth round stones from the beach. It was not the practice at first to pave the whole width of a street, but only a strip in the middle; the Neck was so paved. In the same manner the sidewalks were paved with cobble-stones, bricks, or flags, of only width enough for a single passenger; in some instances, where flag-stones were used, the remaining space was filled with cobble-stones. It is probable that the first paving was done in a fragmentary way before 1700, but in 1703–04 the town voted £100 for this purpose, "as the selectmen shall judge most needful, having particular regard to the highway nigh old Mrs. Stoddard's house." An order for paving 42 rods of Orange Street was made in 1715. From this time sums were regularly voted, and the foundation laid for the most cleanly city in America.

As to sidewalks, a lady who came to Boston in 1795 from New York, and was much struck with the quaint appearance of the town, writes: —

"There were no brick sidewalks, except in a part of the Main Street (Washington) near the Old South, then called Cornhill. The streets were paved with pebbles; and, except when driven on one side by carts and carriages, every one walked in the middle of the street, where the pavement was the smoothest." *

It is not believed that there was a sidewalk in Boston until after the Revolution. At this time State Street was without any, the pavement reaching across the street from house to house.

It is probable that those inhabitants whose business or pleasure took them from home after dark must for a long time have lighted their own way through the devious lanes and by-ways of the town. We can imagine the feelings of a pair of fond lovers who, taking an evening stroll, are bid by the captain of the watch to "Stand!" while he throws the rays of a dark lantern upon the faces of the shrinking swain and his mistress. Yet, although street-lamps were said to have been used as early as 1774, until 1792 there seems to have been no action on the town's part towards lighting the streets, when we read that the "gentlemen selectmen propose to light the town," early in January of that year, "and to continue the same until the sum subscribed is expended." Those gentlemen that proposed to furnish lamps were requested to have them "fixed" by a certain day, so that the lamplighter may have time to prepare them for lighting. To the public spirit of the citizens, then, is due the first shedding of light upon the gloomy ways of the town. Gas was not used to illuminate the streets until 1834, though the works at Copp's Hill were erected in 1828. In December of that year gas was first used in the city.

The springs which supplied the older inhabitants gave place to wells, and these in their turn gave way to the demand for an abundant supply of pure water for the whole town.

* Quincy Memoir.

Wells had to be sunk a depth varying from fifteen feet on the low ground to one hundred and twenty feet on the elevated portions, and the water was usually brackish and more or less impregnated with salt. Water was therefore introduced from Jamaica Pond, in West Roxbury, by a company incorporated in 1795. The pipes used were logs, of which about forty miles were laid. The trenches were only three to three and a half feet in depth, which did not prevent freezing in severe weather, while the smallness of the pipe, — four-inch mains, — rendered the supply limited.

Under the administration of Mayor Quincy the subject of a new supply of water was agitated. In 1825 a great fire occurred in Kilby Street, destroying fifty stores, and the want of water as a means for the subduing of fires became evident. Twenty years were spent in controversy before action was taken, but in August, 1846, ground was broken at Lake Cochituate by John Quincy Adams and Josiah Quincy, Jr. In October, 1848, the work was completed, but the growth of Boston has rendered this source insufficient in less than forty years, and the waters of Nashua River are to be made tributary.

Boston has enlarged her territory by annexation of South Boston, in 1804; Washington Village, in 1855; Roxbury, in 1868; Dorchester, in 1870; Charlestown, Brighton, and W. Roxbury, in 1874. East Boston, though forming a part of Boston since 1637, had neither streets nor local regulations until the incorporation of the East Boston Company; public officers first set foot upon the island in 1833. There was then but one house in the whole of that now populous ward, comprising six hundred and sixty acres. South Boston, when annexed, had only ten families on an area of five hundred and seventy acres, and but nineteen voters. There being at this time no bridge, the inhabitants were obliged to come to Boston *via* the Neck. The building of a bridge was the condition of annexation. South Boston was taken from the territory of Dorchester. Roxbury, itself a city, brought a large accession to Boston, to which it had long been joined in fact. Dorchester, settled a few months earlier than Boston, has become a ward of the metropolis. These two towns brought an increase to the population of about forty thousand, and a territory of nearly seven thousand acres.

Communication between Boston and the surrounding towns was at first wholly by the Neck. The people of Chelsea thus had a circuit of at least a dozen miles, and a day's journey before them, to go to town and return. There was a ferry established at Charlestown and Winnisimmet (Chelsea) as early as 1635, — five years after the settlement of Boston. We find by the records that Thomas Marshall "was chosen by generall consent for ye keeping of a Ferry from ye Mylne Point vnto Charlestown and Wynneseemitt, for a single p'son sixpence, and for two, sixpence; and for every one above ye number of two, two pence apiece." Ships' boats were first used, then scows, and this continued to be the only means of transit until 1786. Four years previous to this the Marquis Chastellux states that he was one hour making the voyage from Winnisimmet in a scow filled with cattle, sheep, etc. Seven tacks were required to bring them safely to land.

A bridge to Cambridge was agitated as long ago as 1739. The obstruction to the passage of ferry-boats by ice was a serious inconvenience. Charles River Bridge, from the Old Ferry landing to Charlestown, was the first constructed. The first pier was laid on the 14th June, 1785, and the bridge thrown open for travel in little more than a year. This was considered at the time the greatest enterprise ever undertaken in America, and its successful completion was celebrated by a public procession, consisting of both branches of the Legislature, the proprietors and artisans of the bridge, military and civic societies. Salutes were fired from the Castle, Copp's and Breed's Hill. This was only eleven years after the battle of Bunker Hill. Thomas Russell was first president of the corporation.

West Boston Bridge, to Cambridge, was opened in November, 1793. Dover Street, or Boston South Bridge, was next opened in the summer of 1805. Cragie's, or, as it used to be called, Canal Bridge, from the Middlesex Canal, was next completed in August, 1809, from what was then known as Barton's Point, on the Boston side, to Lechmere's Point in Cambridge. By a bridge thrown across from Lechmere's Point to Charlestown, the long detour around Charlestown Neck was avoided. The Western Avenue, or Mill Dam, as it was long called, was opened with great ceremony July, 1821. The South Boston Bridge, from what was respectively Windmill and Wheeler's Point, at the foot of Federal Street, to South Boston, was completed in 1828, and shortened the journey into Boston, by way of the Neck, about a mile. Warren Bridge met with great opposition from the proprietors of Charles River Bridge, but was opened as a public highway December, 1828. This completes the list of the older avenues of travel to the mainland; but we have now a magnificent iron structure to South Boston, recently erected, while the numerous railway bridges spanning the river enable the city to stretch its Briareus-like arms in every direction for traffic.

WINTHROP FORDING THE RIVER.

Coaches are first mentioned as being in use in Boston in 1668–69. Captain Anthony Howard appears to have owned one in 1687, for he was fined twenty shillings that year "for setting a coach-house two feet into ye streete at ye N. End of ye Towne." * In 1798 there were 98 chaises and 47 coaches, chariots, phaetons, &c. in all Boston. In October, 1631, Governor Winthrop went on foot to Lynn and Salem, and until there were roads it is obvious there was little use for wheeled vehicles, even for such as could afford them. In 1750 there were only a few carriages, and these, chariots and coaches. Four-wheeled chaises were in use in families of distinction. The first public coach or hack used in Boston was set up in 1712 by Jonathan Wardell, at the sign of the Orange Tree, head of Hanover Street. One

* Town Records.

was also set up by Adino Paddock, in 1762, who called it the "Burling Coach," from its London prototype. Paddock was a coachmaker by trade; we shall have occasion to notice him in these pages. The next public vehicle was a small post-chaise, drawn by a pair of gray horses, and stood at the head of State Street, about 1790. Gentlemen and ladies who attended balls and parties in those times had to walk, unless they could get a cast in a friend's carriage.

Coaches for public conveyance were first established in 1763, when one was put on the route between Boston and Portsmouth, N. H. Bartholemew Stavers was the "undertaker," and his head-quarters were at the sign of the Lighthouse, at the North End. The "Portsmouth Flying Stage Coach," as he styled his carriage, carried six inside passengers, each paying thirteen shillings and sixpence sterling, to Portsmouth. The stage and horses were kept at Charlestown, to save the trouble of ferriage, and set out every Friday morning, putting up at the inns along the road. Returning, the stage left Portsmouth every Tuesday morning. Stavers gave notice "that as this was a convenient and genteel way of travelling, and greatly cheaper than hiring carriages or horses, he hoped ladies and gentlemen would encourage the same." * A stage was put on the route to Marblehead in 1769, by Edward Wade. His carriage was a post-chaise, suited for ladies and gentlemen, and he himself might be "spoken with at the widow Trefry's in Fish (North) Street."

Railways were early under discussion by the people of Boston, but no decisive steps were taken until 1825. The first road chartered in the State was the Experiment Railroad at Quincy. Next came the Lowell, incorporated in 1830, followed by the Worcester, Providence, and others. The Lowell was the first opened for public travel, in June, 1835, closely followed by the Worcester in July of the same year; the Providence was also opened in 1835, with a single track. The Maine was opened from Wilmington to Andover in 1836; to South Berwick, 1843. The Eastern comes next, in 1838, in

* Drake, p. 664.

which year it was opened to Salem. George Peabody was the first president. The Old Colony began operating in November, 1845, the Fitchburg in 1845, and the Hartford and Erie in 1849, under the name of the Norfolk County Road. It is a curious fact, that both of the great railway stations in Boston stand on ground reclaimed from the sea.

We have taken the reader through the settlement, physical features, and successive phases of the growth of the Old Town, and now that we are about to commence our rambles together, we warn him to be prepared for changes that will make it difficult and often impossible to fix localities accurately. For fifty years our men of progress have been pulling down the old and building up the new city. The Great Fire of 1872 left few of its original features, except in the North End, and in and about Dock Square, which, notwithstanding the sweeping changes incident to the extension of Washington Street northward, retains much the same appearance that it did forty years ago.

DAY AFTER THE GREAT FIRE, COURT-HOUSE STEPS.

CHAPTER I.

KING'S CHAPEL AND THE NEIGHBORHOOD.

History of the Chapel. — Establishment of the Church of England. — Chapel Burial-Ground. — Boston Athenæum. — Academy of Arts and Sciences. — Historical Society. — The Museum. — The Old Corner. — Royal Custom House. — Washington. — H. G. Otis. — Daniel Webster. — Tremont Street. — Howard Street. — Pemberton Hill. — Endicott. — Captain Southack. — Theodore Lyman, Senior. — John Cotton. — Sir Henry Vane. — Samuel Sewall. — Gardiner Greene. — Earl Percy. — Bellingham. — Faneuil. — Phillips. — Davenport. — Oxenbridge. — Beacon Street. — School Street. — Latin School. — Franklin Statue. — City Hall. — Otis. — Warren. — Mascarene. — Cromwell's Head. — The Old Corner Bookstore. — Anne Hutchinson. — The French Church. — Catholic Church. — Second Universalist. — Province Street. — Chapman Place. — James Lovell. — Wendell.

WE choose King's Chapel for our point of departure, as well from its central position as from the fact that its vicinage is probably the oldest ground built upon in Boston, Blackstone's lot alone excepted.

GOVERNOR SHIRLEY.

The exterior of King's Chapel does not present any remarkable architectural features. It has an air of solidity and massiveness that seems to bespeak the intention of its builders that it should remain where it was placed. This purpose is likely to be set at naught by the proposed removal of the Chapel northwardly, to widen School Street. So improbable an idea never entered the heads of the founders; but we make nothing nowadays of taking up blocks of brick or stone bodily, and moving them whither we list.

King's Chapel is the fifth in the order of Boston churches. The architect was Peter Harrison, of Newport, R. I., and the plan embraced a steeple, which Mr. Harrison thought essential to his general design, and would have a "beautiful effect." For want

KING'S CHAPEL AS IT APPEARS IN 1872.

of funds, however, the steeple was neve" built. Governor Shirley laid the corner-stone on the 11th of August, 1749, and after giving the workmen £ 20 (old tenor) to drink his health, went into the old church, which was still standing, where a service appropriate to the occasion was held by Rev. Mr. Caner, the rector.

Mr. Harrison had been requested to present drawings with both a double and single tier of windows. Two rows were adopted, the lower ones giving that prince of punsters, Mather Byles, an opportunity of saying that he had heard of the canons of the church, but had never seen the port-holes before.

The stone for the chapel came from Braintree, and was taken

from the surface of the ground, no quarries being then opened. The rough appearance of the stone is due to the limited knowledge of the art of dressing it which then prevailed.

Greenwood's little work on King's Chapel gives the following facts. It was first erected of wood in the year 1688, enlarged in 1710, and, being found in the year 1741 in a state of considerable decay, it was proposed to rebuild it of stone. A subscription for this purpose was set on foot, and Peter Faneuil (of Faneuil Hall memory) was chosen treasurer of the building-fund. The building was to be of stone, and was to cost £25,000 (old tenor). It was not to be commenced until £10,000 were subscribed.

Among the first subscribers were Governor William Shirley, Sir Charles Henry Frankland, and Peter Faneuil. The Governor gave £100; Sir H. Frankland, £50; Faneuil, £200 sterling. Faneuil died in 1742, and the matter was for some time laid aside, but was revived by Mr. Caner in 1747. A new subscription was drawn up. Governor Shirley increased his gift to £200, and Sir H. Frankland to £150 sterling. For the subscription of Peter Faneuil the society was obliged to sue his brother Benjamin, who was also his executor, and recovered it after a vexatious suit at law.

The new chapel was built so as to enclose the old church, in which services continued to be held, in spite of its ruinous condition, until March, 1753, when the society was obliged to remove to Trinity. The congregation having applied for the use of the Old South on Christmas day, a verbal answer was returned granting the request on condition "that the house should not be decorated with spruce," etc.

Efforts to obtain money to complete the chapel were made in every direction. Among others, Captain Thomas Coram, founder of the Foundling Hospital in London, who had resided in this country, was applied to by a gentleman then in London; but no sooner had he mentioned the object of his visit than he was obliged to listen to a burst of passionate reproaches for some alleged slight the vestry of King's Chapel had formerly put upon him. The old gentleman finally told his visitor, with an oath, "that if the twelve Apostles were to apply to him in behalf of the church, he would persist in refusing to do it."

The portico was not completed until 1789. In that year General Washington was in Boston, and attended an oratorio in the chapel, which had for its object the completion of the portico. The general was dressed in a black velvet suit, and gave five guineas towards this purpose.

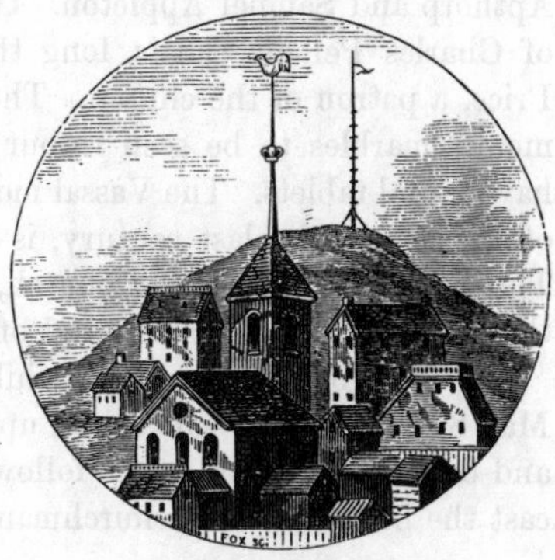

OLD KING'S CHAPEL.

The old building, which gave place to the present one, had an apology for a tower, on the top of which was a crown, and above this a cock for a vane. A gallery was added after the enlargement in 1710, and the pulpit was on the north side. Opposite was a pew for the governors, and near it another for officers of the British army and navy. In the west gallery was the first organ ever used in Boston, given to the society by Thomas Brattle. A bell was purchased in 1689, and a clock was donated in 1714 by the gentlemen of the British Society. The walls and pillars were hung with the escutcheons of the King, Sir Edmund Andros, Governors Dudley, Shute, Burnet, Belcher, and Shirley, and formed a most striking contrast with the bare walls of the Puritan churches of the town. In the pulpit, according to the custom of the times, was an hour-glass to mark the length of the sermons, while the east end was adorned with an altar-piece, the Ten Commandments, Lord's Prayer, etc. The emblems of heraldry have disappeared. It was the usage of the church to place the royal governors at the head of the vestry.

As you enter the chapel, at your left hand is the monument of William Vassall, erected by Florentine Vassall, of Jamaica, in 1766. To the right is a beautiful monumental tablet dedicated to the memory of the young men of the chapel who fell in the late civil war.

On the south side are mural tablets to William Sullivan, John Lowell, Thomas Newton, — an original founder, — and Frances Shirley, wife of the Governor. Within the chancel are busts of Greenwood and Freeman, rectors, and of their successor Dr. Peabody. The burial-ground side contains tablets to Charles Apthorp and Samuel Appleton. Over the vestry are the names of Charles Pelham Curtis, long the treasurer, and of William Price, a patron of the church. These are about the only monumental marbles to be seen in our city churches, though others have mural tablets. The Vassal monument, a beautiful specimen of the art in the last century, is by Tyler, a London sculptor. These add interest to the church, and reflect in a modest way the glories of old St. Paul's and of Westminster Abbey.

The first bell was cracked, while tolling for evening service, May 8, 1814. The wits seized upon the accident with avidity, and commemorated it in the following effusion (Paul Revere re-cast the bell, and some churchman answered the innuendo): —

"The Chapel church,
Left in the lurch,
Must surely fall;
For church and people
And bell and steeple
Are crazy all.

"The church still lives,
The priest survives,
With mind the same.
Revere refounds,
The bell resounds,
And all is well again."

The present organ of King's Chapel was procured from England in 1756, and paid for by private subscription. It cost £500 sterling, and was said to have been selected by the immortal Handel himself, though the great *maestro* was then blind. Over this organ a crown and a couple of gilt mitres are placed which have a history of their own.

In the year 1775, when Boston was in a state of siege, the British military and naval officers worshipped in King's Chapel, as they had in fact done during the previous years the town was in occupation of the British soldiers. The burial of three soldiers of the Sixty-fifth Regiment are the last-recorded interments in the Chapel cemetery previous to the evacuation of the town in March. The rector, Dr. Caner, went to Halifax with the king's troops, taking with him the church registers, plate, and vestments. The service, which had in part been presented by the King, amounted to two thousand eight hundred ounces of silver. It was never recovered.

When the society of King's Chapel were ready to rebuild, in 1748, they desired an enlargement of the ground for their site a few feet northwardly, also a piece of ground at the east side, on part of which then stood the Latin School. After a good deal of negotiation between the town and the church committee, the church erected a new school-house on the opposite side of the street on land belonging to Colonel Saltonstall, where the Latin School remained up to a comparatively recent time. The removal of the old school-house was viewed with no favorable eye by the townspeople, and Joseph Green, a Harvard graduate of 1726, and a noted wit, expressed the popular feeling thus:—

> "A fig for your learning! I tell you the town,
> To make the church larger, must pull the school down.
> 'Unhappily spoken!' exclaims Master Birch;
> 'Then learning, it seems, stops the growth of the church.'"

After the departure of the royal troops, the popular *furor* against everything savoring of their late allegiance to the throne found expression in the removal of the royal emblems from public buildings, changing the names of streets and everything that bore any allusion to the obnoxious idea of kingly authority. King's Chapel was therefore newly baptized Stone Chapel, a name that has in turn been discarded for the old, high-sounding title of yore. In the reign of Queen Anne the church was called "Queens Chappell."

The establishment of the Church of England in Boston was attended with great opposition. The Puritans, who had fled from the persecutions of that church in the old country, had no idea of admitting it among them in the new. In 1646 a petition praying for the privilege of Episcopal worship, addressed to the General Court at Boston, caused the petitioners to be fined for seditious expressions, and the seizure of their papers. Charles II., after his accession, wrote to the colony requiring, among other things, that the laws should be "reviewed" so as to permit the Episcopal form of worship, the use of the Book of Common Prayer, etc. The chief people and elders of the colony looked upon the efforts of the profligate Charles II. in behalf of religious liberty as they would upon the quoting of Scripture by his Satanic Majesty, and paid little heed to the mandate of the merry monarch of whom his favorite Rochester wrote, —

> "Here lies our sovereign Lord the King,
> Whose word no man relied on;
> Who never said a foolish thing,
> And never did a wise one."

The King, when over his bottle, commanded Rochester to write him a suitable epitaph, "something appropriate and witty." The Earl, seizing his pen, wrote as above, and for his keen effusion remained some time in disgrace.

In 1686, in the reign of James II., the first Episcopal services were held in the Old Town House, which then stood on the site of the Old State House. Rev. Robert Ratcliff was the first Episcopal clergyman, and came over in the Rose frigate in May, 1686. The town, however, continued to refuse the use of any of the meeting-houses, and the society were unable to buy land on Cotton (now Pemberton) Hill to build on. Edward Randolph — the first officer of customs that Boston had, a man specially hated for his successful efforts to have the king revoke the colonial charter — may be considered as chiefly instrumental in setting up the Episcopalians in Boston. Randolph was also at this time one of his Majesty's council for New England.

Sir Edmund Andros, who arrived in Boston in December, 1686, after having several conferences with the ministers on the subject of using one of the meeting-houses for Episcopal services, sent Randolph, on Wednesday, the 22d of March, 1687, to demand the keys of the South Meeting-house, now Old South. On Good Friday, which was the following Friday, the sexton opened the doors by command of Andros "to open and ring the bell for those of the Church of England."

But time, which makes all things even, gave the Old South Society a signal revenge for what they considered little less than sacrilege. King's Chapel, abandoned by its rector and congregation when the town was evacuated, remained closed until the autumn of 1777, when it was occupied by the Old South

Society, whose house had been converted into a British riding-school. This society used the Chapel about five years.

King's Chapel stands as a monument to mark the resting-place of Isaac Johnson, the second white inhabitant of Boston. The locality of the grave is unknown, and is likely to remain so, owing to the many changes, both past and prospective, in the old burial-ground. Johnson, under whose direction the settlement of Boston mainly proceeded in its incipient steps, selected for himself the square enclosed by Tremont, Court, Washington, and School Streets. So says tradition on the authority of Chief Justice Sewall. Johnson died in September, 1630, and was buried at his own request at the southwest end of his lot. This solitary grave was the nucleus around which gathered the remains of the first settlers, and constituted the first place of sepulture in the town. The old church of 1688 was erected on the burying-ground, it is conjectured by authority of Andros; the town would not have permitted the use of the public burying-ground for this purpose.

Johnson's history has a touch of romance. He married Lady Arabella, daughter of the Earl of Lincoln. She left her native land and a life of ease to follow her husband to the wilds of America. She died very soon after her arrival, in Salem, and was probably buried there; but the location of her grave, like that of her husband, who so soon followed her, is unknown. Johnson's death was said to have been hastened by the loss of his amiable and beautiful wife. It was to the memory of the Lady Arabella that Mrs. Sigourney wrote, —

> "Yet still she hath a monument
> To strike the pensive eye,
> The tender memories of the land
> Wherein her ashes lie."

It is a popular belief that the Chapel Burying-Ground, or "Old Burying-Place," as it was first called, contains the mortal remains only of such as were of the Episcopal faith; but this is very far from being the case. The dust of Governor Winthrop, of John Cotton, Davenport, Oxenbridge, and Bridge, pastors of the First Church, and of other Puritans of the sternest type, lie under the shadow of a detested Episcopal edifice. Besides these, the remains of Governor Shirley and of Lady Andros repose here. Here may be seen on the tombstones the arms and escutcheons of the deceased, carrying us back to the days of heraldry. Under the Chapel are vaults for the reception of the dead.

SHIRLEY ARMS.

As we look through the iron gate into the enclosure, the curious arrangement of the gravestones strikes us. In the centre the headstones form a sort of hollow square, as if to repel further aggression upon the territory of the dead, while at the sides and walls the same plan is observed. This peculiar arrangement was the *chef d'œuvre* of a former Superintendent of Burials; many stones were removed from their original positions, and now give effect to the proverb, "to lie like a tombstone." What would the future or even present seeker after the grave of an ancestor do in such a case of perplexity? Doubtful, in a certain sense, of the legend "Here lies," he would restrain his emotion, fearing that the tear of affection might fall on the ashes of a stranger.

King's Chapel Burying-Ground is by no means exempt from the ghostly legends that usually attach to cemeteries. One is recorded of a negro-woman, whose coffin the careless carpenter having made too short, severed the head from the body, and, clapping it between the feet, nailed down the lid to conceal his blunder. Another is related of a person who was asserted to have been buried alive. A hue-and-cry was raised, the corpse was exhumed in the presence of a mob which had gathered, and it needed the assurance of the doctors who examined the remains to set the affair at rest. The mob, disappointed of its expected sensation, proposed to bury the old woman who had raised the uproar, but did not execute the threat.* Interments ceased here in 1796.

* Dealings with the Dead.

Next northerly from the burying-ground once stood an old wooden building covered with rough cast. It was the residence of some of the rectors of King's Chapel, and of Dr. Caner, the last one. This building was occupied by the Boston Athenæum in 1810, and was taken down over sixty years ago, to give place to the stone building occupied later as a Savings Bank and by the Historical Society. The Athenæum, now so conspicuous among literary institutions, owes its origin to the Anthology Club, an association of gentlemen for literary purposes. They conducted a periodical called the Monthly Anthology, and in it published proposals in 1806 for subscriptions for a public reading-room. Success following this effort, it was determined to add a library, and trustees were appointed for the management. The rooms were first opened in Joy's Buildings, on the west corner of Congress and Water Streets; then in Scollay's Building in Tremont Street; and later, in the location first mentioned.

The Boston Athenæum became incorporated in February, 1807, and occupied three rooms in the old rough-cast building. The first was the news or reading room; the second, the library of the Athenæum and American Academy; the third, the private library of John Quincy Adams, until it was removed to a building erected for it at Quincy.

Mr. Shaw, in his history published in 1817, gives the following particulars with regard to the library at that time: "The library of the Athenæum contains upwards of ten thousand volumes. The collection in history and biography is very complete, and in American History unrivalled; under this head may be noticed three thousand pamphlets. Twenty-one foreign and about twelve American periodicals are received." In 1822 the Athenæum was removed to Pearl Street, near the corner of High, to a building partly purchased and partly presented by James Perkins. At this time the library possessed seventeen thousand five hundred volumes and ten thousand tracts. It now contains over one hundred and eighty thousand volumes.

The Athenæum was removed in 1849 to Beacon Street, where its spacious picture gallery, containing many valuable works of art belonging to the institution, long continued one of its most attractive features, as it was for many years about the only place in Boston where public exhibitions of paintings were held. The growing needs of the library, however, compelled the removal of the best pictures to the Art Museum. Stuart's fine head of Washington, now to be seen there, belongs to the Athenæum. The price paid for it was fifteen hundred dollars. This institution has received munificent contributions; among others may be named twenty-five thousand dollars nobly donated at once by John Bromfield. Thomas H. Perkins was a generous benefactor, and many other eminent Bostonians have aided it handsomely.

The corner-stone of the elegant freestone building on Beacon Street was laid in April, 1847. The design was by Edward C. Cabot, but some interior alterations were made under the direction of Billings. The site was the estate of Edward B. Phillips, but the proprietors had purchased the ground on which the Museum stands in Tremont Street, with the intention of building there. This ground was sold. The original members of the Anthology Club, founders of the Athenæum, were John Sylvester, John Gardner, William Emerson, Arthur M. Walter, William S. Shaw, Samuel C. Thacher, Joseph S. Buckminster, Joseph Tuckerman, William Tudor, Jr., Peter O. Thacher, Thomas Gray, William Wells, Edmund T. Dana, John C. Warren, and James Jackson.

The Athenæum is managed by trustees elected by its shareholders or "proprietors." Among those trustees we find the names of John Hancock, Daniel Webster, Charles Sumner, O. W. Holmes, Francis Parkman, and W. H. Prescott. The library is rich in works of art, and in files of early newspapers. It also has the Bemis collection of works on international law, including state papers; also one of the best sets of United States documents in the country; besides a large part of Washington's private library, acquired by purchase, with many other works relating to that great man.

The Academy of Arts and Sciences is the oldest institution with literary objects in Boston, and the second in America. It was instituted in 1779, and received a charter the next year, in which the design of the Academy is stated to be, "the promotion of the knowledge of the antiquities of America and of the natural history of the country." The number of members is limited to two hundred.

Governor Bowdoin was the first president, followed by John Adams, Edward A. Holyoke, J. Q. Adams, Nathaniel Bowditch, John Pickering, and other distinguished persons. Count Rumford left a legacy within the control of the Academy to advance the cause of science. The society occupied a room in the Athenæum building until recently.

The Historical Society originated as early as 1791. On the 24th of January, Hon. Judge Tudor, Rev. Drs. Belknap, Thacher, and Eliot, Judge Winthrop of Cambridge, Rev. Dr. Freeman, Judge Minot, Hon. W. Baylies of Dighton, Judge Sullivan, afterwards governor of Massachusetts, and Thomas Wallcutt, met and organized. The meetings were first held in Judge Minot's office in Spring Lane, but the use of a corner room in the attic of Faneuil Hall was soon obtained, "a place as retired and recondite as explorers into the recesses of antiquity would think of visiting." In 1791 the society occupied the Manufactory House in Hamilton Place. In 1793 the society was offered a room in the Tontine Crescent, on the south side of Franklin Street, over the arch, the entrance into Arch Street. Charles Bulfinch, William Scollay, and Charles Vaughan, who reclaimed Franklin Street from a quagmire, made this offer, and here the society remained until 1833, when it removed to its late quarters in Tremont Street, from which it has lately moved to new quarters on the Back Bay. The situation in Franklin Street presented the singular phase of a building without land, as it rested upon an arched passageway.

Governor Gore was president in 1806. In 1838 the society's collections amounted to six thousand volumes and manuscripts. The society possesses many relics of historic interest. It has portraits of Governors Endicott, Winslow, Pownall, Dummer, Belcher, Winthrop, Hutchinson, Strong, Gore, etc. That of Winslow is supposed to be a Vandyke. The swords of Governor Carver, Myles Standish, Colonel Church, Governor Brooks, Sir William Pepperell, and those of Captain Linzee and Colonel Prescott, worn at Bunker's Hill, are the property of the society. Not the least curious among these relics is a silk flag presented by Governor Hancock to a colored company called the "Bucks of America," bearing the device of a pine-tree and a buck, above which are the initials "J. H." and "G. W." There is also a gun used at the capture of Governor Andros by the Bostonians in 1689; the samp-bowl of King Philip, and the lock of the gun with which he was killed.

The library of the society has a value not to be estimated in dollars and cents. It was the foundation of materials for the history of New England, many of which have been published in the society's valuable collections.

Among other valuable donations to the society may be mentioned the papers and documents of General William Heath of Revolutionary fame, besides the magnificent library of Thomas Dowse of Cambridge, containing about five thousand volumes, many being of the greatest historical interest.

The Museum building, which covers twenty thousand feet of land, and cost a quarter of a million, is one of the attractive objects of the street and of the city. For many years its rows of exterior lights have been a lamp in the path of the pedestrian and a lure to its votaries. On its boards have stood in times past the elder Booth and Mrs. George Barrett. Booth, of whom a capital likeness in crayon, by Rowse, hangs in the main hall, deserves to be classed with Kean, Kemble, and the giants of the stage. His unfortunate *penchant* for convivial indulgence has given rise to many anecdotes. On one occasion, while playing at the Howard, Tom Ford, the manager, stipulated that Booth should submit to be locked in his room by a certain hour, in order that the actor might not be in a condition to disappoint the audience, as was sometimes the case. The chagrin of the manager may be imagined at finding the tragedian intoxicated when he came to fetch him to the theatre. Booth had bribed a waiter to bring liquor to his door, where successive glasses were emptied by means of a straw through the key-hole. As Richard III. Booth was incomparable. He often became greatly excited in the combat scene, and on one occasion it is stated that he attacked W. H. Smith, the veteran actor, since deceased, in dead earnest, driving him from the stage, and pursuing him into the street.

WILLIAM WARREN.

William Warren, the comedian, made his first appearance at the Museum in 1847. Adelaide Phillips was a *danseuse* at this house in the same year.

The present Museum covers the site of the Columbian Museum, which was destroyed by fire in January, 1807. The Columbian Museum originated in the exhibition of wax-works at the American Coffee House in State Street, opposite Kilby, as early as 1791. Mr. Bowen, the proprietor, removed to what was called "the head of the Mall," at the corner of Bromfield's Lane (now Street) in 1795. This building was burnt in January, 1803; but Mr. Bowen was enabled to reopen his Museum in Milk Street, at the corner of Oliver, in May of that year. In 1806, a brick building five stories high was erected by Doyle in rear of, and reached by a passage from, Tremont Street.

The destructive element soon swept away this edifice. It took fire about midnight, and was consumed with all its contents; not an article was saved. The event was signalized by a painful disaster. A large crowd of spectators had collected in the burying-ground adjoining, when the walls fell, killing nine or ten boys, from twelve to fifteen years old. Dr. William Eustis, afterwards Governor of Massachusetts, resided then in Sudbury Street, and with other physicians lent his aid on the occasion. The undismayed proprietors had a new two-story building erected by June, 1807, which continued until 1825, when the collection was sold to the New England Museum.

The New England Museum — formed from the New York Museum, which was opened in 1812, in Boylston Hall; from Mix's New Haven Museum, added in 1821; and from the Columbian — was opened by Mr. E. A. Greenwood, July 4, 1818. It was situated on Court Street, and extended from Cornhill to Brattle Street, occupying the upper stories. In 1839 Moses Kimball became the proprietor, and these several establishments, merged in the New England, constituted the present Museum, first located on the present site of Horticultural Hall in 1841, and in 1846 where it now stands.

At the corner of Court and Tremont Streets was the residence of John Wendell, an old Boston merchant of the time of Governor Shirley. He married a daughter of Judge Edmund Quincy, and was the nephew of Hon. Jacob Wendell, a leading Bostonian in the troublous Revolutionary times.

The Royal Custom House was located in Wendell's house in 1759, at which time George Cradock, Esq., a near neighbor of Wendell's, was collector.

The old building long standing here, shown in the engraving, is the one in which Washington lodged during his visit in 1789, as was set forth on the small tablet placed in the Court Street front. At the time Washington occupied it, it was kept by Joseph Ingersoll as a boarding-house. The coming of Washington to the town he had delivered in 1776 was marred by an act of official punctilio on the part of Governor Hancock, which caused the greatest mortification alike to the people and the illustrious visitor

WASHINGTON'S LODGINGS.

On the arrival of the general on the Neck, he was met by the suite of the governor, but not by the governor, whose views of State sovereignty would not admit of his acknowledging a superior personage within his official jurisdiction. The day was cold and raw, and Washington, chagrined at the absence of the governor, was about to turn his horse's head to depart, when he was prevailed upon by the authorities of the town to enter it.

A long delay had occurred at the Neck, and many people caught what was called the "Washington cold." The general wore his old continental uniform, and rode on horseback with his head uncovered, but did not salute the throngs that lined his way. On arriving at the Old State House, Washington would not ascend to the balcony prepared for him at the west end, until assured that the governor was not there; and after the passage of the procession before him, retired to his lodgings. To add to the coldness of his reception, a cold dinner awaited him; but his landlord procured and placed before his guest a fish of great excellence, and thus saved his credit at the last moment.

Washington himself declared the circumstance had been so disagreeable and mortifying that, notwithstanding all the marks of respect and affection he had received from the inhabitants of Boston, he would have avoided the place had he anticipated it.*

Governor Hancock, perceiving that he had made a *fiasco*, hastened to repair it. General Washington had declined his invitation to dinner, so the governor caused himself to be carried next day to the general's lodgings, where he presented himself swathed in flannels as a victim of gout. The general received the governor's excuses with due civility, whatever may have been his private convictions, and so the affair terminated.

Madam Hancock, indeed, related afterwards that the governor was really laid up with gout, and that Washington shed tears when he saw the servants bringing the helpless man into his presence. Governor Brooks, and Hon. Jonathan Jackson,

* Hundred Boston Orators.

then Marshal of the District, dined with the general on the day of his arrival, but did not hold this view, and the affair was freely discussed at table. Hancock seems to have yielded to the popular pressure which condemned his conduct. He was said to have been jealous of Washington's elevation to the Presidency. The general returned the governor's visit, was affable among friends, but stood on his dignity when strangers were present.

Harrison Gray Otis was one of the first who occupied this old corner for a law office. In his day it was considered quite on one side, though only a few paces distant from the Court House. Mr. Otis came upon the stage a little before the opening of the Revolutionary conflict. He remembered seeing Earl Percy's reinforcements mustering for their forced march to Lexington. A pupil of Master Lovell at the Latin School, in 1773, he was removed to Barnstable during the siege of Boston, where he quietly pursued his studies, graduating at Harvard at eighteen. He was an able lawyer, and until the advent of Mr. Webster, — about which time he relinquished practice, — was the acknowledged leader of the Boston bar. Judge Story thought him the greatest popular orator of his day. His personal appearance was elegant and attractive; his voice, strong and melodious, often sounded in Faneuil Hall.

Mr. Otis was prominently identified with public affairs. In politics he was a Federalist, and a leader of that party in Congress from 1797 to 1801. He was also an influential member of the celebrated Hartford Convention. In 1817, after filling a number of State offices, Mr. Otis went into the United States Senate; and became mayor of his native city in 1829. He was the grandson of Harrison Gray, treasurer of the colony and a Royalist, and nephew of James Otis, the patriot. Gifted in oratory, with a winning manner and polished address, Harrison Gray Otis ranks high among Boston's public men. One of the public schools is named for him.

In the building we are recalling was once the law office of the great expounder of the Constitution, Daniel Webster, who first came to Boston in 1804, and studied law with Christopher Gore, afterwards Governor of Massachusetts. He kept school a short time for his brother Ezekiel, in Short Street, since Kingston. Edward Everett, who lived with his mother in Newbury Street, was then about ten years old, and went at this time to Webster's school.

It is related of Mr. Webster, that when a young man, about to begin the study of law, he was advised not to enter the legal profession, as it was already crowded. His reply was, "There is room enough at the top." Mr. Webster removed to Portsmouth, N. H., returning to Boston in 1816, and in 1820 he was a member of the Massachusetts Constitutional Convention. His orations at the laying of the corner-stone of Bunker Hill Monument, June 17, 1825, when Lafayette was present, and also on its completion, June 17, 1843, are familiar to every school-boy. An unsuccessful candidate for the Presidency in 1836, he entered the cabinet of General Harrison in 1840, as Secretary of State, negotiating the long-disputed question of boundary with Great Britain by the Ashburton treaty. His great reply to Hayne of South Carolina, in the Senate, in which he defended New England against the onslaughts of the Southern Senator, made him the idol of the people of Boston. This speech, which opens with the graphic simile of a ship at sea in thick weather, her position unknown and her crew filled with anxiety, was, it is said, delivered without preparation, amid the gloomy forebodings of the New England men in Washington. His wife, even, who heard the fiery harangue of Hayne, feared for the result; but the "Northern Lion" reassured her with the remark that he would grind the Southern Senator "finer than the snuff in her box."

Notwithstanding the sledge-hammer force of Webster's eloquence he was often at a loss for a word, but when it came to him it was exactly the right one. His clearness of expression is well illustrated by the following anecdote of David Crockett, who, having heard Mr. Webster speak, accosted him afterwards with the inquiry, "Is this Mr. Webster?" "Yes, sir." "Well, sir," continued Crockett, "I had heard that you were a very great man, but I don't think so. I heard your speech and understood every word you said."

Mr. Webster's hesitation for a suitable expression is well described by the following anecdote. At a meeting in Faneuil Hall he was arguing in favor of the "Maysville Road" bill, with his usual power, and remarked, "I am in favor, Mr. Chairman, of all roads, except, except —" Here he stuck, at fault for a word, until Harrison Gray Otis, who sat near him on the platform, said in a low voice, "Say except the road to ruin." Mr. Webster adopted the suggestion, and used it as if he had merely paused to make his remark more effective.

In Bench and Bar, it is related that, while Webster was Secretary of State, the French Minister asked him whether the United States would recognize the new government of France. The Secretary assumed a very solemn tone and attitude, saying, "Why not? The United States has recognized the Bourbons, the French Republic, the Directory, the Council of Five Hundred, the First Consul, the Emperor, Louis XVIII., Charles X., Louis Philippe, the —" "Enough! Enough!" cried the Minister, perfectly satisfied by such a formidable citation of consistent precedents.

Mr. Webster lived in Somerset Street, and also at the corner of High and Summer Streets, during the different periods of his residence in Boston. The site of the house in Somerset Street is now covered by the mammoth new Court House. It was occupied successively by Uriah Cotting, Daniel Webster, Abbott Lawrence, and Rev. Ephraim Peabody of King's Chapel. Webster's residence in High Street is marked by a splendid block of stores, aptly styled "Webster Buildings." Here he resided at the time of Lafayette's visit in 1825, and received the distinguished Frenchman on the evening of the 17th of June.

Mr. Webster was a genuine lover of nature and of field sports, and was a good shot. He delighted in his farm at Marshfield, and in his well-fed cattle. Gray's Elegy was his favorite poem, and he was accustomed to repeat it with great feeling and emphasis. Of his two sons, Edward died in Mexico, a Major of the Massachusetts Volunteers; Fletcher, Colonel of the Twelfth Massachusetts Volunteers in the War of the Rebellion, was killed near Bull Run in 1862.

Daniel Webster's Residence, Somerset Street.

With two such distinguished lights of the profession as Otis and Webster before them, it is no wonder the old corner retains its magnetism for the disciples of Sir William Blackstone.

Having now passed down one side of ancient "Treamount" Street, we will repair to the corner of Howard Street, and go up the other side, following the practice of the fathers of the town, who numbered the streets consecutively down on one side and up the other. This is still the custom in London, and was doubtless imported with many other old-country usages.

Old "Treamount Street" began in 1708, at the extreme corner of Court Street and Tremont Row, as they now are, and extended around the base of what was first called Cotton Hill (so called as late as 1733), from the residence of Rev. John Cotton; subsequently Pemberton Hill, from James Pemberton, a later resident at the north end of what is now Pemberton Square. It was at first merely called a highway, like the other principal avenues, received very early the name of street, and was at the northerly part called Sudbury Lane, 1702. It terminated at Beacon Street. Pemberton Hill, a spur of Beacon, now marks a level of about eighty feet below the summit of the original hill, it having been cut down in 1835.

On the brow of the hill, later the residence of Gardiner Greene, was the mansion of Governor Endicott, that uncompromising Puritan who, in 1629, sent the obnoxious Episcopalians home to England, and afterwards cut out the cross from the King's standard because it "savored of popery." John Endicott was sent to America by the Massachusetts Company, in England, of which Mathew Cradock was governor, as their agent, and was governor of the colony which settled at Salem in 1628. He was the successor of Winthrop, as governor, in 1644, and again in 1649, and removed to Boston in the former year. Endicott filled a number of important offices; was appointed Sergeant Major-General in 1645, and in 1652 established a mint, which, though without legal authority, continued to supply a currency for more than thirty years. Governor

Endicott opposed the crusade of Rev. John Cotton against the wearing of veils by ladies, and had a warm personal discussion

ENDICOTT CUTTING OUT THE CROSS.

with that eminent divine. His portrait is more like a cardinal of Richelieu's time than a Puritan soldier. His head is covered by a close-fitting velvet skull-cap, from which the curling iron-gray hair is escaping down his shoulders ; a broad linen collar, fastened at the throat with cord and tassel, falls upon his breast, while his small white right hand is grasping a gauntlet richly embroidered. Endicott's forehead is massive, his nose large and prominent; but a gray mustache which decorates his upper lip effectually conceals the expression of his mouth, while a long imperial of the French fashion hides a portion of the chin. His whole countenance, however, indicates strength, resolution, and courage. The mutilation of the flag was not an act of bravado at a safe distance from punishment, but of conscience; and his portrait shows us that, having once formed a conviction, he would pursue it regardless of consequences.

Captain Cyprian Southack had a comfortable estate of two acres, in 1702, lying on the northerly and easterly slope of the hill. Howard Street, which was first named Southack's Court for him, subsequently Howard Street, from John Howard the philanthropist, ran through his lands. Captain Southack served under the famous Colonel Benjamin Church in an expedition against the French and Indians in 1704, in which he commanded a small vessel, called the Province Snow, of fourteen guns. When Admiral Sir H. Walker arrived in Boston in 1711, with a fleet and five thousand men destined to act against the French in Canada, he took up his residence with Southack in Tremont Street. The captain was to lead the van of the expedition.

In 1717 the pirate ship Whidah, commanded by the notorious Samuel Bellamy, was wrecked on the rocks of that part of Eastham, now Wellfleet. The council despatched Captain Southack to the scene of the disaster. His powers are indicated by the following original document:—

"By virtue of power to me, given by his Excellency Saml. Shute, Esq., Govt., and the Admiral, bearing date April 30th, 1717, to seize what goods, merchandise, or effects have or may be found or taken from the Pirate ship wreck at Cape Codd, and those taken up by Joseph Done, Esq., in carting and bringing in to me the subscriber for his Majesty's service at Mr. Wm. Brown's at Eastham.

"CYPRIAN SOUTHACK.

"EASTHAM, May 6, 1717."

Bellamy's ship was purposely run on shore by the captain of a small vessel he had captured the day before. The captain was to have received his vessel from the pirate in return for piloting him into Cape Cod harbor, but, distrusting the good faith of his captor, run his own vessel so near the rocks that the large ship of the pirate was wrecked in attempting to follow her. A storm arose, and the rest of the pirate fleet, thrown into confusion, shared the fate of their commander. Captain Southack buried one hundred and two bodies. A few that escaped the wreck were brought to Boston and executed. For a long time—as late as 1794—copper coins of William and Mary, and pieces of silver, called cob money, were picked up near the scene of the wreck. The violence of the sea moved the sands upon the outer bar, so that the iron caboose of the vessel was visible at low ebb.*

Theodore Lyman, senior, father of the mayor of that name, owned and occupied a mansion on the corner of Howard and Tremont Streets in 1785. A beautiful green lawn extended in front of his residence. These charming oases in the midst of the desert of brick walls have long ceased to exist except in the public squares. This lot was also intended to have been used by the Brattle Street Church Society when they rebuilt in 1772–73; but Governor Hancock, by the present of a bell,

* Massachusetts Historical Collections.

induced them to rebuild on the old site. This location was also occupied by Holland's Coffee House, afterwards the Pemberton House, destroyed by fire in 1854.

Passing the estate of John Jekyll, Esq., one of the earliest collectors of the port of Boston, 1707, and a great friend of his neighbors the Faneuils, we come to that of Rev. John Cotton, the spiritual father of Boston. John Cotton, as stated in our introductory chapter, was vicar of St. Botolph's Church in Boston, England, but inclined to the Puritan form of worship. Cited to appear before the notorious Archbishop Laud for omitting to kneel at the sacrament, he fled to America, and arrived in Boston in 1633, three years after the settlement. Here he became a colleague of the Rev. John Wilson in the pastorate of the First Church. He was a man of great learning, well acquainted with Latin, Greek, and Hebrew, and published many sermons and controversial works. He died from the effects of exposure in crossing the Cambridge ferry, and has a memorial erected to his memory in his old church of St. Botolph's, England, through the liberality of Edward Everett and other Bostonians.

The house of Mr. Cotton stood a little south of the entrance to Pemberton Square, near the street, as nearly as it can be located. It was then considered the oldest in Boston, and the back part, which remained unaltered, had the small diamond panes of glass set in lead. His ample estate extended back over the hill as far as Dr. Kirk's Church in Ashburton Place, and embraced all the central portion of what is now Pemberton Square.

This house had a still more distinguished tenant in Henry Vane the younger, who resided in it during his stay of two years in Boston, making some additions to the building for his own greater comfort. Sir Harry, whose eventful history is familiar, was received with great respect by Winthrop and the people of the town, on his arrival in 1635. His father, Sir Henry, was Secretary of State and Treasurer of the Household under James I. and Charles I. Alienated from the Church of England, young Harry Vane refused to take the oath of allegiance, and became a Republican and a Puritan. He was only twenty-four when chosen governor of Massachusetts Colony. During his administration the religious controversy between the congregation and the new sect of Familists, of which Anne Hutchinson was the acknowledged exponent, broke out. Sir Harry, opposed by Winthrop, was defeated at a second election of governor, but was immediately chosen a representative from the town to the General Court. Returning to England, in 1637, he was elected to Parliament and knighted in 1640. He is said to have presented the bill of attainder against the Earl of Strafford. Disliking Cromwell's dissolution of the Long Parliament, Vane withdrew from public affairs until 1649, when he became member of the Council of State, with almost exclusive control of naval and foreign affairs of the Commonwealth. At the restoration of Charles II. he was thrown into the Tower, and executed on Tower Hill, London, June 14, 1662. His bearing at the place of execution was manly and dignified, and he has been described by Forster as one of the greatest and purest men that ever walked the earth: —

> "Vane, young in years, but in sage counsel old,
> Than whom a better senator ne'er held
> The helm of Rome, when gowns, not arms, repelled
> The fierce Epirot and th' Afric bold,
> Whether to settle peace, or to unfold
> The drift of hollow states hard to be spelled;
> Then to advise how war may, best upheld,
> Move by her two main nerves, iron and gold,
> In all her equipage; besides, to know
> Both spiritual power and civil, what each means,
> What severs each, — thou hast learned what few have done,
> The bounds of either sword to thee we owe;
> Therefore on thy firm hand Religion leans
> In peace, and reckons thee her eldest son."

Judge Samuel Sewall, Chief Justice of the colony, in whose family the estates of Cotton and Bellingham became united, lived here in 1689. He was repeatedly applied to to sell a piece of his land to the Episcopalians to build a church upon, but refused. He married a daughter of John Hull, the celebrated mint-master, with whom he got, at different times, a snug portion of Master Hull's estate. He was one of the judges during the witchcraft trials of 1692, but afterwards expressed contrition for his share in that wretched business. Stoughton, on the contrary, on one occasion, indignant at the governor's reprieve of some of the victims, left the court exclaiming, "We were in a way to have cleared the land of these. Who is it obstructs the course of justice I know not. The Lord be merciful to the country!"

Judge Sewall was a considerable proprietor, owning a large estate on Beacon Hill, known in his time as Sewall's Elm Pasture. Through this were laid out anciently Coventry, Sewall, and Bishop-Stoke Street, the latter named from his English birthplace. The judge left a diary, now in possession of the Historical Society, containing much contemporary history. He attended the Old South, and related to Rev. Dr. Prince the story of Johnson's settlement and burial in Boston.

Patrick Jeffrey, who married Madam Haley, sister of the celebrated John Wilkes of the North Briton, became a subsequent possessor of the Cotton estate. Somerset Street, named from John Bowers of Somerset, Mass., crosses the Jeffrey or Cotton estate, and the former conveyed to the town, in 1801, so much of that street as passed through his property.

Another proprietor of the Cotton estate was Gardiner Greene, well remembered as one of the wealthiest citizens of Boston. By purchase of his neighbors, Mr. Greene became possessed of the larger portion of Pemberton Hill, which he greatly beautified and improved. The hill was terraced, and Mr. Greene's mansion — which, though substantial, had no special marks of elegance — was reached by long flights of steps. Mr. Greene is said to have owned the only greenhouse then existing in Boston, and his grounds, adorned by nature and art, made altogether the finest private residence in the town.

Mr. Greene's third wife was a sister of Lord Lyndhurst, son of the celebrated painter, Copley, and a Bostonian, who became a peer of the realm and Lord Chancellor of Great Britain. He was called the "Nestor of the House of Lords," and was noted for his dry caustic humor. Once, when Lord Brougham, speaking of the salary attached to a certain appointment, said it was all moonshine, Lyndhurst, in his waggish way remarked, "Maybe so, my Lord Harry; but I have a confounded strong notion that, moonshine though it be, you would like to see the first quarter of it."

Gardiner Greene's residence was occupied in 1775 by a noble tenant, Percy, afterwards Earl of Northumberland, gallant, chivalrous, and brave,—

> "Who, when a younger son,
> Fought for King George at Lexington,
> A major of dragoons."

Percy it was who saved the royal troops from destruction at Lexington, on the ever memorable 19th of April, 1775. He seems to have changed his quarters quite often, for, about the time of the affair at Lexington, he was ordered by General Gage to take possession of the Hancock house on Beacon Street. He also resided some time with Mrs. Sheaffe, widow of the collector, in Essex Street. We shall call on him at his several habitations.

Richard Bellingham, Esq., Governor of Massachusetts in 1635, in 1641, and again in 1654, and from 1666, after the death of Endicott, until his own decease in 1672, was the next neighbor of Cotton. Anne Hibbins, who married William Hibbins, an early settler of Boston, for many years in the service of the Colony, was a relative of Governor Bellingham. This unfortunate woman, denounced for witchcraft, was executed in 1656, when an accusation was equivalent to condemnation, and forfeited her life to the superstitious bigotry of the period. Governor Bellingham served the colony as governor and deputy for twenty-three years; was ordered by Charles II. to England with other obnoxious persons, but prudently declined going, by advice of the General Court. Bellingham, whose intellect was said to have been impaired, was an unrelenting persecutor of the Quakers. His house stood on the spot afterwards occupied by the residence of Lieutenant-Governor Phillips, opposite the north end of the Chapel Burying-Ground, and about midway from the entrance to Pemberton Square to Beacon Street.

The Bellingham estate was also the property of Peter Faneuil, who received it from Andrew, his uncle, in 1737. The house, a fine old stone mansion, stood on the hillside some distance back from the street. Opening into the cellar was a curious cylindrical brick vault, resembling in shape a wine-cask, and used as a wine-cellar by the more modern occupants. It was about fifteen feet in diameter by twenty-five feet long; and as it formed no part of the original cellar, which was amply sufficient for ordinary purposes, was considered to have been a place of concealment for smuggled goods.

The following description of the Faneuil house is from Miss Quincy's Memoir: "The deep court-yard, ornamented by flowers and shrubs, was divided into an upper and lower platform by a high glacis, surmounted by a richly wrought iron railing decorated with gilt balls. The edifice was of brick, painted white; and over the entrance door was a semicircular balcony. The terraces which rose from the paved court behind the house were supported by massy walls of hewn granite, and were ascended by flights of steps of the same material. A grasshopper yet glittered on a summer-house which commanded a view only second to that from Beacon Hill."

Such was the mansion at the time of its occupancy by Governor Phillips. Andrew Faneuil erected on this estate the first hothouse in New England. The deed to him describes the mansion as "a stone house."

The Faneuils were French Huguenots from La Rochelle, ever memorable from its siege and gallant defence, and came to America after the revocation of the Edict of Nantes. The name was always pronounced "Funel" by all old Bostonians, including Edward Everett, and is so cut on the tombstone in the Granary. Peter Faneuil is best known as the munificent donor of Faneuil Hall to the town of Boston. He was born at New Rochelle, near New York, in 1700; was the wealthiest Bostonian of his day, and after having lived only forty-two years, died suddenly of dropsy in 1742. Like many of his contemporaries, he was a slaveholder, and there is a sort of poetic justice in the fact that the first steps for the emancipation of slaves in Boston were taken in Faneuil Hall.

Peter Faneuil lived in a style worthy his position as a prince among merchants. He owned a chariot and coach, with English horses, for state occasions, and a two and four wheeled chaise for ordinary purposes. He had five negroes, and fourteen hundred ounces of plate, among which is enumerated "a large handsome chamber-pot." His cellar was bursting with good wine, arrack, beer, Cheshire and Gloucester cheeses, — what wonder his decease was sudden! — and he died owner of eight buildings in Cornhill and King Street, with many vessels and parts of vessels.

To retrograde a little, next north of Peter Faneuil's once dwelt Rev. John Davenport, who came over to Boston in 1637. He was one of the founders of New Haven, Connecticut. When the Regicides, as Charles I.'s judges Goffe and Whalley were styled, were forced to live in concealment, Davenport took them into his own house. Returning to Boston he became, in 1668, pastor of the First Church, but died in 1670, after holding his charge but a short time, and lies in the "Old Burial-Place," opposite where he once lived. The estate of Rev. John Davenport remained for nearly a century the property of the First Church, and was occupied by Foxcroft, Clarke, and others.

Lieutenant-Governor William Phillips, by birth a Bostonian, became the proprietor of the Faneuil mansion and estate in 1791, which was confiscated in 1783 by the Commonwealth. Governor Phillips also acquired the Davenport estate in 1805, which gave him a magnificent homestead, well worthy one of the solid men of Boston. He was in office from 1812 to 1823. Mr. Phillips made a most liberal use of the fortune he inherited, was a great benefactor of the Massachusetts General Hospital during his life, and made valuable bequests to Phillips Academy, Andover Theological Seminary, and other institutions.

Rev. John Oxenbridge, another pastor of the First Church,

lived on the site of the Pavilion in 1671. A former occupant was Colonel Samuel Shrimpton, who at one time owned Noddle's Island (East Boston), and gave his name to what is now Exchange Street, once Shrimpton's Lane. Rev. John Oxenbridge was educated at Oxford and also at Cambridge, was a popular preacher and a fluent writer. Dying in 1674, he was interred, like his predecessor Davenport, in the Old Burying-Place opposite. George Cradock, Collector of Boston, lived here in 1728.

We have now reached the corner of Beacon Street, which was first styled the lane leading to the Almshouse, a rather humble designation for the most aristocratic street of Boston. The Albion corner was once occupied by James Penn, ruling elder of the First Church, and a citizen of note. It became later the estate of Samuel Eliot, father of Mayor Eliot, noted for his reforms in the Fire Department. Both the Albion site and that of the block of houses west of it were occupied by Mr. Eliot's mansion-house and gardens. He was a true gentleman of the old school, wedded to the customs of a past generation. In the coldest weather he appeared in his customary cocked hat, small clothes, and ruffled shirt bosom, without cloak or overcoat. All the estates, from the Albion to the Pavilion, inclusive, are now covered by Houghton & Dutton's Department Store.

From the array of honorable names presented, Tremont Row was once entitled to be called the Rotten Row of Boston. Endicott, Vane, Bellingham, governors of the Colony; Phillips, lieutenant-governor of the State; and the eminent divines Cotton, Davenport, and Oxenbridge, all found a residence here.

We continue our perambulations through School Street, which, receiving its name from the old Latin School, was called Latin School Street. Its limits were the same as now, and it was first called the lane leading to Centry Hill. It was laid out in 1640.

Below the old King's Chapel stood the Latin School, whose situation and removal to the opposite side of the street has already been described. It originated in 1634, and Philemon Pormont was "intreated to become schoolmaster for the teaching and nourtering of children with vs." This was the beginning of that educational system in which Boston takes so just a pride. The grounds extended down the street nearly to the Franklin statue. The building itself was of one story, large enough to accommodate a hundred scholars. Franklin went to the Latin School one year, entering in 1714, at the age of eight years; his statue is, therefore, becomingly placed near his *alma mater*. John Hancock also attended the school, entering in 1745; his much-admired and striking autograph was doubtless acquired on its hard benches. Robert Treat Paine, the elder, Lieutenant-Governor Cushing, James Bowdoin, Cotton Mather, Samuel Adams, Sir William Pepperell, and a host of names famous in our history, prepared here for future high stations.

The early masters were men of erudition and high consideration in the town. Ezekiel Cheever ranks at the head of the old pedagogues. He was one of the founders of New Haven, and a teacher for seventy years at New Haven, Ipswich, Charlestown, and Boston.

John Lovell presided over the school, as usher and principal, from 1717 until 1775, when the siege put an end to it for a time. He decamped with the Royalists in 1776. He delivered the first public address in Faneuil Hall on the death of its founder. Lovell's house adjoined the new school, and after the evacuation General Gage's coach and phaeton, with harness entire, were found there.

Of the school on the opposite side of the street, which, till 1844, stood on the site of the Parker House, many distinguished Bostonians have been pupils, among whom Harrison Gray Otis, Rev. Dr. Jenks, R. C. Winthrop, Charles Sumner, and the sculptor Greenough are conspicuous.

The Centre Writing School was built in 1790, on the north side of School Street. It was a two-story wooden building, and was pulled down in 1812, as it then obstructed the front of the new Court House. This was the school of Master James Carter. The pupils were accommodated by an enlargement of the Latin School.

The statue in bronze of Benjamin Franklin, in the grounds

of the City Hall, is by Richard S. Greenough, and was cast by the Ames Manufacturing Company at Chicopee, Mass. It is eight feet high, and stands on a pedestal of granite, capped with a block of *verd antique* marble. Four bas-reliefs represent different periods of Franklin's career. It was publicly inaugurated September 17, 1856.

When Franklin worked in the printing-office of Mr. Watts, Little Wild Street, London, he was called by his fellow-workmen the "Water American," because he refused to drink anything else, while they drank their five pints of beer apiece daily. When he went to England afterwards, as agent for Massachusetts, he went into this office, and going up to a particular press (now in this country), said to the two workmen, "Come, my friends, we will drink together. It is now forty years since I worked like you at this press, a journeyman printer."

Franklin's celebrated toast at Versailles will not lose by repetition. At the conclusion of the war he, with the English Ambassador, was dining with the French Minister Vergennes; a toast from each was called for. The British minister began with, "George III., who, like the sun in its meridian, spreads a lustre throughout and enlightens the world." The French ambassador followed with, "Louis XVI., who, like the moon, sheds its mild and benignant rays on and illumines the world." Our American Franklin then gave, "George Washington, commander of the American armies, who, like Joshua of old, commanded the sun and moon to *stand still*, and they obeyed him."

The City Hall stands on ground sold to the town by Thomas Scotto in 1645. The foundation of the present building was laid in 1862 with appropriate ceremonies. It is built of Concord granite, and was designed by Messrs. Bryant and Gilman. The first Town House was erected between 1657–59, at the head of State Street, of wood, where the Old State House now stands. A legacy had been left by Captain Robert Keayne, in 1656, for this purpose, which was supplemented by subscriptions from Governors Endicott, Bellingham, and others. This building was consumed in the fire of 1711; another, built of brick in 1712, was burnt in 1747, with the early books, records, and valuable papers. In 1748 the Town House was rebuilt. Faneuil Hall was also used as a Town House for nearly eighty years, and the first city government was organized there. In 1830 the city government removed to the Old State

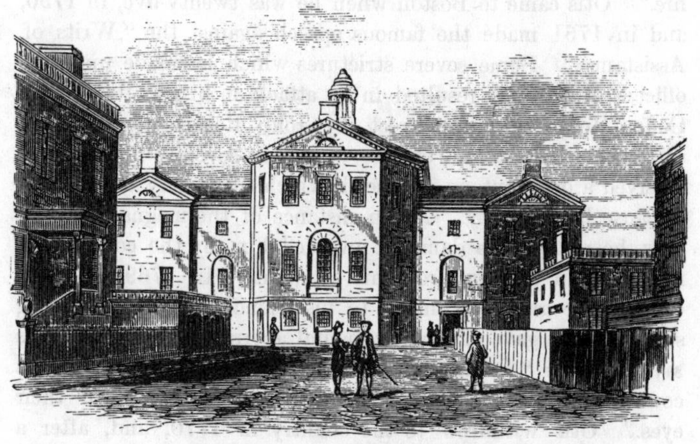

THE OLD COURT HOUSE AND CITY HALL.

House, which was, on September 17, dedicated as the City Hall. In 1840 the old County Court House, on the present site, was remodelled for a City Hall, and continued to be so used until the erection of the present building and its dedication in 1865.

Our view of the Old Court House is taken from School Street, and shows how the building and surroundings appeared in 1812. In the left foreground is Barristers' Hall, and to the right the wall and enclosure of Dr. Samuel Clarke's house is seen.

The County Court House, referred to as occupying this site, was built in 1810, of granite. The main building was octagonal, with wings at each side. It was one hundred and forty feet long, and was occupied by the offices of Probate, Registry of Deeds, and the County Courts. This building was called Johnson Hall, in honor of Isaac Johnson, tradition having ascribed to this spot the location of his house,—a name which does not seem to have been generally adopted.

Next the county property, in 1760, once lived one of the greatest of the ante-Revolutionary patriots, James Otis, "whose electric eloquence was like the ethereal flash that quenched its fire." Otis came to Boston when he was twenty-five, in 1750, and in 1761 made the famous speech against the "Writs of Assistance." Some severe strictures which he made upon the officers of customs resulted in an attack on him at the British Coffee House in King Street, by John Robinson, a commissioner of customs, and others. Otis was severely injured, and received a deep cut on the head, which ultimately contributed to cause his insanity. As an instance of the magnanimity of Otis, he refused the damages awarded him by the court, upon receiving an apology from his assailant. In 1769 Otis was causing the greatest concern to his friends for the increasing symptoms he gave of coming mental aberration. John Adams says of him: "I fear, I tremble, I mourn for the man and his country; many others mourn over him with tears in their eyes." Otis withdrew to the country in 1770, and, after a brief lucid period, during which he resumed practice in Boston, he was killed at Andover in May, 1783, by a stroke of lightning, at the age of fifty-eight.

Upon the ground where the Niles Building now is, was the house of Jean Paul Mascarene, a French Huguenot of Languedoc. He went to England and entered the army, coming in 1711 to Nova Scotia, of which he became Lieutenant-Governor, and ultimately rose to the rank of Major-General. He died in Boston in 1760. The house was of two stories, of brick, and painted white. The Mascarene family were loyalists, and retired to Nova Scotia when the Revolution began.

Dr. John Warren, the youngest brother of Joseph Warren, killed at Bunker Hill, next occupied the premises. The old house and gardens are still remembered by many. Dr. Warren served in the American army as hospital surgeon, and was long the most eminent surgeon in New England. On the day of Bunker Hill, the anxiety of the doctor for his brother led him to attempt to pass a guard, who gave him a bayonet wound, the mark of which he carried to his grave. Dr. Warren was the father of Dr. John C. Warren, scarcely less eminent in his profession than his father. The old doctor died in 1815, and was buried from King's Chapel, Dr. James Jackson delivering the eulogy. Both Joseph and John Warren were born in the old wooden house on Warren Street, in what was formerly Roxbury. The original mansion, being ruinous, was rebuilt on the site of the old in 1846, partly of the old materials, by Dr. John C. Warren. Many a pilgrimage is paid to the birthplace of the hero who placed himself, against the advice of friends, in the post of honor and of danger.

The Cromwell's Head, a famous tavern, was on the spot where the building numbered 19 now stands, which is to-day, as of yore, devoted to the replenishing of the inner man. It was kept by Anthony Brackett in 1760, by his widow from 1764 to 1768; and later by Joshua Brackett. Its repute was good, for we find the Marquis Chastellux alighting there in 1782, before paying his respects to M. de Vaudreuil, commander of the French fleet that was to convey away Rochambeau's army.

The sign of this hostelry was the effigy of the Lord Protector Cromwell, and it is said hung so low that all who passed were compelled to make an involuntary reverence. The royal officers would not allow it to remain; it was too suggestive of the overthrow of kingly authority; but Brackett, in whose eyes this circumstance gave it additional value, replaced it after the evacuation. Mine host Brackett's *carte* is surmounted by a *fac-simile* of the sign, from a plate by Paul Revere, and shows that besides board, lodging and eating, one might have wine, punch, porter, and liquor, with due care for his beast, for certain pounds, shillings, and pence. Brackett's, no doubt, commanded the patronage of his neighbors we have been noting. Rare Ben Jonson's lines might have been a trumpet-call to his votaries, —

> "Wine is the word that glads the heart of man,
> And mine 's the house of wine. *Sack* says my bush,
> *Be merry and drink sherry,* that 's my posie."

But mine host of Cromwell's Head had in 1756 a more distinguished guest, for in that year Lieutenant-Colonel Washington visited Boston accompanied by Captain George Mercer of Virginia and Captain Stewart. He came to refer a question of command to General Shirley who had succeeded Braddock in the military control of the colonies. This was after the disastrous campaign that ended in Braddock's defeat. Washington's next visit was with the commission of the Continental Congress as commander-in-chief.

The corner familiarly known as the "Old Corner Book-Store," where have gathered the disciples of black-letter and

THE OLD CORNER BOOKSTORE.

red-line for so many years, is probably the oldest brick building standing in Boston. It bears the date of 1712, and its erection is supposed to have occurred soon after the great fire of 1711. It is one of the few old landmarks remaining, but aside from its literary associations the corner has only a single historical incident worth noting.

Anne Hutchinson, who fills a chapter in the history of Boston commemorative of the ecclesiastical tyranny of its founders, lived here about 1634. She was the leader of the sect of Antinomians, and daughter of Rev. Francis Marbury of London, — an ancestor of Governor Thomas Hutchinson, and rector of several London parishes. Her mother was great aunt of John Dryden the poet. She was a woman of consummate ability and address, for we learn that Rev. John Cotton was ensnared by her, while Winthrop wavered. The latter, however, became her bitter enemy, and pursued her with great vindictiveness. For a time she had all Boston by the ears, and even public business halted.

Islebius, a German, appears to have founded the sect of Antinomians about 1600. It held the "law of Moses to be unprofitable, and that there is no sin in children." "Mistris Hutchison," as Governor Winthrop calls her, after a two days' trial was banished in 1638, and went to Rhode Island, the haven of religious refugees. Going afterwards to New York, she fell a victim to an Indian foray. Her followers in Boston, a numerous faction, were disarmed. Winthrop says "she was a woman of haughty and fierce carriage, a nimble wit and active spirit, a very voluble tongue, more bold than a man, though in understanding and judgment inferior to many women."

At the conclusion of Mrs. Hutchinson's trial she was addressed by Governor Winthrop as follows: —

"Mrs. Hutchinson! the sentence of the court you hear is, that you are banished from out of our jurisdiction, as being a woman not fit for our society, and are to be imprisoned 'til the court shall send you away."

Mrs. H. "I desire to know wherefore I am banished."

Winthrop. "Say no more; the court know wherefore, and is satisfied."

Just before you came to the Universalist Church, ascending School Street towards Tremont, was the little church of the French Huguenots of Boston. This was the church of the Faneuils, Baudoins, Boutineaus, Sigourneys, and Johonnots; their names are not quite extinct among us, although the orthography may be changed in some instances. The church was built of brick, about 1704, was very small, and for a long time its erection was opposed by the town. Before building, the French occupied one of the school-houses. Queen Anne presented a large folio Bible to this church, which afterwards fell into the possession of Mather Byles ; and Andrew Faneuil gave in his will three pieces of plate for communion and baptism, besides his warehouse in King Street. Pierre Daillé was the first minister, deceased in 1715, and was succeeded by Le Mercier. A singular incident led to the discovery of Daillé's gravestone. While laborers were excavating a cellar on the Emmons estate on Pleasant Street they suddenly uncovered the stone which bore the following inscription :—

Here lyes ye body of y^{e}
Reverend Mr. Peter
Daille minister of y^{e}
French church in
Boston died the
21 of May 1715
In the 67 year
Of his age.

After the dissolution of the society, the house of the French Church fell into the hands of the Eleventh Congregational Society, which arose during the excitement caused by the coming of Whitefield. Mr. Crosswell was the pastor, dying in 1785, when the house passed to the Roman Catholics. Mass was first celebrated in the church in November, 1788. It was removed in 1802.

The Second Universalist Church stood next below the corner estate, now occupied by the Five Cents Savings Bank, opposite to the Niles Building. It was erected in 1817, after preliminary action in the preceding year by a meeting held at the Green Dragon Tavern. It was much enlarged and improved in 1837, and entirely remodelled in 1851. Rev. Hosea Ballou was the first pastor. Rev. E. H. Chapin preached here from 1846 to 1848, when he removed to New York, and Rev. A. A. Miner until the removal to Columbus Avenue.

Province Street received its name in 1833, from its vicinity to the Province House. Before that time it was Governor's Alley. Chapman Place was Cooke's Court, from Elisha Cooke, a resident of colonial times, who was agent with Increase Mather in England to obtain a new charter for the colony. The house of Elisha Cooke becomes distinguished as the residence of Governor Burnet until the Province House could be made ready. The house was a two-story brick, with dormer windows, and faced the east. In front was a small court-yard.

Loring, in the "Hundred Boston Orators," says: "The residence of James Lovell during the Revolution was on the estate where Chapman Hall is now located, and his family witnessed, on the house-top, the burning of Charlestown during the battle of Bunker Hill. While Mr. Lovell was imprisoned in the Boston jail, in Queen Street, in consequence of General Howe having discovered a prohibited correspondence, proving his adherence to the Revolutionary cause, his devoted wife was daily accustomed to convey his food to the prison door." Chapman Hall was in Chapman Place, and is now succeeded by the Parker House.

James was a son of that Master Lovell of whom mention has been made. He had been usher of that school, and master of what is now the Eliot School. He was among the prominent Revolutionary patriots, and had first been imprisoned and finally carried to Halifax on the evacuation. After being exchanged in 1776, Master Lovell became a member of the Continental Congress; was receiver of taxes in 1784, and after being Collector of the port, was for a long time Naval Officer. His son married Helen, one of Mr. Sheaffe's handsome daughters.

Besides having replaced the Latin School, the Parker House also occupies the ground where there long remained an old brick mansion, erected early in the last century by Jacob Wendell. He was a wealthy merchant, and colonel of the Boston Regiment in 1745; afterwards a councillor, and a director in the first banking institution in the province. His son Oliver, also a leading Bostonian, was the grandfather of Oliver Wendell Holmes, the only "autocrat" who has ever flourished in Boston. Wendell's garden reached to Tremont Street.

Oliver Wendell was, like his father, a leading merchant of

Boston. He was a selectman during the siege, and joined in the congratulatory address to Washington when it was terminated by the evacuation. The following original document shows us that Wendell was trusted by the commander-in-chief:—

The United States of America to the Subscribers Dr.

To one month's services by Land and Sea, from March, 25th 1776, to April 25th, Strictly watching the communication from the Town of Boston to the British fleet Laying in Nantasket Road in Order to apprehend and seize any British Spies who might have Concealed themselves in the Town in order to Carry Intelligence to our Enemies of the Proceedings of the American Troops then in the Town of Boston, by Order of Major Generall Greene.

Thirty Days Each man at 12/ p Day is £ 108.—

BENJ WHEELER
BENJ[A] BARNARD
ANDREW SYMMES JR
JOSHUA BENTLEY
JOHN CHAMPNEY
THOMAS TILESTON

Rec the within Contents in full

OLIVER WENDELL

The following is indorsed on the back:—

Pay unto Oliver Wendal Esquire one hundred eight pounds Lawful money for the use of the signers of the within account, he being employed by Major General Greene by my order to engage a number of persons for the within service in March 1776 when the Enemy evacuated Boston.

Given under my hand at
Camp Fredericksburg Novem 12 1778

Hon Major Genl. Gates

G. WASHINGTON

To Ebenezer Hancock Esq Paymaster Genl
Eastern Department

Sir,—Pay the above sum of one hundred and eight pounds Lawful money to Oliver Wendell Esq in consequence of the above order for which this with his receipt shall be your sufficient Warrant By the Generals command

HORATIO GATES

John Armstrong Jr
Aid de Camp Head Quarters 25th November 1778

Joseph Green, beyond comparison the keenest wit of his

time, lived in School Street. He was a merchant, — Dr. Byles terms him a distiller, — and accumulated a handsome property. He was the general satirist, epic, and epitaph writer of his day, and wielded a trenchant pen, of which none stood more in awe than Governor Belcher. His epitaph on the countryman whose *forte* was raking hay, in which he excelled all but his employer, is as follows : —

> "He could rake hay ; none could rake faster,
> Except that raking dog his master."

Green, who was well advanced in life when the Revolutionary struggle begun, removed to England, where he engaged in business, residing in the parish of St. Andrew, Holborn, London. He died in London in 1780. There is a portrait of Joseph Green, by Copley, in the possession of the heirs of Rev. W. T. Snow. Green often ran a tilt with Mather Byles, unhorsing his clerical opponent with his goose-quill lance. His residence was between the house of Dr. Warren and the Cromwell's Head.

FROM A PLATE BY PAUL REVERE.

CHAPTER II.

FROM THE ORANGE-TREE TO THE OLD BRICK.

Hanover Street. — General Warren. — The Orange-Tree. — Concert Hall. — Brattle Street. — Samuel Gore. — John Smibert. — Nathaniel Smibert. — Colonel Trumbull. — The Adelphi. — Scollay's Buildings and Square. — Queen Street Writing School. — Master James Carter. — Cornhill. — Brattle Street Parsonage. — Old Prison. — Captain Kidd. — Court Houses. — Franklin Avenue. — Kneeland. — Franklin. — Edes and Gill. — Green and Russell. — First Book and Newspaper printed in Boston. — Rufus Choate. — Governor Leverett. — John A. Andrew. — Henry Dunster. — Town Pump. — Old Brick. — General Knox. — Count Rumford. — John Winslow.

STANDING at the head of Hanover Street, we are sensible that improvement has ploughed a broad furrow through the North End. Away before us stretches a broad avenue, where once vehicles passed each other with difficulty. As the old street was, there were places where it was no great feat to jump across. This was the old highway from Winnisimmet Ferry to Treamount Street, first called Orange-Tree Lane, from the tavern at its head. Hanover Street extended at first only from Court to Blackstone Streets. Why this name, a perpetual reminder of a detested House, should have been retained, when Queen retired before Court, and King succumbed to State, we cannot otherwise answer than by supposing the changes during the Revolution spasmodic, rather than systematic efforts of republicanism.

As we look down this street, a little way on our left stands the American House. On the ground it covers lived that early martyr to American freedom, General Joseph Warren, who in 1764, after his marriage, took up his residence and the practice of medicine on this spot. He went to Brattle Street Church, near by. In 1774, while the "Boston Port Bill" was in operation, there was a good deal of suffering in consequence of the closing of the port, and at this time Colonel Putnam, better known as "Old Put," came to Boston with a drove of sheep for the inhabitants, and was Warren's guest.

It was Warren who caused the alarm to be given of the British expedition to Concord, by sending Paul Revere on his famous night ride, and gave timely warning to Hancock and Adams. There are many stories of the manner of Warren's death at Bunker Hill, some of them highly colored. He was killed after the retreat began, a little way in the rear of the famous redoubt. General Howe, who knew Warren well, said his death was equal to the loss of five hundred men. Colonel John Trumbull, who, when in England in 1786, painted his picture of the Battle of Bunker Hill, gives the following relation of the fall of Warren by Colonel Small, who was on the field, and is represented by Trumbull endeavoring to save the life of Warren :—

"At the moment when the troops succeeded in carrying the redoubt, and the Americans were in full retreat, General Howe, who had been wounded by a spent ball, was leaning on my arm. He called suddenly to me, 'Do you see that elegant young man who has just fallen?' I looked to the spot to which he pointed. 'Good God!' he exclaimed, 'I believe it is my friend Warren; leave me then instantly, — run, — keep off the troops, — save him if possible!' I flew to the spot. 'My dear friend,' I said to him, 'I hope you are not badly hurt.' He looked up, seemed to recollect, smiled, and died. A musket-ball had passed through the upper part of his head."

The body lay on the field until the next day, when it was recognized by Dr. Jeffries and John Winslow of Boston, and interred on the spot where he fell. General Howe's solicitude does not seem to have extended to Warren's remains, which, however, received a soldier's burial. After the evacuation the body was disinterred and deposited in King's Chapel, and subsequently in St. Paul's, Tremont Street. The ball which killed Warren is now in possession of the Genealogical Society. It is a common ounce musket-ball, and does not look at all flattened. It must ever appear unaccountable why General Ward, at Cambridge, did not attempt to recover the body of the President of the Provincial Congress. The usages of war must have been well known to him, and Howe was not the man to refuse the request.

Thus died in "the imminent deadly breach" the young hero at the early age of thirty-four. President of the Committee of Safety, of the Provincial Congress, and Major-General, he declined the command at Bunker Hill, taking the place of a common soldier. Deeply hurt by the reflections cast upon the courage of his countrymen, he is said to have exclaimed, "I hope I shall die up to my knees in blood." To the remonstrances of his friend, Elbridge Gerry, who begged him not to go to Bunker Hill, Warren replied, "*Dulce et decorum est pro patria mori.*"

Adjoining the American House on the west are Codman's Buildings, covering the ground where stood the famous Earl's Coffee House in bygone days. It was established in 1806, and was the headquarters of the New York, Albany, and other mail coaches.

"Go call a coach, and let a coach be called."

On the north corner of Hanover Street was the Orange-Tree Tavern, which designated the northerly end of Treamount Street in 1732, and beginning of Hanover Street in 1708. It continued a tavern until 1785, when it was advertised to be sold. The name was from the sign of an orange-tree, and the inn was noted for the best well of water in the town, — never dry nor known to freeze. Here was the first hackney-coach stand we have an account of, set up by Jonathan Wardwell, keeper of the Orange-Tree, in 1712. He was succeeded by Mrs. Wardwell, who kept the house in 1724.

Concert Hall, of which a considerable moiety is now in the street, was on the southerly corner, and was also a tavern, kept, in 1792, by James Vila. The site was first known as Houchin's Corner, from a tanner of that name who occupied it. The building was of brick, though it underwent various alterations until torn down in 1869, to make way for the widening of Hanover Street. Concert Hall was owned by the family of Deblois until 1679. Before the Revolution it was a resort of the

Concert Hall (Court and Hanover Streets). From a Water-color.

Friends of Liberty, and as early as 1755, after the installation of Jeremy Gridley as Grand Master of the Masons in North America, it was used by the Grand Lodge for occasions of meeting or festivity, and continued to be so used until the present century. Here have met Gridley, the Warrens, Revere, Tomlinson, Oxnard, Webb, and others. Here Captain Preston was dallying on the evening of the fatal 5th of March, 1770, when he was summoned in hot haste to begin the first act of the great conflict of the American Revolution. The American prisoners captured at Bunker Hill are said to have been tried by a military court in Concert Hall. In 1768 the obnoxious Commissioners of Customs ventured to return from the Castle, while the town was under the control of the newly arrived British troops, and had an office here, with a sentinel at the door. And here came Samuel Adams and James Otis to remonstrate with them.

According to the "News Letter," concerts were held in the old hall as early as January, 1755, when "a concert of musick" was advertised to take place there, tickets at four shillings each. Governor Hancock gave, in 1778, a grand ball in Concert Hall to the officers of D'Estaing's fleet, at which three hundred persons were present. The Society of the Cincinnati also held meetings in this hall, and the Massachusetts Mechanic Charitable Association had their first meetings therein. Peter B. Brigham was for about forty years mine host of Concert Hall.

A little east of Concert Hall on Hanover Street lived William Cooper, Town Clerk of Boston for nearly half a century. His term embraced the Revolutionary period, during which he was an ardent friend of the Whig cause. He was a brother of the patriotic pastor of Old Brattle Street Church.

Brattle Street was opened in 1819, from Court Street to the Church. Before this it was a narrow way, known first as Hillier's Lane, and sometimes as Belknap's, and as Gay Alley. Looking towards the site of the old church we notice, on the north side of the street, a continuous row of granite buildings, uniform in their general appearance. This was the first block of stone buildings erected in Boston.

At the head of Brattle Street lived Samuel Gore, elder brother of Christopher, afterwards governor of the Commonwealth. Gore was a painter, and was one of those stout-hearted mechanics who furnished the muscle of the Revolution while Adams and Otis supplied the brain. One of the Tea Party of 1773, Gore was one of those who seized the two brass guns, Hancock and Adams, from the gun-house in Tremont Street, and conveyed them to the American lines under the very eyes of the British. These two guns are now in Bunker Hill Monument.

The celebrated Scotch painter, John Smibert, owned and occupied the premises between Brattle Street and Cornhill in 1743, having acquired part through his marriage with Mary Williams of Boston, and part by purchase. The biographers have but little to say about this pioneer of the fine arts in America. He was before West or Copley, and is said to have influenced the works of the latter, as well as those of Allston and Trumbull.

Smibert must have had a large and lucrative custom, for he was possessed of property in Boston and Roxbury, which he bought from time to time, and at his decease left in his studio thirty-five portraits, valued by the appraisers at £60 5*s.* 8*d.* Thirteen "landskips" were estimated at the moderate sum of £2 13*s.*, while four historical pieces, "and pictures in that taste," were considered worth £16. Two conversation pictures, whatever they may have been, were thought worth £23 6*s.* 8*d.* His negro girl, Phillis, went for £26 13*s.* 4*d.* He kept his horses and chaise, in which he used to take his wife, Mary Smibert, to Lynde Street Church to hear good Dr. Hooper.

Smibert came over to America in 1728 with the Dean, afterwards Bishop Berkeley, settling in Boston in 1730. The largest known work of Smibert's in this country is his picture of Berkeley and family, in which the portrait of the artist is introduced. This painting is now in the possession of Yale College. His portrait of Jonathan Edwards is said to be the only one extant of that learned and eminent divine.

Nathaniel Smibert, son of John, took up the profession of his father. He went to the Latin School, under Master Lovell, in his early youth, but soon turned to his father's brush and easel, with the promise of making a finished artist, but died at the early age of twenty-one, deeply regretted by all who knew him.

Colonel John Trumbull, aide-de-camp to Washington during the siege, retired in disgust from the service in 1777, on account of the date of an appointment to the rank of colonel, by Gates, being rejected by Congress. He then resumed his study of painting in Boston, amidst the works of Copley, and in the room which had been built by Smibert, and in which remained many of his works. Governor Hancock sat for his portrait to Trumbull while the latter was in Boston. Hancock was president of the Congress which ignored Trumbull's rank, and had also spoken rather slightly of his family being well cared for by the government, on seeing the latter at the headquarters of Washington. Trumbull was stung by the ungenerous remark, and when, after having served as a volunteer in the expedition to Rhode Island in 1778, he fell ill on his return, he at first repelled the advances of Governor Hancock, who, by considerate attentions, repaired his original offence. Trumbull was a historical painter. The Trumbull Gallery at Yale contains fifty-seven pictures by him. An engraved likeness of Governor Yale, for whom the college was named, is one of the first you see on entering the gallery. The following is his epitaph in the churchyard at Wrexham:—

> "Born in America, in Europe bred,
> In Africa travel'd, and in Asia wed,
> Where long he lived and thrived ; at London dead.
> Much Good, some Ill he did ; so hope all 's even,
> And that his soul through Mercy 's gone to heaven."

Trumbull exhibited, in 1818, in Faneuil Hall, his picture of the Declaration, which John Randolph irreverently called the shin-piece. The venerable John Adams went to see it, and, pointing to the door next the chair of Hancock, said, "There, that is the door out of which Washington rushed when I first alluded to him as the man best qualified for Commander-in-Chief of the American Army." *

* Miss Quincy's Memoir.

Colonel Trumbull's historical paintings in the rotunda of the Capitol at Washington have gained him a world-wide reputation; his "Sortie from Gibraltar" is now in the Museum of Fine Arts. He was a fellow-student with Stuart, under West.

The paint-room of the Smiberts and of Trumbull continued to be occupied by various artists of lesser note until 1785. At this time Mrs. Sheaffe occupied the abode of the Smiberts as a boarding-house. This lady has acquired celebrity through her children. In those days painters sometimes styled themselves limners. One of Mrs. Sheaffe's boarders varied the monotony of portrait painting by doing hair-work in the neatest manner. Part of the Smibert estate went to make the present Brattle Street.

This locality, after having served the New England Museum, was, in course of time, appropriated by the Adelphi Theatre. John Brougham was, in 1847, associated with Mr. Bland as manager, with Mrs. Brougham and Mr. Whiting in the *corps dramatique.* The Adelphi was a side-splitting affair, defying the conventionalities of the modern stage. An open bar stood in the rear of the auditorium, to which the audience were invited to repair upon the falling of the curtain.

One of the greatest changes that has occurred in Boston is the transformation of the over-crowded thoroughfares around what was known as "Scollay's Buildings" into the spacious, pleasant area we now call Scollay Square. All of the original is gone except the distinctive appellation, and what has existed in some form for two centuries has vanished

"Like the baseless fabric of a vision."

The Scollays were Scotch, from the Orkneys. John Scollay is mentioned, in 1692, as lessee of Winnisimmet Ferry. Another John Scollay, of the Revolutionary period, was a man of considerable note in Boston. He was one of the first Fire-Wards of the town, and a selectman during the siege. His son, William, is the one for whom the buildings and square were named. The name, however, and his proprietorship only date back to about 1800. William Scollay was a commander of the Cadets, an apothecary at No. 6 Old Cornhill, and resided on the site of the Museum in Tremont Street. He was prominently identified with Charles Bulfinch and others in the improvement of Franklin Street.

A long row of wooden buildings at one time extended from the head of Cornhill to nearly opposite the head of Hanover Street. Both ends of this wedge-shaped range of houses, with the point towards Hanover Street, were cut off at various times, leaving only the brick structure of Scollay, since removed. Scollay's Building was supposed to have been erected by Patrick Jeffrey, who came into possession in 1795. Neither age nor incident render the building an object of special interest.

Opposite to where Cornhill now opens into Court Street was erected, in 1683–84, the second school-house in the town. The first being styled the Latin School, this was termed the Free Writing School. It is clearly mentioned in 1697, and continued to be used until 1793, when it became private property, the school — then known as the Centre Reading and Writing School — being removed to School Street. The first master here was Samuel Cole.

The preamble to the first law establishing schools reads thus: —

"It being one chief project of Satan to keep men from the knowledge of the Scriptures, as in former times keeping them in unknown tongues; to the end, therefore, that learning may not be buried in the graves of our forefathers, in church and Commonwealth, it is enacted," etc.

The school-house is brought into notice in 1744, by a somewhat curious affair. It appears that Captain W. Montague, afterwards a British Admiral, came ashore from his ship, the frigate Eltham, then lying in Nantasket Roads, and, accompanied by a party from his vessel, indulged in a regular sailor's lark on shore. In the course of their rambles the party committed some depredations on the school-house, for which warrants were issued against some of the offenders.

James Carter was the most famous of the masters of this old school. He was a pedagogue of an extinct type, and after a long term of service, continuing almost to the time of his death, was buried December 2, 1797. His house adjoined the school-house on the west. Turell's Museum once occupied the old school-house, part of which was removed upon the completion of Cornhill, to afford a free passage into Tremont Street.

Green and Russell, one of the old printing houses of Boston, transacted business in an old building that stood on the site of Scollay's, in 1755. Joseph Russell, one of the partners, carried on the business of an auctioneer, in which he was very successful, and became the owner of the property. William Vassall, a royalist refugee, in 1776, was the next proprietor, followed by Jeffrey. The Colonial Custom-house stood very near this locality in 1757, but we have been unable to discover its exact site.

Cornhill owes its name, no doubt, originally, to its London prototype. It is the second street which has borne the name in Boston, and was first called Market Street, as it opened a new route to Faneuil Hall Market. The stores erected in this street were the first raised on granite pillars in Boston. Uriah Cotting built the street in 1817. To his genius Boston owes a debt not yet suitably recognized. Mr. Cotting's remains lie beneath an humble tomb in Granary Burying-ground, but we may appropriately apply to him the epitaph of Sir Christopher Wren: —

"Reader, if thou seekest his monument, look around."

Opposite to us, on the premises of the Adams Express Company, was the old Parsonage House of Brattle Square Church, given to it by Mrs. Lydia Hancock in 1765. She was the wife of Thomas Hancock (uncle of the patriot), and resided in the old house, as also did her father, Colonel Daniel Henchman, grandson of the old Indian fighter. Henchman was a bookseller and bookbinder, and Thomas Hancock served his time with him. Colonel Henchman established the first paper-mill in the colony, at Milton. Since their day it was the residence of the pastors of the church, — last, that of Dr. Lothrop. This house has been noted as one of the dwelling-places of James Otis.

The Old Prison stood on the spot where now the massive

granite Court House is placed. From it the street was very early named Prison Lane, changed to Queen Street in 1708, and to Court in 1784. What the Old Prison was like is left to conjecture, but we will let an old master of the imaginative art describe it: "The rust on the ponderous iron-work of its oaken door looked more antique than anything else in the New World. Like all that pertains to crime, it seemed never to have known a youthful era." The fancy of Hawthorne in locating a blooming rose-bush on the grass-plot beside the prison door is striking. Here were confined the victims of the terrible witchcraft delusion.

"Who is he? one that for lack of land
Shall fight upon the water."

This heavy oaken door stood between the notorious pirate, William Kidd, and liberty. He arrived in Boston in June, 1699, with his sloop, and was examined before the Earl of Bellomont and the Council of the province. On the 6th of June Kidd was seized and committed to prison with several of his crew, and his vessel taken possession of. When arrested, Kidd attempted to draw his sword and defend himself. By order of the king, he was sent to England in a frigate, and arrived in London April 11, 1700. He was examined before the Admiralty, and afterwards before the House of Lords, where great efforts were made to implicate the Earl of Bellomont and other of the lords in Kidd's transactions. The pirate, after a long confinement, was finally hung at Execution Dock. He died hard. The rope broke the first time he was tied up, and he fell to the ground; a second trial proved more successful.

It has been claimed that Kidd was not a pirate. He was an officer in the British navy prior to 1691, married in this country, and had commanded a merchant ship owned by Robert Livingstone, a wealthy New York merchant. When, in 1695, the coast of New England was infested with pirates, Livingstone proposed to the Earl of Bellomont to employ Kidd to go in pursuit of them, and offered to share the expense of fitting out a vessel. Application was made to the home government for a thirty-gun ship, and a commission for Kidd for this purpose; but, the government being then unable to furnish a vessel, the Earl of Bellomont, Lords Halifax, Somers, Romney, Oxford, and others contributed, with Livingstone, to fit Kidd out in the Adventure Galley. He received a commission from the Court of Admiralty in December, 1695, authorizing him to cruise against the king's enemies.

Once at sea, Kidd turned pirate, reversing the adage "Set a rogue to catch a rogue," and made several captures; but his exploits preceded him, and on his return to New England he was arrested. The search after the pirate's hidden treasure has continued ever since. A pot of dollars was dug up in 1790 on Long Island, supposed to have been Kidd's. The fate of the freebooter has often been lamented in the melancholy ditty, —

"My name was Captain Kidd, as I sailed," etc.

The Old Prison, ugly and uncouth, gave place to a new in 1767, designed by Governor Bernard. This was, two years later, destroyed by fire, the prisoners being with difficulty rescued; some of them were badly burned.* The site was then appropriated by a Court House built of brick, about the Revolutionary period, three stories high, with a cupola and bell. Before the erection of the County Court House (City Hall), in 1810, this building was used by all the courts of law held in the county.

At this time the County Jail was in an old stone building situated between the Old Court House, just described, and the New. On the ground where it stood was formerly an old wooden building called the Debtor's Jail. The County Jail and Municipal Court House were, in 1822, situated in Leverett Street.

In 1851 the keys of the Old Prison in Court Street were found under the office of the Leverett Street jail, where they had lain since 1823. They were three in number; were from twelve to eighteen inches in length, and of a most primitive construction. The keys weighed from one to three pounds each, and when attached to the jailer's girdle, must have been

* Drake's History of Boston.

weighty arguments to his wards. These keys, when found, were over a hundred years old. What a tale they could tell!

In September, 1833, the corner-stone of the present Court House was laid, and it was completed in 1836. The building is massive and unattractive. Within its granite walls the fugitive slave cases were tried, and here also Professor John W. Webster received the death sentence for the murder of Dr. Parkman.

The little alley which enters Court Street opposite the easterly side of Court Square is not unknown to fame. It is today Franklin Avenue, but was very early called Dorset's Lane, and in 1722 was a part of Brattle Street. Daniel Webster's first office was on the northerly corner of this alley. On this corner where also was the Advertiser building Samuel Kneeland began the printing business in 1718, in quite another fashion. Thomas, in his History of Printing, says:—

OLD PRINTING-PRESS.

"William Brooker, being appointed Postmaster of Boston, he, on Monday, December 21, 1719, began the publication of another newspaper in that place. This was the second published in the British Colonies, in North America, and was entitled 'The Boston Gazette.' James Franklin was originally employed as printer of this paper; but in two or three months after the publication commenced Philip Musgrave was appointed Postmaster, and became proprietor of it. He took the printing of it from Franklin, and gave it to Kneeland. Kneeland also published here, in 1727, 'The New England Journal.' He occupied the office for about forty years."

This is also the location assigned James Franklin, the brother of Benjamin, who, as we have mentioned, printed "The Boston Gazette," on Monday, December 21, 1719. He began, August 6, 1721, the publication of "The New England Courant," the third newspaper in the town. It was, like the other papers, printed on a half-sheet of foolscap, and, being of a more progressive cast than the others, soon fell under the ban of rigid Puritans like Rev. Increase Mather. The first number of this paper, made famous by Benjamin Franklin's connection with it, has been reprinted, and the whole contents might easily be contained in a single column of one of our present journals. Two very primitive woodcuts, one representing a war ship under full sail, the other a postman galloping over a village, adorn the pages.

Benjamin became his brother's apprentice at the age of twelve, in 1718. He soon began to write clandestinely for the paper, and thrust his productions furtively under the office door. But his essays were approved and printed. In 1723, James Franklin being forbidden to publish the Courant, it was issued under the name of his younger brother, and bore the imprint, "Boston, printed and sold by Benjamin Franklin, in Queen-Street, where advertisements are taken in."

Benjamin Franklin remained but a short time with his brother after this. The old press on which he worked fell into the possession of Major Poore, of West Newbury, Mass., who obtained it of Isaiah Thomas's heirs. It bears no date, and is old enough to be located at any time since printing began, without danger of dispute. Major Poore was confident of the authenticity of this press, tracing it by Thomas to the office of James Franklin. The building, interesting by its association with the early history of printing in Boston, became a bookstore, ornamented with a head of Franklin, and disappeared a great many years ago. The amusing *rencontre* of Franklin with his future wife, Miss Reed, of Philadelphia, will always excite a smile.

The house was occupied for eighty years as a printing-house, by Kneeland and others. In 1769 it became the office of Edes and Gill, who continued there until hostilities commenced, in 1776. Edes and Gill printed a copy of the "Stamp Act," in a pamphlet of twenty-four pages. They also published "The Boston Gazette and Country Journal," a successor of the Gazette of Franklin, Kneeland, etc., which had been discontinued.

Edes and Gill, when they printed the Stamp Act, occupied premises on the south side of Court Street, about on the present site of the Scollay Building. In their back office, on the old corner, the council for the destruction of the tea was held, of which Samuel Adams was the master spirit. The Gazette, under the control of Edes and Gill, was the paper in which Adams, Otis, Warren, Quincy, and other leaders of popular feeling, wrote, and became conspicuous for its able political articles. We present two specimens of the renowned British Stamps.

Over the printing-office was a long room in which were wont to meet the active patriots. They took the name of the Long Room Club. Samuel Adams was the leader. Hancock, Otis, Samuel Dexter, William Cooper, town clerk, Dr. Cooper, Warren, Church, Josiah Quincy, Jr., Thomas Dawes, Samuel Phillips, Royal Tyler, Paul Revere, Thomas Fleet, John Winslow, Thomas Melvill, and some others, were members. In this room were matured most of the plans for resistance to British usurpation, from the Stamp Act to the formation of the Provincial Congress at Watertown.

After the avenues from the town were closed by General Gage, Edes made his escape by night, in a boat, with a press and a few types, with which he opened an office in Watertown, and printed for the Provincial Congress of Massachusetts. John Gill, his partner, remained in Boston and was imprisoned for printing treason, sedition, and rebellion. Green and Russell, in 1758, became occupants of the corner, and printed the "Weekly Advertiser" therein, which may be considered the progenitor of the present journal of that name.

Court Street was long the headquarters of the newspaper

press. During exciting political controversies abuse sometimes waxed warm. In the language of a writer at the beginning of the present century, —

> "Press answers press; retorting slander flies,
> And Court Street rivals Billingsgate in lies."

The first book printed in Boston was an election sermon preached to Governor John Leverett, the Council, and Deputies of the Colony, May 3, 1676. It was a small quarto pamphlet of sixty-three pages. John Foster was the printer.

The first regular newspaper was the "News Letter," issued April 24, 1704, by John Campbell, Postmaster of Boston at that time. Bartholomew Green was the printer. Green continued to print it until the close of 1707. The building in which the News Letter was printed stood very near the east corner of Avon Street, on Washington.

Tudor's Buildings were so named for Colonel William Tudor, who lived on the site. He was a member of the old Boston Bar, having studied with John Adams. He was colonel and judge-advocate-general in the Revolutionary army, on the staff of Washington. Colonel Tudor was also a member of the Massachusetts House and Senate, Secretary of State 1809–10, and one of the founders of the Historical Society. Fisher Ames, Judge Parker, afterwards Chief Justice, and Josiah Quincy, studied law with him. Young's Hotel now occupies the site.

It is related that Colonel Tudor was once presented at the court of George III. by our ambassador, Rufus King. His Majesty catching the name, ejaculated in his disjointed way: "Eh! what, what, Tudor, Tudor, — one of us, eh?"

Rufus Choate, who as an advocate left no successor at the Boston bar, had an office in the gloomy granite block that formerly stood below the Court House, on the site of the Sears Building. He had also, for a time, an office on Tremont Row. Choate came to Boston in 1834, after having studied law in the office of William Wirt at Washington. He was not long in taking the place left vacant by Mr. Webster.

Besides pathos, which he could bring to bear with overwhelming effect, Choate possessed a fine humor. It is said that, coming into court one day to hear a decision against him from Chief Justice Shaw, who was by no means a handsome man, Choate addressed his Honor in these words: "In coming into the presence of your Honor I experience the same feelings that the Hindoo does when he bows before his idol, — I know that you are ugly, but I feel that you are great." *

Mr. Choate's face possessed great mobility, and his voice was capable of the most varied modulation. When pleading a criminal cause he held court, jury, and auditory alike in a spell, and seldom failed to sway the jury by his eloquence. He had the magnetism of a natural orator, and could make his auditors weep or laugh at will. Mr. Choate held the offices of State representative and senator; was elected to Congress from the Essex district; and succeeded Webster in the Senate in 1841. In 1853 he was attorney-general of Massachusetts and a member of the Constitutional Convention. He retired from practice in 1858, on account of failing health, and died in Halifax in 1859, while *en route* to Europe. He was sixty years old when this event occurred.

Where now stands the stately Sears Building was once the habitation of Governor John Leverett, during whose administration occurred King Philip's war. Leverett went to England in 1644, and served under Cromwell,

"From Edge-Hill Fight to Marston Moor."

Charles II. made Leverett a knight, — a title which he never assumed. Few names connected with the colony are more honorable than Governor Leverett's. He commanded the Ancient and Honorable Artillery; was agent of the colony in England; on terms of intimacy with the Protector, major-general, and deputy-governor. He died in 1679. Governor Leverett's house was afterwards in State Street, next east of the old Exchange. Before the adoption of the Federal Constitution the post-office was located on this corner. In the building since taken down was once the law office of John A. Andrew, a man whose memory is warmly cherished by the soldiers of Massachusetts in the Rebellion, who gave him the name of the war governor.

* Bench and Bar.

On the northeast corner of Court and Washington Streets was the estate of Henry Dunster, first president of Harvard College. Here also stood the Town Pump, yielding its cooling fluid to our thirsty ancestors, or drenching some maudlin vagrant of the kennel. Here is Hawthorne's invocation from the Town Pump to the passers-by :—

"Like a dramseller on the Mall at muster-day, I cry aloud to all and sundry, in my plainest accents, and at the very tiptop of my voice : Here it is, gentlemen ! Here is the good liquor ! Walk up, walk up, gentlemen, walk up, walk up ! Here is the superior stuff ! Here is the unadulterated ale of Father Adam,— better than Cognac, Hollands, Jamaica, strong beer, or wine of any price ; here it is by the hogshead or single glass, and not a cent to pay ! Walk up, gentlemen, walk up, and help yourselves !"

Public notices and proclamations were affixed to the Town Pump.

A little south of the Sears estate is the Rogers Building, around which is a vacant space now known as Cornhill Court and Court Avenue, once Cornhill Square.

This is the site of the second location of the First Church of Boston, removed from State Street in 1640. In 1808 the society sold this site to Benjamin Joy, on which he erected a brick structure, and the church was removed to Chauncy Street. From the church the space around it took the name of Church Square. The old meeting-house was of wood, but after standing seventy-one years, was destroyed by the great fire of 1711, and was then rebuilt of brick. After the building of the Second Church in Hanover Street this house took the name of the "Old Brick." It

OLD BRICK CHURCH.

was of three stories and decorated with a bell-tower and clock. This clock was, without doubt, the first placed in any public position in the town. The records show that in 1716–17 the town voted to obtain a town clock to be set up in some convenient place in Cornhill. Before this the bells were called clocks. The bell of the Old Brick sounded the alarm on the evening of the Massacre of March 5, 1770.

On the corner of State Street, nearly opposite the Old Brick, was the bookstore of Daniel Henchman, and later that of Wharton and Bowes. In this shop Henry Knox, afterwards one of the most famous generals of the Revolutionary army, was an apprentice. Here he acquired, by reading, the rudiments of the military art. The store was the resort of the British officers, who were very friendly with the future general. At eighteen Knox was lieutenant of the grenadier company of the Boston Regiment, — a company distinguished for its martial appearance and the precision of its evolutions. He was one of the watch on board the tea ship before the tea was destroyed, and he also was early at the scene of the Massacre in King Street. In Knox's account of this affair he said, "Captain Preston seemed much agitated. Knox took him by the coat and told him, 'for God's sake to take his men back again, for if they fired, his life must answer for the consequences.' While I was talking with Captain Preston the soldiers of his detachment had attacked the people with their bayonets. There was not the least provocation given to Captain Preston or his party." Knox, after serving his time, published for himself. "A Dissertation on the Gout," etc., bears his imprint in 1772.

After Lexington Knox escaped with his wife from Boston; Mrs. Knox concealing within the lining of her cloak the sword he subsequently wore through the war. She accompanied her husband through all his campaigns. The Marquis Chastellux, who visited the headquarters of the American army in 1782, says: "We found Mrs. Knox settled in a little farm where she had passed part of the campaign; for she never quits her husband. A child of six months and little girl of three years old formed a *real* family for the general. As for himself, he is between thirty and forty, very fat, but very active, and of a gay and amiable character. From the very first campaign he was intrusted with the command of the artillery, and it has turned out it could not have been placed in better hands. It was he whom M. du Coudray endeavored to supplant, and who had no difficulty in removing him. It was fortunate for M. du Coudray, perhaps, that he was drowned in the Schuylkill, rather than be swallowed up in the intrigues he was engaged in."

Knox's corpulency was the subject of an ill-timed pun from Dr. Byles. An intimacy existed before the war, and when, on the day Boston was evacuated, Knox marched in at the head of his artillery, the doctor audibly remarked, "I never saw an ox fatter in my life." Knox did not relish the joke from the old tory, and told Dr. Byles he was a "—— fool."

The graduate of the little shop in Cornhill was volunteer aid at Bunker Hill, commanded the artillery during the siege of Boston, and became Secretary of War. His greatest service, perhaps, was the bringing of more than fifty cannon, mortars, and howitzers from Ticonderoga, Crown Point, etc., to the lines before Boston. This feat was accomplished early in 1776, the ordnance being dragged on sledges in midwinter almost through a wilderness.

Knox was a generous, high-minded man. His portrait, by Gilbert Stuart, hangs in Faneuil Hall. A gunning accident having injured one of his hands, it is concealed in the picture.

The celebrated Benjamin Thompson, a native of Woburn, afterwards a count of the German Empire, was, like Knox, an apprentice to a shopkeeper in Union Street at the time of the Massacre. He was at the American lines in Cambridge at the time of Bunker Hill, and accompanied Major, afterwards Governor Brooks until they met the retreating Americans. After endeavoring unsuccessfully to obtain a commission in the Continental army, he turned loyalist. He was sent to England by General Howe after the fall of Boston, but returned to America and raised a regiment of horse, called the "King's Dragoons."

After the war he was knighted, and became Sir Benjamin Thompson. The Elector of Bavaria, whose service he entered in 1784, made him a count, with the title of Count Rumford, that being the ancient name of Concord, N. H., where Thompson had formerly resided. Rumford went afterwards to Paris, and married the widow of the celebrated Lavoisier, from whom, however, he afterwards separated.

The Rumford Professorship at Harvard testifies to the remembrance of this distinguished man for his native country. He left a munificent bequest to the College for the advancement of the physical and mathematical sciences.

John Winslow, one of Knox's compatriots, and a captain in Crane's Artillery during the Revolutionary War, was a hardware merchant with his uncle, Jonathan Mason, at No. 12 Cornhill, just south of the present Globe newspaper office. He remained in Boston during the siege, and buried the Old South communion plate in his uncle's cellar; his uncle was deacon of that church. It was Winslow who recognized the body of Warren, the day after the battle of Bunker Hill. He was at Ticonderoga, Saratoga, and White Plains, and held a number of State offices after the war. Winslow lived in Purchase Street, just north of the Sailors' Home.

Within fifty years dwellings were not infrequent in this part of Boston. Many such are located in Washington Street, Court Street, and Cornhill. It was a common custom for the family of the storekeeper to live over the store, as the custom is in some parts of Old England to this day.

CHAPTER III.

FROM THE OLD STATE HOUSE TO BOSTON PIER.

Captain Keayne. — Coggan, first Shopkeeper. — Old Cornhill. — Old State House. — First Church. — Stocks and Whipping-Post. — John Wilson. — Wilson's Lane. — United States Bank. — Royal Exchange Tavern. — William Sheaffe. — Royal Custom House. — Exchange Coffee House. — "Columbian Centinel." — Benjamin Russell. — Louis Philippe. — Louis Napoleon. — Congress Street. — Governors Dummer and Belcher. — First United States Custom House. — Post-Office. — Bunch of Grapes. — General Lincoln. — General Dearborn. — First Circulating Library. — British Coffee House. — Merchants' Row. — First Inn. — Lord Ley. — Miantonimoh. — Kilby Street. — Oliver's Dock. — Liberty Square. — The Stamp Office. — Broad Street. — Commodore Downes. — Broad Street Riot. — India Street and Wharf. — Admiral Vernon. — Crown Coffee House. — Butler's Row. — The Custom House. — Retrospective View of State Street. — Long Wharf. — The Barricado. — T Wharf. — Embarkation for Bunker Hill.

THE earliest settler on the southwestern corner of State Street was Captain Robert Keayne, who has left his name to us in connection with a legacy to build a Town House. He was also the first commander of the Ancient and Honorable Artillery, and was by business a tailor. Captain Keayne fell under the censure of court and church for selling his wares at exorbitant profits, — we have before mentioned that the authorities regulated the prices of goods, products, etc. His will, of nearly two hundred pages, is devoted largely to an effort to relieve himself of this charge. What would Washington Street say to-day to such a regulation?

The opposite or northwest corner of State Street was occupied by John Coggan, one of the names in the original Book of Possessions. He has the distinction of establishing the first shop for the sale of merchandise in Boston. From this small beginning dates the traffic of Boston.

Having crossed ancient Cornhill, which name applied to that

Southwest View of the Old State House, in 1791.

part of Washington Street from Dock Square to School Street, and in which congregated the early booksellers, we are at the head of old King Street. Before us is the earliest market-place of the town, on the space now occupied by the Old State House. King Street was changed to State in 1784, but it was frequently called Congress Street before the present name was settled on.

OLD STATE HOUSE IN 1791.

> "And mark, not far from Faneuil's honored side,
> Where the Old State House rises in its pride.

The early history of this edifice has been given in connection with the City Hall, as its progenitor. Besides being used as a Town House and by the Colonial Courts, it has been occupied by the General Court of the Colony and of the State, by the Council of the Province, and as a barrack for troops. It was the first Exchange the merchants of Boston ever had, and is still used for business purposes. In it met the Convention to ratify the Constitution of the United States before adjourning to Federal Street Church. In the west end was located the Post-Office, in its beginning, and again in 1838, when a force of fifteen clerks was sufficient for the transaction of its business. In 1832 it was again slightly damaged by fire.

Under its shadow the Massacre was enacted by a detachment of the 29th British Regiment, the result of constant collisions between the people and the soldiery. At the time of its occupation by the British troops,—admitted by Governor Bernard in 1768,—James Otis moved to have the Superior Court held in Faneuil Hall, "not only as the stench occasioned by the troops may prove infectious, but as it was derogatory to the honor of the court to administer justice at the mouths of cannon and the points of bayonets." This referred to the establishment of the main-guard opposite, with two field-pieces pointed toward the Old State House.

The following was the interior arrangement of the building after the fire of 1747. The eastern chamber was originally occupied by the Council, afterwards by the Senate. The Representatives held their sittings in the west chamber. The floor of these was supported by pillars, and terminated at each end by doors, and at the east end by a flight of steps leading into State Street. On the north side were offices for the clerks of the supreme and inferior courts. In the daytime the doors were kept open, and the floor served as a walk for the inhabitants who thronged it during the sessions of the courts. After the removal of the Legislature to the new State House the internal arrangement was changed to suit later occupants.

In the Chamber of Representatives, according to John Adams, "Independence was born" and the struggle against the encroachments of the mother country sustained for fourteen years by the Adamses, Bowdoins, Thachers, Hancocks, Quincys, and their illustrious colleagues. According to Hutchinson, in this chamber originated the most important measures which led to the emancipation of the Colonies, — with those giants who, staking life and fortune upon the issue, adopted for their motto,

> "Let such, such only, tread this sacred floor,
> Who dare to love their country, and be poor."

It was customary to read the commissions of the royal governors in presence of the court, attended by military display, in the Court House, as it was then called. The news of the death of George II., and accession of George III., was read from the balcony; the latter was the last crowned head proclaimed in the Colonies.

The popular indignation against the Stamp Act found vent, in 1766, in burning stamped clearances in front of the Town House. A council of war was held by Gage, Howe, and Clinton, here before Bunker Hill. On the 18th July, 1776, the Declaration of Independence was read from the east balcony by William Greenleaf, Sheriff. All the Continental troops in the vicinity of Boston were paraded in State Street, and at its conclusion fired thirteen volleys commemorative of the thirteen Colonies. Here the Constitution of Massachusetts was planned. In 1778 Count D'Estaing made a splendid entry into Boston with his fleet, and was received by Governor Hancock in the Council Chamber.

After the Revolution it became the place of meeting of the Legislature, and has been ever since called the Old State House, — except during the interval when it was the City Hall, — and this name is its customary appellation. In October, 1789, Washington received the homage of the people, from a temporary balcony at the west end. A triumphal arch was thrown across the street there, and a long procession passed before him, whose salutations he occasionally returned. In January, 1798, the Legislature took possession of the new State House.

The building has undergone material alterations, especially in the roof, which gives it a more modern appearance, and the steeple or tower was once considerably higher than at present. The sun-dial, which formerly adorned the eastern gable, has been superseded by a clock; the rampant Lion and Unicorn have been renewed at the east end. There have been a lottery office, engine-house, and even a newspaper published in the old building, — the latter printed in 1805, in the Senate Chamber, and called the "Repertory." After the Grand Lodge of Masons was burnt out of the Exchange Coffee House it occupied quarters in the Old State House. At the great fire of 1711, by which it was destroyed, several gentlemen, at imminent risk of their lives, succeeded in saving the Queen's portrait. The building is now in the custody of the Bostonian Society.

The old First Church of Boston was situated on the ground now covered by Brazer's building, until its removal to another location. Here preached John Wilson and John Cotton, and here came Winthrop and Bellingham, with their zealous Puritan followers. An inscription, cut above the State Street entrance, records these leading facts in the history of this hallowed spot.

In an old two-story wooden house which stood upon the site of Brazer's Building were located the first United States Bank, and also the first government Post-Office. The former remained here until the erection of the building on the site of the Exchange; the Post-Office was removed here from Cornhill. Jonathan Armstrong was postmaster, and easily performed, from his perch on a high stool, all the duties pertaining to his office.

The figure of a winged Mercury, well executed in wood by Simeon Skillin, a North End carver, was placed over the door of the Post-Office in State Street. The tutelar deity was represented in the act of springing from a globe. In one hand he held his emblematic rod, in the other a letter directed to the president of the Branch Bank.

In front of the old meeting-house stood the whipping-post, and probably the stocks, though this latter engine has been located in front of the Old State House. In later years, the stocks and pillory were a movable machine, on wheels, and had no fixed position. Both were used as a means of enforcing attendance, or punishing offences against the church, and their location at its very portal served, no doubt, as a gentle reminder to the congregation.

THE STOCKS.

It is recorded that in the year 1753 a woman stood for an hour in the pillory near the Town House, amid the scoffs and jeers of the multitude. The Scarlet Letter is no myth; Hawthorne had but to turn to the criminal records of the Colony for the dramatic incidents he has related. The General Court enacted in 1695 a law to prevent marriages of consanguinity, the declared penalty of breaking which was that the man or woman offending should be set upon the gallows for an hour, with a rope about the neck, and in the way from thence to the common jail be severely whipped. The offenders were forever to wear a capital letter "I," cut out of cloth of a color different from their clothes, on the arm or back, in open view. If the culprit removed the letter, he or she was to be further whipped. No doubt there were Hester Prynnes thus branded and scourged in State Street.

Public whipping was inflicted as late as 1803, and the writer has talked with eye-witnesses of it. By order of the Supreme Judicial Court of Massachusetts, two men were placed in the pillory, in the year mentioned, in State Street. Pierpont, the owner, and Storey, master of the brig Hannah, having procured a heavy insurance on their cargo, for a voyage to the West Indies, the vessel was sunk in Boston harbor, November 22, 1801, and a large portion of the insurance collected. Fraud being proved, both as to the lading and loss of the brig, the Court decreed that Pierpont and Storey be set in the pillory in State Street two several times, one hour each time, and imprisoned two years, and pay the costs of prosecution. The sentence was duly executed, the pillory being placed near "'Change" Avenue. The Sheriff usually performed the whipping by deputy. The whipping-post became a perambulating affair, and at one time was stationed in West Street. Its acknowledged utility appears by the Sessions Justice's famous charge, which lays down the law in somewhat startling phrase.

THE PILLORY.

"Gentlemen of the grand jury: You are required by your oath to see to it, that the several towns in the county be provided according to law with,

Pounds and schoolmasters,
Whipping-posts and ministers."

John Wilson, first pastor of the First Church, owned land on Cornhill and State Street; the lane bearing his name, and running through his tract, was deservedly called Crooked Lane. His dwelling was on the site of the Globe Bank, demolished in 1873 to widen the narrow way, which is now lost in the extension of Devonshire Street northward.

Wilson's Lane was chiefly remarkable for the number and excellence of its eating-houses. This circumstance, with its old name, calls to mind Tom Hood's lines: —

> "I've heard about a pleasant land, where omelets grow on trees,
> And roasted pigs run crying out, 'Come eat me, if you please.'
> My appetite is rather keen, but how shall I get there?
> 'Straight down the Crooked Lane, and all round the Square.'"

The Merchants' Bank succeeded to the location of the United States Branch Bank, which was in its day a building of considerable architectural pretension. The two columns which now support the front of the Merchants' Bank performed a like service for its predecessor, and when taken down were fluted to correspond more nearly with the plan of the new building. Observation will show that the granite is of a different color from that used in the rest of the façade. The United States Bank building was built of Chelmsford granite, in imitation of a Grecian temple. It was at first proposed to take the site of the Old State House, but the project — happily for the existence of this old monument — was abandoned. The structure was erected in 1824; Solomon Willard was the architect; Gridley Bryant, master-mason. The columns referred to were brought from Chelmsford on ponderous trucks built for the purpose. On account of their great weight the proprietors of the bridges refused to permit the passage of the teams, and they were accordingly brought over the Neck. The moving of such unwieldy masses of granite — a marvel when it was first attempted — was eclipsed by the transporting of the columns for the Court House and Custom House.

The pediment was a favorite resort for pigeons, which becoming somewhat troublesome, by order of Gardiner Greene, the president, a wooden cat was placed on the accustomed perch of the feathered visitors. They were at first a little shy, but soon ceased to have any fear of the sham grimalkin. It was then removed to the directors' room, and presided for a long time over the deliberations of the board.

The United States Bank was established in 1791, and the charter expired in 1812, but was revived in 1816, and finally dissolved in 1836. The bank originated in the want of money to carry on the government. The directors were appointed by the parent bank at Philadelphia, and the dividends which the bank declared were made up from the business of all the branches. Under the charter of 1816 the capital was thirty-five millions, of which the government owned seven. The attempt to permanently establish a bank under government control, like the Bank of England, proved a failure, as is well known. The removal of the deposits by General Jackson affected the Boston branch but little, but it brought to light a defaulting official. The receiving teller, whose name was John Fuller, finding discovery inevitable, put forty thousand dollars into his pocket one afternoon and absconded. In 1836 Congress revived the charter, but Jackson vetoed it. A bank under the old title, established by the State of Pennsylvania, went into operation in the latter year, and continued until 1841.

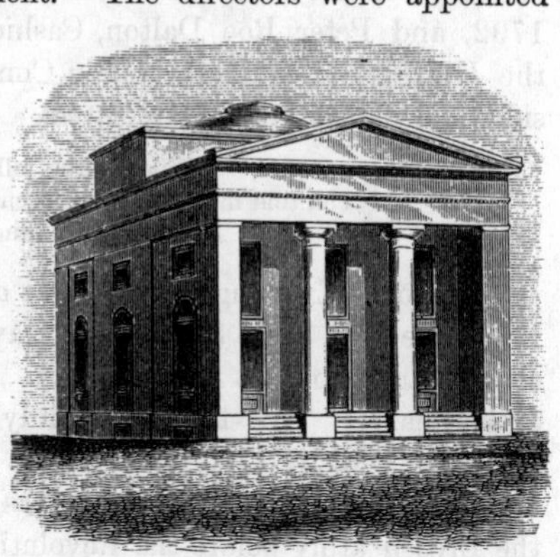

UNITED STATES BANK.

The old United States Bank was erected on the site of the Exchange, in 1798, and bore on its front an American eagle, with its wings outstretched, as if in the act of swooping upon the bulls and bears of the street. On the expiration of the charter the State Bank purchased the building, and the eagle was afterwards removed to Faneuil Hall, where it is one of the curiosities to be seen there. It is made of clay baked in an oven at the South End; and the fractured edges chipped away by relic-hunters have the appearance of broken pottery or tile.

Formerly the proud bird of Jove, and emblem of our republic, was in the centre of the hall, guarded by an iron railing. The iron gates of the old bank now guard the entrance to the Cemetery on Washington Street, near the St. James Hotel; a rather singular transition from the shrine of Mammon to the abode of death. Thomas Russell was the first President in 1792, and Peter Roe Dalton, Cashier. The next location of the United States Bank was in Congress Street, on the west side, and not far from State Street.

"— Where 's the jolly host
You told me of? 'T has been my custom ever
To parley with mine host."

The Royal Exchange Tavern was on the southwest corner of Exchange and State Streets, and gave the name of Royal Exchange Lane to that thoroughfare. Shrimpton's Lane was an earlier name. This tavern certainly dates back to 1727, and was then kept by Luke Vardy. At the time of the Massacre one Stone was the landlord. It was a resort for the officers of the British army before the Revolution. At the beginning of the present century it was kept by Israel Hatch, and was a regular stopping-place for the Providence stages.

The rencontre between Henry Phillips and Benjamin Woodbridge, which ended in a duel on the Common, had its beginning in this house. After the fire of December, 1747, which destroyed the Town House, the General Court was held at Vardy's for the few remaining days of the session. The Royal Exchange was also a favorite hostelry of the Masons, Vardy being of the fraternity. At a Masonic procession on St. John's day Joseph Green notices the jolly landlord thus:—

"Where 's honest Luke? that cook from London;
For without Luke, the Lodge is undone.
'T was he who oft dispell'd their sadness,
And filled the Brethren's hearts with gladness.
Luke in return is made a brother,
As good and true as any other,
And still, though broke with age and wine,
Preserves the token and the sign."

The Royal Custom House, at the time of the Massacre, was

on the southeast corner of Exchange and State Streets. Joseph Harrison was Collector, and William Sheaffe Deputy. With the sentinel on duty at this point began the affray in State Street. The sentinel, abused, beaten, and likely to be overpowered, loaded his piece and shouted for assistance to the post of the main-guard, which was opposite the south door of the Town House. The deplorable results which followed are familiar. The old Custom House had a balcony, from which shots were fired at the populace during the Massacre.

This circumstance, elicited during the investigation into the affair by the town authorities, did not tend to improve the relations between the people and the obnoxious officers of the customs. The town desired these officials to be present during the investigation and use the privilege of questioning the witnesses. Sheaffe, however, was the only one who attended. He had been a long time connected with the Custom House; as deputy under Sir Henry Frankland, and as his successor when Sir Henry was removed for inattention to his duties. Sheaffe issued the famous Writs of Assistance. He was the father of the celebrated Sir Roger Hale Sheaffe, and a devoted loyalist. Sheaffe lived in the vicinity of Scollay Square in Court Street. He had some pretty daughters, of whom Sabine, in his "Loyalists," says: —

"Susanna, Mr. Sheaffe's oldest daughter, married Captain Ponsonby Molesworth, a nephew of Lord Ponsonby.

"The family account is, that on the day of the landing of a regiment of British troops in Boston, a halt was made in Queen (Court) Street opposite Mr. Sheaffe's house; that Susanna, attracted by the music and the redcoats, went upon the balcony; that Molesworth soon saw her, was struck by her great beauty, gazed intently upon her, and at last said to a brother officer, who, like himself, was leaning against a fence, 'That girl seals my fate.'"

Margaret, another daughter of Mr. Sheaffe, was remarkable for her beauty; so handsome, according to tradition, "no one could take her picture." Previous to her marriage, Lafayette, who admired her, said to her lover, "Were I not a married man, I'd try to cut you out."

At the time of the Massacre the Custom House was in a building used as a dwelling by Bartholomew Green and family. King Street was then full of dwellings, the occupants using the lower floor for their business. This Green, a printer by profession, had, according to Thomas, the peculiar faculty of recognizing at sight any vessel belonging to the port of Boston. Perpetually on the watch, as soon as a vessel could be discovered with a spy-glass he knew its name, and gave information to the owner. He had some small office in the Custom House at one time.

He who stood on the balcony of the Old State House in 1770 might count five taverns of repute in King Street. The Bunch of Grapes was the best punch-house, but Vardy's, the nearest, was probably most frequented by the barristers and officers of the court.

EXCHANGE COFFEE HOUSE.

From our stand-point, at the lower end of the Old State House, Devonshire Street opens at our right hand. The Pudding Lane of yore is suggestive of good living. Accordingly we find the well-remembered Exchange Coffee-House was situated in Congress Square, once known by the singular title of Half-Square Court. The name of this house owes its origin to the fact that the principal floor was intended to be used by the merchants as an Exchange. It was a mammoth affair of seven stories, far in advance of the wants of its day, and was completed in 1808, having occupied two years and a half in building; it cost half a million. An unsuccessful speculation, it was the means of ruining many of the mechanics who were employed in building it. Destroyed by fire November 3, 1818, it was rebuilt in a less expensive manner, and occupied as a tavern until 1853, when it was demolished, giving place to the buildings known as the "City Exchange."

The front of the Coffee House, on Congress Street, was ornamented with six marble Ionic pilasters, and crowned with a Corinthian pediment. It had entrances on the State Street side and from Devonshire Street. The building was of an irregular shape, rather like a triangle with the apex cut off, and contained about two hundred and ten apartments. It was in the very centre of business, and was a stopping-place for stages going or returning from town. A number of Masonic Lodges occupied the upper stories.

Captain Hull made the Exchange his quarters when he was in port during the war of 1812. At the rooms of the Exchange was kept a register of marine news, arrivals, departures, etc. When Hull arrived in Boston after his fortunate escape from the British fleet in July, 1812, he wrote with his own hand in this book the following: —

"Whatever merit may be due for the escape of the Constitution from the British fleet, belongs to my first officer, Charles Morris, Esq.

"ISAAC HULL."

On his arrival, after the memorable action with the Guerriere, Hull was the recipient of flattering attentions from the merchants, and indeed the whole population vied to do him honor. Hull, with straightforward manliness, wrote on the journal of the Coffee House a well-deserved tribute to the services of this same Lieutenant, afterwards Commodore Morris, who was severely wounded in the fight.

Dacres, who became Hull's prisoner after this engagement, lodged at the Exchange. Of him it is related, that when he went up the side of the Constitution, after leaving his own ship, Hull, eager to soothe the feelings of his gallant adversary, stepped forward, offered his hand, and said, "Dacres, my dear fellow, I am glad to see you!" The reply of the discomfited Briton was, "D—n it, I suppose you are." The twain became afterwards firm friends.

President Monroe visited Boston in July, 1817. He took apartments at the Exchange Coffee House. On the 4th a sumptuous dinner was served, at which the following guests were present. It would be hard to find a more distinguished company. General Swift, Superintendent of West Point Academy, presided, assisted by Commodore Perry and Mr. Mason. The other guests were ex-President John Adams, Governor Brooks, Lieutenant-Governor Phillips, General H. Dearborn, President Kirkland, Chief Justice Parker, Judges Story, Jackson, Davis, and Adams, Generals Cobb and Humphreys of the old army, Hon. Messrs. Pickering and Fales, Commodores Bainbridge and Hull, and other naval officers. The President returned the visit of the venerable John Adams, and the two walked, arm in arm, over the farm at Quincy, like any two plain country gentlemen.

The fire which consumed the Coffee House was destructive. The keeper, Mr. Barnum, lost $ 25,000. Eleven printing-offices, the Grand Lodge of the State, and several other Masonic Lodges were burned out.

Next below Brazer's Building was once the printing-office of the "Columbian Centinel," established in 1784. It was then the size of a sheet of commercial post writing-paper, and published semi-weekly. Benjamin Russell was the editor, a name well known in the annals of Boston journalism. Russell was an apprentice to Isaiah Thomas of the celebrated Worcester Spy. Thomas had the ill luck to be drafted in 1780, and young Russell volunteered in his place. During his service he witnessed the execution of André, at Tappan, as one of the guards. Russell published the Centinel until 1824.

When the Duc de Chartres, afterwards Louis Philippe, was in Boston, an exile from his native country, he was in the habit of visiting the Centinel office to obtain the news from abroad, and, it is said, occasionally wrote articles for the paper. The Centinel was, at this time, distinguished for the accuracy of its information in regard to the war then waging between republican France and combined Europe. An atlas which had belonged to Louis enabled the editor to describe the topography of the battle-fields minutely, and thus surpass his contemporaries. Louis Napoleon, late Emperor of the French, was, if report speaks true, at a later day, an *habitué* of the Centinel office. Thus the representatives of two opposing dynasties have eagerly scanned the columns of the same republican newspaper for intelligence that was to make or mar their fortunes. The Centinel was the leading Federalist organ of New England, and was ably conducted.

Next is Congress Street, named for the National Legislature. The founders of Boston called it Leverett's Lane, from Elder Thomas Leverett, who owned the tract through which it passes. It was subsequently Quaker Lane, from the old Quaker Meeting-house situated therein. Congress Street, at its junction with State, was once only eleven feet wide; and Exchange, even now scarcely deserving the name of street, was once as narrow as Wilson's Lane, but was widened through its entire length. The lower part of State, where it meets Long Wharf, was also widened, — a proceeding so repugnant to one of the proprietors, that he took his gun and threatened to shoot any one that attempted to remove his building. It was effected, however, without bloodshed.

The Exchange Building stands partly upon ground which once belonged to Elder Thomas Leverett, who emigrated from Boston, England, where he had been an alderman, and a parishioner of Rev. John Cotton. He was a man of property and distinction in the province. His more distinguished son, afterwards governor, became the owner of this property, which he parted with in 1656. It became afterwards two estates, each having a proprietor of consequence.

Andrew Belcher, one of the most wealthy merchants of Boston, and a contemporary with old André Faneuil, lived, in 1691, in the westerly part of this estate, which is described as "fronting on the Broad Street near the Exchange." This was before they had found a name for the street. Belcher's house was of brick. He also owned two brick warehouses, "the one bigger and the other less," lying near the Town Dock; an estate at the south corner of Washington and Bedford Streets, one in Wing's Lane, and other valuable property. He had been one of the Provincial Council, and was a representative in 1698 and 1701.

Jonathan Belcher, afterwards governor of "the Massachusetts," was in his tenth year when Andrew, his father, came from Charlestown to live in Boston. While in Europe, the Bostonian was presented at court, and made so favorable an impression on George I. that the King appointed him governor in 1730. The year previous he had gone again to England as agent for the colony, — a position he had not obtained very creditably, according to Hutchinson. Governor Belcher became very unpopular, and was superseded, in 1741, by Governor Shirley; but was afterwards appointed governor of New Jersey. Shaw says Governor Belcher's house was after the model of Julien's, which is represented in another place; he adds that it was standing a few years before he wrote, in 1817. Mr. Belcher was a very opulent merchant. His residence was in Orange Street, now Washington, in 1732. He was one of the foremost in organizing the Hollis Street Church, and gave the Society land to build it upon. During his administration occurred the great religious revival, caused by the visit of Whitefield, and Faneuil Hall Market was built. Governor Belcher's son, Jonathan, of Boston, became lieutenant-governor of Nova Scotia. He was an able jurist, and had been also Chief Justice of that province.

Governor Leverett sold a part of his estate, next east of Governor Belcher's, to Jeremiah Dummer, goldsmith, in 1677. This Jeremiah, father of two distinguished sons, was himself a conspicuous man in the affairs of the town, and in 1708 this corner of Kilby Street is called "Justice Dummer's Corner."

William Dummer, the elder son, lieutenant-governor of the colony from 1716 to 1729, was a captain in the Ancient and Honorable Artillery in 1719. He was acting chief-magistrate during a great part of his term, the governor, Samuel Shute, being absent from his post. The principal events of Governor Dummer's term were the establishment of a linen manufactory in the town, and the introduction of inoculation for the small-pox, during one of its periodical visits, by Dr. Boylston. This terrible distemper, which had scourged Boston with great violence at different times, was arrested by this simple expedient, which the Western world owes to the efforts of a woman. Lady Mary Wortley Montagu accompanied her husband to the Porte, where he was ambassador, in 1716. While there she witnessed the custom among the Turks of *engrafting* for the small-pox. She at once devoted her extraordinary epistolary powers to procure the introduction of this great boon into England, and, by great exertions, happily succeeded. Franklin's paper was established while Dummer was acting-governor. Governor Dummer provided in his will for the manumission and care of his three negroes. He attended Hollis Street Church, living close at hand at the time.

Jeremiah Dummer, the younger, was born in the old homestead in State Street. He graduated at Harvard in 1699, and studied at the University of Utrecht, where he took a degree. A polished scholar and writer, he is known in public life as the Massachusetts Agent in England, 1710–21. He published an eloquent defence of the New England charters when they were threatened in the latter year.

In a building adjoining the west side of the old Exchange was the first United States Custom House; General Benjamin Lincoln was the first collector, and retained the position until 1808. He occupied part of the house for a dwelling. A distinguished Revolutionary soldier, General Lincoln fought from the lakes to Savannah. He was with Gates at Saratoga as second in command, and with D'Estaing in the assault on Savannah. The fortune of war made him a prisoner to Sir H. Clinton in May, 1780, with the garrison of Charleston. Again, at Yorktown, he had the satisfaction of seeing the army of Cornwallis lay down their arms. In Shays' Rebellion of '87 Lincoln commanded the State forces; he was also lieutenant-governor in this year. General Lincoln's portrait, by F. A. Durivage, — copied from Sargent's picture in the Historical Society's Collection, — is in the collector's room at the Custom House.

The Merchants' Exchange, also the Sub-Treasury and Post-Office, was one of the most imposing edifices in State Street. It was erected in 1842, and stood here until 1890, when the new Exchange Building rose in its stead.

The first action in regard to a post-office appears to have been an order of the General Court, November 5, 1639, as follows: —

"For the preventing the miscarriage of letters, it is ordered, that notice bee given, that Richard Fairbanks, his house in Boston, is the place appointed for all letters, which are brought from beyond seas, or to be sent thither; are to be brought unto him, and he is to take care that they bee delivered or sent according to their directions; provided that no man shall be compelled to bring his letters thither except hee please." His house was in Cornhill.

Somewhat later it seems to have become the custom to bring letters to the Exchange, in the Town Hall, to run the hazard of being forwarded by visitors; but this proved so precarious a method that the Council, in 1677–78, appointed John Hayward Postmaster for the whole colony. John Campbell, publisher of the News-Letter, was Postmaster about 1704.

In 1711 the Post-Office was in Old Cornhill, and, when the great fire occurred in October of that year was removed to the south side of Milk Street, opposite Rev. Mr. Pemberton's. It was removed back to Cornhill soon after this. William Brooker was Postmaster in 1719. In 1754 the Post-Office was in Cornhill, at the house of James Franklin, Postmaster; in 1770 it was still in Cornhill, between King Street and Dock Square; Tuthill Hubbard was Postmaster in 1771. Between this date and 1788 it occupied the corner of Court and Washington Streets (Sears Building), and in the latter year was removed to 44 Cornhill, where New Cornhill now enters Washington Street.

Post-routes were first established in 1711, to Maine and Plymouth once a week, and to New York once a fortnight. In 1829 the Post-Office was located on the corner of Congress and Water Streets, and employed eight clerks; and in 1838 in the Old State House, as related. After the Great Fire of 1872 the Old South was used for a post-office until the completion of the present stately edifice, which narrowly escaped destruction at that time.

The Bunch of Grapes Tavern was on the west corner of Kilby Street (formerly Mackerel Lane) and State. The New England Bank replaced the inn, until, in turn, itself displaced by the stately Exchange Building.

SIGN OF THE BUNCH OF GRAPES.

> "As ancient is this hostelry
> As any in the land may be."

Francis Holmes kept it as early as 1712; Rebecca, his widow, in 1726; William Coffin, 1731–33; Edward Lutwych, 1733; Samuel Wethered, 1734–50; Henry Laughton (date uncertain), Rebecca Coffin, 1760; Joseph Ingersoll, 1764–72; Captain John Marston, 1775–78; William Foster, 1782; Colonel Dudley Coleman, 1783; James Vila, 1789, in which year he removed to Concert Hall; Thomas Lobdell and Mrs. Lobdell, 1789; and perhaps also some others for short periods.

The Bunch of Grapes was the chosen resort of the patriot leaders prior to the Revolution, and as such is associated with many important acts of those eventful years. Among others, Washington, Lafayette, and Stark were entertained there. One act of far-reaching import was the initial organization of the Ohio Company in March, 1786, which founded Marietta.

Recrossing the street, we find that the Custom House was, in 1810, situated on the lower corner of Change Avenue, formerly Pierce's, and afterwards Flagg Alley. General Henry Dearborn, of Revolutionary fame, succeeded the venerable General Lincoln as Collector in 1809, the latter having resigned on account of the Embargo. It is said that General Lincoln wrote to President Madison, "that he had fought for the liberties of his country, and spent his best years in her service; and that he was not, in his old age, to be made an instrument to violate what he had assisted to acquire." *

General Dearborn continued to be Collector until appointed by Madison Senior Major-General, and ordered to the Canada frontier in 1812. His long and glorious career of public service extended from Bunker Hill, in 1775, to the capture of York, in 1813. At the latter place, now Toronto, was captured the royal standard of England, the only one that ever fell into our hands. This trophy is in the naval museum at Annapolis. By the intrigues of his enemies the veteran was displaced from his command, but was refused the court of inquiry he solicited. He was minister to Portugal in 1822. General Dearborn lived in what was afterwards the Sun Tavern, on Batterymarch Street, more recently occupied by a Glass Company. He married James Bowdoin's widow, and was a man of very imposing presence.

H. A. S. Dearborn, son of the old warrior, succeeded to the collectorship. The younger General Dearborn held a number of offices, and is known as an author of several historical works. At the time of the Dorr Rebellion in Rhode Island he was Adjutant-General of Massachusetts, and was removed for loaning the State arms to suppress that affair.

When the Custom House was located on the north side of State Street, the front was ornamented with two figures carved in wood; one representing Hope leaning on the traditional anchor, the other Justice holding the scales aloft. These memorials are now preserved in the insurance office occupying the same site.

In 1810 the building in Custom House Street was completed, and occupied in December of that year, but was soon found too contracted for the government business. The United States Custom House had, for short periods, locations in Merchants' Row, on the northeast corner of Corn Court, and in Half-Court Square, now Congress Square. The tablet in the building in Custom House Street is from the old Custom House.

On this site was established, in 1764, the first circulating

* Miss Quincy's Memoir.

library in Boston, by John Mein, the most extensive bookseller of the day. His place was called the London Bookstore, and his stock contained, according to his advertisement, ten thousand volumes.

Thomas says Mein came from Glasgow, in 1764, with Robert Sandeman. His shop was first on the north corner of what is now Franklin and Washington Streets, where, in addition to books, he sold Irish linens, etc. The firm at this time was Mein and Sandeman.

John Mein is also associated with early printing in Boston, having been connected with John Fleming, in 1767, in the publication of the Boston Chronicle, the first semi-weekly in New England.

The paper fell under the ban of popular censure, and was suspended in 1770, it having espoused the cause of the mother country. Mein was exhibited in effigy on Pope Day, 1769, and in the unique and horrible pageant was carried a lantern with this acrostic :—

> " Mean is the man, M—n is his name,
> Enough he 's spread his hellish fame ;
> Infernal Furies hurl his soul,
> Nine million times from Pole to Pole."

Mein was afterwards the subject of a personal attack, and took refuge with the soldiery, making a final escape from the profane poetry and hard blows of the wrathful " Bostoneers " soon after, to England.

As we are now among the Insurance Offices, it becomes appropriate to state that the first in the town was established by Joseph Marion, in 1724. His office was called " The Sun Fire Office in Boston," and was located near the site of the Globe Bank, 22 State Street.

Where the beautiful marble building numbered 66 now stands was the British Coffee House, an inn kept by Mr. Ballard in 1762. It was of some prominence, and divided with its neighbors the patronage of the military and civilians. The repeal of the Stamp Act was celebrated here, and at the Bunch of Grapes in March, 1767. It was also the scene of the unfortunate collision between James Otis and John Robinson, one of the Customs Commissioners referred to in connection with Otis's residence. Otis went to the Coffee House alone, by appointment, and was immediately attacked by Robinson and his friends. A young man who went to the assistance of Otis was roughly handled and put out of the house.

The house seems to have been preferred by British officers; for we find one of them, Surgeon Bolton, delivering a harangue from the balcony, ridiculing the orations of Warren and Hancock, and abusive of the Whig patriots, while the main-guard, paraded in front, furnished an audience. Under the new *régime* this tavern was styled the American Coffee House. It became a place of public vendue, in 1786, by a firm who sold books in the chamber and jackasses in the street. The Massachusetts Bank long occupied its site.

Merchants' Row seems to have retained its original designation, being thus described in 1708. Andrew Faneuil's warehouse was on the lower corner in 1732. This was then the lower end of King Street. The Row followed an irregular, serpentine course to the wharf on the southerly side of the Town Dock.

In Corn Court is the reputed site of the first public house, kept by Samuel Cole in 1634. It is now thought that it was on Washington Street, nearly opposite Water Street. Governor Vane, in 1636, invited Miantonimoh, the Narragansett chief, to Boston, and the sachem repaired thither with a considerable retinue. The attendants of the chieftain were dined at Mr. Cole's, doubtless with many a grunt of satisfaction, for their landlord bore a good name, as we shall learn, from high authority. In what manner Cole fed his score of painted Narragansetts does not transpire. It must have vexed the spirit of the jolly Boniface full sore to know how to place his guests at table. They did not know the use of chairs, so he may have seated them, according to their custom, in a circle on the floor, with his iron pot of meat in the centre, into which each might plunge his hand until satisfied. However, Indians were no uncommon sight in the town in those days.

Lord Ley, Earl of Marlborough, who was killed in a naval engagement with the Dutch in 1665, visited Boston in 1637. He lodged at Cole's inn, and when urged by Governor Winthrop to partake of his hospitality declined, saying that the house where he was was so well governed, he could be as private there as elsewhere. Lord Ley accompanied Sir Harry Vane back to England. His lordship's reply was not, it is said, relished by the governor, who considered himself slighted and his hospitality and position neglected.

Kilby Street, which once boasted the euphonious name of Mackerel Lane, extended first only from State Street to what is Liberty Square, the portion beyond being known as Adams Street until 1825. Mackerel Lane was very narrow until the great fire of 1760, and crossed the creek in Liberty Square by a bridge at the foot of Water Street. On the map of 1722 wharves line the east side of Kilby Street, and until about 1800 Oliver's Dock came up to this street. Broad and India Streets had no existence until 1808–09.

Oliver's Dock was originally marsh, and through Liberty Square a creek ran up as far west as Spring Lane. This was Governor Winthrop's marsh, and the head of this cove was in the vicinity of the spring mentioned in the Introduction. Shaw states that

"The greater part of Congress Street is made land. An aged gentleman, who lived near the spot, says that when the foundation of Joy's Buildings (corner of Congress and Water) was preparing, the remains of the hull of an old vessel, or large boat, with fragments of canvass and tarred rope, were dug up; which shows the place had been once used as a graving-yard, or some similar purpose. From a view of the ground, there is reason to believe that the greater part of Congress Street, the whole of Kilby Street and Liberty Square, are built on flats, once covered by salt water."

In noticing the great storm and tide in 1723 the writer says, —

"We could sail in boats from the southern battery (Rowe's Wharf) to the rise of ground in King Street."

In very high tides the water has flowed up to the corner of

State Street and Merchants' Row. Sound logs have been dug up at the bottom of this street, which, from the appearance of knots and branches, were supposed to have been felled near at hand.

Oliver's Dock, so named from Peter Oliver, is noted as the scene of an episode of the Stamp Act riots of 1765. A building newly erected on the northeast corner of Kilby Street and Liberty Square was supposed by the people to be intended for a stamp office, and was torn down and thrown into the dock. Liberty Square derives its name from this circumstance. It was so named at the Civic Feast in honor of the French Revolution January 24, 1793, when a liberty-pole sixty feet in length, surmounted by the horns of the ox that had been roasted on Copp's Hill for the feast, was raised, and a salute of fifteen guns fired. The procession, after passing through the principal streets, pausing at Liberty Stump (where Liberty Tree had stood), and at the residences of "Citizens" Hancock and Adams, as they were then styled, then governor and lieutenant-governor, halted in State Street, where tables were laid from the Old State House to near Kilby Street. The roasted ox was there dispatched by the crowd amid a scene of confusion. In the afternoon an entertainment was provided at Faneuil Hall at which Samuel Adams presided. "Liberty and Equality" were toasted and sung, but as the bloody character of the French Revolution became manifest in the execution of Louis XVI., which had occurred three days before, the Civic Feast was not repeated.

The first directory published in Boston was printed by John Norman, at Oliver's Dock, in 1789. It contained 1,473 names. The directory of 1899 contains 242,000 names.

Broad Street next invites attention. It was built, in 1808, by that great public benefactor, Uriah Cotting, whose improvement of Cornhill is already noticed. Until this street was laid out Batterymarch marked the water-line to its junction with Kilby Street. Broad Street was at first occupied for business, but the subsequent building of India Street rendered it unavailable for this purpose, and it became the headquarters of a respectable class of residents; these were ousted in their turn by the Irish, who swarmed to this country in great numbers after the war of 1812. Among the early residents of Broad Street we find Lieutenant, afterwards Commodore John Downes, who served with distinction in the navy. He was in the attack on Tripoli under Preble, and with David Porter in the Pacific, where, in command of the Essex Junior, — to use the language of a contemporary, — "he played the devil among the whalers."

Broad Street was, in June, 1837, the scene of a riot between the firemen and Irish. The affair grew out of an attempt of Engine No. 20 while proceeding to a fire, to pass through the ranks of an Irish funeral cortege. This was resented, and led to a regular Donnybrook scrimmage, resulting in many broken heads, but no loss of life. Military force was used to put down the riot, which assumed serious proportions, but no powder was burned. The affray led to the disbandment of the whole fire department.

India Street, flanked by India and Central Wharves, was built, the year after Broad Street, by Mr. Cotting. About midway of Central Wharf was formerly an arched passage-way, which presented the singular feature of a building supported by it, but having no land belonging to it, — to use a military phrase, it was in the air. There were formerly a number of these arches, — not the least among the curious objects to be seen in Boston, — but few are yet existing.

Two other taverns remain to be noticed, of which the first is the Admiral Vernon. The name was from Edward Vernon, the admiral, who was known while he lived under the *sobriquet* of Old Grog. In bad weather he was in the habit of walking the deck in a rough grogram cloak, and thence had obtained the nickname. Whilst in command of the West India Station, and at the height of his popularity on account of his reduction of Porto Bello with six men-of-war, he introduced the use of rum and water by the ship's company.* The Admiral Vernon was on the lower corner of State Street and Merchants' Row,

* Notes and Queries.

and was kept by Richard Smith about 1743, and in 1775 by Mary Bean.

The first house on Long Wharf was the Crown Coffee House, noticed in 1718. It was kept by Widow Anna Swords in 1749, being then owned by Governor Belcher, while Governor William Dummer owned the next estate easterly. Richard Smith, of the Admiral Vernon, kept it in 1749, and Robert Shelcock in 1751. It was, like the Admiral Vernon, a water-side resort, but is not known to possess any associations of marked interest. It stood where the building now is, having a westerly front on State Street, but the street has been widened here. Like the other inns, it was used as a dwelling by the proprietors.

Peter Faneuil's warehouse was, in 1742–43 (the year of his death), below the Admiral Vernon, from which he carried on his large business with the West Indies and Europe. Peter was not averse to a little sharp practice upon the King's revenue, for we find an extract of one of his letters which requests advice, — "*also what good French brandy is worth, and if it be possible to cloak it so as to ship it for rum.*" * Otherwise, Peter seems to have placed a high estimate upon his commercial honor, and his charities were numerous and open-handed.

If you enter the little passage-way just below Merchants' Row, you will find a range of brick buildings, bounded north by Chatham Street and south by the passage-way. This is Butler's Row, and you may yet see the name cut in stone on the southeast corner of the block. Peter Butler, an old proprietor, had a warehouse and wharf here. Andrew, Peter, and Benjamin Faneuil all had warehouses on, or bounding upon, Butler's Row. These were all merchants of high standing, which marks the locality as one of importance to the mercantile class.

Seventy years ago the space between Batterymarch and State Streets was occupied by a ship-yard and wharves. Where the old Custom House stands, on Custom House Street, large vessels have been built and launched.

The massive proportions of the new Custom House, which contains about the same number of cubic feet of stone as Bunker

* Dealings with the Dead.

State Street in 1825, looking West.

Hill Monument, stand on a foundation recovered from the sea. Begun in 1837, it took three years to make a secure foundation. The building is cruciform, of the Grecian Doric order, and has the peculiarity that the roof is covered with granite tiles, rendering it completely fire-proof. Its position is not conspicuous, but it is one of the noticeable public edifices in Boston. It was completed in 1849, at a cost of over a million. A. B. Young, M. A., was the architect.

We may now take a retrospective view of State Street. It is the busy mart and exchange of the city, sacred to the worship of Mammon. Bills, stocks, and bonds are its literature, and in its vaults are fifty millions of dollars. Here Shylock meets Antonio, and daily takes his pound of flesh. It is our Rialto, our Bourse, our Royal Exchange. But time was when Perez Morton dwelt where the Union Bank's strong coffers are, and John Coburn took gentlemen boarders just below the Post-Office, — this, too, within the present century.

Since Boston was, State Street has been a favorite theatre of military displays, — the train-bands of the hard-visaged Puritans, the solid tramp of the newly arrived British soldiery in 1768, and of the reinforcements in 1774. Through State Street marched the 5th and 38th to embark for Bunker Hill, and the tread of Rochambeau's gallant Frenchmen has wakened the echoes of the old street. Since those more stirring scenes it has been the custom and delight of the citizen soldiery to "march up State Street." The bayonets of many a gallant regiment have glittered in the sunlight here, ere they marched to the front in the late civil war. Here, too, Burns, a poor fugitive was conducted by the whole police and military force of the city to the ship which took him back to slavery. But we have changed all that.

The fire of 1711 left its mark in State Street, destroying all the upper part, the Town House, and the Old Meeting House. An attempt was made to save the bell of the latter, and several sailors ascended the cupola for that purpose ; but the flames cut off their retreat, and they perished in the falling ruins. In 1747 the Town House was again destroyed. In the great fire of

1760 the street was again scourged by the devouring element, scarcely a building being left in the part below Kilby Street.

State Street was also the scene of a fatal affray in August, 1806, between Charles Austin and Thomas Oliver Selfridge, in which the former was killed. This affair made a great noise, and the day was long remembered as "Bloody Monday." James Sullivan was then Attorney-General, while the defence of Selfridge was conducted by Samuel Dexter and Christopher Gore. The origin of the difficulty was political feud; but, according to Mr. Sargent, the immediate cause was a dispute between other parties, about *seven roast pigs and ten bushels of green peas.* Austin was killed between the Old State House and the corner formerly occupied by the Traveller Office.

Long Wharf and State Street are so firmly united that they may be considered one to all intents and purposes. Before the wharf was built the lower part of State Street terminated at the Governor's Dock. The subject of building a wharf at the bottom of King Street was mooted, as early as 1707, by Oliver Noyes and others. In 1709–10 the town voted to accept the proposals of Noyes and his associates to build a wharf, with a sufficient common sewer, from Andrew Faneuil's corner to low-water mark, to be of the width of King Street. As originally projected, the wharf was to have a public way on one of its sides, thirty feet wide, for the use of the inhabitants and others forever. At about the middle a gap, sixteen feet wide, was to be left for the passage of boats; the end was to be left free for the town to plant guns on, if occasion required. The name of the wharf was, first, Boston Pier. M. l'Abbé Robin describes the pier as "a superb wharf, advancing nearly two thousand feet into the sea, wide enough along its whole length for stores and shops." On the map of 1722 there appears almost a continuous row of buildings on the north side; on Price's plan of 1743 the end of the wharf is fortified.

The "T" of Long Wharf, formerly known as Minott's T (from Stephen Minott), is a part of the ancient structure known as the Barricado, or Old Wharf, which was a line of defence connecting Scarlett's Wharf, at the foot of Copp's Hill, with the

South Battery at the foot of Fort Hill. It enclosed the Town Cove, in which the shipping lay. The Barricado extended in straight lines from the wharf to the terminal points, making an angle at the junction with Long Wharf, with the point towards the town. It was built of wood, and had openings on each side of Long Wharf for vessels to pass through. Apprehensions of invasion from the Dutch or French caused its construction. Atlantic Avenue now follows, substantially, the line of the Barricado. It crossed Long Wharf on the neck of the T, and two little islands to the north and south of the wharf furnished points of *appui*. Central Wharf was laid out over one of these islands, and large trees and stones, which had been used in building the Barricado, were found when excavations were making for the wharf. The other island was removed. The Old Wharf, being for defence only, was only wide enough to work guns upon. It fell into gradual decay, and the last vestiges disappeared long ago. "T" Wharf, which name has sometimes erroneously been connected with the Tea Party, has always been noted for an excellent old well of water, from which ships were supplied. Minott and Andrew Faneuil owned it in 1718.

When, in November, 1745, after that extraordinary and successful expedition, which resulted in the reduction of Louisburg, Governor Shirley returned home in the Massachusetts Frigate, a splendid reception awaited him. He first landed at the "Castle," where he passed the night, coming up to Boston in the morning in the Castle barge. About noon he landed, with his retinue, at Long Wharf, under salutes from all the shipping in the port and the acclamations of the people. Here they were received by the dignitaries of the province and town, and by Colonel Wendell's regiment of militia, a Chelsea company, the Troop of Guards, and another Troop of Horse, with the Cadets under Colonel Benjamin Pollard. The ringing of bells, illuminations, and fireworks prolonged the joyful occasion.

General Thomas Gage landed at Long Wharf in May, 1774, and was received by the Troop of Guards, a regiment of militia, and the Cadets, under the command of Lieutenant-Colonel

Coffin. The reception was in the midst of a drenching rain, but was, nevertheless, attended by a great concourse of people. Six years before this umbrellas — or "umbrilloes," as they were called — were first used in Boston, and were, doubtless, put in requisition on this occasion. Nearly all the British troops that set foot in Boston landed at this wharf. It was also the scene of the embarkation of the 5th and 38th for Breed's Hill, who left so many of their number on its green slope.

The stores on the wharf, deserted by most of their owners, were used during the siege for the storage of military and naval stores, of which a considerable quantity was recovered by Quartermaster-General Mifflin, — besides General Gage's chariot, which was taken out of the dock broken, — when our forces entered the town. After the evacuation, the British fleet remained for some time anchored at Nantasket, and was a source of continual alarm to the people. General Benjamin Lincoln organized a force which embarked from Long Wharf and took positions at Long and Pettick's Islands, Hull, Point Alderton, and elsewhere. The battery on Long Island sent a shot through the upper works of Commodore Banks's ship, when he signalled the fleet to get under way, blew up the lighthouse, and vexed the waters of Boston harbor no more.

When the news of the Embargo of 1812 reached the town it caused the greatest consternation. All the vessels that could get away before the port closed did so. Sunday, April 5, was as busy a day as any of the remaining six. Long Wharf, and every other, was crowded with trucks, sailors, and longshoremen. About fifty sail went to sea before the flag of Embargo was raised on Fort Hill.

The embarkation of the troops which were to force the American works at Breed's Hill, from this wharf and from the North Battery (Battery Wharf), was a scene to be remembered. The ships of war furnished the boats, which were in charge of Collingwood, — afterwards so famous as Nelson's lieutenant, — then a midshipman. Frothingham graphically describes the display: —

"When a blue flag was displayed as a signal, the fleet, with field-pieces in the leading barges, moved towards Charlestown. The sun was shining in meridian splendor; and the scarlet uniforms, the glistening armor, the brazen artillery, the regular movement of the boats, the flashes of fire, and the belchings of smoke formed a spectacle brilliant and imposing."

> "Hark, from the town a trumpet! The barges at the wharf
> Are crowded with the living freight, and now they're pushing off.
> With clash and glitter, trump and drum, in all its bright array,
> Behold the splendid sacrifice move slowly o'er the bay!"

THE BRAZEN HEAD.

CHAPTER IV.

BRATTLE SQUARE AND THE TOWN DOCK.

Old Cornhill. — Paul Revere. — Amos and Abbott Lawrence. — Boylston's Alley. — Barracks of the 29th. — Blue Anchor. — Brattle Street Church. — General Gage. — Howe, Clinton, and Burgoyne. — John Adams. — Headquarters of Stage-Coaches. — Dock Square. — The Conduit. — Town Dock Described. — Quincy Market. — Origin of Markets in Boston. — The Triangular Warehouse. — Roebuck Passage. — Clinton Street. — The Old Market Museum. — Old Cocked Hat. — Faneuil Hall. — D'Estaing. — Lafayette. — Jackson. — Prince de Joinville. — Jerome Bonaparte. — Lord Ashburton. — The Portraits. — Corn Court. — Hancock House. — Talleyrand. — State Custom House. — The Conscription Riot.

OUR way lies through that part of Old Cornhill from State Street to Dock Square. The Town Pump, which has been referred to, stood in the middle of Cornhill, on a line with the north side of Court Street, giving room for vehicles to pass on either side. In 1771 we find it made use of as a point of direction to the shop opposite.

At No. 50 Cornhill, or next south of Goldthwait's carpet store, we find Paul Revere, a man whose name occurs frequently in connection with the history of Boston. Descended from the sturdy old Huguenots, whose ancient family name was Rivoire, Paul Revere began business as a goldsmith, but, erelong, took up the art of engraving on copper, in which he was self-taught; a fact evident enough in his early attempts.

Of his engravings of Dr. Mayhew, and the Rescinders, he might have said with Beau Brummel, "These are my failures." "The Massacre," "Cromwell's Head," etc., show a somewhat truer hand. But

"Copperplate, with almanacks
Engraved upon 't, and other knacks,"

did not fill the measure of Revere's ingenuity. He put in operation the first powder-mill in the province, visiting Philadelphia — where was the only mill in the Colonies — for this purpose.

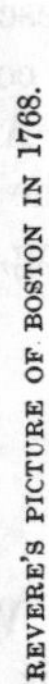

REVERE'S PICTURE OF BOSTON IN 1768.

The proprietor would only permit the Boston mechanic to go through his mill; but this was enough, and the Provincial Congress soon had powder. Revere was of the Tea Party; was lieutenant-colonel of a regiment of militia raised after the evacuation; and was in the ill-starred Penobscot expedition of 1779. After the peace of 1783 he established a cannon and bell foundry at the North End, and, later, works at Canton for the manufacture of malleable copper bolts, spikes, etc. A company at the latter place still bears his name. Paul Revere was also the first President of the Mechanic Charitable Association.

When the engraver was at work upon the caricature of the seventeen members of the Legislature who voted, in 1768, to rescind the resolution to issue a circular to the Colonies calling a convention to oppose taxation without representation, entitled "A warm place, Hell," Dr. Church, who afterwards betrayed the patriot cause, dropped in, and, seeing what Revere was doing, seized a pen and wrote:—

> "O brave Rescinders! to yon yawning cell,
> Seventeen such miscreants will startle hell.
> There puny villains damned for petty sin,
> On such distinguished scoundrels, gaze and grin;
> The outdone devil will resign his sway,—
> He never curst his millions in a day."

When Amos Lawrence first came to Boston, in 1807, from his native town of Groton, he began business in Cornhill, on the corner which makes the turn into Dock Square. We are assured that the rental of $ 700 per annum seemed, at that time, to presage ruin to the future millionnaire. Mr. Lawrence, whom we find set down as a shopkeeper, removed afterwards to the situation on the opposite side of Cornhill, now occupied by a well-known carpet firm. At this time he boarded with Mrs. Dexter, in Portland Street, as did also his brother Abbott, an apprentice in his store. The munificent public and private charities of Amos Lawrence will long perpetuate his memory. To Williams College he gave upwards of $ 40,000, and to Bunker Hill Monument large sums and personal effort.

Abbott Lawrence, the apprentice, became an eminent Boston merchant, besides holding many offices of public trust. He was the founder of the city of Lawrence; was in the City Council in 1831, a member of Congress two terms, and minister to England from 1849 to 1852. He also founded the Lawrence Scientific School at Cambridge, endowing it munificently.

We have mentioned among the peculiar features of the town the arches, which in various places tunnel the buildings, and furnish a short cut from street to street. One of these formerly led from the foot of Cornhill into Brattle Street, but was obliterated in extending Washington Street. It was here long prior to the Revolution. At the time of the Boston Massacre, and for two years previous, Brattle Square was a sort of *place d'armes* for British troops, and in the alley began a collision between some grenadiers of the 29th and a few citizens on the evening of the memorable 5th of March.

As early as 1734 John Draper, who published the Boston News-Letter in 1732, and was printer to the Governor and Council, lived on the east corner, and from him it took the name of Draper's Alley. In 1776 Benjamin Edes, the printer, took the house next to Draper, part of which formed the alley, so that its later occupation by a large printing firm was entirely legitimate. The passage was known both as Draper's and Boylston's Alley.

Opposite the opening into Brattle Street was Murray's Barracks, in which the 29th were quartered. This regiment was thoroughly hated by the Bostonians before the Massacre, and after this tragedy, in which it was the chief actor, there is little question that it would have been exterminated in detail but for its removal to the Castle. It is a singular fact that a major of the 29th, Pierce Butler, became a citizen of the United States and a Senator from South Carolina, becoming, in 1812, an advocate for war against his native country. The officers of the 29th lodged at Madame Apthorp's. Her house stood in the angle now covered by the Quincy House.

Where the City Tavern gave place to the extension north of Washington Street once stood the Blue Anchor Tavern. Still another Blue Anchor is found in Cornhill, very near the site of the Globe newspaper building. This old tavern was kept in 1691 by George Monck, and as early as 1664 by Robert Turner. Savage says: "At the sign of the Blue Anchor, Turner furnished lodgings and refreshments to members of the government, to juries, and to the clergy, when summoned into synod by our General Court." The rooms in the Blue Anchor were designated as the "Cross Keyes," "Green Dragon," the "Anchor and Castle Chamber," and the "Rose and Sun Low Room." * What should we think in these days of such a bill as the following abstract of an election dinner to the General Court in 1769 presents?—204 dinners, 72 bottles of Madeira, 28 of Lisbon, 10 of claret, 17 of port, 18 of porter, 50 "double bowls" of punch, besides cider. A double bowl of punch held two quarts, enough to satisfy thirsty Jack Falstaff himself.

The City Tavern, or City Hotel as it was sometimes called, was one of the most noted stage-houses, whose bustle and activity of a morning, when the lumbering stage-coaches rattled out of the stable yard, and over the cobble-stone pavements at a brisk trot, enlivened all this locality. It was also a favorite hostelry of the novelist Hawthorne.

We have before us another striking example of the ever changing conditions incident to the growth of our city. Here, where the Old Brattle Street Church had stood for a hundred years, the stately Wakefield Building stands to-day.

The first building was erected in 1699, of wood, and was for a time known as the "Manifesto Church," in consequence of a declaration of principles by it, in answer to a protest from the older churches against its more liberal form of worship. The old church was never painted, and the tower and bell were on the west side, while the entrance was at the south side. Its ruinous condition caused it to be rebuilt of brick, as it lately stood. John S. Copley, the painter, made a plan for the new building, but it was rejected on account of the expense, and that of Major Thomas Dawes accepted. Governor Hancock gave a thousand pounds, and a bell, on which was inscribed,—

"I to the Church the living call,
And to the grave I summon all."

* Whitmore's Notes to John Dunton's Letters.

This was the church of Colman, the Coopers, Thacher, Buckminster, Edward Everett, Palfrey, and Lothrop, an array of clerical talent unsurpassed in the Boston pulpit. General Gage quartered the 29th in the church and vicinity, taking up his

BRATTLE STREET CHURCH.

own quarters in the house opposite. Gage told Mr. Turell that he had no fears for his men while quartered within such walls. Nevertheless, the night before the evacuation a twenty-four pound shot from Cambridge struck the tower, and falling to the ground was picked up by Mr. Turell, and in 1824 was imbedded in the masonry, where it remained until the work of demolition began.

When the society sold the church, they reserved the ancient quoins, pulpit, bell, and cannon-ball. The bell given by Governor Hancock became cracked, and was sold; the present one having been purchased in London in 1809. The society voted to make Mr. Wakefield the custodian of the cannon-ball, to be placed by him in the front of his new building on the old site, but this purpose was not carried into effect. The rustic quoins, of Connecticut stone, have been placed inside the tower of the new church on Commonwealth Avenue. One of these, which had the name of John Hancock inscribed upon it, was mutilated by the King's soldiers, who owed a special spite to King Hancock, as they styled him. Dr. John Greenleaf's name was on another of the quoins.

WINDOW OF BRATTLE STREET CHURCH, WITH BALL.

During the occupation by troops, services appear to have been held occasionally in the church, as the Boston Gazette, of September 21, 1775, states that "the Rev. Dr. Morrison received a call to preach in the elegant new church in Brattle Street, vacated by the flight of Dr. Cooper, and on Sunday he delivered an excellent discourse to a genteel audience." The tenor of this discourse was upon the fatal consequences of sedition, and was adapted to the "genteel" audience. Of the pastors, besides Cooper, noted as a zealous coworker with the patriots, there was Buckminster, who had taught Daniel Webster at Exeter Academy, and was one of the originators of the Anthology Club; Everett, whom Lafayette styled the young American Cicero, who left the pulpit for a distinguished career in public life; and others who have been prominent in our annals.

Besides Governors Hancock and Bowdoin and their families, Joseph Warren, Harrison Gray Otis, Madame Scott, Daniel Webster, John Coffin Jones, and many other distinguished Bostonians, have sat under the ministration of the pastors of Old Brattle Street.

General Thomas Gage, whom some wit proposed to create Lord Lexington, Baron of Bunker Hill, on account of his disasters here, was well acquainted with Washington, having fought under Braddock at Fort du Quesne, where he (Gage) led the advance. Washington, in July, 1775, became his adversary. Another of these intimacies existed between General Charles Lee and Burgoyne, who had served together in Portugal.

Gage succeeded Hutchinson as governor, in 1774, when it was determined by the Ministry to crush the rising spirit of rebellion in the Colonies. He was at first well received, but the course of events soon led to a wide separation between him and the people. After Lexington, Gage proclaimed martial law, offering pardon to all offenders except Samuel Adams and John Hancock. Bunker Hill followed, and the British general soon found himself shut up in the town. In October he resigned and returned to England, being succeeded by Howe. Howe, Clinton, and Burgoyne, all arrived in Boston in the Cerberus, May 25, 1775. As they came up the harbor they met a packet outward bound, and Burgoyne hailed the master and inquired the news. Learning that Boston was closely besieged by the provincials, he demanded, "How many regulars are there in thé town?" Being answered about five thousand men, he exclaimed, "What! ten thousand peasants keep five thousand King's troops shut up; well, let us get in and we'll soon find elbow-room." This name stuck to Burgoyne, and on a second visit to Boston, when the fortune of war had made him a prisoner, he landed at Charlestown Ferry, — where the bridge now is, — but was extremely annoyed by an old woman, who, perched on a neighboring shed, kept crying out, "Make way there, — elbow-room, — elbow-room."

In 1768 John Adams, the future president, but then a young barrister, took up his residence with Mr. Bollan in Brattle Square. The house was known as the White House. His son, John Quincy Adams, was then only a year old. In his diary Mr. Adams remarks that "the town was full of troops, and through the whole succeeding fall and winter a regiment was exercised by Major Small directly in front of my house." On the night of the Massacre Mr. Adams was passing the evening at the house of Mr. Henderson Inches at the South End, where a club, of which Adams was a member, used to assemble. Thinking the alarm was for a fire, he snatched his hat and cloak, and went out to assist in putting it out. He did not reach the Town House until the affair was ended, and passed on, through the little alley we have taken in our route, to Brattle Street. The 29th were drawn up in front of their barracks, and Adams had to pass along their ranks to reach his lodgings, but not a word was spoken on either side. At this time he lodged in Cole Lane, now Portland Street.

Mr. Adams was elected to the General Court of Massachusetts in 1770, though laboring under some obloquy on account of his defence of Captain Preston. He has been called the father of our navy, as the act passed under Washington's administration authorizing the construction of six frigates, was vitalized by him, while at a still earlier day, in the Continental Congress of 1775, he drew up a code of regulations for a navy, that has formed the basis for the government of that branch of the service. Ambassador to England and Holland, and finally Chief Magistrate, John Adams, by a coincidence, died on the same day as Thomas Jefferson, July 4, 1826. Mr. Adams was termed by Jefferson the "Colossus" of Congress.

Before leaving Brattle Square and its vicinity, it must not be forgotten that this street, with Elm and Union, formed the great headquarters of the stages before the day of railways. Wilde's and Doolittle's were chief among the taverns for stage travel, and on a clear morning the air resounded with the crack of the whips and halloo of the drivers. The starting of the stages was always witnessed by a gaping crowd, and their diurnal passage over the country roads was an event to the dwellers along the route, scarcely equalled by the later advent of the iron horse. The Tony Wellers of the box were great men in the eyes of the stable-boys and country lasses. One at least among them has reached the eminence of M. C., while another presided over the traffic of a great railway.

In exploring Dock Square, we find that the old Town Dock, from which its name is derived, flowed up to a point opposite the entrance of Elm Street, formerly Wing's Lane. On the brink of the Dock was a watch-house, and in the space formed by the junction of North (Anne), Union, and Elm Streets was the Flat Conduit. This conduit was merely a reservoir of water, about twelve feet square, but was deep enough for Moses Bradford to be drowned, while trying to save a boy who had fallen into it. It is mentioned as early as 1656, and was constructed perhaps not long after the fire of 1653. Anne Street was originally Conduit Street as far as Cross, and Union Street is described in 1732 as leading from the Conduit to the Mill Pond.

Before Faneuil Hall was built — as early as 1708 — the space it covers and which surrounds it was occupied as a market-place, and at the foot of Merchants' Row the Dock was crossed by a swing-bridge, in two equal parts. That part of the Dock lying west of Merchants' Row was filled up about 1780; it was known as the Market Dock. The lower section of the Dock was narrower, and is now covered by North Market Street. At the time of the improvement of this region by Josiah Quincy, in 1826, the Town Dock came up as far as the head of Faneuil Hall Market, or, as this name is now applied to the market in Faneuil Hall, we will say Quincy Market, which the popular will has christened it. On the old plans of 1738 the Town Dock was flanked by Woodmansie's wharf on the south, and by Borland's, Bridgham's, Hill's, and Pitt's wharves on the north. The Mill Creek, connecting the Mill Cove with the Town Cove, emptied into the latter on a line with, and a little south of Blackstone Street.

In the primitive order of things, it is apparent that the tide covered all the level ground in Dock Square, as indicated on all early plans, and all east of Union Street from Creek Lane on the west. Between the Mill Creek and the Town Dock was a triangular tongue of land, or rather marsh. All of the north side of the Dock seems to have been known at one time as the Fish Market. Shaw says, "The chief part of the town was built on the cove or bay which has since been called the Town Dock." The first paragraph in the town records establishes the fact that in 1634 this was the chief landing-place.

The improvement by Mr. Quincy was the greatest enterprise of the kind that had been undertaken in Boston. By reference to Quincy's History, we learn that "a granite market-house, two stories high, 535 feet long, covering 27,000 feet of land, was erected at a cost of $150,000. Six new streets were opened, and a seventh greatly enlarged, including 167,000 feet of land, and flats, docks, and wharf rights obtained to the extent of 142,000 square feet. All this was accomplished in the centre of a populous city, not only without any tax, debt, or burden upon its pecuniary resources, but with large permanent additions to its real and productive property." This improvement also facilitated the opening of Fulton and of Commercial Streets, the latter making direct communication north and south instead of a long *détour* through North Street. S. S. Lewis was the projector of Commercial Street.

Quincy Market, though not at once pecuniarily successful, soon became so. It is a monument to Mr. Quincy's genius and perseverance. Any other man would have succumbed to the obstacles he had to encounter, but he pressed on to the accomplishment of his purpose. He invested the sluggish town with new life, and brought into practical use a new watchword,— *Progress.* At a very early hour Mr. Quincy was in the habit of mounting his horse, and riding through every quarter of the town, remedying evils or projecting new enterprises.

The interior of the market has always been a scene of attraction to visitors, and a model of its kind. Admirable system and order prevails. Here are haunches that would have caused the royal sword to leap from its scabbard, as when

> "Our second Charles of fame facete,
> On loin of beef did dine;
> He held his sword pleased o'er the meat,
> 'Rise up, our famed Sir-loin!'"

Here are sausages in festoons; roasting pig that would have made Charles Lamb's mouth water; vegetables in parterres, and fruits from every clime. Here one may have fish, flesh, fowl, or good red herring. The countenances of those who seek their daily food before the stalls is a study. The poor woman lingering over the coveted joint far beyond her slender purse is jostled by the dame who gives *carte blanche* to her purveyor. What quantities we eat! Sydney Smith thought he had eaten wagon-loads more than was good for him. The open mouths of the gazers upon this scene of plenty have been likened to so many graves yawning for the slaughtered herds.

Yet plenty has not always prevailed in the town. Putnam came with his drove of sheep to succor the inhabitants in 1774. In 1775 the Town Bull, aged twenty years, was killed and sold for the use of the generals and officers, at eighteen pence sterling per pound. Perhaps Gage, in Brattle Square, with his subordinates, Howe, Clinton, and Burgoyne, sat in gloomy conclave over a tough morsel of the patriarch, hoping vainly that "good digestion might wait on appetite."

Faneuil Hall Market was begun in 1824, the corner-stone laid in 1825, and was finished in November, 1826. It occupied a little more than two years in building. North and South Market Streets were built at the same time, and are respectively sixty-five and one hundred and two feet wide. The difference in the width of these streets, and in fact the position of the market itself, is due to the refusal of the heirs of Nathan Spear to part with their estate on any terms. By the increased width of South Market Street, the difficulty was overcome, as the city then took the estate for the street with a clear legal conscience. Codman's, Spear's, Bray's, and the wharves extending between North Market and State Streets towards the present line of Commercial Street, were reclaimed in this great improvement, and converted into solid ground, and Chatham Street was laid out.

Benjamin Faneuil, Jr., was in business in Butler's Row in 1767, which, before the improvements, entered Merchants' Row between Chatham and State Streets. This Benjamin was the nephew of Peter, of noble memory, and was one of the consignees of the tea ships whose cargoes were emptied into the dock in 1773.

As a merchant, John Hancock had a store at the head of

what is now South Market Street, or, as it was then described, "Store No. 4, at the east end of Faneuil Hall Market. A general assortment of English and India Goods, also choice Newcastle Coals, and Irish Butter, cheap for Cash. Said Hancock desires those persons who are still indebted to the estate of the late Hon. Thomas Hancock, Esq., deceased, to be speedy in paying their respective balances to prevent trouble." *

In Winthrop's Journal, a market is mentioned as set up by order of the court in March, 1634. Its locality is not mentioned, but it is believed to have been on the site of the Old State House. In 1734 the town located three markets, and appropriated £300 towards their erection. They were situated in North Square, Dock Square, and on the present ground of Boylston Market. A bell was rung daily at sunrise to give notice of the opening, and one o'clock P. M. was the hour of closing. On the 4th of June the three markets were opened for the first time, and the people and dealers flocked in great numbers to them.

The market in Dock Square was always the most frequented. Faneuil Hall, of which we shall presently relate the history, did not long provide sufficient accommodations. At the time of Mr. Quincy's improvements there was a row of sheds, for the sale of vegetables, on the north side of Faneuil Hall, in what is now the street. The neighboring streets were often obstructed with market-wagons, while farmers were compelled to occupy Union Street with their stands, nearly to Hanover, and Washington, almost to Court Street. In 1819 a number of citizens erected what was known as the City Market, in the large building at the foot of Brattle Street, demolished for the extension of Washington Street; the upper part was occupied as a Gallery of Fine Arts. The General Court refused to incorporate the proprietors, and the city subsequently rejected the offer of the market as a donation.

Retracing our steps along North Market Street, the first object of interest is the Triangular Warehouse, which stood on the border of the town dock, opposite the swing-bridge, until

* Boston Evening Post, December 25, 1764.

taken down in 1824 to make room for the sweeping changes then inaugurated. Its site is now covered by the buildings at the head of North Market Street, with a moiety in Merchants' Row and Clinton Street.

This singular old building was built of brick, of two stories, on a stone foundation, with a tower at each angle ; a tower also rose from the centre of the roof. Each of these towers terminated in a pointed roof of slate, and were capped with a stone ball set in lead, except the middle tower, which had a wooden one. The strength with which it was constructed, with the quaint architecture, led for a time to the supposition that it was intended for a Custom House, or some other similar purpose, but no proof being found to support the belief, the opinion became general that it was erected by London merchants for a warehouse, about 1700.

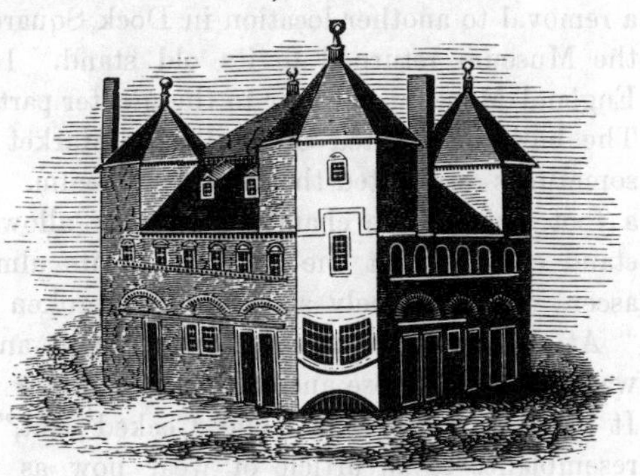

TRIANGULAR WAREHOUSE.

One side of the Triangular Warehouse fronted Roebuck Passage, which has become, by transition, the extension of Merchants' Row. The passage, named from a tavern called the Roebuck, within its limits, was a tortuous defile a hundred feet in length, varying in width from thirteen to twenty feet, but was still the main thoroughfare from the market north and south. The tavern itself was a building with a projecting upper story, and was a notorious resort of doubtful repute. It was the scene of at least one deadly affray. Richard Whittington, a descendant of the Lord Mayor of London, is said to have been the builder.

Clinton Street was one of the new avenues which arose out of the chaos of this region. The Old Mill Creek crossed it at the point where now stands the New England House, the last of the Boston coffee-houses. The hotel is built on made land. The course of the creek was altered at this point, so as to flow through the lower part of Clinton Street into the harbor, instead of following its old channel into the dock. To effect this plan, the city bought Governor Eustis's wharf, through which the creek found an artificial outlet. Blackstone Street has taken the place of the creek.

Opposite the north side of Faneuil Hall is a little alley, and on the alley, with a front on North Street, was an old landmark. This lofty wooden building of five cramped stories was the Old Boston Museum, established in 1804, by Philip Woods. After a removal to another location in Dock Square for a short time, the Museum returned to its old stand. In 1822 the New England Museum fell heir to the greater part of the collection. The building fronted originally on Market Square, and was sometimes designated the Market Museum. The timbers were a foot square; the chambers scarcely allowed a tall man to stand erect, whilst the staircase in its almost perpendicular ascent was extremely suggestive of broken bones.

At the corner formed by North Street and Market Square was another of those ancient structures now extinct among us. It was known as the "Old Cocked Hat," from its fancied resemblance to an article of wear now as obsolete as itself. Under the western gable, fronting Dock Square, was the date of 1680. The building was of wood, covered with plaster on the outside, with which were mixed fragments of broken glass. Various ornamental figures were traced upon this rough surface. On two sides, south and southwest, the water once flowed, and in digging not far from here some years ago to settle a disputed boundary question, the capstan and ring-bolt of the old wharf were uncovered within the present sidewalk.

The "Old Cocked Hat" was of two stories, the upper projecting, and is supposed to have been built the year following the destructive fire of August 3, 1679, which began about midnight and raged till midday of the 4th. A hundred and fifty dwellings and warehouses, with several ships and their

ANCIENT HOUSE IN DOCK SQUARE.

cargoes, were consumed. This old house was at first a dwelling, and for a time, according to Snow, the principal apothecary's shop of the town was kept there. It was taken down in July, 1860.

The fame of Faneuil Hall is as wide as the country itself. It has been called the "Cradle of Liberty," because dedicated by that early apostle of freedom, James Otis, to the cause of liberty, in a speech delivered in the hall in March, 1763. Somewhat of its early history has appeared in the account of the town government. Its walls have echoed to the voices of the great departed in times gone by, and in every great public exigency the people, with one accord, assemble together to take counsel within its hallowed precincts. Though much too small for popular gatherings of the present day, its long use for this purpose, with the many glorious associations that cluster around it, still mark it as the centre from which the voice of the people of Boston should proceed.

The Old Market-house, mentioned as existing in Dock Square in 1734, was demolished by a mob in 1736–37. There was contention among the people as to whether they would be served at their houses in the old way, or resort to fixed localities, and one set of disputants took this summary method of settling the question. Pemberton says, this mob were "disguised like clergymen."

In 1740, the question of the Market-house being revived, Peter Faneuil proposed to build one at his own cost on the town's land in Dock Square, upon condition that the town should legally authorize it, enact proper regulations, and

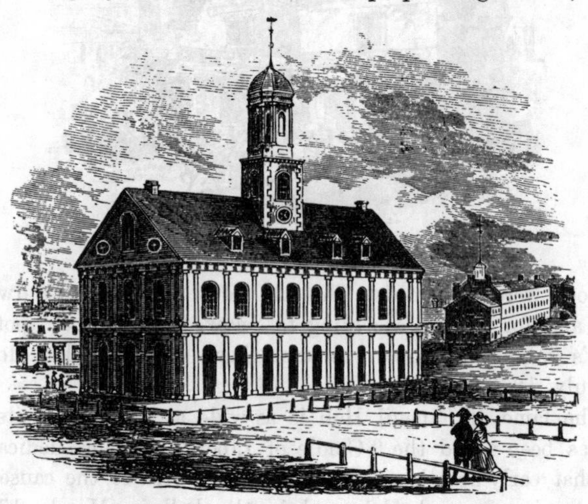

FANEUIL HALL BEFORE ITS ENLARGEMENT.

maintain it for the purpose named. Mr. Faneuil's noble offer was courteously received, but such was the division of opinion on the subject, that it was accepted by a majority of only seven votes, out of seven hundred and twenty-seven persons voting. The building was completed in September, 1742, and three days after, at a meeting of citizens, the hall was formally accepted and a vote of thanks passed to the donor. Hon. Thomas Cushing, the moderator of the meeting, the selectmen, and representatives of the town, were appointed a committee, "to wait upon Peter Faneuil, Esq., and in the name of the town, to render him their most hearty thanks for so bountiful a gift." Besides this, the town voted that the hall should be called Faneuil Hall forever; to procure Mr. Faneuil's portrait to be placed therein; and later, to purchase the Faneuil arms, carved and gilt by Moses Deshon, to be fixed in the hall.

The first architect of Faneuil Hall was John Smibert the painter; Samuel Ruggles was the builder. It was not at first intended by Faneuil to build more than one story for the market, but with noble generosity he went beyond his original proposal, and built another story for a town hall. The original size of the building was forty by one hundred feet, just half the present width; the hall would contain one thousand persons. At the fire of January 13, 1763, the whole interior was destroyed, but the town voted to rebuild in March, and the State authorized a lottery in aid of the design. The first meeting after the rebuilding was held on the 14th March, 1763, when James Otis delivered the dedicatory address. In 1806 the Hall was enlarged in width to eighty feet, and by the addition of a third story.

But little is left of the original building, but a rule has been laid down for such as may be curious to trace the old outline: "Take a northeast view of the Hall, — there are seven windows before you in each story, — run a perpendicular line, from the ground, through the centre of the middle window to the top of the belt, at the bottom of the third story, carry a straight line from that point nearly to the top of the second window, on the right, in the third story. That point is the apex of the old pediment. From that point draw the corresponding roof-line down to the belt, at the corner; and you have a profile of the ancient structure."

A grasshopper, which still decorates the vane, made by that cunning artificer Deacon Shem Drowne, was long thought to be the crest of the Faneuils; especially as a similar insect adorned the vane of the summer-house in Tremont Street. But the arms were extant not many years ago on some of Peter Faneuil's plate, in the possession of his descendants, and disproved this theory. No better reason has been assigned for the adoption

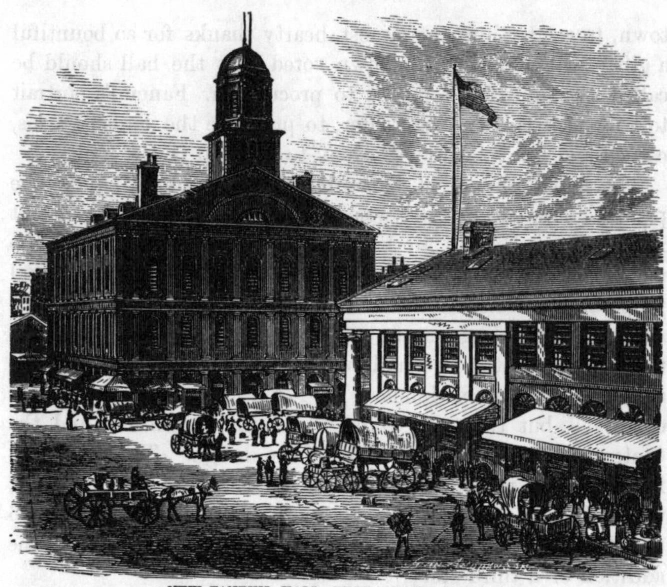

NEW FANEUIL HALL, WITH QUINCY MARKET.

of the grasshopper than that it was an imitation of the vane of the Royal Exchange, London.

Curiously enough, the first public oration delivered in Faneuil Hall was a funeral eulogy, pronounced on the death of Peter Faneuil, March 14, 1743, by Master Lovell of the Latin School. In the course of his address the orator said, "May Liberty always spread its joyful wings over this place. May Loyalty to a king under whom we enjoy that Liberty ever remain our character." Master Lovell, himself a tory fugitive when Boston was freed from the British occupation, did not dream of the fulfilment of his wish — divested of its dependence on a king — when he uttered it.

Faneuil Hall was illuminated, by a vote of the town, on the news of the repeal of the Stamp Act, and the selectmen were requested to make provision for drinking the king's health. During the winter of 1775 – 76 the British officers, under the patronage of General Howe, fitted the hall into a very neat theatre, devoted chiefly to performances ridiculing the patriots. The Sunday after the battle of Lexington there was a meeting held in the hall by the citizens to agree with General Gage on regulations under which the people might leave the town. The strictness with which the Sabbath was then observed testifies to the importance the subject had assumed. Gage communicated with the meeting through Captain Sheriff, his aide-de-camp, the proposal that the inhabitants might be allowed to depart after surrendering their arms. Many of the old provincial officers, men who had served at Louisburg, were present, and viewed with deep chagrin the proposition to give up the arms they had worn in many honorable campaigns. Gage had the bad faith afterwards to render his promise nugatory by appointing a Town Major, to whom applications were made. This officer discriminated against those whose attachment to the patriot cause was known.

In Faneuil Hall is the rendezvous of the "Ancient and Honorable Artillery Company." Its original designation was the "Military Company of the Massachusetts"; it was also styled, at different periods, "The Artillery Company" and "The Great Artillery." The name "Ancient and Honorable" was not applied until 1720; no military organization can dispute its title to be the oldest band of citizen-soldiery in America. The company was formed in 1637, and at once applied for an act of incorporation, which was not granted, the rigid Puritans fearing to establish a privileged military body which might, on occasion, subvert the government. The Prætorian Band of the Romans and the Templars of Europe were cited to enforce this wise determination. The company was, nevertheless, permitted to choose a captain and make use of the common arms in their exercise. A charter was granted in 1638.

Captain Keayne, the first commander, has been noticed. The charter prohibited any other military company from parading on the days appointed by law for the "Artillery"; and this exclusive privilege was maintained against the "Winslow Blues," in 1808, when that company assembled in Faneuil Hall on one of the field-days of the "Ancients."

It does not appear what the uniform of the company — if any was adopted — was at the beginning. Blue and buff was supposed to be the dress in 1738. By 1770 the corps stood arrayed in gold-laced hats, blue coats, buff under-clothes, and silk stockings, with white linen spatterdashes. In 1772 an order was issued that wigs and hair should be clubbed. Some few changes were made in 1787, when shoulder-straps, to secure the cross-belts, and a black garter, worn below the knee, were adopted; the hair to be worn *en queue.* Chapeau-bras and cockade, with black plume, eighteen inches long, took the place of the old cocked-hat in 1810, with red facings for the coat instead of buff.

The company was assembled by beat of drum, which remained the practice for many years. On days of parade the drummer passed through the principal streets beating the rappel vigorously. The colors were displayed on these occasions from Colonel Daniel Henchman's bookstore, at the corner of King Street and Old Cornhill, — the vacant area which then existed under the Old State House serving the corps for a rendezvous until the town provided an armory in Faneuil Hall. In 1743 halberds were used by sergeants, and pikes and half-pikes by the captain and lieutenant.

The roll of the "Ancients" presents a host of names distinguished in Colonial and Revolutionary history. To enumerate them would be impossible within our limits. The old custom of "Artillery Election," when the old officers retire and the new are commissioned by the governor, is still scrupulously observed. The "Election Sermon" is still preached as in the days of Colman and Sewall.

During the reception of Count D'Estaing in September, 1778, a superb entertainment was given him at Faneuil Hall, at which five hundred guests were present.

When Lafayette was in Boston, in 1784, the merchants gave him a dinner at Faneuil Hall. At every toast thirteen cannon were discharged in Market Square by Major Davis's train of Artillery. The picture of Washington had been concealed by drapery, and when in the course of the banquet it was unveiled, the Marquis rose to his feet, clapped his hands, and seemed deeply moved as he gazed on the features of his old commander. The audience was not less affected than the distinguished guest. The Marquis was fond of identifying himself with the Americans, and in this way won their love and admiration. Being asked by a lady on one occasion if the black cockade was not the color worn by the Continental officers, he replied : "Yes, madame, but we added the white out of compliment to the French when they joined us."

The following anecdote is related by Mr. Dean, in his memoir of Daniel Messinger : —

"An amusing incident occurred once at a dinner given Prince Jerome Bonaparte in 1804. It is stated on the authority of Josiah Quincy, that after dinner Colonel Daniel Messinger sang the favorite old song of 'To-morrow.' As the audience joined in the chorus of 'To-morrow, To-morrow,' a cloud came over the countenance of the Prince, and taking his next neighbor by the arm he exclaimed, 'To Moreau ! To Moreau ! Is it a song in honor of General Moreau ?' He was quickly undeceived, and smiled when he found that no one but himself was thinking of the great rival of his brother."

President Jackson visited Boston in June, 1833, accompanied by Secretaries Cass and Woodbury, and Mr. Poinsett of South Carolina. The occasion was the opening of the new Dry Dock at Charlestown, and the docking of the frigate Constitution. The President held a public reception in Faneuil Hall. Commodore Hull, Mr. Winthrop, and Mr. Van Buren were present. The Vice-president was described as a tight, snug, compact, vigorous-looking little body, with a bright, keen, twinkling little eye and winning smile. Both he and Mr. Woodbury were very bald. Mr. Cass was not present.

The visit of the Prince de Joinville to Boston in November, 1841, was rendered memorable by a grand ball given in his honor at Faneuil Hall. The Prince had come over to New York in *La Belle Poule* frigate, the same that conveyed the ashes of the great Napoleon from St. Helena to France. The town was all agog for the expected visit of the Prince, and when he appeared at the ball simply attired in a blue naval uniform, the enthusiasm was extreme. The Prince wore no decoration, except the ribbon of the Legion of Honor, and devoted himself assiduously to the ladies to whom he was introduced. The old hall was beautifully decorated with flags and devices specially designed for the occasion.

Alexander Baring, Lord Ashburton, negotiator with Mr. Webster of the treaty which bears his name, was welcomed to Boston in Faneuil Hall, August 27, 1842, by Mayor Chapman. From him Ashburton Place takes its name. As one of the great house of Baring Brothers, he resided some time in the United States. He and Webster were on terms of close intimacy.

The Earl of Elgin, while governor-general of Canada, visited Boston to attend the jubilee upon the opening of the Grand Trunk Railway. He was accompanied by a numerous staff, and received the honor of a grand ball at Faneuil Hall. Among the officers who accompanied him, none attracted more attention than those of a Highland regiment, — stalwart, bare-legged fellows in bonnet, kilt, and tartan.

Among the attractions to the old Cradle of Liberty, the portraits which adorn the walls are not the least, and it is to be regretted that some which have hung there and would now be highly prized were either destroyed or spirited away by vandal hands. Shortly after the death of Mr. Faneuil, Governor Shirley informed the selectmen that he had received his Majesty's picture through the hands of the Duke of Grafton, and soon after the likeness of George II. was hung in the hall. The town had solicited the portraits of Colonel Barré and General Conway, their able defenders on the floor of Parliament. The request was complied with, and the pictures sent over in 1767, but they disappeared from the hall when the British evacuated the town, that of Faneuil with the rest.

The west end of the hall is covered with paintings. The large picture by Healey, representing Webster replying to Hayne, first attracts the eye. The portraits of John Hancock, Samuel Adams, and Joseph Warren are copies, the originals being deposited in the Museum of Fine Arts. The Adams has been called Copley's master-piece, and was painted for Governor Hancock, but on the sale of his effects became the property of S. A. Wells, and finally of Adam W. Thaxter, who presented it in 1842 to the city. The full length of Peter Faneuil is a copy of a smaller painting in the Historical Society's possession. It is by Colonel Henry Sargent, and was presented by Samuel Parkman, as was also the full length of Washington, by Stuart. The portraits of Rufus Choate and Abraham Lincoln are by Ames, that of Governor Andrew by Hunt. General Henry Knox is by Gilbert Stuart. Commodore Preble, one of the only two he ever sat for, is probably a Stuart. The superb clock was the gift of the school children.

Corn Court took its name from the corn market which was once held on the south side of the Town Dock. Entering its recesses, unknown to half the town, we find the oldest inn in Boston, now called the Hancock Tavern. This has been called the site of Samuel Cole's old inn. Altered in some respects, the building presents a front of brick, with wooden side-walls. A dilapidated sign, bearing the weather-stained features of Governor Hancock, hung here within remembrance.

This was the old Brasier Inn, at which Talleyrand sojourned when in Boston in 1795. He afterwards became the guest of Mr. William Lee, in Water Street. Mr. Lee's residence, a two-story wooden house, stood near the site of the new Post-Office, and was taken down many years ago. Talleyrand, the future prime minister and evil genius of Napoleon, was banished from France, and made his way to the United States, accompanied by the Duc de la Rochefoucauld Liancourt and M. de Beaumetz. At the same time Robespierre proscribed him in France, Pitt also proscribed him in England. He went first to Philadelphia, where Congress was sitting, and entered freely into the political questions then being agitated. He was intimate with Jefferson, and intrigued with the opposition to prevent the accomplishment of a treaty between England and the United States. On his return to France, after an absence of little more than a year, he was accused of having worn the white cockade in America. He wrote from the United States to Madame de Genlis: "I think no more of my enemies; I occupy myself in repairing my fortune."

Talleyrand visited the studio of Gilbert Stuart. The latter, who was a great physiognomist, after an attentive examination of the features of his visitor, remarked to a friend, "If that man is not a villain, the Almighty does not write a legible hand." Talleyrand was no friend to the United States, as was soon manifest in the capture of our vessels by the French cruisers when he came into power, which resulted in a quasi state of war with the French Republic.

M. de Talleyrand returned to Europe in an American vessel, commanded by a man named Vidal, to whom he took a great liking. He signalized his arrival in Hamburg by an amour, which, in its deplorable results, made the language of Stuart prophetic. His adventure with the young and beautiful Baroness de S——, a pupil of Madame de Genlis, is a matter of history. The unfortunate lady, better known as "Cordelia," being deserted by Talleyrand, put an end to her life with a small American penknife, the gift of her lover, which she thrust into her heart. Upon her table was found an open note directed to M. de Talleyrand. The contents were as follows:—

"I have burnt all your letters. They did no honor to my memory nor to your heart. You are the author of my death; may God forgive you, as I do!

"CORDELIA."

The brick building now occupied as a wine store, on the south side of Faneuil Hall, is one of the antiquities of the neighborhood, having stood for nearly a century unmoved amid the mutations that have swept over that locality.

Opposite the southeast corner of Faneuil Hall was located the Custom House under the State government, James Lord, Collector. Hon. James Lovell was Collector in 1789.

Dock Square was the scene of one of the incidents of the Conscription Riots of 1863. The mob, after a fruitless assault upon the gun-house in Cooper Street, proceeded in this direction with intent to supply themselves with arms from the stores of the dealers in weapons. They were so promptly met, however, by the police force, which behaved with signal bravery on this occasion, that no serious results followed, and, the military soon arriving on the ground, the riot fell still-born.

CHAPTER V.

FROM BOSTON STONE TO THE NORTH BATTERY.

The North End. — Boston Stone. — Painter's Arms. — Louis Philippe. — Union, Elm, and Portland Streets. — Benjamin Franklin's Residence. — The Blue Ball. — Lyman Beecher's Church. — Benjamin Hallowell. — Green Dragon. — Pope Day. — St. Andrew's Lodge. — Mill Pond. — Causeway. — Mill Creek. — North Street. — Sir D. Ochterlony. — Eastern Stage-House. — Cross Street. — The Old Stone House. — New Brick Church. — The Red Lyon. — Nicholas Upshall. — Edward Randolph. — North Square. — Sir H. Frankland. — Major Shaw. — Pitcairn. — Old North Church. — Cotton, Samuel, and Increase Mather. — Governor Hutchinson. — General Boyd. — Fleet Street. — King's Head Tavern. — Bethel Church. — Father Taylor. — Hancock's Wharf. — Swinging Signs. — First Universalist Church. — First Methodist. — New North. — Ship Tavern. — Noah's Ark. — Salutation Tavern. — The Boston Caucus. — The North Battery. — Trucks and Truckmen.

WE now invite the reader to accompany us into the North End, a section of the town which became settled after the more central portion we have been traversing. It contains more of its original features than any other quarter; many of its old thoroughfares are but little altered, and retain their ancient names. As for the buildings, as we plunge deeper into this region, we shall find some of those old structures that still link us to the olden time. Weather-stained, tottering, and decrepit as they are, not many years will elapse before the antiquary will seek in vain for their relics.

Imbedded in the rear wall of a building which fronts on Hanover Street, and presents its westerly side to Marshall Street, is the Boston Stone. Of the thousands who daily hurry through this narrow way, the greater part are unconscious of its existence. The stone bears the date 1737, and seems to have got its name from the famous London Stone, which served as a direction for the shops in its neighborhood, as did the Boston Stone for its vicinity. It was brought from England about 1700, and was used as a paint-mill by the painter who then occupied a little shop on these premises. The spherical stone which now surmounts its fellow was the grinder, and was for a time lost, but was discovered in digging the foundation for the present edifice. The larger stone is only a fragment of the original, which was split into four pieces when placed in its present position. Its capacity is said to have been nearly two barrels.

Following the custom of the times, the painter placed in the front of his house the coat of arms carved in wood now in the Hanover Street front, from which his dwelling was known as the "Painter's Arms." Though it bears the date of 1701, the coat of arms, representing probably the guild of painters, appears in excellent preservation. In 1835 the old "Painter's Arms" was taken down, and the tablet transferred to the building which replaced it.

Opposite to Boston Stone is an antiquated but well-preserved brick building standing quietly aloof from the neighboring and busy street. This building makes the corner — on Creek Lane — of a row of three or four venerable brick structures extending towards Blackstone Street. These were built shortly after the peace by John Hancock, and are to this day called "Hancock's Row." Times were depressed, and Hancock's bounty gave employment to many deserving and needy artisans. The row at first extended to the creek whose waters have long since ceased to flow.

The building first mentioned was the office of Ebenezer Hancock, brother of the governor, and deputy paymaster-general of the Continental army. Here, when the town was under the government of Greene and Heath and Gates, a sentinel paced before the door, never, we may believe, deserted by the needy officers of the Continental line. The lower floor has groaned beneath the weight of the French crowns sent us by his Most Christian Majesty, our excellent ally, brought over by the fleet of D'Estaing.

How the poor fellows' eyes must have sparkled when they received their long arrears in King Louis's bright silver crowns! The order of Gates or Heath was now a talisman to unlock the strong-box of the paymaster, and for once it was not empty. Two and a half million livres, in silver, were brought to Boston at one time.

William Pierce was a well-known barber at Boston Stone in 1789, and he continued to follow his calling until nearly a hundred years old. His shop was a sort of exchange for the gossip current at the North End, and was frequented by many celebrated residents of that locality. It was Pierce's boast that he had shaved Franklin, and he related that Franklin told him he was born at the corner of Union and Hanover Streets. He had also preserved a tradition that the Hancocks formerly resided in Hatters' Square. John Norman, also known as an engraver of some repute, had his printing-office at Boston Stone in 1784.

At the corner of Marshall and Union Streets lived, in 1798, James Amblard, a tailor. Amblard, a Frenchman by birth, had the honor of being the host of the Duc de Chartres, afterwards Louis Philippe, during his residence in Boston, to which allusion has been made. While awaiting funds from Europe, Louis found himself obliged to resort to teaching the French language here, until he and his brothers were relieved by remittances from their mother. The Duke returned to London in 1800, and resided at Twickenham. According to Mr. Nason, the future king of France was intimate with the father of Wm. B. Fowle, Esq., the educator, and often played chess with him of an evening, presenting on his departure a set of chessmen still preserved in the family.

Union Street was named from the British Union. Creek Lane reminds us of the mill creek to which it led. Cole Lane, or Cold Lane, has taken the name of Portland Street, and at first extended only as far as the Mill Pond. Elm Street was Wing's Lane. Elm, Hanover, and Salem Streets were all widened under the town government; before this they were the merest lanes.

Emerging from Union Street into Hanover, we stand on the corner which disputes with Milk Street the honor of being the birthplace of Benjamin Franklin. The student who patiently investigates the claims of the rival localities will be likely at last to exclaim with Mercutio, —

"A plague o' both the houses!"

Franklin's own statement, as given by himself to a person worthy of credit, was that he was born on this now famous corner, while other evidence goes to contradict it. That his early youth was passed here is certain. Here he practised the art of making tallow candles for his father, and employed his leisure in throwing rubbish into the neighboring Mill Pond. From here he wended his way through Hanover and Court Streets to the Latin School, and, after his father's business became distasteful to him, to his brother's printing-office in Queen Street.

The sign of Josias Franklin, father of Benjamin, was a Blue Ball, suspended by an iron rod from the front of his shop, which stood at the southeast corner of Hanover and Union Streets. Before the streets were numbered, and while the buildings were scattered, it was the universal custom among the inhabitants to designate their shops by some emblem. Thus we find the "Heart and Crown," "Three Nuns and a Comb," and "Brazen Head" in Cornhill, "Three Doves" in Marlborough Street, "Tun and Bacchus" and "Three Sugar Loaves and Canister" in King Street. This last was thus distinguished from the "Two Sugar Loaves" in Cornhill:—

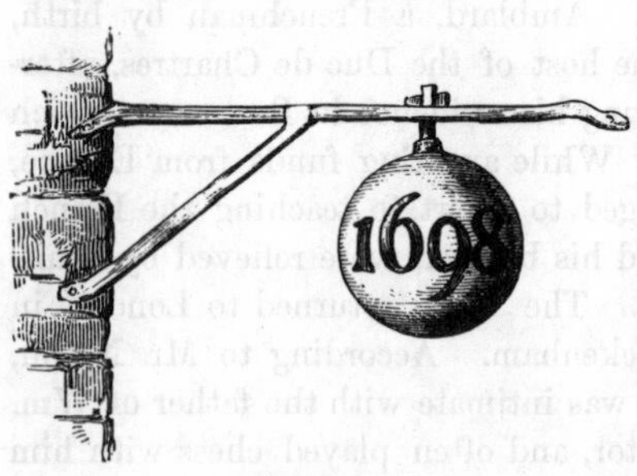

THE BLUE BALL.

"Oft the peasant with inquiring face,
Bewildered, trudges on from place to place;
He dwells on every sign with stupid gaze,
Enters the narrow alley's doubtful maze,
Tries every winding court and street in vain,
And doubles o'er his weary steps again."

The old house was quite small and of two stories, to which a third was added in later times. It was partially destroyed by fire in 1858, and in the same year the city took the building to widen Union Street. When the widening of Hanover Street took place, the old site was partially taken for that street. In the same way, by the plan of cutting off wholly from one side of the street, a number of quite noted landmarks disappeared. It was the intention of the owners to have removed the Franklin building to another location, but it was found impracticable. Two relics of it are, however, preserved. The Blue Ball came into the possession of General Ebenezer W. Stone of Boston, and from the original timbers was made a chair which was presented to the Mechanic Charitable Association.

SIGN OF THREE DOVES.

There are two original portraits of Franklin in the Public Library, — one by Duplessis, presented by Hon. Edward Brooks; the other by Greuze, presented by Gardner Brewer.

Midway between Elm and Union Streets once stood the church of Dr. Lyman Beecher, the eminent divine, father of Henry Ward Beecher. The church was erected in 1826, and consumed by fire on the night of the 31st December, 1829. Report says, a quantity of liquor was found by the firemen in the cellar. It was built of rough granite, had a central tower, and in general appearance was not unlike the old Brattle Street. After the destruction of their house, the society united in building the church in Bowdoin Street, which was completed in June, 1831. Dr. Beecher was the first pastor, having been settled in March, 1826, but in 1832 he removed to Cincinnati.

The society was originally formed from members of Park Street, the Old South, and Union Churches.

The Hanover Church stood on the site of Benjamin Hallowell's old residence, which was ransacked by the same mob that pillaged Lieutenant-Governor Hutchinson's house in August, 1765. Mr. Hallowell was a comptroller of customs, and as such, regarded with special hatred by the populace. The mob destroyed or carried off everything of value, including a small sum of silver. Hallowell then removed to an elegant mansion at Jamaica Plain, which was afterwards confiscated. One of his sons, B. Carew, became a distinguished British admiral. Hon. John Coffin Jones also lived on the Hallowell estate. Captain Henry Prentiss, a Revolutionary soldier and one of the Tea Party, lived also on this spot. He was a distinguished merchant and ship-owner.

The Green Dragon Tavern in Union Street was the greatest celebrity among all the old Boston hostelries. It stood facing towards the street, on a little alley running from Union Street around by the rear, but by the increased width of the street the site now abuts upon it, and is marked by a freestone tablet set in the wall with a dragon sculptured upon it in bas-relief.* This was the sign of the old tavern, which was on the west side of Union, a short distance from Hanover Street. In early times it was the property of Lieutenant-Governor Stoughton, and was used as a hospital during the Revolution. It was a two-story brick building with pitch roof. From above the entrance projected an iron rod on which was crouched the fabled monster of antiquity.

William Stoughton, Lieutenant-Governor from 1692 to his death in 1701, was one of the "Council of Safety" which deposed Andros. As Chief Justice of the Court he has acquired a fearful celebrity in connection with the witchcraft trials.

We have seen that Warren, John Adams, Revere, and Otis were neighbors. The former was the first Grand Master of the first Grand Lodge of Masons who held their meetings in the

* Many think the tablet incorrectly placed.

Green Dragon. The rest of the patriots came here to plan or to confer. How much "treason" was hatched under this roof will never be known, but much was unquestionably concocted within the walls of the masonic lodge. It is upon their record that they adjourned on account of the memorable Tea Party, for which they furnished no inconsiderable number.

Paul Revere says: "In the fall of 1774 and winter of 1775 I was one of upwards of thirty, chiefly mechanics, who formed ourselves into a committee for the purpose of watching the movements of the British soldiers and gaining every intelligence of the movements of the tories. We held our meetings at the Green Dragon Tavern. This committee were astonished to find all their secrets known to General Gage, although every time they met, every member swore not to reveal any of their transactions except to Hancock, Adams, Warren, Otis, Church, and one or two more." The traitor proved to be Dr. Church, who was afterwards arrested for treasonable correspondence with the enemy.

The early meetings of the Massachusetts Charitable Association, organized in 1795, were held here and at Concert Hall. It was always a favorite resort for the mechanics of the North End. When the convention was sitting which was to consider the adoption of the Federal Constitution, a great mass meeting of Boston mechanics assembled in the Green Dragon, which gave so emphatic an expression in favor of its acceptance that Samuel Adams said, "If they want it, they must have it."

One of the old customs long observed in Boston was the celebration of Pope Day, as November 5th, the anniversary of the Gunpowder Plot, was called. A bitter animosity existed between the North and South Enders, whose line of demarcation was the Mill Bridge on Hanover Street. Each section had its procession and its pope, and when the rival parties met, a battle ensued with fists, sticks, and stones, and one or the other of the popes was captured. The North End pope was never, it is said, taken but once.

Pope Day was a saturnalia. A stage was erected on wheels, on which was placed a figure of the pope seated in a chair.

Behind this was a female scarecrow called Nancy Dawson, with effigies of Admiral Byng and the Devil hanging from a gallows. Much ill-blood arose from these conflicts, the effects of which remained until the anniversary came round again. Governor Hancock, considering this foolish rivalry prejudicial to the patriot cause, used every effort to subdue it, but without effect. He at last gave a supper at the Green Dragon Tavern, which cost him $1,000, to which he invited all the leading men of both parties, and invoked them in an eloquent speech to lay aside their animosity for their country's sake. The appeal was successful, and the rival parties shook hands before they separated. From that time Pope Day ceased to agitate the warring factions.*

The Green Dragon, also known as the "Freemason's Arms," is specially noted in the annals of Masonry in Boston. It was purchased by St. Andrew's Lodge before the Revolution, and remained in their possession more than a century. The lodge was organized under a charter from the Grand Lodge of Scotland in 1756, and was chiefly composed of residents of the North End. There were several lodges in the British regiments that landed in Boston in 1768 and 1774, and St. Andrew's Lodge united with them in organizing a Grand Lodge. The first Lodge of Freemasons met in Boston July 30, 1733. It was the first in the Colonies, receiving authority from Lord Montague, Grand Master of England. Daniel Webster styled the Green Dragon the Headquarters of the Revolution, a name to which it has an undoubted claim. In the Green Dragon the Sandemanians held their first meetings in America. In later times it was kept by Daniel Simpson, the veteran musician. On the corner where once stood the Baptist Church building was formerly a brewery.

The Mill Pond, or Cove, mentioned in the Introduction, once covered all the tract embraced within North and South Margin Streets, being divided from the sea on the northwest by the Causeway, now Causeway Street. The station-house of the Boston and Maine Railroad stood in the midst of this Mill

* General Sumner's Reminiscences.

Pond, until with the Lowell, Eastern, and Fitchburg it took a site beyond the Causeway rescued from the sea. The high ground sloping away from Green and Leverett Streets once marked the boundary of the Cove in that direction, whilst the eastern margin, reaching to Distill-house Square, included all of Haymarket Square. On the northern shore the water covered Endicott Street, reaching to Prince, below Thacher, and penetrated to the rear of Baldwin Place, almost to Salem Street. When the Second Baptist Church was situated in Baldwin Place, candidates for baptism were immersed in the rear of the church. Before Endicott Street was laid out, about 1836, over a part of what was known as the "Old Way," Prince Street was the thoroughfare to Charlestown. The Mill Pond thus embraced an area as large as the Common.

FIRST BAPTIST CHURCH IN 1853.

The origin of the Causeway was in a footpath of the Indians over a more elevated part of the marsh. One Mr. Crabtree raised and widened this primitive path into a dam to retain the waters of the pond.

In 1643 the town granted Henry Simons and others a tract, including the Mill Pond and flats west of the Causeway, on condition of their building one or more corn-mills, and bridging the Mill Creek at Hanover and North Streets. Mills were accordingly erected at the west end of the creek called the South Mills, and at either end of the Causeway. The North Mills stood very near the junction of Thacher and Endicott Streets. These were a grist-mill and a saw-mill; a chocolate-mill stood at a little distance beyond in after times.

In 1804 the grant came into possession of the Mill Pond Corporation. The town in 1807 released the original obligation to maintain the mills and bridges forever, and the work of filling commenced, Copp's and Beacon Hills furnishing the material for this purpose. The process of filling occupied twenty-five years before it was fully completed, and during that time the Mill Pond was the receptacle for all the rubbish from the streets.

The Mill Creek, whose outlet into the Town Dock has been traced, was doubtless in some form an original feature of the peninsula. The want of an early map is keenly felt in any effort to establish the structure of the original surface. Winthrop says, the north part of the town "was separated from the rest by a narrow stream which was cut through a neck of land by industry." Hanover Street was this neck, and all north of the creek was an island known in times past as the "Island of Boston." An order of the court in 1631, levying £30 on the several plantations for clearing a creek and opening a passage to the new town, supports the view that a small water-course existed here which finally became a means of communication between the Town Dock and Mill Cove.

The creek, at first furnishing a supply of water for the tide mills, became in process of time a canal, with walls of stone, wide and deep enough to permit the passage of boats and even sloops from the harbor on the east to the river on the west. As such, it was an extension of the Middlesex Canal, incorporated in 1793, and of which Loammi Baldwin was engineer. The boats entered the canal at Chelmsford on the Merrimack, and passed on to the wharves on the east side of Boston, a distance of thirty miles. Blackstone Street, named from the founder of Boston, is built upon the bed of the canal.

The old Mill Bridge thrown over Hanover Street was rebuilt in 1686; was taken up in 1793 and replaced by a stone arch over which the pavement was continued. At North Street where the creek crossed was a drawbridge, from which this street was sometimes called Drawbridge Street. The passage of vessels being discontinued, the creek, which had an average width of twenty feet, was planked over here.

The North End was but three streets wide in older times. These were North, Hanover, and Salem Streets. The former, besides a number of aliases already given, was known along its course first as the Fore, or Front Street, and also as Anne, Fish, and Ship Street. Hanover was Middle Street from the Mill Creek to Bennet Street, beyond which it was North Street. Salem was called Back Street as far as Prince, and at one period Green Lane. All these retain their original names in part, except North, which has ever enjoyed a reputation not inferior to the Seven Dials of London or Five Points of New York. Crowded at one time through its entire length with brothels and low dram-shops, Anne Street took a new name before its character was improved.

"And on the broken pavement here and there,
Doth many a stinking sprat and herring lie;
A brandy and tobacco shop is near,
And hens, and dogs, and hogs are feeding by,
And here a sailor's jacket hangs to dry.
At every door are sunburnt matrons seen,
Mending old nets to catch the scaly fry;
Now singing shrill, and scolding eft between;
Scolds answer foul-mouthed scolds; bad neighborhood, I ween."

Laid out along the original water-front, wharves extended from Anne Street into the harbor. Over these Commercial Street since extended. In colonial times Anne Street bore a better reputation, and many of the magnates of the town found their residence in it. It was widened in 1859 and greatly improved, and is now for the most part devoted to business purposes.

At the lower corner of North and Centre Streets, formerly called Paddy's Alley, stands an old two-story brick house. The front wall has apparently been rebuilt, but the remainder of the structure bears the genuine stamp of antiquity. This was the home of Sir David Ochterlony, Bart., son of a royalist, and a Bostonian by birth.

It was not those alone who served under their country's flag that gained celebrity during the Revolutionary War. Among those who entered the British service were seven young Bostonians, who arrayed themselves against their native land, and finally became generals or admirals in that service. Their names are General John Coffin, Thomas Aston Coffin, Bart., Roger Hale Sheaffe, Bart., Admiral Sir Isaac Coffin, General Hugh McKay Gordon, B. Hallowell, and Sir David Ochterlony.

The latter, before whose home we are pausing, was a Latin-School boy, went to India at eighteen, served in the Indian wars, and was at the great conflict of Delhi. For his services in India Ochterlony was made a major-general in 1814 and baronet in the year following. The name indicates his Scotch origin. Unlike his famous companions, Sir David did not find himself compelled to serve against his countrymen.

At a little distance from this corner we find in Centre Street the old brick stable of the Eastern Stage-House, the headquarters for many years of stages bound to Portland and the eastward. It was kept by Colonel Ephraim Wildes, and ranked with Earl's, Doolittle's, and other principal rendezvous of this kind.

The entrance on North Street was by a large arch, through which you passed into a court-yard of large area. Descending from the coach you entered the main building by a flight of steps, where good cheer and hearty welcome always awaited the tired traveller.

Cross Street, in 1708, extended from the Mill Pond to the sea. At the corner of Anne was the Cross Tavern; its name was, like Middle and Back, descriptive. It was an important thoroughfare in former times, but is chiefly interesting to the antiquarian on account of the Old Stone House that stood between Hanover and North, about midway on the east side. The interest which attached to it was chiefly on account of its age, though conjecture has assigned to it the uses of a jail and garrison house under the old colony. It was built of rough stone, with the large brick chimneys on the outside, and stood for about two hundred years. It was very early described as the "Stone House of Deacon John Phillips in the cross street." Tradition has ascribed to it the first place of meeting of the town overseers, and Pemberton vouches for the finding of loopholes in the walls while it was under repair. None of these garrison houses, so commonly erected in the scattered villages for defence against the Indian foe, are known to have been built in Boston. The Old Stone House was removed in 1864, and a part went to make the foundation of an East Boston church. Savage's Police Record gives the following description of the Old Stone House, which he says, "at first consisted of two wings of uniform size joining each other and forming a right angle. Each wing was forty feet long, twenty feet wide, and two stories high, the wings fronting the south and west. There was one door in the end of each wing on the first story, and a single circular window in the second story over the doors; there were also two circular windows in each story of each wing in front, but neither door nor window in either wing in the rear. The foundation walls were four feet thick or more; the walls above ground were two feet in thickness, and built entirely of small quarried stones, unlike anything to be seen in this neighborhood, and were probably brought as ballast from some part of Europe."

Passing the Old Hancock School, now a police-station, and Board Alley, so narrow a drunken man could not fall to the right or left, we arrive at Richmond Street, formerly Bridge Lane, and according to some authorities the old Beer Lane.

The "New Brick" or "Cockerel" Church was first built on this spot in 1721, and originally came out of the New North Church. The figure of the cock was placed upon the first vane in derision of Rev. Mr. Thacher, whose Christian name was Peter. A fierce controversy at the ordination of Mr. Thacher as pastor of the New North Church caused the division which led to the formation of the society of the New Brick. Dr. Eliot says, "that when the cock was placed upon the spindle, a merry fellow straddled over it and crowed three times to complete the ceremony." This church went by the name of the "Revenge Church," until Dr. Lathrop took charge and healed the breach with the parent church.

The New Brick, a name given to distinguish it from the Old Brick in Cornhill, originally fronted upon Hanover Street, but now stands sidewise upon that street and facing towards Richmond. It is one of the very few church buildings occupying their original sites. In 1845 it was rebuilt of brown stone, and pulled down in 1871 during the widening of Hanover Street. The historic rooster is seen on Paul Revere's picture of 1768. It is now, after having breasted the storms of a century and a third, adorning the spire of a Cambridge church.

Passing through Richmond to North Street, we find ourselves in a region where even that veteran antiquary, Jonathan Oldbuck, would have felt at home;

> "Where winding alleys lead the doubtful way;
> The silent court and opening square explore,
> And long perplexing lanes untrod before."

At our left hand the ground rises towards the triangular enclosure known as North Square. In front of us, on the northeast corner of North and Richmond, is a brick building to which tradition has long attached the importance of standing on the site of the first Colonial Custom House, under Edward Randolph and his successors. Evidence is wanted to support this statement, — an important one in the investigation of the old landmarks; but the tradition is firmly fixed in the minds of old residents of the North End, and is generally credited. When the old building was taken down, about twenty years ago, many a pilgrimage was made to it and the wish expressed that its walls could speak.

NEW BRICK CHURCH.

Randolph was Collector in 1681, but the "Bostoneers," as Hutchinson calls them, refused to recognize his office. He had been appointed "Collector, Surveyor, and Searcher" in New England. His authority was treated with contempt by Governor Leverett, who sat with his hat on while the King's letter of appointment was being read before the Council. His public notification of the establishment of his office posted at the Town House was torn down by an officer of the Court. In 1682, fearing they had gone too far in resistance to the King's commands, the Court established a Custom House, but the loss of the Colonial Charter soon followed.

The removal of the papers belonging to this department at the evacuation of Boston leaves few materials wherewith to establish its history, and these are connected by imperfect links. The old building was long known as the "Red Lyon Inn," prominent among the early North End taverns. The tablet in the front of the building bears the initials of the Wadsworths, former proprietors. The old "Red Lyon" gave its name to Upshall's wharf below, which became Red Lyon Wharf. The ordinary itself was one of the oldest, and was kept by Nicholas Upshall probably as early as 1654, when he had a number of soldiers billeted upon him, and certainly in 1666. He was one of the first to feel the rigor of the persecution of the Quakers. He was banished, imprisoned, and at length in his old age died a martyr to the faith which, amid all his sufferings and hardships, he seems stoutly to have upheld. He was in Boston as early as 1637, and then owner of all the property on the north-east side of Richmond Street from Hanover Street to the water. His first banishment was for an attempt to bribe the keeper of Boston jail to give food to two starving Quaker women in his charge. Upshall was one of the first members of the Ancient and Honorable Artillery Company; his remains lie in Copp's Hill Cemetery, and his friends the Quakers were not forgotten in his will.

As little as North Square is known to the present generation, few localities can surpass it in the interest which attaches to the historic personages who have dwelt within its confined area. But our readers shall judge as we proceed.

Standing before an entrance still narrow, all old residents of the North End well remember that the original opening was once even more cramped than now, and scarce permitted the passage of a vehicle. The point made by North Street reached considerably beyond the present curbstone some distance into the street, both sides of which were cut off when the widening took place. This headland of brick and mortar, jutting out into old Fish Street as a bulwark to protect the aristocratic residents of the square, was long known as "Mountfort's Corner," from the family owning and occupying it. It was the established custom of those early times to fix the limits of the streets from corner to corner. Thus Fish Street is described in 1708 as "from Mountjoy's corner, lower end of Cross Street, northerly to the sign of the Swan, by Scarlett's Wharf."

Opposite to us, reached by a little alley from the street, was the residence of Dr. Snow, the historian of Boston. Where we stand, a narrow passage opens at our left hand, through which, beyond the crazy tenements, one might pass out to the Second Church. Through this passage Governor Hutchinson is said to have passed from his residence to the old church, a door having been constructed in the rear of that edifice expressly for his excellency's convenience.

Fronting the street and bounding upon this alley was the residence of Francis Shaw, father of Samuel Shaw, the Revolutionary soldier, and grandfather of Robert G. Shaw, the wealthy merchant and philanthropist. In this house were the quarters of the old Major of Marines Pitcairn, and Lieutenant Wragg of the same corps. Troops were scattered in detachments throughout the North End, a *cordon* extending from the works on Copp's Hill to the South Battery. North Square was the rendezvous for those nearest the battery, and Pitcairn appears to have been intrusted with the supervision of his quarter.

Young Shaw, who became a major in the Continental army, served in the Revolution from the beginning to its close, first as a lieutenant in Knox's artillery, rising by successive grades to be a captain of artillery in 1780. He was secretary of the officers who formed the Society of the Cincinnati, major and aide-de-camp to General Knox, his old commander, at the peace, and was appointed by him to a post in his bureau when secretary-at-war. In 1794 Major Shaw received an appointment as consul to China from Washington, and sailed for that country in the first American ship that ever set sail for those shores. On this voyage he died, and his epitaph may be seen on the

North Square, with Paul Revere's Birthplace, in 1872.

family monument in Copp's Hill. The company of artillery attached to the Boston regiment gave to the Continental service upwards of forty young men, most of whom became distinguished officers of that arm.

A tradition is preserved that Wragg, the lieutenant of marines, one day made some remark at the family board disparaging the "rebels," whereupon he was challenged by young Samuel Shaw. The interposition of Pitcairn, it is said, prevented a hostile meeting.

Proceeding up the square, which still preserved its cobblestone pavement, we first passed a ruinous wooden building said to have been once in the family of Commodore Downes, and come to another somewhat fresher specimen of the same order. This was the habitation of Paul Revere, and his probable birthplace. From this house he gave the striking exhibition of transparencies on the evening of the anniversary of the Massacre. We have found Revere at his shop in Cornhill, and briefly alluded to his engraving on copper, his first efforts having been on silver plate. He also engraved the plates, made the press, and printed the paper money for the Provincial Congress at Watertown. The house has not altered in appearance in fifty years.

On the other side of the square stood the old Town Pump, in front of the former Naval Rendezvous. One of the old town watch-houses was near at hand.

Among the older families resident here were the Holyokes. The father of the celebrated President of Harvard was a respectable soap-boiler.

Nowhere in Boston has Father Time wrought such ruthless changes, as in this once highly respectable quarter, now swarming with Italians in every dirty nook and corner. In truth, it is hard to believe the evidence of our own senses, though the fumes of garlic are sufficiently convincing. Past and Present confront each other here with a stare of blank amazement, in the humble Revere homestead, on one side, and the pretentious Hotel Italy on the other; nor do those among us, who recall something of its vanished prestige, feel at all at home in a place where our own mother-tongue no longer serves us.

Yet this contracted space was once the court end of the town. It was first called Clark's Square, from an old resident, and afterwards Frizell's Square. Where now is a brick block facing the square was built the Second Church in Boston, better known as the Old North. This was the church of the Mathers, — Samuel, Increase, Cotton, and Samuel the son of Cotton. Built in 1650, it was destroyed by fire in 1676, and rebuilt the next year. Both houses were of wood, and the latter edifice was pulled down in the winter of 1775–76 for fuel, as were also upwards of a hundred other wooden buildings. General Howe sanctioned the act.

Dr. Lathrop says: "No records of the Old North Church exist for more than a year after the memorable 19th of April. At this time most of the churches in town were broken up, and the greatest part of the inhabitants went into the country. While the pastor and members were dispersed, a number of evil-minded men of the King's party obtained leave of General Howe to pull it down." The society then joined the New Brick, which took the name of the Second Church.

Cotton Mather, the son of Increase and grandson of John Cotton, is regarded as the most celebrated of the Boston clergy. A Bostonian by birth, he graduated with honor at Harvard, and was a scholar of high attainments. Mather was a prolific author, and his numerous works are valuable contributions to the early history of New England. He was a firm believer in witchcraft, and his name is identified with the persecution of the unfortunates who fell under the ban of suspicion.

Samuel and Increase Mather were sons of Rev. Richard Mather, who was settled in Dorchester in 1636. Both were men of learning and high consideration. Increase received the first degree of D. D. conferred in America. He went to England as agent of the colony, and returned in 1692 with the new charter. Unlike his son, he did not pursue the witchcraft delusion, which desolated so many homes and left an indelible blot upon our history.

Cotton Mather lived on Hanover Street, in a house built by Captain Turell. It was not far from the Cockerel Church on the opposite side of the street, and was afterwards occupied by Master Harris of the North Grammar School. Samuel Mather lived on the east side of Moon Street, about midway from Sun Court to Fleet Street, on the corner of what was formerly known as Moon Street Court. The house was demolished about 1832, and a tobacco warehouse erected on the site, which became afterwards a Catholic Church. Increase Mather lived on North Street, near Clark, in a house afterwards used as a seamen's boarding-house.

During the year 1676, when great scarcity prevailed, Dr. Increase Mather procured from his friends in Dublin a ship-load of provisions. Boston paid this debt of long standing with interest, when she sent by R. B. Forbes a ship laden with food for the starving in Ireland.

The following version of the humorous pen photographs of the Boston clergy of 1774 is from Mrs. Crocker's memoir. There were two distinct productions, which appear somewhat intermixed in the published versions. The lines given here were the first to appear, and were attributed to Dr. Benjamin Church. They were the rage of the town: —

"Old Mather's race will not disgrace
 Their noble pedigree,
And Charles Old Brick * both well and sick
 Will plead for liberty.
There 's puffing Pem, † who does condemn
 All Freedom's noble sons,
And Andrew Sly, ‡ who oft draws nigh
 To Tommy skin and bones. §
In Brattle Street we seldom meet
 With silver-tongued Sam, ‖
Who smoothly glides between both sides
 And so escapes a jam.
There 's Penuel Puff, ¶ is hearty enough,
 And so is Simeon Howard;
And Long Lane Teague ** will join the league
 And never prove a coward.

* Chauncy. † Pemberton. ‡ Eliot. § Hutchinson.
‖ Cooper. ¶ Bowen. ** Moorhead.

There 's little Hopper,* if you think proper,
In Liberty's cause so bold,
And John Old North,† for little worth,
Won't sacrifice for gold.
There 's puny John‡ from North Hampton,
A meek mouth moderate man,
And colleague stout,§ who, without doubt,
Is linked in tory clan."

According to Mrs. Crocker, the residence of Samuel Mather in North Square was built by Captain Kemble, who in 1673 was condemned to stand in the stocks two hours for lewd and unseemly conduct in saluting his wife at the step of the door, on the Sabbath day, when he first met her after three years' absence. His daughter, Mrs. Sarah Knight, kept in the same house a school, said to have been the first writing-school in that part of the town, from 1701 till her death in 1708. Dr. Mather afterwards occupied the same premises. All three of the Mathers are interred in Copp's Hill. Mrs. Crocker, here referred to, was a granddaughter of Cotton Mather. It was she whom Franklin told that he was born at the Blue Ball in Union Street.

On the corner of Garden Court and Prince Streets, formerly Bell Alley, was the residence of Sir Charles Henry Frankland, who was Collector of Boston in 1741 under Governor Shirley. He was said to have been removed from this office for inattention to its duties. Sir Charles led a romantic and eventful life. On one of his official visits to Marblehead he met with the lovely Agnes Surriage, maid-of-all-work at the inn. The attachment he conceived for her appears to have been returned, though Sir Charles did not offer her marriage.

"The old, old story, — fair and young,
And fond, — and not too wise, —
That matrons tell, with sharpened tongue,
To maids with downcast eyes."

Sir Charles had a fine estate at Hopkinton, Mass., where he delighted to pass the time with his beautiful companion. Returning to England, Agnes was made to feel the scorn of her noble lover's family, and the pair went to Portugal. They were at Lisbon during the great earthquake of November 1,

* Stillman. † Lathrop. ‡ Hunt. § Bacon.

1755, in which Sir Charles, while riding out, was overwhelmed by the falling ruins. The faithful Agnes succeeded in reaching and rescuing the entombed baronet, and carried him bruised and bleeding to their apartments. For this act of heroism the poor Marblehead girl became Lady Frankland. She survived her lord, and resided, until the breaking out of the Revolution, principally on the estate at Hopkinton, when she returned to England. The following lines were addressed to Sir H. Frankland on receiving the present of a box of lemons, by S. M. (supposed to be Samuel Mather), February 20, 1757 :—

"You know from Eastern India came
The skill of making punch, as did the name ;
And as the name consists of letters five,
By five ingredients it is kept alive.
To purest water sugar must be joined,
With these the grateful acid is combined ;
Some any sours they get contented use,
But men of taste do that from Tagus choose.
When now these three are mixed with care,
Then added be of spirit a small share ;
And that you may the drink quite perfect see,
Atop the musky nut must grated be."

The Frankland estate at Hopkinton came into the Rev. Mr. Nason's hands, who wrote a most interesting account of its former possessor. Sir Charles attended King's Chapel in Boston. The house in which the baronet resided was built by William Clark, for whom the square and wharf were named. He was contemporary with the elder Hutchinson, Faneuil, Belcher, and Hancock, who may be said to have controlled in their day the commerce of Boston. He was also a Councillor of the Province, and a man of marked distinction in the affairs of the town. Clark, it is said, met with reverses in the French wars, losing forty sail of vessels, which so impaired his fortune and depressed his spirits that he died soon after. He was one of the original attendants at Christ Church, and is buried in Copp's Hill in a tomb on which is blazoned the family arms.

The Clark-Frankland house was a monument of human pride. In all colonial Boston we have not met with its peer, and it was

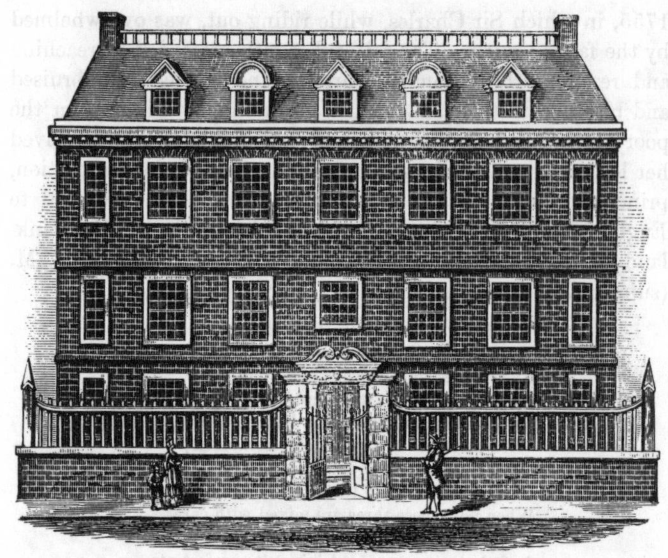

SIR H. FRANKLAND'S HOUSE.

without doubt built to outvie that of Hutchinson, Clark's wealthy neighbor. A brick dwelling of three stories was, in itself, a unique feature for the period in which it was constructed; its solid brick walls were traversed by belts at each stage. The tiers of windows at either end of the front were narrower than the others, and opened upon closets that would have gladdened the eyes of modern housekeepers and put modern architecture to the blush. The entrance door was low, a common fault in our old builders; but what was unusual, the different flats or stories were ten feet in the clear. The dormer windows in the roof varied enough in form to break the monotony of the outline.

Entering by the front on Garden Court upon a hall twelve feet wide, you were ushered into a reception-room, or saloon, at the right of the hall of entrance. You walked on a floor curiously inlaid with alternate squares of pine and cedar, much after the fashion in vogue at the present day. Exactly in the middle of the floor was a centre-piece of a yard square, on which the mechanic had expended his utmost skill. The pieces of variegated wood were beautifully interwoven around a shield bearing the family device, — a bar with three white swans. This was before the day of carpets, when floors were kept brightly polished, even by the poorer classes.

The walls were wainscoted around and divided by wooden pilasters into compartments with panels, on each of which was painted armorial bearings, landscapes, or ruins. Similar panels in the wainscot were ornamented with various devices. A heavy moulding of wood, supported by the gilded capitals of the pilasters, enclosed the ceiling. One of the panels of this room bore an exact resemblance of the building, from a copy of which our engraving is taken.

The house was similarly finished with wooden pilasters in every story. Some of the mantels were exquisitely carved in imitation of fruit and flowers. There has been preserved a picture taken from a compartment built expressly for it into the wall, representing two children richly attired and of a tender age. Conjecture has been busy as to the authorship of this really fine work of art. It is evidently antecedent to Copley, and may have been from the pencil of Smibert. This relic, together with others, was in the possession of Rowland Ellis, of this city.

After the death of the baronet, he gave the house to the widowed Lady Agnes, who resided in it for a time. It ultimately came into possession of the Ellis family, during whose occupancy the entrance was somewhat enlarged, and the old wooden fence replaced by one of iron. The native hue of the brick had been improved upon with yellow paint. The conversion of old Bell Alley into an extension of Prince Street cut off a considerable portion of the building, and it was taken down. Mr. Cooper, the novelist, visited the Frankland house and examined it minutely before he wrote "Lionel Lincoln," in which the house is described as the residence of Mrs. Lechmere and located in *Tremont* Street. Mr. Cooper talks about the "salient lions" of the tesselated floor, into which a fertile imagination converted the peaceful swans of the Clarks. It should be observed that the coat of arms in Copp's Hill bears a leafless branch, and is otherwise different from the escutcheon of the floor.

Redford Webster, an old Boston apothecary, and father of John White Webster, the slayer of Dr. Parkman, also lived in the house we have been describing.

Next to Sir Charles Frankland, on Garden Court, resided Thomas Hutchinson. Under his administration, as lieutenant-governor and governor, were enacted the most turbulent scenes that preceded the Revolution. By birth a Bostonian, his love for office led him at length into a position of antagonism with his countrymen. Bancroft describes him as sordid and avaricious, smuggling goods and using every means to put money in his purse. By his townsmen he was nicknamed "Stingy Tommy." He held at one time the offices of lieutenant-governor, member of the Council, commander of the castle, judge of probate, and chief justice of the Supreme Court. Dr. Franklin, in 1772, obtained possession in England of some of Hutchinson's confidential letters, which he forwarded to this country. They showed that Hutchinson had advocated the most repressive measures by the home government.

On the night of the 26th of August, 1765, during the Stamp Act troubles, the mob attacked and sacked the governor's elegant mansion, destroying his furniture, drinking his wine, and scattering the streets far and wide with the *débris.* The governor and family escaped personal violence, but an irreparable injury occurred in the destruction of the valuable library and manuscripts, — for Hutchinson was a man of literary tastes and scholarly attainments. Hutchinson at first took refuge with his sister at the house of Dr. Samuel Mather in Moon Street. The mob, however, demanded his person, and he was compelled to retreat by a back way to the house of Thomas Edes, a baker, guided by little Hannah Mather, as she herself relates. Here he remained during the night, returning to his brother's house to breakfast. The next day he was compelled to open court without gown or wig, both having been destroyed by the mob.

The Massacre increased his unpopularity, although he appeared on the scene and censured the unauthorized and fatal action of Captain Preston. The destruction of the tea in December, 1773, was followed in a few months by the governor's departure for England, where he died.

The governor's mansion-house has been minutely described by Lydia Maria Child in the "Rebels." The house was of brick, painted a neutral tint, and was ornamented in front with four Corinthian pilasters. One of the capitals of these is now in the Historical Library. The crown of Britain surmounted each window. The hall of entrance displayed a spacious arch, from the roof of which a dimly lighted lamp gave a rich twilight view. The finely carved and gilded arch in massy magnificence was most tastefully ornamented with busts and statues. The light streamed full on the soul-beaming countenance of Cicero, and playfully flickered on the brow of Tulliola. The panelling of the parlor was of the dark, richly shaded mahogany of St. Domingo, and ornamented with the same elaborate skill as the hall just quitted. The busts of George III. and his young queen were placed in front of a splendid mirror, with bronze lamps on each side covered with beautiful transparencies, one representing the destruction of the Spanish Armada, the other giving a fine view of a fleet of line-of-battle ships drawn up before the Rock of Gibraltar. On either side of the room were arches surmounted with the arms of England. The library was hung with tapestry, representing the coronation of George II., interspersed with the royal arms. The portraits of Anne and the Georges hung in massive frames of antique splendor, and the crowded shelves were surmounted with busts of the house of Stuart. In the centre of the apartment stood a table of polished oak. The gardens of the old mansion extended back to Hanover and to Fleet Streets. In 1834 the building was taken down, and ceased to be a noted attraction of the North End. Governor Hutchinson received a pension and was reimbursed for his pecuniary losses, but died at last, it is said, of a broken heart. On Pope Day Hutchinson's effigy was often exhibited with two faces.

The Hutchinson House was built about 1710 by Thomas Hutchinson, father of the governor, who was born in it the year following. The estate was entailed to the male heirs, but was confiscated and sold for a mere song. The premises afterwards became the property of William Little, at which time Mrs. Child visited them.

General John P. Boyd also lived in the Hutchinson house. He had been in the service of the native East Indian princes, with a force raised and equipped by himself. Returning to the United States, he re-entered the army as colonel of the 4th infantry, and commanded at Fort Independence when the embargo of 1809 was laid. General Boyd distinguished himself greatly at Tippecanoe, Williamsburg, and Fort George during the campaigns of 1811–13. He was naval officer of Boston in 1830.

Fleet Street, formerly Scarlett's Wharf Lane, is another of those names by which the Bostonians loved to testify their love for Old London. It is an old street, bearing this name in 1708. From the lower end projected Scarlett's Wharf, now a part of Atlantic Avenue, while from the junction of Fleet and North the latter anciently took the name of Ship Street, to its terminus at Battery Wharf, from the ship-yards that lined its course.

The "King's Head," another inn of "y[e] Olden tyme," was at the northwest corner of Fleet and North Streets, by Scarlett's Wharf. It belongs to the first century of the settlement; was burnt in 1691 and rebuilt. James Davenport kept it in 1755, and his widow in 1758. The site was long a bake-house kept by Joseph Austin. This neighborhood must bear off the palm for inns, being, before the construction of Long Wharf, the chief commercial centre of the town.

In North Square were barracks for British troops at the time of the battle of Lexington. These troops were mustered in the square the night of the expedition, and sentinels, posted at all the entrances, turned the citizens from the spot. The preparations for this affair were so secretly conducted that Gage hoped his intentions would escape discovery until the blow was struck. No changes were made in the disposition of the troops, except to detach the grenadier companies. Dr. Lathrop, the pastor of the Old North, occupied a wooden building erected on the site of his old church after its demolition, in front of which were some handsome elm-trees destroyed by the gale of 1815.

The Catholic Chapel, which stands on the east side of North Square, was long the scene of the labors of Father E. T. Taylor, the eloquent Methodist preacher. His parishioners were the sailors that found themselves in port for the time being, and having himself followed the sea, Father Taylor was peculiarly fitted to preach to the seafaring class. His discourses were filled with graphic illustrations from the language of the ocean, and went straight to the comprehension of his hearers. Frequently he would have his audience wrought up to the highest pitch of excitement by some graphic picture. On one occasion a rough, weather-beaten mariner became so interested in the preacher's wonderful portrayal of the impending destruction of a gallant vessel, that, forgetful where he was, he exclaimed, — "Let go your best bower; nothing else will save you." Father Taylor quickly turned the interruption to good purpose. He was chaplain to the frigate sent with supplies to the famishing Irish, and spoke in Cork and Glasgow. A daughter married Hon. Thomas Russell, Collector of Boston. Father Taylor lived in the building at the corner of Prince Street, erected on the Frankland estate.

In 1676, November 27, happened the greatest fire that had occurred in the town up to this time. It broke out early in the morning near the Red Lyon, and consumed forty-five dwellings, the Old North Meeting-House, and several warehouses. The wind blew with great violence, carrying flakes of fire across the river and endangering Charlestown. Hubbard, in his History of New England, says the fire occurred "through the carelessness of a boy called up to work very early in the morning, who falling asleep, as was said, the candle set the house on fire." A change of wind from southeast to south, with a copious rain, arrested the flames at last. Increase Mather's dwelling was burned in this fire, and he then removed to the north corner of Hanover and North Bennet Streets, afterwards the home of Revs. Andrew Eliot and John Eliot.

Clark's Wharf, subsequently Hancock's, was the most noted in the early history of the town, but was gradually rivalled by Long Wharf. It now coincides with the north side of Lewis's Wharf, although it originally formed no part of it. Thomas Hancock was the principal proprietor in 1761, owning seven eighths, as appears by an original statement of the income for that year. This wharf formerly opened into Fish, now North Street, and John Hancock's warehouses were upon it.

In June, 1768, John Hancock's sloop Liberty arrived from Madeira loaded with wine. As she was lying at Hancock's Wharf, says Drake's History, Thomas Kirk the tidewaiter came on board, and was followed by Captain John Marshall, who commanded Hancock's ship, the London Packet, with five or six others. These persons confined Kirk below until they had removed the wine from the ship, of which no entry was made at the Custom House. The next morning the master of the sloop entered, it is said, a few pipes of wine, and made oath it was all he brought. It was resolved to seize the vessel, and Joseph Harrison, collector, and Benjamin Hallowell, comptroller, repaired to the wharf and affixed "the broad arrow." Apprehensive of the mob which had collected on the wharf, the sloop was moored under the guns of the Romney frigate.

The exasperated people now turned upon the officers, and beat and maltreated them so that Mr. Harrison was for some time confined to his bed, while his son, Richard Acklom, who was not present in any official capacity, was very roughly used. Hallowell and Irving, inspectors, fared no better. The mob broke the windows of Mr. John Williams, inspector-general, and also those of Mr. Hallowell's house, and finished by dragging the collector's boat to the Common, where they burnt every fragment of it. The revenue officers retired after this affair to the Castle, where they remained until the arrival of the troops in October.

On the 4th of July, ominous day to British rule, the 38th regiment landed at Hancock's Wharf, and marched to the Common and encamped. When the British retreated from the town they scuttled a new ship of 300 tons then lying at this wharf, and left behind about 1,000 bushels of salt and 3,000 blankets.

Opposite the head of Hancock's Wharf, which we remind our readers once extended to the present North Street, was the North End Coffee House kept in 1783 by David Porter, who advertised that he had taken the Coffee House, where "gentlemen shall be entertained in a genteel manner." This was the father of David Porter of renown, and grandfather of the late Admiral David D. Porter. The elder Porter was himself an old ranger of the main, having commanded the private-armed vessels Aurora and Delight in the Revolutionary War. At the peace he took the Coffee House, located at one of the most important wharves of the town, but soon removed to Baltimore, where he engaged in trade. The Coffee House was occupied in 1789 by Robert Wyre, distiller, and was for some time known as the Philadelphia Coffee House. The same house was afterwards the dwelling of Jonathan Amory, and later, of Colonel John May. It had, however, a prior importance, having been built and inhabited by Edward Hutchinson, brother of Thomas.

David Porter, the hero of the Essex, was born, it is said, in Charter Street. He entered the navy as midshipman in 1798, and fought his way to a captaincy in 1812. He was in the Constellation when she captured L'Insurgente ; first officer in that busy little craft the Enterprise before Tripoli ; of the frigate New York, under Rodgers ; and of the Philadelphia, under Bainbridge, when he became a prisoner for eighteen months. He sailed from New York in the Essex, thirty-two guns, in July, 1812, and soon captured the British sloop Alert of twenty guns. Going around to the Pacific he annihilated the British whale-fishery, and captured the Nocton packet with £ 1,100 sterling on board, without finding a cruiser to molest him. Blockaded by the British ships Phœbe and Cherub in Valparaiso, he attempted to get to sea, but losing some of his spars by a sudden squall, was forced to anchor. Here he maintained a bloody and determined resistance until his ship was on fire and incapable of fighting, when his flag was hauled down. Porter afterwards commanded the Mexican navy, and filled the post of minister from his native country to Turkey.

Returning through Fleet Street to Hanover, we find that the use of swinging signs, and carved figures for the shop fronts or houses of entertainment is by no means as unusual as has been supposed. To be convinced of this, it is only necessary to walk over the district we are describing. Jack is represented in every conceivable attitude. We are in no danger of losing our reckoning, for quadrant or sextant are pendent from every corner, while a jolly tar with spyglass to his eye forever scans the neighboring shipping. Female heads, with features as weird as those of the famed lady of the Red Rover, gaze from the entrance of some ship artisan, while figures of Venus, Hebe, or Mary Ann start forth as if in the act of leaping from the painter's window to the pavement below.

The First Universalist Church was at the corner of North Bennet and Hanover Streets. It was a wooden building erected by seceders from the Old North, with Rev. Samuel Mather for their pastor. After the decease of Mather, in 1785, the house passed by purchase into the hands of the Universalists. The first pastor of the society was the Rev. John Murray, the father of American Universalism, who, it is said, was greeted with a shower of stones when he first attempted to preach in Boston. While the building stood, it was the last of the old wooden churches, but after ninety-six years of service it was succeeded by the brick edifice built in 1838, now a Baptist Seamen's Bethel.

The brick chapel, on the north side of North Bennet Street, and only a few paces from Hanover, was the second house of worship of the Methodists in Boston. They first occupied a small wooden structure in Methodist Alley, now Hanover Avenue. The society, which has now such numerical strength in the land, had, it is asserted, its beginning among the British soldiers who arrived in 1768, a few of whom were Methodists. In 1772 Mr. Boardman, colleague of Pillmore, the first Methodist preacher sent to America by Wesley, formed a small society, which soon dissolved. In October, 1784, Rev. William Black, of Halifax, preached in the Sandemanian Chapel, on Hanover, near Cross Street, and in the Second Baptist Church. The building in Methodist Alley was dedicated in May, 1796, and continued to be used by the society until September, 1828, when the North Bennet Street Chapel was dedicated.

A distressing accident occurred at the laying of the corner-stone of this chapel. The floor gave way under the pressure of the great number of people attending the ceremony, and precipitated the living mass into the cellar beneath. No lives were lost, but many received serious injuries.

The famous eccentric preacher, Lorenzo Dow, occasionally preached in the little church in Methodist Alley. He was extremely theatrical in his manner, but an effective speaker. In this small house the preacher might almost shake hands with his hearers in the front seats of the gallery.

The New North Church is one of the monuments still preserved in the North End. Seventeen substantial mechanics formed the nucleus of this, the Second Congregational Society in this part of the town. In 1714 they erected a small wooden building at the corner of Clark and Hanover (North) Streets, "unassisted by the more wealthy part of the community except by their prayers and good wishes." This house required enlargement, in 1730, to accommodate its increasing congregation; and in 1802 was superseded by the present edifice. In 1805 a bell from the foundry of Paul Revere was placed in the tower. John Webb was the first minister, the two Mathers assisting at the ordination. In 1870 the church was raised bodily, and moved back to conform to the increased width of the street, it having been sold to the Catholics a few years before.

NEW NORTH CHURCH.

The installation of Rev. Peter Thacher, in 1719, as Mr. Webb's colleague, was attempted to be prevented by the minority opposed to him, who assembled at the house of Thomas Lee, in Bennet Street, next the Universalist meeting-house, resolved to resist the progress of the minister and the council which met at Mr. Webb's, on the corner of North Bennet and Salem Streets. A crowd gathered and matters looked serious, when Mr. Webb led his party out by a back way to the church, thus out-manœuvring the rival faction. The house of Dr. Eliot, of the New North, is still standing. It is next but one to the north corner of Hanover and Bennet Streets, is of wood, and appears in good preservation.

On the southwest corner of North and Clark Streets stood, within thirty years, an ancient brick building, reputed to be over two hundred years old. It was certainly built as early as 1650, and probably dated back a few years anterior. It had been one of the oldest inns or ordinaries in Boston, and was called the "Ship Tavern." It stood at the head of or opposite Clark's shipyard, and was kept by John Vyal in 1663. Vyal's was a favorite resort of the King's Commissioners, who were sent over by Charles II., after the restoration, with instructions to visit the New England Colonies, and adjust all matters of dispute. Colonel Richard Nichols, a soldier of Turenne, Colonel George Cartwright, Sir Robert Carr, and Samuel Maverick, the founder of East Boston, composed the commission.

Sir Robert Carr having assaulted a constable at the Ship Tavern, Governor Leverett sent a letter requesting Sir Robert to attend at his house to answer the complaint lodged against him. Carr replied as follows: —

Sr Yors I receyved last night in answer to wh as I am Sr Robert Carr I would have complyed wth yor desyres, but as I am wth ye Kyng's Commission, I shal not grant yor requests, both in respect of his Majestyes honor and my oune duty, and rest yours

Boston Jan. 23. 1666. ROBERT CARR

For Major General John Leverett, these *

A second summons to Carr was received with a reply more insulting in its tenor than the first, and the bellicose commissioner seems to have avoided the arrest.

As far back as Vyal's proprietorship the tavern was known

* Hist. and Antiq. of Boston.

as the "Noah's Ark," doubtless from the fancied resemblance of the ship on its sign to the Ark of Scripture. By this name it was subsequently known until its disappearance in 1866, both in the proprietor's deeds and by common repute.

The old Ship Tavern, or Noah's Ark, was probably built by Thomas Hawkins, whose shipyard was below. It became later the property of Thomas Hutchinson, father of the governor, and was given by him to his daughter Hannah, the wife of Rev. Samuel Mather. The original building was of two stories, to which a third was added by a modern proprietor. The walls were of brick, laid in the English Bond, with overhanging eaves, and roof with projecting Lutheran windows. A seam in the old front wall was attributed to the earthquake of 1663. It was altogether a remarkable specimen of the antique style of buildings, of which not a single pure specimen is now existing in Boston.

Besides the tavern, Vyal carried on a brew-house, one of the first of which we find any mention, at the corner of Clark and North Streets, where Mathews' Block stood. This brew-house obtained a wide reputation both in the Colonies and abroad, rivalling Burton's or Alsopp's of our day. The old tavern of Vyal was used as a barrack by the British troops. While there, a contagion broke out among them which carried off a large number.

What is now Harris Street, next north of Clark, was once known as White-Bread Alley, and is so laid down on the maps. It was so named from the circumstance that the first penny rolls ever offered for sale in Boston were baked there by Madam Tudor. She was an Englishwoman, and began by sending her little son, afterwards Deacon John Tudor, around among the neighbors with her bread. She died at ninety, and the business was continued by her son.

We next come to Salutation Street, raised in modern times from the meaner appellation of "alley" without any particular pretension to the dignity. Its singular name comes from the old Salutation Tavern, in former times at the corner of the alley and North Street. A grotesque sign, descriptive of the meeting of two gentlemen of the era of small clothes, cocked hats, etc., in the act of greeting each other, gave the hostelry its name. Samuel Green kept there in 1731, and William Campbell in 1773.

The Salutation, also called the Two Palaverers, while kept by Campbell, was the rendezvous of the famous North End Caucus. In the "Hundred Boston Orators" it is stated that this Revolutionary association originated with Warren, and that the resolutions for the destruction of the tea were there drawn up. It consisted at first of sixty-one members. Dr. John Young was the first president. When the best means of ridding Boston of the regulars was under discussion, Hancock, who was a member, exclaimed, "Burn Boston and make John Hancock a beggar, if the public good requires it."

The word "caucus" is said to occur first in Gordon's "History of the American Revolution," Vol. I. p. 365, published in 1788. He says that more than fifty years previous to his time of writing, "Samuel Adams and twenty others in Boston, one or two from the North End of the town, where all the ship business is carried on, used to meet, make a caucus, etc." From the fact that the meetings were held in a part of Boston where all the ship business was carried on, Mr. Pickering, in his Vocabulary (Boston, 1816), infers that "caucus" may be a corruption of "calkers," the word "meeting" being understood. This derivation has been adopted by others.

A few steps bring us to Battery Street, likewise an alley in 1708, receiving its name from the North Battery below, to which it conducted. It formerly ran from Charter Street to the Battery, but now to Hanover Street only.

The first mention of what was afterwards called the North Battery occurs in the records in January, 1644, when a work at Merry's Point was agreed upon. There was, however, no definite action taken until 1646, when there appear propositions about a fortification at the North End, "att Walter Merry's point." Johnson's "Wonder-Working Providence" speaks of the forts on Copp's and Fort Hill as "the one well fortified on the superficies thereof with store of great artillery well mounted.

The other hath a very strong battery built of whole timber and filled with earth," the latter being the North Battery. In 1706 a project was brought before the town to extend the North Battery one hundred and twenty feet, with a breadth of forty feet, and £1,000 were voted for the improvement and security of the work. John Steele had command in 1750.

The town sold the North Battery to Jeffrey and Russell. It became Jeffrey's Wharf between 1789 and 1796, and is now Battery Wharf, in memory of its ancient purposes.

The 52d, 43d, and 47th British regiments, with companies of grenadiers and light infantry, embarked from the North Battery on the day of Bunker Hill, as did also the 1st Battalion of Marines, led by Major Pitcairn, of Lexington fame, who fell a victim to the murderous fire from the fatal redoubt while gallantly urging on his men to the attack.

When Lord Howe evacuated Boston the North Battery was armed with seven twelve-pounders, two nine-pounders, and four six-pounders, — all rendered unserviceable. From its position the work commanded the entrance to Charles River as well as the Town Cove; and was deemed of the highest military importance in those days of short-range artillery.

While in the neighborhood of the prominent wharves, we may appropriately refer to the long trucks once used in Boston for conveying heavy merchandise. As long ago as 1720 trucks were used, when we find, by an order regulating them, none were to be "more than eighteen feet long; to employ but two horses in one team; to carry no more than one ton at a load; and wheel tires to be four inches wide; the driver to go at the head of the thill horse, which he must govern by a halter to be kept in the hand." These ponderous vehicles finally disappeared, and with them that distinctive body of men, the "Boston Truckmen," who once formed a leading and attractive feature of our public processions, with their white frocks and black hats, mounted on their magnificent truck-horses. Hardy and athletic, it would have been hard to find their equals on either side of the water. The long jiggers now used are scarcely less objectionable than the old trucks.

CHAPTER VI.

A VISIT TO THE OLD SHIPYARDS.

Early Ship-Building. — Boston Shipyards. — Massachusetts Frigate. — New England Naval Flag. — First Seventy-Four. — Hartt's Naval Yard. — The Constitution. — Her Launch, History, and Exploits. — Anecdotes of Hull, Bainbridge, and Decatur. — Old Ironsides Rebuilt. — Josiah Barker. — Nicholson. — Preble. — Stewart. — Other Distinguished Officers. — Escape from the British Fleet. — Anecdote of Dr. Bentley. — Action with the Guerriere. — The Java. — Cyane and Levant. — Relics of Old Ironsides. — Affair of the Figure-Head. — Captain Dewey. — The Frigate Boston. — Capture of Le Berceau. — The Argus.

WE have now brought the reader among the shipyards, which were in bygone days a principal feature of the North End. The first ship built in the vicinity of Boston was the "Blessing of the Bay," at what is now Medford. It was a bark of thirty tons ordered by Governor Winthrop, and was launched on the 4th of July, 1631. In 1632–33 a "shippe of a hundred tunnes" was launched in the same town, so that the Medford shipwrights seem to bear off the palm in establishing this industry in our neighborhood. The first mention of ship-building in Boston occurs in 1640, and a hundred years later there were on the stocks at the same time forty topsail vessels with seven thousand tons' capacity.

ANCIENT SHIP.

As early as 1645 Captain Thomas Hawkins built the Seafort, a fine ship of four hundred tons, at his yard at the foot of Clark Street; she was lost on the coast of Spain. John Richards succeeded to the yard on the north of the Ship Tavern in 1688. Clark's yard was the same in 1722. In 1708 Joshua

Gee had a shipyard at the foot of Copp's Hill, and fourteen years later there were no less than six yards lying around the base of the hill, two below Fort Hill, and another beyond the causeway at West Boston. In 1745 was built the Massachusetts Frigate, which, under command of Captain Edward Tyng, accompanied Sir William Pepperell's expedition against Louisburg, where she rendered efficient service, capturing the Vigilant, French man-of-war of sixty-four guns, — more than double her own force. According to Captain G. H. Preble's "Notes on Early Ship-Building," "when it was designed to reduce Louisburg, Governor Shirley directed Captain Tyng to procure the largest ship in his power. He accordingly purchased one on the stocks nearly ready for launching, and made such improvements upon her that she was able to carry twenty-four to twenty-six guns." On her return to Boston this frigate brought Governor Shirley and lady, who had been to the theatre of war. They met with a splendid ovation at the hands of the Bostonians, as we have related elsewhere.

We may appropriately mention here the colors which were used on the sea by the colony before 1700, a representation of which is given herewith. The field and cross were red, the tree green, and the union white. The tree appears as a distinctive emblem on the coins as well as the flag.

NEW ENGLAND FLAG.

Pemberton, in his description of Boston, written in 1794, says : —

"Ship-building was formerly carried on at upwards of twenty-seven dock-yards in the town at one and the same time, and employed a large number of mechanicks. In one of the yards, twelve ships have been launched in twelve months. In all the dock-yards, I am credibly informed there have been upwards of sixty vessels on the stocks at one time. Many of the ships built here were sent directly to London with naval stores, whale oil, etc., and to the West Indies with fish and lumber. The whale and cod fishery employed many of our smaller craft. They were nurseries, and produced many hardy seamen. About the year 1750, when paper money was suppressed in this then colony, the sale of ships lying in England, on account of the owners here, occasioned a loss to them from twenty to forty per cent. Few ships were built here, and ship-building gradually declined. Vessels are now built in the country towns not far from where the timber grows.

"The harbor of Boston is at this date" (November, 1794), continues Pemberton, "crowded with vessels. Eighty-four sail have been counted lying at two of the wharves only. It is reckoned that not less than four hundred and fifty sail of ships, brigs, schooners, and sloops, and small crafts are now in port."

The first war-ship built in Boston was a seventy-four, laid down at the yard of Benjamin Goodwin, — afterwards Tilley's Wharf, — a short distance from Charlestown Bridge. She was ordered by the Continental Congress, and Thomas Cushing, afterwards lieutenant-governor, then agent of the government, took possession of the dwelling-house, stores, wharf, and yard of Goodwin for this purpose. In 1784, the exigency having passed by, the ship was sold on the stocks by Thomas Russell as agent of the United States. This was probably the first seventy-four begun in the United States.

It is stated in Emmons's excellent "History of the Navy" that the America, built at Portsmouth in 1782, the command of which was destined for the renowned Paul Jones, was the first vessel of this class built for our navy. She appears to have been the first afloat. The America, awarded by a unanimous vote of Congress to the conqueror of the Serapis, was given to the French, to supply the loss of the Magnifique, lost in Boston harbor in the above year. Her fate is a matter of uncertainty.

SHIP OF THE TIME OF THE PILGRIMS.

Edmund Hartt's shipyard will be forever famous in our annals as the place where the Pride of the American Navy was built. The Hartts were a family of shipwrights. Besides Edmund, there were Edward, Zephaniah, and Ralph the mast-maker. Edmund lived opposite his yard, in what was then Ship Street. He was one of the original trustees of the Mechanic Charitable Association.

Before the establishment of government dockyards, private yards were used for building national vessels, and Hartt's went for a long time by the name of "Hartt's Naval Yard." Thornton's yard on the map of 1722 corresponds with Hartt's, which is now known as Constitution Wharf.

The frigates Constitution and Boston and brig Argus were all built here. All three are known to fame; but the glorious career of Old Ironsides is indelibly associated with the downfall of England's naval supremacy. The proud boast of Waller —

> "Others may use the ocean as their road,
> Only the English make it their abode" —

was rendered obsolete by the deeds of a navy unborn when he wrote.

In consequence of the depredations of the Algerine corsairs upon our commerce, an act was passed at the first session of the Third Congress to provide, by purchase or otherwise, four ships to carry forty-four guns and two to carry thirty-six. This act was approved by President Washington, March 27, 1794. The keel of the Constitution was accordingly laid by Mr. Hartt in November of that year, and preparations made for setting her up. Mr. Cooper, in his Naval History, says her keel was laid on Charlestown Neck, — a situation somewhat remote from her actual birthplace, — and has also incorrectly stated the date of her launch, an error into which many historians have been led by the two unsuccessful attempts made before she finally passed to her destined element.

Peace being concluded with the Dey of Algiers, work was ordered stopped on three of the new frigates, and the materials sold. The act of July 1, 1797, approved by President John Adams, makes the first official mention of the Constitution. The President was authorized to cause the frigates United States, Constitution, and Constellation to be manned and employed.

The names of all who contributed by their labor to the

building of Old Ironsides deserve to be perpetuated, but the records of the Navy Department having been destroyed when Washington was captured in 1814, the loss of the mechanics' rolls has been supplied only after diligent search. She was designed by Joshua Humphries of Philadelphia, and constructed under the superintendence of Colonel George Claghorn of New Bedford. Captains Barry, Dale, and Truxton of the navy agreed with Mr. Humphries upon the dimensions of the Constitution, and Mr. Humphries prepared the drafts, moulds, and building instructions. Her masts and spars were made in the yard between Comey's Wharf and the shipyard ; Paul Revere furnished the copper bolts and spikes, drawn from malleable copper by a process then new ; and Ephraim Thayer, who had a shop at the South End, made the gun-carriages for the frigate. He afterwards made those used on the gunboats built under Jefferson's administration. Isaac Harris, who worked as an apprentice in the mast-yard in 1797, put new sticks into the frigate during the war of 1812. To him is said to belong the honor of first applying in this country the important improvement of making ships' masts in sections. He constructed the first shears used at the Navy Yard at Charlestown for placing the heavy masts of war-vessels in position. A brave act is recorded of him in connection with the Old South, and we shall presently allude to him in connection with a very celebrated flag-raising. The anchors of the Constitution were made in Hanover, Plymouth County, Mass.

CONSTITUTION'S FIGURE-HEAD CARRIED IN THE WAR OF 1812.

Mr. Hartly of Boston, father of a subsequent naval constructor, assisted Colonel Claghorn ; and Captain Nicholson, who was appointed her first commander, exercised a general supervision, in which he was aided by General Jackson and Major Gibbs of Boston. Under the orders of Colonel Claghorn, Edmund Hartt was the master carpenter. The frigate's sails were made in the Old Granary, at the corner of Park and Tremont Streets, where now stands Park Street Church.

No other building in Boston was large enough. The Messrs. Skillings of Boston were the carvers of the figure-head and stern ornaments and of the cabin. She first carried at her prow a figure of Hercules with uplifted club. This was shot away before Tripoli, and seems to have been exchanged at the beginning of 1812 for a Neptune, which is alluded to in the old song,—

> "By the Trident of Neptune, brave Hull cried, let 's steer,
> It points to the track of the bullying Guerriere."

She subsequently bore a plain billet-head scroll, long preserved at Charlestown Navy Yard by the thoughtful care of some unknown commander at that station. Finally, the bows of the gallant old craft were decorated with a bust of General Jackson. The Constitution first carried an English battery; her frame was live-oak.

> "Day by day the vessel grew,
> With timbers fashioned strong and true,
> Stemson and keelson and sternson knee,
> Till, framed with perfect symmetry,
> A skeleton ship rose up to view."

At length came the 20th September, 1797, the day on which Colonel Claghorn had announced that he would launch the Constitution. People poured into the town from all quarters. The day was pleasant, but cold, and the neighboring wharves were crowded with spectators, who received warning that the passage of the vessel into the water would create a swell that might endanger their safety. About six hundred people went over to Noddle's Island, where they could obtain a fine view of the expected launch. At high water, twenty minutes past eleven, the signal was given, but the ship only moved about eight feet. Her colors were then lowered, and the assembled multitude dispersed with disappointment and anxious forebodings.

Owing to an accident to the United States, launched at Philadelphia, by which she ran off the ways an hour before it was intended, damaging her keel and injuring several people, the ways of the Constitution were laid too level, to prevent a similar accident. Part of the site of Hartt's yard was natural, and part artificial; the latter sank under the immense weight. The vessel might have been forced off, but the constructor decided not to attempt a measure so hazardous.

On Friday, the 22d, a second effort was made to get the frigate afloat. She moved a little and then stuck fast. Grave doubts were now expressed as to the practicability of moving her, and the "ill-fated ship," as the superstitious now regarded her, remained seemingly fixed in her position.

Saturday, October 21, a third attempt was made, the high tides having afforded an opportunity of completing the ways. The day was lowering and cold, with an easterly wind. But few people assembled, the general belief being that this would, like the other attempts, prove abortive. A few dignitaries, specially invited, gathered within the narrow limits of the yard. At half past twelve P. M. all was ready.

"And at the mast-head,
White, blue, and red,
A flag unrolls the stripes and stars."

Commodore James Sever stood on the heel of the bowsprit, and, according to the usage of the time, baptized the ship with a bottle of choice old Madeira from the cellar of Hon. Thomas Russell, a leading Boston merchant. A few invited guests, among whom were some ladies, stood on the vessel's deck. At last, at the given signal, —

"She starts, — she moves, — she seems to feel
The thrill of life along her keel;
And, spurning with her foot the ground,
With one exulting, joyous bound,
She leaps into the ocean's arms!"

We have extracted the following incident of the launch from the manuscript of Captain Preble's "History of the Flag": —

"We are glad to be able to record the name of the person who first hoisted our flag over her, little imagining the glorious history she would make. When the Constitution was about ready to launch, Commodore Nicholson, who had charge and superintendence of her construction, left the shipyard to get his breakfast, leaving express orders not to hoist any flag over her until his return, intending to reserve the honor to himself. Among the workmen upon her was a shipwright and calker named Samuel Bentley, who, with the assistance of another workman named Harris, bent on and hoisted the stars and stripes during the commodore's absence. When the commodore returned and saw our flag, contrary to his orders, floating over her, he was very wrathy, and expressed himself in words more strong than polite to the offending workmen. Could he have foreseen the future of the noble frigate he would have been still more excited. He had, however, the satisfaction of being the first to command her, and we know she was the first of the new frigates to carry the fifteen stars and stripes under canvas upon the deep blue sea. Bentley died in Boston in 1852. The fifteen stars and stripes were worn by her before Tripoli and throughout the war of 1812."

In Emmons's Naval List the Constitution is described as a ship of 44 guns, 400 men, 1,576 tons, and cost, ready for sea, $302,719. She has been several times rebuilt, but the original model, tonnage, and general appearance were preserved. In 1833 the frigate was taken into the new Dry Dock at Charlestown in the presence of the Vice-President Mr. Van Buren, Lewis Cass, Secretary of War, the Secretary of the Navy Mr. Woodbury, and other distinguished personages. The President, General Jackson, was to have been present, but was prevented by illness. Commodore Hull had charge of her on this interesting occasion, and his clear voice was frequently heard ringing from the quarter-deck of his former glory. Loammi Baldwin, engineer of the Dry Dock, also assisted at the ceremony. The frigate was entirely dismantled and dismasted, with all her gingerbread-work stripped off preparatory to a thorough overhauling. Her hull presented a most venerable appearance, the bottom being covered with mussels, many of which were gathered as relics.

Here she was rebuilt by Josiah Barker, the eminent naval constructor of the Vermont and Virginia ships-of-the-line, the frigate Cumberland, sloops-of-war Marion, Cyane, Bainbridge, and many others. Mr. Barker's first shipyard occupied the site of the present Navy Yard. There is now in this yard one of the famous umbrellas, used to warp the frigate away from Broke's squadron, in July, 1812.

The Constitution first moved under canvas July 20, 1798, proceeding to sea August 13. The roll of her commanders embraces in their order Samuel Nicholson, who had been a lieutenant with Paul Jones in his action with the Serapis; Edward Preble, styled "the father of our navy," who had served in the old Protector and Winthrop, and who in 1804 gallantly laid Old Ironsides under the walls of Tripoli; Isaac Hull, fourth lieutenant of the old bark in her first cruise, executive officer in 1800, and finally in 1812, as commander, the victor in the famous action with the Guerriere; William Bainbridge, a tried officer of the old navy, captured in the Philadelphia at Tripoli in 1803, and subsequently conqueror in December, 1812, of the Java, British frigate; Charles Stewart, who closed the war so gloriously for his flag by the capture of two British frigates, the Cyane and Levant. This action was fought on a beautiful moonlight evening off Madeira after peace was concluded, but by the terms of the treaty the capture was legalized.

Besides these names, so illustrious in the pages of naval warfare, the Constitution was commanded a short time in 1804 by the brave but ill-fated Decatur; by John Rodgers; by Jacob Jones; by T. Macdonough, J. D. Elliott, and others, whose deeds have passed into history. The brave Lawrence, gallant David Porter, Charles Ludlow, and Charles Morris have served in her as first-lieutenants, while Isaac Chauncey was a master commandant, and Shubrick a lieutenant. The latter officer, promoted to rear-admiral, was the last survivor among the officers of the battle with the Cyane and Levant, in which he was engaged.

The first crew of the Constitution were, with few exceptions, natives of Massachusetts. Her career and exploits are as familiar as household words. No ship was ever so loved by a nation, not even the famous old Victory of Nelson. Good luck pursued her without the intervention of the horse-shoe which Nelson carried nailed to his mast-head.

"Aye, put her atop on the log-book of fame,
Her voice always roared from the van,
When she bore down in thunder and darkness and flame,
Crash foundering each foe that before her came,
The old sailors' love flashes up at her name,
For her yards Young Americans man."

The first cruise of Old Ironsides under Nicholson and the second under Talbot are void of any interesting features, and it was not until Preble commanded her in the Mediterranean, in 1803, that she fired a broadside at an enemy.

Cooper says that Preble was appointed to the Constitution as first lieutenant under Commodore Nicholson, but got relieved, his relations with his commander not being cordial. Preble hoisted his flag on board the Constitution, May 21, 1803. The ship, having been lying in ordinary for ten months, was unfit for immediate service, and the commodore caused a thorough overhauling of the vessel to be made, personally scrutinizing every rope and timber in her. Under his orders she achieved her early reputation, and was, when he turned her over to Decatur, a ship to be proud of. After lying some time in President's Roads taking in powder, etc., the Constitution weighed anchor and sailed on her famous cruise to the Mediterranean, Sunday, August 14, 1803.

Her escape from the British squadron in July, 1812, was due to Yankee ingenuity. The method by which this was accomplished is, it is believed, understood by few. The Constitution carried two umbrellas, so called, made of stout spars attached to a central one precisely like an umbrella frame. These were covered with canvas, and were capable of being expanded or closed ; the weight of the iron-work caused them to sink. While the becalmed British vessels were towing with their boats, Hull caused his umbrellas to be carried out ahead and warped his vessel up to them, so contriving, that while one was being hauled in the other was being put in position. In this way, he left his pursuers astern before they discovered the means employed to escape them. These umbrellas are now in the Charlestown Navy Yard, where, it is hoped, they may be preserved with care. The Constitution ran into Marblehead on Sunday.

While Dr. Bentley, pastor of the Second Church at Salem, was in the midst of his sermon, some one called out under the window of the church, "The British fleet is chasing the Constitution into Marblehead." The minister instantly dismissed his congregation, seized his hat, and ran out of the church, following the men and cannon towards the scene of action. Being a short, thick-set man, and the mercury at eighty-five, the good doctor soon gave out, when he was lifted astride one of the cannon, and in this way proceeded to the beach. Dr. Bentley was a Boston boy, graduate and tutor at Harvard, and for a long time an editor of the Salem Gazette and Salem Register.

The following anecdotes of Hull are printed in Miss Quincy's Memoir:—

"Toward evening on the 29th of August, 1812, a frigate (recognized as the Constitution) came in under full sail and dropped her anchor beside Rainsford Island,—then the quarantine ground. The next morning a fleet of armed ships appeared off Point Alderton. As they rapidly approached, the Constitution was observed to raise her anchor and sails and go boldly forth to meet the apparent enemy; but as the frigate passed the leader of the fleet, a friendly recognition was exchanged instead of the expected broadside. They joined company, and the Constitution led the way to Boston. It was the squadron of Commodore Rodgers returning unexpectedly from a long cruise.

"A few days afterwards, Hull, who had just taken the Guerriere, came with Decatur to breakfast at Quincy. When this incident was mentioned, Hull said, 'I must acknowledge I participated in the apprehensions of my friends on shore. Thinking myself safe in port, I told my officers to let the men wash their clothes, and get the ship in order to go up to Boston; and being excessively fatigued, went to my stateroom. I was sound asleep when a lieutenant rushed down, exclaiming, 'Captain, the British are upon us!—an armed fleet is entering the harbor!' No agreeable intelligence, certainly; for I was wholly unprepared to engage with a superior force. But determined to sell our lives as dear as I could, I gave orders to clear the decks, weigh anchor, and get ready for immediate action. I confess I was greatly relieved when I saw the American flag and recognized Rodgers.' In speaking of the conflict with the Guerriere, he said, 'I do not mind the day of battle; the excitement carries one through: but the day after is fearful; it is so dreadful to see my men wounded and suffering.'

"These naval officers formed a striking contrast. Hull was easy and prepossessing in his manners, but looked accustomed to face 'the battle and the breeze.' Decatur was uncommonly handsome, and remarkable for the delicacy and refinement of his appearance."

Hull, who had a good deal of the bluff sailor about him, exclaimed when he saw the mast of the Guerriere go by the board, — "Huzzah, my boys, we 've made a brig of her." A shipmaster, prisoner on board the Guerriere, gives an interesting relation of his experience during the action. While the Constitution was manœuvring for position, Captain Dacres asked his prisoner, "Do you think she will strike without firing?"

Obtaining permission to retire into the cockpit, the captain says: —

"Within one moment after my foot left the ladder the Constitution gave that double-shotted broadside which threw all in the cockpit over in a heap on the opposite side of the ship. For a moment it seemed as if heaven and earth had struck together; a more terrific shock cannot be imagined."

After the firing had ceased, the prisoner returned to the deck, and continues: —

"What a scene was presented, and how changed in so short a time, during which the Guerriere had been totally dismasted and otherwise cut to pieces, so as not to make her worth towing into port. On the other hand, the Constitution looked perfectly fresh, and even those on board the Guerriere did not know what ship had fought them. Captain Dacres stood with his officers surveying the scene, — all in the most perfect astonishment."

"At this moment a boat was seen putting off from the hostile ship. As soon as within speaking distance, a young gentleman (Midshipman, late Commodore Reed) hailed and said, 'Commodore Hull's compliments, and wishes to know if you have struck your flag?' At this Captain Dacres appeared amazed, but recovering himself and looking up and down, he deliberately said, — 'Well, I don't know; — our mainmast is gone, our mizzenmast is gone, and upon the whole you may say we have struck our flag.'"

The little hurt received by the Constitution in this engagement — her hull showing only here and there a scar — gave her the name of Old Ironsides, by which she was familiarly known. Her crew, indeed, affirmed that the Guerriere's shot fell harmless from her "iron sides."

Old Ironsides arrived in Boston on a Sunday, about noon, from this cruise. The ship was soon surrounded by boats eager to learn the news, which was communicated to the first that came alongside. Instantly the word was passed to the other boats, "The Constitution has captured the Guerriere!" The men cheered, swung their hats, and spread the joyful tidings to the shore, where thousands gathered on the wharves took up the refrain until it echoed from one extremity of the town to the other.

> "On Brazil's coast she ruled the roast
> When Bainbridge was her captain;
> Neat hammocks gave, made of the wave,
> Dead Britons to be wrapped in."

Bainbridge, who succeeded Hull in the command of the Constitution, next fought a well-contested action with the Java on the coast of Brazil, December 29, bringing his own ship victoriously out of the fight. The Java, indeed, only struck her flag after the loss of every mast and spar, bowsprit included. Her gallant commander, Lambert, was mortally wounded. The disabled condition of his prize, with the great distance from our own shores, compelled Bainbridge to destroy the Java, as Hull had destroyed the Guerriere. When the officers of the Java left the Constitution at St. Salvador, they expressed the warmest gratitude for the humane and generous treatment they had experienced.

Bainbridge returned to Boston from this cruise, arriving on the 15th of February. He was received on landing by a salute of artillery, and a procession was formed at Faneuil Hall headed by the "Boston Light Infantry" and "Winslow Blues," which escorted the commodore to the Exchange Coffee House, where the company sat down to a superb banquet. Hull and Rodgers walked with Bainbridge in the procession, and shared the applause bestowed upon him. At the dinner Governor Gore presided, assisted by H. G. Otis, Israel Thorndike, T. L. Winthrop, William Sullivan, and others. The Legislature being in session passed complimentary resolutions.

The commodore, with some of his officers, visited the Federal

Street Theatre, where they were immediately recognized by the audience, which rose up as if by one impulse, while cheer upon cheer shook the house from pit to dome. The veteran Cooper, who on that night was playing Macbeth, flung his bonnet in the air and joined in the applause.

In June, 1813, Stewart was appointed to command her, and proceeded to sea December 30, although Boston was then blockaded by seven of the enemy's ships. She returned in April, 1814, and was chased into Marblehead by the frigates Tenedos and Junon. The country was alarmed, and the local militia from Newburyport to Boston marched to defend the frigate; one Boston company, the New England Guards, proceeded as far as Charlestown, when they learned that the pursuit had been abandoned. They then found that their cartridge-boxes were empty.

In December, 1814, Stewart sailed on his second cruise and encountered, February 28, off Madeira, the British frigates Cyane and Levant, which were both captured after a contest in which the Constitution was handled with consummate skill by her commander. Of the prizes, only the Cyane succeeded in reaching the United States, the Levant being recaptured by Sir George Collier's squadron, which suddenly appeared off Port Praya, where Old Ironsides was quietly lying with her captives. All three vessels were compelled to cut their cables and run for it. The Cyane arriving first at New York, great anxiety was felt for the Constitution, and on her arrival at that port on the 15th of May, 1815, the ship and commander were greeted with the utmost enthusiasm.

On the 4th of July, 1828, Old Ironsides returned from a long cruise in the Mediterranean to the place of her nativity. As she passed up to the Navy Yard, the roar of her guns mingled with the echoes from the Castle and from Constitution Wharf, the place of her birth. The guns were firing peaceful salutes instead of round shot and grape, but the presence of the idolized frigate gave additional *éclat* to the national holiday.

It was at one time decided to break her up, and orders had actually been issued to this effect. The destruction of her old timbers seemed like an act of sacrilege, and gave rise to Holmes's much admired lines expressive of the universal feeling of condemnation. To the poet's impassioned outburst is due the preservation of the Constitution on the roll of the American Navy: —

"O, better that her shattered hull
Should sink beneath the wave;
Her thunders shook the mighty deep,
And there should be her grave.
Nail to the mast her holy flag,
Set every threadbare sail,
And give her to the god of storms,
The lightning, and the gale."

From the old timbers were made a number of relics which have no doubt been highly prized by their possessors. Mr. Barker, the constructor, sent a cane to Joshua Humphries, her original designer. In 1836 a beautiful coach was built entirely of the wood of the old frigate at Amherst, Mass., intended as

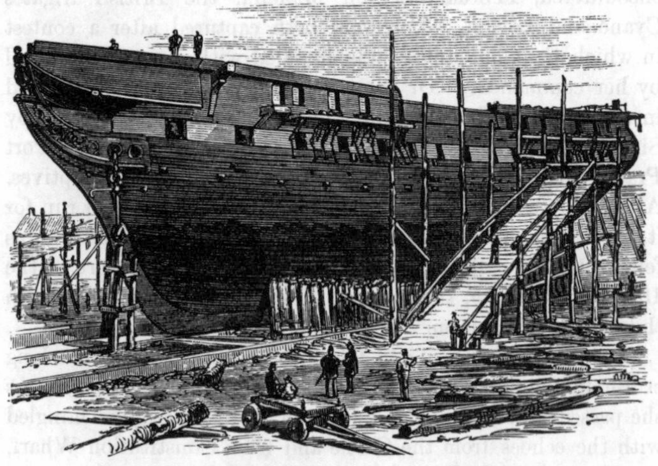

THE CONSTITUTION HAULED UP ON THE WAYS.

a New-Year's present to General Jackson from several gentlemen of New York City. Commodore Hull presented canes from the original wood to President Jackson, Mr. Van Buren, and Mr. Poinsett at the time the ship was docked.

The captured flags of the Cyane, Levant, Guerriere, and Java are in the Naval Academy at Annapolis, but of her original battery, before which the "wooden walls of Old England" went down, no traces have been found. One of the guns was dented by the enemy's shot; but we have reason to apprehend that these dogs of war were broken up and treated as so much old iron.

The Constitution carried out Ministers Barlow and Cass to France, and brought home Mr. Livingstone and family. Her flag has been seen in nearly every sea, and her deck has been trod by many noble personages. In 1822, while in the Mediterranean, she was visited by Lord Byron, who, while endeavoring to preserve his incognito, was much embarrassed at finding all the officers on deck in full uniform to receive him. Lord Byron was accompanied by Count Gamba, father of the Countess Guiccioli. A beautifully bound volume of his poems was lying on the cabin table, which he took up with evident pleasure at the delicate compliment implied.

An episode of this visit caused Byron to remark, "that he would rather have a nod from an American than a snuff-box from an emperor." This is in pleasing contrast with the surly saying of Johnson, — "I am willing to love all mankind except an American." At this time Commodore Jacob Jones flew his broad pennant on board the old craft.

After Old Ironsides had emerged a new ship from Mr. Barker's hands, there happened to her an adventure that awakened at the time the most intense excitement in Boston, and which, from its peculiar aspects, was soon communicated all over the seaboard. This was known as the "Affair of the Figure-Head." Andrew Jackson was President, and had been greeted with the consideration due his official station during his visit to Boston of the previous year. Under this outward courtesy, however, was an undercurrent of political antagonism, apparent enough in the public prints of the day. Cheers were raised for Mr. Clay in Faneuil Hall at the time of General Jackson's reception there. The old political party which controlled Boston was putting on the new title of "Whig," under which it subsequently fought. Not even the LL. D. conferred upon the President at Harvard could reconcile the opposition with the acts of his administration.

The appearance of the frigate Constitution, therefore, with a figure-head of President Jackson was greeted with a storm of disapproval. When it was known that it was the intention of Commodore Jesse D. Elliott, the then commander of the Navy Yard, to thus ornament the frigate's bows, and that Laban S. Beecher, the well-known Boston carver, was at work upon it, threats were freely made that she would not be allowed to go to sea with the obnoxious image. Large bribes were also offered to the artist to destroy his work, but he remained true to his employers, working on the figure-head in his garret, which served alike as his *atelier* and citadel. Alarmed, however, by the menaces against Beecher, and thinking the head no longer safe in his custody, Commodore Elliott caused its removal by an armed boat's crew to the Navy Yard, where it was placed in the engine-house and finished by Beecher at his leisure. The figure represented the President in the Hermitage scene, holding in his hand a scroll with the motto, "The Union it must be preserved." Beecher was also engaged upon the busts of Hull, Bainbridge, and Stewart for stern ornaments of the frigate.

The graven image was placed at the Constitution's stem, but on the 3d of July (1834) was discovered to have been mutilated, — the head being sawed completely off, leaving only the body of the Chief Magistrate. The affair caused a great noise. It was committed during the prevalence of a violent thunder-storm, with sentinels pacing the ship's deck, while she herself lay moored between two seventy-fours (the Independence and Columbus) off the yard. The act was a daring one, and conjecture was for a long time busy as to its author, who, however, maintained a prudent reserve until the excitement caused by the affair had time to cool. What this excitement was may be understood when it is stated that the people of Wheeling, Va., rang the bells, assembled in public meeting, and passed resolutions approving the act.

On the night in question, Captain Dewey, a Boston ship-master, obtained a small row-boat, and dropped quietly down with the tide to where the frigate lay moored. Securing his boat he proceeded to his work, in the accomplishment of which he had to cut through a copper bolt. Several times the sentry on deck looked over the bow, — hearing perhaps the noise of the saw, — when the workman ceased his labor for the time. The rain poured in torrents, which, with the intense darkness, favored the bold operator. The head of Jackson, like a victim of the seraglio, fell into a sack. Dewey pulled to the shore and repaired to meet some friends at a public-house, where his success was duly celebrated.

In this plight the Constitution — she was then in commission — proceeded to New York, where, in due time, a second figure-head bearing the same features took the place of the headless one. To secure it from a similar mutilation, a copper bolt of extraordinary thickness was placed perpendicularly in the head. At the Charlestown Navy Yard may be seen the bust of General Jackson from which the original was modelled.

In March, 1835, the Constitution sailed from New York for the Mediterranean as flag-ship of Commodore Elliott, since which time her history is that of a useful but peaceful ship. At the outbreak of the Rebellion she was lying at Annapolis, where she would doubtless have shared the fate of the government vessels at Norfolk and elsewhere, had not our soldiers opportunely secured the place. Edward E. Preble, a grandson of the commodore, was on board the Constitution at this time. After being used as quarters for the midshipmen of the Naval Academy at Newport and Annapolis, she was, in 1871, towed round to Philadelphia and laid up. She is now an object of much interest to visitors at the Charlestown Navy Yard.

From sources already mentioned it is ascertained that she captured eight armed vessels carrying one hundred and fifty-eight guns, and ten unarmed prizes. From this statement it will be seen that her crews shared more hard knocks than prize money.

The next war-vessel built at Hartt's yard was the Boston frigate of seven hundred tons, so called because she was built by the subscription of Boston merchants and others, and given a free-will offering to the government. She was designed, probably, by Mr. Hartt, and built under his superintendence. Her rate was to have been a thirty-six, but she mounted only twenty-eight guns. On the 22d of August, 1798, her keel was laid, and in April, 1799, President Adams appointed Captain George Little, of Massachusetts, to command her. June 12 she hauled into the stream, and sailed on her first cruise July 24, 1799. She was declared to be one of the handsomest vessels that ever floated.

The names of those persons who contributed to build the Boston are worthy of preservation. A notice appeared in the Centinel of June 27, 1798, that a subscription would be opened in the chamber over Taylor's Insurance Office (corner of State and Kilby Streets) at one o'clock, "where those who wish to join in this testimonial of public spirit" might affix their signatures. At this meeting $115,250 was raised, of which Hon. William Phillips gave $10,000. This subscription was subsequently increased to $130,000; the frigate cost $137,969. David Sears, Stephen Higginson, Eben Parsons, John Codman, Joseph Coolidge and Son, Theodore Lyman, Boot and Pratt, and Thomas Dickinson gave $3,000 each. Samuel Parkman and Samuel Elliott gave $4,000 each. Benjamin Joy, James and T. H. Perkins, Thomas Walley, John Parker, Stephen Higginson, Jr., Abiel Smith, and Thomas C. Amory are down for $1,500 each. St. Andrew's Lodge gave $1,000. Benjamin and Nathaniel Goddard and Josiah Quincy gave $500. The givers of smaller sums are not less deserving of mention, but are too numerous for our limits.

The Boston got to sea during the hostilities with France, and soon distinguished herself on the West India station by capturing Le Berceau, a ship of twenty-four guns and two hundred and twenty men; Les Deux Anges, ship of twenty guns; three barges, and three unarmed prizes. At this time she was one of Commodore Talbot's squadron. The next year, under command of Captain McNeil, the Boston carried a minister to France and joined the Mediterranean fleet.

Captain Little brought Le Berceau, his prize, into Boston early in November. The Frenchman was completely dismasted in the engagement, but was repaired and restored to the French under treaty stipulations. For circumstances attending this capture, Captain Little was court-martialled, the court sitting on board the Constitution, but was honorably acquitted. In her action with Le Berceau the Boston had four killed and eight wounded. The French prisoners were confined at the Castle.

In 1812 the Boston was reported unworthy of repair, and in 1814, when the British were advancing on Washington, she was burned to prevent her falling into the enemy's hands.

The brig Argus, sixteen guns, two hundred and twenty-six tons, was built at Hartt's yard in 1803, at a cost of $ 37,420. She was designed by Mr. Hartly. In August, 1813, having landed Mr. Crawford, our Minister to France, at Havre, she proceeded to cruise off the English and Irish coasts, and captured and burnt so many vessels that the Irish declared the Channel was all ablaze. Between the Shannon and the Liffey she captured twenty vessels, most of which were burnt. On the 14th August, 1813, the Argus fought and was captured by the British brig Pelican, of twenty-one guns. Lieutenant Wm. H. Allen of the Argus was mortally wounded early in the conflict; he was Decatur's first lieutenant when he took the Macedonian. The Argus had also been a busy cruiser during the war with Tripoli. Both Hull and Decatur had commanded her.

CHAPTER VII.

COPP'S HILL AND THE VICINITY.

Copp's Hill. — British Works. — Ancient Arch. — Wm. Gray. — Old Ferry. — Reminiscences of Bunker Hill. — The Cemetery. — Curious Stones, Epitaphs, etc. — Old Funeral Customs. — Charter Street. — Sir Wm. Phips. — John Foster Williams. — John Hull. — Colonial Mint. — Christ Church. — Revere's Night Ride. — The Chimes. — The Vaults, — Legends of. — Major Pitcairn. — Love Lane. — North Latin School. — Prince Street. — Salem Church. — North End Heroes. — Captain Manly. — Massachusetts Spy. — First Baptist Church. — Second Baptist Church. — Draft Riot, 1863.

WE pursue our way, after our long halt among the ship-yards, around the base of Copp's Hill. The hill itself is the early Mill Field of 1632 and later, so called because the windmill used to grind the settlers' corn was brought from Cambridge in this year and placed upon the summit. This was the first windmill erected in the town. The appearance of Copp's Hill, which name is from William Copp, an early possessor, is very different to-day from what it was in 1800. At that time the hill terminated abruptly on the northwest side in a rugged cliff almost inaccessible from the water-side. Southerly, the ground fell away in an easy descent to the bottom of North Square and the shore of the Mill Pond, while to the eastward a gradual slope conducted to the North Battery. The beach at the foot of the headland, opposite Charlestown, was made into a street with earth taken from the summit of the hill, which was where Snow-Hill Street now crosses it. This made Lynn Street, — now Atlantic Avenue extension, — and afforded a continuous route along the water.

Going north, the rising ground at Richmond Street indicates the beginning of the ascent. The hill has been known as Windmill Hill and as Snow Hill; but our ancestors were never at a loss for names, as appears in the redundancy of their street nomenclature. The foot of the hill, at the northeasterly side, went in old times by the name of New Guinea, on account of its being exclusively inhabited by blacks. A representation is here given of the kind of windmill used by the first settlers of Boston. Its architecture differs entirely from the mills used by the French in Canada, the old stone mill at Newport, or of the western settlements of the French. It is a copy of one set up at West Boston, the design for which may have been brought from the Low Countries.

ANCIENT MILL.

The work erected by the British from which they bombarded the Americans on Bunker Hill and set fire to Charlestown, was on the summit of the eminence, near the southwest corner of the Burial Ground. It was a small affair, consisting, when it was visited in the following year (1776), of only a few barrels of earth to form parapets. Three twenty-eight pounders, mounted on carriages, were left spiked within. The battery was covered by a small earthwork to the rear designed for the infantry. Traces of these works remained until the summit was levelled in 1807.

At the foot of Henchman's Lane, when the work of excavation was proceeding at this point, there was uncovered an arch built of brick, of large dimensions, with an opening at the water side. There was originally a high bank at this place, — the arch spanning the then Lynn Street and communicating with the cellar of a house on the north side. Sixty odd years ago, when digging for the foundation of the houses on the east side of the street, the remains of the arch were found, and are still to be seen in the cellar of the house opposite Henchman's Lane.

Those who examined it while it was intact are of the opinion that it was intended as a place of concealment for smugglers and their contraband goods. Many speculations were indulged as to its origin and its uses, the theory that it was a retreat for pirates being the favorite one. Time has disclosed that it was built by a Captain Gruchy during the French wars, and used as a place of deposit for captured goods. Perhaps the captain was a free-trader, or fitted out privateers to prey upon the commerce of the French king. Gruchy was a subsequent owner of Sir William Phips's house, his land running down the hill to the water's edge.* He built him a wharf of two captured vessels, which he sunk for the purpose. These old arches were a unique feature of Old Boston, and doubtless began to be built about the time Randolph made the attempt to collect the king's excise. Another is noted built by Edward Hutchinson from his house on North Street.

Lynn Street is described in 1708 as from the North Battery northwesterly to the Ferry-way at Hudson's Point; it retained this name until after 1828. Before it was built into a thoroughfare this street was only a narrow way around the beach. Henchman's Lane is coeval with Lynn Street in receiving its name, which was from Captain Daniel Henchman, father of the bookseller, who lived within its precincts.

We next come to Foster Street, in the lower part of which was formerly the cannon and bell foundry of Paul Revere. Up to the time of the establishment of these works both cannon and bells were imported; but Revere cast brass guns successfully, and some of his bells still hang in our steeples. Hollow-ware, stoves, and a variety of articles for domestic use were manufactured at this foundry, erected previous to 1794.

The rain had been falling as we continued our walk through the filthy street along the water. The air was filled with the stench arising under the warm sun from the mud and garbage of the gutter, and from every door and window of the over-crowded tenements peered forth a swarm of dirty humanity. Some one has called the Irish the finest peasantry in the world, but perhaps he had not seen them herded together in our cities. Musing on these disenchanting features of our antiquarian pursuit, we cast our eyes upward in the direction of Christ Church steeple, which serves us as a guide and beacon, —

* The shore end of the tunnel was traced to the cellar of these premises.

"And lo! from out a dirty alley,
Where pigs and Irish wont to rally,
I saw a crazy woman sally,
Bedaubed with grease and mud."

The reader knows what a trifle will suffice to collect a crowd in the city. Let a single individual stop in one of our crowded thoroughfares and gaze intently in any direction, he will be instantly surrounded by a curious, gaping multitude. We quickened our pace, and left behind us the throng gathering around the poor creature crazed with drink, blaspheming, and tearing her hair by handfuls. In this manœuvre we were anticipated by a prudent policeman who turned the corner in our front.

The new Public Park under Copp's Hill takes in Gray's Wharf, built by Hon. William Gray, better known by the sobriquet of "Billy." Beginning at the lowest round of the ladder, he climbed to the highest mercantile eminence, and at the time of his death, in 1825, was the largest ship-owner in America, perhaps in the world. He was the owner at one time of sixty square-rigged vessels, whose sails whitened every sea. Mr. Gray, after acting in the State Legislature, was elected lieutenant-governor with Elbridge Gerry in 1810. He was a Democrat in politics, sustaining the embargo, notwithstanding it inflicted a heavy loss upon him. He lived in Summer Street, in the mansion previously occupied by Governor Sullivan.

There were few to whom the face of the old merchant was not familiar. He was an early riser, and performed a considerable amount of work before breakfast. Affable in intercourse, unostentatious in manner, Mr. Gray was also a man of practical benevolence. He aided the government largely in 1812, and it is said but for him the Constitution would not have got to sea and electrified the nation by her exploits. Mr. Gray was the first president of the State Bank, the first democratic banking institution that obtained a charter in Massachusetts. After the Treaty of Ghent, Mr. Gray presided over a public dinner given to John Quincy Adams, at which the venerable patriarch, John Adams, was also present. Mr. Gray's old homestead in Salem afterwards became the Essex Coffee House.

Benjamin Goodwin, mentioned in the preceding chapter in

connection with the seventy-four, lived in a house between Charter and Lynn Streets extending from one street to the other. Goodwin's Wharf extended from a point opposite his house, and was sixty to eighty rods east of the bridge. He carried on a distillery, bake-house, and blacksmith-shop. The premises were seized by order of the British general, and occupied by his troops at the time of the battle of Bunker Hill. The soldiers afterwards wantonly destroyed much of the property and some of the buildings, Mr. Goodwin's damages being estimated at £1,500, lawful money.

Hudson's Point, the extreme northwest point of the town, was named from Francis Hudson, the ferry-man. It is first called "ye Mylne Point," in the grant of the ferry to Thomas Marshall in 1635. At this point were established both the ferries to Charlestown and Chelsea. To be exact, the Ferry-way was, in 1720, between Mr. Gee's and Hudson's Point, and Mr. Joshua Gee, the boat-builder, owned the present property of the Gas Company, his residence being in Prince Street, a short distance from his yard. This Mr. Gee was also owner of a large tract on Copp's Hill, between Charter, Prince, and Snow-Hill Streets. The town voted in 1720 to move the General Court to take action about a bridge at this place, but no action followed.

Among the reminiscences of the old Ferry, besides being the probable landing of Winthrop's company and the place where the first white woman jumped ashore, it is noted as the point of debarkation for the British wounded from Bunker Hill. Their admitted loss in this battle was two hundred and twenty-six killed, eight hundred and twenty-eight wounded, though estimates have been made as high as fifteen hundred. In Frothingham's account of the battle is the following description of the harrowing scene: —

"The wounded during the whole night and the next day were conveyed to Boston, where the streets were filled with groans and lamentation. A letter of June 30, 1775, says: 'I have seen many from Boston who were eyewitnesses of the most melancholy scene they ever beheld in this part of the world. The Saturday night and

Sabbath were taken up in carrying over the dead and wounded; and all the wood-carts in town, it is said, were employed, — chaises and coaches for the officers. They have taken the workhouse, almshouse, and manufactory house for the wounded.' The physicians, surgeons, and apothecaries of Boston rendered every assistance in their power. The processions were melancholy sights. 'In the first carriage,' writes Clarke, 'was Major Williams, bleeding and dying, and three dead captains of the 52d. In the second, four dead officers; then another with wounded officers.' The privates who died on the field were immediately buried there, — 'in holes,' Gage's report states. 'On Monday morning,' a British account says, 'all the dead officers were decently buried in Boston in a private manner, in the different churches and churchyards there.'"

Francis Rawdon, afterwards Marquis of Hastings, and George Harris, afterwards a peer, were both officers of the 5th, and wounded. The 5th, 59th, and the Welsh Fusileers were terribly cut up.

The first act of the British commander before the Lexington expedition, which had a hostile look, was the hauling of the Somerset man-of-war from the stream where she had been lying into Charles River, so as to command the Ferry-ways. This is stated in the Salem Gazette of April 18, 1775, and was to prevent communication of the intended movement to the country. This vessel served to cover the disorderly retreat of the regulars over Charlestown Neck on their return from Lexington and Concord. We shall see that the Somerset's watch was ill-kept, and that a North End mechanic looked into the muzzles of her guns as he carried Warren's errand and spread the tidings abroad. The Somerset went ashore on Cape Cod during the war, and her officers and crew were made prisoners by the militia, and sent to Boston.

When Burgoyne's army was near Cambridge as prisoners of war, some of the officers pushed on over the ferry into Boston; but their hopes of comfortable quarters and good cheer were speedily dashed, for they were all peremptorily ordered back to the prisoners' camps at Union, Winter, and Prospect Hills, where barracks had been prepared for them. Burgoyne himself had the privilege of *entrée* into the town, which he improved as we have seen, though times were changed since he stood on Copp's Hill and saw his comrades-in-arms advance up the hillside across the river to storm the American redoubt. Burgoyne's graphic account of the battle written to Lord Stanley has supplied the best English narration of the battle of Bunker Hill. A rapier once belonging to the general is in possession of a descendant of that Benjamin Goodwin whose property was so ill-used by the king's troops.

Copp's Hill Burying-Ground, first called the North Burying-Place, was the second place of sepulture within the town. About three acres is enclosed by the cemetery walls, made up of several tracts. The first was conveyed to the town in 1659, and composed the northeastern part. An additional parcel was conveyed in 1711 by Samuel Sewall and his wife Hannah, the daughter of John Hull, for the purpose of enlargement. In the conveyance was reserved "one rodd square in which Mrs. Mary Thatcher now lyeth buried," which they had previously conveyed to Joshua Gee. The deed also gave the right of way across the burying-ground, so that a small piece of private property, without any restrictions as to its use, exists in the midst of the cemetery. Another strip of land was added on the Hull Street side in after years. On the Snow-Hill Street side the hill has been cut down twenty feet, the cemetery being there protected by a heavy granite wall. A gun-house once stood in the southeast corner of the new part of the cemetery.

THE MATHER TOMB.

When we are at King's Chapel, or the Granary Burial-Ground, amid the bustle of a crowded thoroughfare, the mind is wholly divested of those feelings of calm and solitude with which we are accustomed to view the last resting-places of the dead. The superstitious do not hurry past, nor do the timid pass by on the other side. The absence of funeral rites for so long a time deprives them of the awe and reverence which such mournful pageants inspire ; the living move on in a continual tide, unbroken except in the still watches of the night, separated only by a narrow barrier from the motionless dead.

But in Copp's Hill it is different. Quiet prevails, and we almost expect to hear the clink of Old Mortality's chisel among the gravestones.

> "Beneath those rugged elms, that yew-tree's shade,
> Where heaves the turf in many a mouldering heap,
> Each in his narrow cell forever laid,
> The rude forefathers of the hamlet sleep."

Copp's Hill is, however, strangely like the Chapel Ground in one respect. The same mathematical precision is observable in the laying out of the walks and arrangement of the stones. While a cemetery may be beautified under a competent hand, what can excuse the wholesale depredations made among the bones of our ancestors of the North End?

Apparently the oldest stone in this cemetery bears the date of 1625, or before the settlement of Boston, being that of Grace Berry; that of Joanna, daughter of William Copp, is dated 1625–6. It is said that these stones were altered in a boyish freak, by George Darracott, from 1695. Many stolen gravestones have been recovered by Supt. MacDonald from drains, chimney-tops, or cellars in the vicinity. The oldest stone, that to two children of David Copp, dated 1661–1678, lay buried many years.

Since the beautiful symbolic customs of the Greeks and Romans, their emblems are to be found in every churchyard. The broken column, the cylinder and sphere, the monumental urn and torch, are types derived from antiquity. The pyramids of Egypt, the tombs by the banks of the Nile, now used by the living, and the splendid mausoleums of the Greeks and Romans, are evidences of the respect and veneration felt for the departed in centuries gone by. Inscriptions were early used by the Greeks until forbidden by Lycurgus, except to such as died in battle. Since then wit, humor, and sentiment have been exhausted on marble or stone. Too many, perhaps, profess a virtue if they have it not; others are facetious, marking the passage of a soul into eternity with a flippant jest. Pope and Byron wrote epitaphs on dogs, and Voltaire on a bird, while Prior demolishes the pretensions of Westminster Abbey in four lines : —

"Nobles and heralds, by your leave,
Here lies what once was Matthew Prior,
The son of Adam and of Eve ;
Can Stuart or Nassau claim higher ?"

The following is from a stone in Copp's Hill : —

"A sister of Sarah Lucas li th here,
Whom I did love most dear,
And now her soul hath took its flight,
And bid her spightful foes good night."

Many of the inscriptions are in rude contrast with the beautifully chiselled armorial bearings here seen, as in King's Chapel Ground, the best executed specimens of mortuary sculpture being usually imported from England. Some of the stones are indeed primitive, being little more than solid blocks, — massy, and scarce shaped into form. Quaint inscriptions, the traditional death's-head and hourglass, greet you on every hand. Many of the older inscriptions are illegible, — what wonder, after more than two hundred years' conflict with the elements ! Is the spirit which prompted the pious work of Old Mortality extinguished in our historical institutions ?

The singular juxtaposition of names strikes the reader of the headstones in Copp's Hill. Here repose the ashes of Mr. John Milk and Mr. William Beer ; of Samuel Mower and Theodocia Hay ; Timothy Gay and Daniel Graves ; of Elizabeth Tout and Thomas Scoot. Here lie Charity Brown, Elizabeth Scarlet, and Marcy White ; Ann Ruby and Emily Stone. The old familiar North End names are here on every side. The Huguenot Sigourneys ; the Grays, of rope-making fame ; the Mountforts, claiming descent from the Norman Conquest. Edmund Hartt, builder of the Constitution ; Deacon Moses Grant and Major Seward of Revolutionary memory, and a host of others who go to swell the ranks of the unnumbered dead.

On the Charter Street side, near the northeast corner of the ground, once grew a beautiful weeping willow, drooping gracefully over the monument of Joshua Ellis. This willow came from the grave of the great Corsican at St. Helena. It was ruined by a gale in 1888.

Interments are now restricted to the tombs, and if we except the occasional pilgrimage of a stranger, the cemetery seems to be the common playground of the children of the neighborhood. By levelling a range of old rookeries, on the Charter Street side, a fine view was opened across Charles River, embracing the monument and spires of Charlestown, with the dismantled war-ships moored in quiet waters below.

Acts of vandalism are recorded with respect to some of the gravestones in the yard. Those of Grace Berry and Captain Daniel Malcolm having served King George's soldiers for target-practice, by which they were splintered, and the inscriptions defaced. The names on some of the old tombs have been obliterated and others substituted. The beautiful coat of arms of the Hutchinsons has been thus desecrated. So says Thomas Bridgman in his Epitaphs. The remains of Thomas Hutchinson, father of the governor, once rested here. Besides the Mathers, Andrew and John Eliot, divines of old celebrity, lie here.

From Copp's Hill Burgoyne and Clinton witnessed the fight on Bunker Hill, and directed the fire of the battery. It was a shell from here that set fire to Charlestown, adding to the grandeur and horror of the scene. Clinton, seeing the ranks of his veterans reel and fall back before the murderous discharges from the redoubt, threw himself into a boat and crossed to the aid of Howe.

The British shipping took a prominent part in this battle, especially the Glasgow, which lay in a position where she swept Charlestown Neck with her guns, thus preventing reinforcements passing over to the Americans, and harassing their retreat from the hill. An American officer told Putnam no one could cross that Neck and live; nevertheless it is stated, on the authority of Major Russell, that a number of Boston school-boys crossed and recrossed during the battle.

The Glasgow was also one of the fleet that brought the British troops to Boston in 1768. The engraving is from an original drawing, and shows the style of naval architecture in the last century.

Out of this tranquillity we can with difficulty conjure up the scene of carnage that once raged upon the hillside yonder. The still, starry night that preceded the battle, when a thousand men, stacking their firelocks, with mattock and spade threw up the first rampart of the Revolution. Gridley, the veteran engineer, marking out the works upon the wet turf, with Pomeroy, Prescott, Putnam, and many more that heard

THE GLASGOW.

"The drum that beat at Louisburg and thundered in Quebec!"

How strangely to their ears must have sounded the cry of the British sentinel, "All 's well!" as he paced where we now stand. To the laborers on that sultry night this cry was hailed at every hour as proof of their undiscovered toil. So the defences grew, hour by hour, until the morning dawned on the eventful day.

In this battle General Gage's military reputation was lost. By his neglect to seize and hold Charlestown heights a battle was forced upon him, with the loss of British prestige and twelve hundred of his bravest soldiers. And Howe, notwithstanding the bitter experience of that day, thought to repeat the experiment at Dorchester Heights before a year had passed.

It was once the custom to hang the escutcheon of a deceased head of a family from the window or over the entrance of a house from which a funeral was to take place until it was over. The last instance noted is that of Governor Hancock's uncle, Thomas Hancock, in 1764. Copies of the escutcheon were distributed among the pall-bearers, rings afterward, and gloves within the century. Scarfs were once given the mourners, but this was prohibited, in 1724, by law.

Before Copp's Hill was built upon so densely, it served the North End population as a place of promenade and recreation. The common was far too distant, and wanted the attraction of the beautiful panorama of the harbor then to be seen from this eminence. The character of this quarter of the town has since then undergone a change, its residents no longer claiming the high standing once their due. The hill, fortunately for its preservation, is not in the line of the movement of traffic, and has experienced little alteration except on the water-side.

After the surrender of Quebec the North-Enders made an unexampled bonfire on Copp's Hill. Forty-five tar-barrels, two cords of wood, a mast, spars, and boards, with fifty pounds of powder, were set in a blaze, and must have cast a ruddy glow over the waters of the bay. This, with a similar illumination on Fort Hill, was paid for by the province, together with thirty-two gallons of rum and much beer for the people.

Charter Street, which makes the northern boundary of the cemetery, takes its name from the Charter of King William III. Under it Maine, Plymouth, and Massachusetts formed a single provincial government. The name has stood since 1708.

Sir William Phips's name is closely identified with the street, both as a resident and for having been the first governor under the new charter. His residence was at the westerly corner of Salem and Charter Streets, which long went by the name of Phips's Corner. The house was of brick, altered by the addition of a third story in the present century, and was used in 1830 as an Asylum for Indigent Boys. The governor's name is remembered in Phips Place, near at hand.

Governor Phips's origin was obscure. An apprentice to a ship-carpenter in early youth, he is naturally found among his craftsmen of the North End. He received knighthood for the recovery of £300,000 of treasure, in 1687, from a sunken Spanish galleon, near the Bahamas, all of which he turned over to the English government, receiving £16,000 as his share. He made two expeditions against Canada in 1690, —

one against Quebec, resulting unsuccessfully, and another in which his fleet captured Port Royal. It is said he received his appointment through the influence of Increase Mather, while the doctor was agent for the colony in England.

The occasion of the governor's arrival in Boston, May, 1692, was one of great rejoicing. On the 16th he was escorted from his dwelling to the State House by the Boston Regiment and companies from Charlestown, with the magistrates and people, not only of Boston, but the neighboring towns. The new charter and the governor's commission were then read from the balcony, according to custom, and the old governor, Bradstreet, vacated his office. A banquet closed the ceremonies.

Dr. Cotton Mather says Phips dreamed when a poor boy that he would become rich and build him a house on the Green Lane, the ancient name of Salem Street. He lived to realize his dream, and become the head of the colony.

Sir William was a man of ungovernable temper. He assaulted Brenton, the collector of the port, and caned Captain Short, of the Nonesuch frigate. He was of large stature and great personal strength, which made these personal conflicts undesirable to his foes. An instance is given of his having acted a Cromwellian part. Having procured, by a bare majority, the passage of an act prohibiting any but residents of the town they represented to be members of the General Court, Sir William rushed into the chamber and drove out the non-resident representatives, who did not stand upon the order of their going, but left the governor master of the field. Governor Phips was a member of the Old North under the ministration of the Mathers. Aside from his impetuous disposition, he is described as a man of sterling traits. He died in London in 1695, and was buried in the church of St. Mary Woolnoth, where a long epitaph commemorates his life and public services.

Hutchinson relates that once in Sir William's absence his wife, whose name was Mary (William and Mary were the reigning sovereigns), was applied to in behalf of a poor woman who had been committed under a charge of witchcraft, and that out of the goodness of her heart she signed a warrant for the woman's discharge, William and Mary, which mandate was obeyed by the keeper of the jail without question.

In Charter Street lived the ancestors of John Foster Williams, who, in the Massachusetts frigate Protector, of twenty-six guns, sunk the English ship Admiral Duff, of thirty guns, during the Revolutionary War. In this action Preble, afterwards commodore, was a midshipman with Williams, who died in Boston in 1814. Foster Street, now Clark, was intended to perpetuate the old family. Paul Revere, the *fidus Achates* of Warren, lived and died in a house in Charter Street which he bought near the close of the war of Independence. It stood near Hanover Street, on the west side, where Revere Place now is.

Spencer Phips, afterwards lieutenant-governor, was originally named David Bennet, but took the name of his Uncle Phips when adopted by him. He also lived in Sir William's house. Spencer Phips was in office while William Shirley was governor, and was of course overshadowed by that remarkable man. Phips was succeeded by Hutchinson at his death in 1757.

Hull Street bounds the cemetery on the south. It is named for John Hull, through whose pasture it was laid out, and was conveyed to the town by Judge Samuel Sewall and wife, on the express condition that it should always bear that name.

John Hull, the primitive owner of this field, is famed as the coiner of the first money in New England. The scarcity of silver in the colony for a circulating medium seems to have rendered the step necessary. The colonists being purchasers as yet, the bullion flowed out of the country.

PINE-TREE SHILLING.

In the "History and Antiquities of Boston" it is remarked : —

"It was no small stretch of authority for a Colony or a Province to presume to coin money ; but this Colony was now very peculiarly situated, and its presumption in taking this step was greatly favored by the recent state of affairs in the mother country."

The mint was established at John Hull, the silversmith's, house, and he and his coadjutor, Robert Sanderson, took oath that all the money coined by them should "be of the just alloy of the English cojne; that every shilling should be of due weight, namely, three penny troj weight, and all other pieces proportionably, so neere as they could." This was, in 1652, the origin of the old pine-tree shilling. Hull's house was the same formerly owned by Rev. John Cotton.

In 1654 an order of the General Court prohibited the transportation out of its jurisdiction of more than twenty shillings "for necessary expenses" by any person. Searchers were appointed "to examine all packs, persons, trunks, chests, boxes or the like." The penalty was the seizure of the whole estate of the offender.

Hull began poor, and ended rich, many of his new shillings finding their way into his own strong-box. He was a very worthy man, and a member of the First Church under Rev. John Wilson. He married Judith, the daughter of Edmund Quincy, ancestor of that family in New England. From her is named that much-dreaded point of Narragansett Bay, where Neptune exacts his tribute from voyagers through the Sound. It is said, moreover, that Hannah Hull, his daughter, received for her wedding portion her weight in pine-tree shillings when she married Judge Sewall, — a statement probably originating in an ingenious computation of the weight of the sum she actually received. "From this marriage," remarks Quincy, "has sprung the eminent family of the Sewalls, which has given three chief justices to Massachusetts and one to Canada, and has been distinguished in every generation by the talents and virtues of its members."

Salem Street was, in 1708, from Mr. Phips's corner in Charter Street to Prince Street ; from thence to Hanover it was Back Street.

Christ Church spire has long dominated over this locality, and served as a landmark for vessels entering the harbor. It is the oldest church in Boston standing on its original ground, having been erected in 1723, — six years before the Old South. Of the fifteen churches built previous to 1750, only a few occupy their original sites ; the others may be found in the new city which has sprung up as if by magic in the old bed of Charles River.

This was the second Episcopal Church erected in the town. It has been in its day considered one of the chief architectural ornaments of the North End. The body of the church has the plain monotonous style peculiar to all the old houses of worship, but the steeple — the design of Charles Bulfinch — beautifies the whole structure. The old steeple was blown down in the great gale of 1804, falling upon an old wooden building at the corner of Tileston Street, through which it crashed, to the consternation of the tenants, who, however, es-

CHRIST CHURCH.

caped injury. In rebuilding, the height was shortened about sixteen feet by Joseph Tucker, the builder. Over the entrance is a plain tablet with the name and date of the house.

CHRIST CHURCH.
1723.

It is generally known that from this steeple — which was visible far and near — warning was given of the intended march to Lexington and Concord. Paul Revere's narrative gives a relation of the method: —

"On Tuesday evening, the 18th of April, 1775, it was observed that a number of soldiers were marching towards Boston Common. About ten o'clock Dr. Warren sent in great haste for me, and begged that I would immediately set off for Lexington, where were Hancock and Adams, and acquaint them of the movement, and that it was thought they were the objects. The Sunday before, by desire of Dr. Warren, I had been to Lexington to see Hancock and Adams, who were at Rev. Mr. Clark's.

"I returned at night, through Charlestown. There I agreed with a Colonel Conant and some other gentlemen that if the British went out by water we would show two lanterns in the North Church steeple, and if by land, one, as a signal; for we were apprehensive it would be difficult to cross Charles River, or get over Boston Neck. I left Dr. Warren, called upon a friend, and desired him to make the signals. I then went home, took my boots and surtout, went to the north part of the town, where I had kept a boat. Two friends rowed me across Charles River, a little to the eastward, where the Somerset lay. It was then young flood; the ship was winding, and the moon was rising. They landed me on the Charlestown side. When I got into town, I met Colonel Conant and several others. They said they had seen our signals."

Within the steeple are hung a chime of bells, placed there in 1744, — the first whose cadences gladdened the town.

"Low at times and loud at times,
And changing like a poet's rhymes,
Rang the beautiful wild chimes."

These bells were from the famous West of England foundry of Abel Rudhall, of Gloucester, whose bells have been heard in many a town and hamlet of "Merrie England." Each had an inscription containing its own and much contemporary history, as follows: —

FIRST BELL.

"This peal of eight bells is the gift of a number of generous persons to Christ Church, in Boston, N. E., Anno 1744. A. R."

SECOND BELL.

"This Church was founded in the year 1723. Timothy Cutler, D. D., the first Rector. A. R. 1723."

THIRD BELL.

"We are the first ring of bells cast for the British Empire in North America. A. R. 1744."

FOURTH BELL.

"God preserve the Church of England. 1744."

FIFTH BELL.

"William Shirley, Esq., Governor of the Massachusetts Bay, in New England. Anno 1744."

SIXTH BELL.

"The subscription for these bells was begun by John Hammock and Robert Temple, Church Wardens, Anno 1743 ; completed by Robert Jenkins and John Gould, Church Wardens, Anno 1744."

SEVENTH BELL.

"Since generosity has opened our mouths, our tongues shall ring aloud its praise. 1744."

EIGHTH BELL.

"Abel Rudhall, of Gloucester, cast us all, Anno 1744."

The chimes or "ring of bells," were obtained in England by Dr. Cutler, and were consecrated there. They were invested with the power to dispel evil spirits, — according to popular belief. The same bells still hang in the belfry. Their carillon, vibrating harmony on the air of a quiet Sabbath, summons the fifth generation for whom they have proclaimed "Glory to God in the highest, and on earth peace, good-will toward men."

The chandeliers used formerly in the church were given by that Captain Gruchy we visited not long since. Mrs. Crocker's relation is, that they were taken from a Spanish vessel by one of Gruchy's privateers, and found their way to a Protestant Church instead of a Catholic Cathedral, as was intended. Dr. Cutler, the first rector, lived on the corner of Tileston and Salem Streets, in close proximity to the church.

The height of tower and steeple is 175 feet, and the aggregate weight of the bells 7,272 pounds ; the smallest weighing 620 pounds, the largest 1,545. General Gage, it is said, witnessed from Christ Church steeple the burning of Charlestown and battle of Bunker Hill.

In this church is the first monument ever erected to the memory of Washington in our country. Dr. Byles, the rector, left Boston in 1775, and went to St. John, New Brunswick, where he was settled as rector and curé of the church of that place. This Dr. Byles was the son of Rev. Mather Byles, the punning parson of Hollis Street. There does not appear to have been a settled pastor after this until 1778.

The interior has been considerably changed by alterations. Formerly there was a centre aisle, now closed, as is also the large altar window. The chancel is decorated with paintings creditably executed by a Boston artist. The walls of the church are of great strength, being two feet and a half thick; the brick are laid in the style of the last century, in what is termed the English Bond, of which but a few specimens remain in Boston.

Like many of the old Boston churches, this has its vaults underneath for the reception of the dead, and with them, of course, its legendary lore. In Shaw it is recorded that

"In 1812, while the workmen were employed building tombs, one of them found the earth so loose that he settled his bar into it the whole length with a single effort. The superintendent directed him to proceed till he found solid earth. About six feet below the bottom of the cellar he found a coffin covered with a coarse linen cloth sized with gum, which, on boiling, became white, and the texture as firm as if it had recently been woven. Within this coffin was another, protected from the air in a similar manner, and the furniture was not in the least injured by time. The flesh was sound, and somewhat resembling that of an Egyptian mummy. The skin, when cut, resembled leather. The sprigs of evergreen, deposited in the coffin, resembled the broad-leaved myrtle; the stem was elastic; the leaves fresh and apparently in a state of vegetation. From the inscription it was found to be the body of a Mr. Thomas, a native of New England, who died in Bermuda. Some of his family were among the founders of Christ Church. His remains, when discovered, had been entombed about eighty years."

Major Pitcairn's remains were interred under this church, and thereby hangs another legend. After being twice wounded, Pitcairn rallied his men for a third assault, and received his death-wound while entering the redoubt, falling into the arms of his own son, who bore him to the boat. He was brought across the river and taken to the house of Mr. Stoddard, boat-builder, near the ferry, where he bled to death in a short time.

Pitcairn was a large, portly man, and so was Lieutenant Shea, whose remains were also deposited under the church. The latter died of fever; and when, some time after the events of the Revolution, the body of Pitcairn was sent for by his relatives in England, it is said that of Lieutenant Shea was forwarded by mistake. The sexton was at a loss to identify the remains, but the presence of a large blistering plaster on the head of the body he sent to England seems to point to a blunder on his part. It has been questioned whether the monument in Westminster Abbey to Pitcairn commemorates his bravery and death on the battle-field, or that of a man who died from inflammation of the brain in his bed.

Pitcairn will always be remembered as the leader of the advance-guard who fired on the provincials at Lexington, and began the great drama of the Revolution. He always maintained that the minute-men fired first, which those present on the American side warmly disputed. This circumstance has associated Pitcairn's name with undeserved obloquy, for he was a brave officer and a kind-hearted man. Of all the British officers in Boston, he alone, it is said, dealt justly and impartially by the townspeople in their disputes with the troops. His men were warmly attached to him, and declared they had lost a father when he fell. Gage sent his own physician to attend him. The bullet which laid the gallant marine low was fired by a negro soldier from Salem. The regiment which he commanded arrived from England in the latter part of December, 1774, in the Asia, Boyne, and Somerset.

Rev. William Montague, rector of Christ Church, was the person to whom Arthur Savage gave the ball which killed Warren at Bunker Hill. The identity of this ball has been disputed by some of the martyr's descendants, on the ground that it was said to have been taken from the body, while Warren received his death from a ball in the head. The controversy was maintained with considerable warmth on both sides, the general opinion favoring the authenticity of the fatal bullet. Arthur Savage was an officer of the customs in Boston, and his statement that he took the piece of lead from Warren's body is worthy of belief. Mr. Montague is said to have been the first American Episcopal clergyman ordained in America who preached in an English pulpit. The English officers billeted in this quarter of the town attended Christ Church.

Tileston Street is the Love Lane of our ancestors, not from the Hymeneal Deity, — else we may believe it would have been the favorite resort of the North End damsels and their love-lorn swains. It was thus named from the Love family, who owned most of the street. Mrs. Susannah Love sold the ground on which the Eliot School was built, and the name of the lane was changed about 1820, for good old Master John Tileston of that school. Master Tileston presided over the school for two thirds of a century, and after he became superannuated his salary was continued ; the only instance of the kind in the history of the town or city. He lived at the westerly corner of Margaret and Prince Streets. Mather Byles is said to have first seen the light in Tileston Street.

The first Grammar School in this part of the town was erected in Bennet Street in 1713, and was called the North Latin School. Recompense Wadsworth was the first master. A writing-school was built on the same lot, on Love Lane, in 1718 ; and in 1741, when an enumeration was made, this school had more pupils than all the others combined. Up to 1800 there were but seven schools in the town, and only nine when Boston became a city. Bennet Street was for some time distinguished as North Latin School Street. The old schools were known later as the North Grammar and North Writing, the subsequent name of Eliot being given to honor the memory of the pastors of the Old North Church. Since the city government went into operation it seems to have passed into a custom to name the schools for the mayors. The old school-house stood by the side of the present one, and was the third in the town. Captain Thomas Hutchinson, father of the too-celebrated lieutenant-governor, built the house and gave it to the town. Three or four edifices have succeeded the original, the present structure having been dedicated on Forefather's Day, 1859. Mather Byles, Edward Everett, and Dr. Jenks are among the distinguished pupils of the school. Edward Everett lived, in 1802, in Proctor's Lane, now the easterly part of Richmond Street, and in 1804 removed to Richmond Street. His mother afterwards removed to Newbury, now Washington Street, to a house nearly opposite the head of Essex Street.

The modern school acquired some notoriety in 1859, from a rebellion of the Catholic pupils against the reading of the Ten Commandments, which caused no little excitement in the old North End. Various attempts have been made from time to time to prohibit the reading of the Scriptures in the public schools, one of which gave rise to the following *mot* of Rufus Choate: "What! banish the Bible from schools! Never, while there is a piece of Plymouth Rock left large enough to make a gun-flint of!"

At Prince Street we reach the old line of division between Salem Street proper and Back Street. The origin of Salem and Lynn Streets are obvious. Back Street was thus distinguished from Fore, through which our readers have followed us in a former chapter. Prince, named from some scion of royalty, has outlived King and Queen. This street was originally from Hanover (Middle) to the sea, but now reaches into North Square, its easterly terminus. The portion between Salem and Hanover was anciently known as Black Horse Lane, from an old tavern on the corner of Back Street. This tavern, corrupted into Black-us-inn, was noted as a place of refuge and concealment for deserters from Burgoyne's army at Cambridge. It was of considerable antiquity, the lane being so called before 1700. The royal regulars had barracks on the corner of Prince and Salem Streets in 1775–76.

Salem Church, at the corner of North Bennet and Salem

Streets, was organized in 1827. Its formation was coeval with the church in Pine Street, and the dedication occurred January 1, 1828, at which time Rev. Justin Edwards, D.D., was installed. On the opposite side of Salem Street was the very curious old house of Major John Bray, whose robbery by the notorious highwayman, Mike Martin, caused a great stir at the time, and for which Martin was hung.

Though we would fain linger in the old North End, other sections claim our attention. In it the spirit of resistance to British tyranny was strongly developed, and it contained less of the tory element than some other quarters of the town. The sturdy mechanics of the North End were ever ready to act in the cause of liberty, no matter what the sacrifice might be. Many of her sons gained a noble reputation in the wars of the republic. There was that old sea-lion, John Manly, who held the first naval commission issued by Washington, in 1775. He took, in the Lee, the dangerous cruising-ground of Boston Bay, and captured, in November, the British ordnance brig Nancy, a prize so important to the Continental army that the camps were wild with joy. Among other pieces taken was a heavy brass mortar, which Old Put mounted with a bottle of rum in his hand, while Mifflin christened it the "Congress." The Lee made other important captures; and in 1776 Manly was given command of the Hancock frigate, in which he captured the Fox, British man-of-war, but was himself taken prisoner by the Rainbow, a much heavier vessel than his own. He commanded afterwards the Jason and Hague, in both of which he gave evidence that he was a worthy comrade of Paul Jones. Manly was a bluff but indiscreet seaman, and for some irregularity was court-martialled. He died in 1793, at his house in Charter Street.

Another naval hero, still more renowned, was Commodore Samuel Tucker of the old Continental navy, who lived in a three-story brick building on the north side of Fleet Street, where now stands a brick stable.

His first cruise was in 1776, with a commission signed by Samuel Adams in his pocket, and a pine-tree flag at his peak, made by the hands of his wife. This intrepid sailor took from the enemy during the war sixty-two sail of vessels, more than six hundred cannon, and three thousand prisoners, and when at length compelled to surrender the old Boston frigate, which he then commanded, to the British squadron at Charleston, he kept his flag flying until Admiral Arbuthnot sent him a special order to lower it. Tucker's reply was, "I do not think much of striking my flag to your present force; but I have struck more of your flags than are now flying in this harbor."

Commodore Tucker carried John Adams to Bordeaux in 1778, "through the six-and-twenty misfortunes of Harlequin." During this voyage the ship was struck by lightning, and the Commodore narrowly escaped death from the fragments of a falling spar. His services, which it is believed were unsurpassed by those of any of his comrades of the old navy, met with tardy requital from the nation. According to his biographer, Mr. Sheppard, he retired in 1793 to a farm in Bristol, Maine. John Adams, in speaking of a visit from Tucker, says, "When I see or hear of or from one of these old Men, whether in civil, political, military, or naval service, my heart feels."

The brave Lieutenant James Sigourney, who commanded the armed schooner Asp, and fell heroically fighting in an engagement with a British flotilla in Chesapeake Bay in 1812, — Captain Samuel Newman, lieutenant in Craft's Artillery in the early part of the Revolution; serving in the navy under Nicholson in the Deane in 1782; killed in St. Clair's battle with the Miami Indians, — Colonel Josiah Snelling, fighting against the Indians and distinguished at Tippecanoe; afterwards at York, Plattsburg, and other fields; finally colonel of the 5th United States infantry, and giving his name to Fort Snelling, — Colonel John Mountfort, brevetted for gallantry at Plattsburg, and distinguished in the Florida war, — Captain Samuel Armstrong, a soldier of 1812, — and Lieutenant Robert Keith, who served under Macomb at Plattsburg; all lived in the North End.

Next north of Christ Church was a large brick building, end to the street, occupied more than seventy years ago as a type and stereotype foundry; a part of the site next the church was afterwards used for an academy. The north corner of Tileston, at its junction with Hanover Street, was the home of Professor Henry J. Ripley, of the Newton Theological Institute.

At the northerly corner of Sheaffe and Salem Streets was the residence of Dr. Samuel Stillman, the well-known pastor of the First Baptist Church from 1765 to his death in 1807. From him Stillman Street takes its name. He preached eloquently in the cause of liberty in his house of worship in the rear of Salem, near Stillman Street. This church, once cowering under the lash of bigotry, seeking to hide itself in an obscure corner of the town, is now translated to that final haven of all the old churches, the Back Bay.

The First Baptist Church, like the Episcopal, had to struggle against the determination of the magistrates, backed by a majority of the people, to permit no other church than their own to obtain a foothold in their midst. A few individuals constituted the church in Charlestown in May, 1665, but were driven by persecution to a private dwelling on Noddle's Island. They erected their church in Boston without exciting the suspicion of the authorities, until its dedication in February, 1679. This act of contumacy was summarily dealt with. The church doors were nailed up, and the following notice posted upon them:—

"All persons are to take notice, that by order of the court, the doors of this house are shut up, and that they are inhibited to hold any meeting, or to open the doors thereof, without license from authority, till the General Court take further order, as they will answer the contrary at their peril.

"Dated at Boston 8th March 1680, Edward Rawson Secretary."

The first house was erected on the banks of the Mill Pond, on the north side of Stillman Street, between Salem and Pond (now Endicott) Streets. This house was replaced by a larger one, also of wood, in 1771, and abandoned in 1829, when the society took possession of the brick building then erected at the corner of Hanover and Union Streets. This was in turn vacated in 1858 for the edifice in Somerset Street.

In Baldwin Place — since become the Home of Little Wanderers — is the house of the Second Baptist Church. This society organized in 1743, and held their first services at the house of James Bownd in Sheaffe Street, near Copp's Hill, removing later to Proctor's School-house, until March, 1746, when they took possession of their new building upon the spot first mentioned. The first house was of wood, and quite small, having near the head of the broad aisle a basin for baptismal purposes. It was superseded, in 1810, by the present brick structure.

In Salem Street was the old printing-office of Zachariah Fowle, — first the master and then the partner of Isaiah Thomas, — in which was printed the old Massachusetts Spy in 1770, until Thomas dissolved his connection with Fowle and opened his office in School Street, near the Latin School. Thomas, whose paper was a high organ of liberty, was ordered to appear once before Governor Hutchinson for a publication reflecting on the executive, but refused to go. He removed his types, press, etc., to Worcester a few days before the battle of Lexington. This was the origin of the Worcester Spy. Later he opened a bookstore at 45 Newbury Street, under the name of Thomas and Andrews, but did not reside in Boston. Oliver Ditson & Co. now occupy the spot.

A few old buildings still remain in Salem, Prince, Charter, and the neighboring streets. Over the apothecary's door, at the corner of Salem and Prince Streets, is an antique head of Æsculapius, or some follower of the curative art, which is the oldest sign now known in the North End. Many years ago it stood at the edge of the sidewalk affixed to a post, but, obstructing the way, it was removed. This is believed to be the oldest apothecary's stand in Boston now used for that purpose. Robert Fennelly was the ancient dispenser of pills and purgatives on this corner.

In the slums of the North End originated the draft riot of 1863. The officers who attempted to serve the notices in Prince Street were cruelly beaten, and the mob, gathering courage from its triumph over a handful of police, reinforced from the purlieus of Endicott, Charlestown, and neighboring streets, made an attempt to seize the cannon kept at the gun-house in Cooper Street, which was held by a little band of regulars from Fort Warren. The rioters had killed and wounded several of the garrison, and had nearly succeeded in demolishing the doors, when the guns were discharged into the mob with fatal effect. After withstanding for a few moments the fusillade from the small arms of the soldiers, the crowd gave way, moving towards Dock Square, where they expected to secure a supply of weapons by breaking open the store of William Reed and other dealers in arms in that vicinity. Eight of the rioters were known to have been killed, but those who fell were removed by their friends, and no authentic data can be given.

CHAPTER VIII.

THE OLD SOUTH AND PROVINCE HOUSE.

Marlborough Street. — Governor Winthrop. — Old South. — Warren's Orations. — Tea-Party Meeting. — British Occupation. — Phillis Wheatley. — Spring Lane. — Heart and Crown. — Boston Evening Post. — Province House. — Samuel Shute. — William Burnet. — William Shirley. — Thomas Pownall. — Francis Bernard. — General Gage. — Lexington Expedition. — Sir William Howe. — Council of War. — Court Dress and Manners. — Governor Strong. — Blue Bell and Indian Queen. — Lieutenant-Governor Cushing. — Josiah Quincy, Jr. — Mayor Quincy.

THAT part of Washington Street lying between School and Summer Streets was, in 1708, named Marlborough Street, from the great duke whom Thackeray irreverently calls Jack Churchill, — the man of Blenheim, Ramillies, Oudenarde, and Malplaquet.

As we stand at the south corner of School Street at its union with Washington, a collection of old buildings faces us extending from the yard of the church nearly to Spring Lane. This, together with the church property, was a part of the estate of one of the greatest men among the early colonists, John Winthrop. It was long thought, with good reason, to have been his first and only place of residence, in Boston, for here bubbled up in its native purity the famous "Governor's Spring," which played so important a part in the settlement of Boston, if, indeed, it did not actually determine it. It is evident, however, that when the frame of Winthrop's house at Cambridge was taken down, and removed hither (probably by rafting it round to what was long known as the "Governor's Dock") it was again set up on the site of the present Exchange Building. His removal to "The Greene" came some years later, and from here the great governor's body was borne to the tomb.

The life of Winthrop is the history of the Colony. It appears in connection with its affairs, or the biographies of his contemporaries. Under his rule church and state were one; and the idea of tolerating any belief but their own was repugnant to the practice, whatever may have been the theory, of the then colonists. Winthrop was one of the first selectmen of Boston, and more than any other moulded its government. The remarkable affair of Anne Hutchinson, in which so many persons of importance were participants, shook to its centre the social and religious fabric Winthrop had assisted to raise, and left him at variance with Sir Henry Vane, next to himself the most considerable man in the infant colony. His rule was iron towards all who professed any but the orthodox faith, until a short time before his death, when, it is said, he refused to sign an order for the banishment of some dissenting person, saying to Dudley that he had done too much of that work already. The Pequot war, begun while Vane was governor, ended under Winthrop. So far as the neighboring Indians were concerned, the governor maintained peace by a firm yet conciliatory policy. The chiefs were entertained at his table, and greatly edified by the governer's domestic economy. Chicataubut refused to eat until his host said grace, and received at his departure a suit of the governor's clothes, in which he strutted home to his wigwam with increased importance.

According to the modern view, the governor did not favor popular government; his opinion being that wisdom resided in the few. As a man he was less inflexible than as a magistrate, for it is related that he reclaimed a thief whom he detected stealing his wood in the following manner. "Friend," said the governor, "it is a very cold season, and I doubt you are poorly provided with wood; you are welcome to supply yourself at my pile till the winter is over." The governor had four wives, and lost not only three of these, but six children. His death occurred on the 26th of March, 1649, at the age of sixty-one. He was entombed in King's Chapel Ground, on the north side. One of his sons became governor of Connecticut, and shares his tomb; a beautiful statue of Winthrop, by Greenough, is in the chapel at Mount Auburn. The governor left a journal of his voyage from England, and of the proceedings in the colony up to his decease, which was edited by James Savage. Some of the admirers of Governor Winthrop's character have declared him worthy of canonization, had we like Rome a sacred calender.

The Old South still stands, one of the monuments of Old Boston. Its existence has been often threatened, and the attempt of the society to sell it, in 1876, aroused the patriotic spirit of Boston as never before since the days of 1861. It is the richest church corporation in the city, and, next to Old Trinity of New York, in the country. The Winthrop estate passed through Thatcher and Mrs. Norton to the church, and in consequence of its central location has become of great value. Its parishioners once dwelt within sight of its steeple, but now few can be found within sound of its bell. Milk Street, Franklin Street, Summer and Winter, Bromfield and School, have not a residence left.

THE OLD SOUTH.

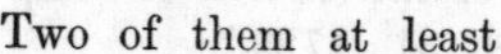

Two of them at least were once filled with the abodes of the most respectable inhabitants of the city, but commerce has said "Move on!" and the the population has vanished before it.

Curiously enough, the Old South, arising from a schism in the First Church, like it originated in Charlestown, where also was organized the First Baptist Society. Like the Baptists, also, this society was proclaimed against, but erected a house of worship, the third in Boston. The theological disputes, questions of doctrine or church government in which this society originated, however interesting, cannot be given here. Thomas Thacher was the first minister, settled in February, 1670. The first house was of wood, and stood until 1729, when it was taken down to give place to the then new brick edifice. In the front was placed, in 1867, a tablet bearing the following inscription, so that all who run may thus read a little of the history of the church: —

> OLD SOUTH.
> CHURCH GATHERED 1669.
> FIRST HOUSE BUILT 1670.
> THIS HOUSE ERECTED, 1729.
> DESECRATED BY BRITISH TROOPS, 1775-6.

This little memorial contains a succinct account of the church even to the last line, "Desecrated by British Troops," which was strenuously objected to by many at the time the tablet was placed there. The occupation of churches by troops has been common in all wars, notably so in the late Rebellion. Such occupation has not been generally considered as calling for a new consecration, and the use of the word "desecrated" is perhaps not fortunate, though the usage of this house was peculiary malicious and repugnant. The name "Old South" goes no further back than the building of the "New South," in Summer Street, in 1717. It was primarily the South Meeting-house, being then considered in the south part of the town. On a stone at the southwest corner of the church is sculptured, "N. E. (Newly Erected) March 31, 1729."

The possession of the South Meeting-house by Sir Edmund Andros has been stated in connection with King's Chapel. From this church, in 1688, was buried Lady Andros, wife of the arbitrary Knight. The governor's house was doubtless in the immediate vicinity of Cotton Hill, as from Judge Sewall's account of the funeral we learn that "the corpse was carried into the hearse drawn by six horses, the soldiers making a guard from the Governor's house down the Prison Lane to the South Meeting House." The tomb of Lady Anne Andros was identified by the care of a relative, who found a slab, with her name inscribed, while repairing her last resting-place.

None of the city churches are so rich in historical associations as this. Here Lovell, Church, Warren, and Hancock delivered their orations on the anniversaries of the Massacre. When Warren delivered his second address in March, 1775, an officer of the Welsh Fusileers, Captain Chapman, held up to his view a number of pistol-bullets, at the same time exclaiming, "Fie! fie!" This was construed to be a cry of fire, and threw the house into confusion until quieted by William Cooper, while Warren dropped a handkerchief over the officer's hand. Many other officers were present with the purpose, as was thought, to overawe the speaker. But Warren was not to be overawed. At the same time the 47th regiment, returning from parade, passed the Old South, when Colonel Nesbit, the commander caused the drums to beat with the view of drowning the orator's voice.

A writer thus describes the events of that day:—

"The day came and the weather was remarkably fine. The Old South Meeting-house was crowded at an early hour. The British officers occupied the aisles, the flight of steps to the pulpit, and several of them were within it. It is not precisely known whether this was accident or design. The orator with the assistance of his friends made his entrance at the window by a ladder. The officers, seeing his coolness and intrepidity, made way for him to advance and address the audience. An awful stillness preceded his exordium. Each man felt the palpitations of his own heart, and saw the pale but determined face of his neighbor. The speaker began his oration in a firm tone of voice, and proceeded with great energy and pathos. Warren and his friends were prepared to chastise contumely, prevent disgrace, and avenge an attempt at assassination."

In the old church Benjamin Franklin was baptized. In the new, was held the famous Tea-Party meeting, adjourned from

Faneuil Hall because the crowd was too great to be contained there. It is believed that Samuel Adams had with others contrived this assemblage to draw off attention from their plans, already matured and waiting only the signal of execution. Certain it is that the Mohawks appeared precisely at the moment when negotiation had failed to prevent the landing of the tea. At this meeting was made the first suggestion to dispose of the tea in the way finally adopted. John Rowe, who lived in Pond Street, now Bedford, said, "Who knows how tea will mingle with salt water?" The idea was received with great laughter and approval. It is from the same Rowe that Rowe Street took its name.

Governor Hutchinson was at this time at his country-seat in Milton, — afterwards occupied by Barney Smith, Esq., — where he received a committee from the meeting, who made a final demand that the cargoes of tea should be sent away. The governor, however, refused to interfere in the matter. It is related that he was afterwards informed that a mob was on its way to visit him, and that he left his house with his face half shaven, making the best of his way across the fields to a place of safety.

During the absence of the committee Josiah Quincy, Jr., made an eloquent speech. When the deputation returned with their unfavorable report, about sunset, the Indian yell was heard at the church door, and the band of disguised Mohawks since so famous in history, filled the street. The meeting broke up in confusion, notwithstanding the efforts of Samuel Adams to detain the people, who rushed forth into the street. The Indians, after their momentary pause, took their way through Milk Street directly to Griffin's, now Liverpool Wharf, opposite the foot of Pearl Street.

The number of the simulated Indians has been variously estimated at from sixteen to eighty. Their disguise was effected in a carpenter's shop, where Joseph Lovering, a boy of twelve, held the candle for the masqueraders. They wore paint and carried hatchets. Under their blankets were concealed many a laced and ruffled coat. "Depend upon it," says John Adams, "they were no ordinary Mohawks."

The women of Boston were not behind the men in their opposition to the tea-duty; many, doubtless, keenly felt the loss of their favorite beverage. The ladies had their meetings, at which they resolved not to use the obnoxious herb. Here is the lament of one matron over her empty urn: —

"Farewell the tea-board, with its gaudy equipage
Of cups and saucers, cream-bucket, sugar-tongs,
The pretty tea-chest, also, lately stored
With Hyson, Congou, and best double fine.
Full many a joyous moment have I sat by ye,
Hearing the girls tattle, the old maids talk scandal,
And the spruce coxcomb laugh at — maybe — nothing.
Though now detestable,
Because I am taught (and I believe it true)
Its use will *fasten slavish chains upon my country*,
To reign Triumphant in America."

The occupation of the Old South by troops was at the instance of General John Burgoyne. It was his regiment, the Queen's Light Dragoons, that set up the riding-school in the House of God, overthrowing its sacred memorials, and transforming it into a circus. These brave troopers never showed their colors outside the fortifications. The pulpit and pews were all removed and burnt, and many hundred loads of gravel carted in and spread upon the floor. The east gallery was reserved for spectators of the feats of horsemanship, while a bar fitted up in the first gallery offered means of refreshment. "The beautiful carved pew of Deacon Hubbard, with the silken hangings, was taken down and carried to ——'s house by an officer and made a hog stye." * The south door was closed, and a leaping-bar placed for the horses. It has been stated that some of the valuable books and manuscripts of Rev. Thomas Prince went for fuel during the winter, as did also the adjoining parsonage house, and the noble sycamore-trees that skirted the grass-plot in front.

After the surrender of Burgoyne his army marched to Cambridge. General Heath, then commanding in Boston, invited Sir John to dine with him, and he appeared in response to the invitation, bringing with him Phillips and Riedesel. After dinner

* Newell's Diary. Thacher's Military Journal.

Burgoyne desired to go out of town by way of Charlestown, and General Heath accompanied him to the ferry. The curiosity to see the prisoners was very great, and the inhabitants crowded the streets, windows, and even the house-tops, to gratify it. As the procession was passing the Province House, General Burgoyne observed to the other generals, "There is the former residence of the governor." Some one in the crowd who heard the remark said, in an audible voice, "And on the other side is the riding-school."

A good anecdote is told of the hero of Portugal and Flanders while the prisoner of Gates. "In the height of jocular conversation Burgoyne told the victor of Saratoga that he was more fit for a midwife than a general. 'Acknowledged,' said Gates, 'for I have delivered you of seven thousand men.'"

While the regulars held possession of the church, an incident occurred which frightened the more superstitious among them, so that it was difficult to maintain a guard, as was the custom, at the church door. Among the troops were a good many Scotch Presbyterians, who were not a little fearful of retributive justice for their abuse of the place. Some one, knowing the Scotch belief in apparitions, appeared to the sentinel as the ghost of Dr. Sewall. The Scot yelled with affright to the guard stationed at the Province House, and was with difficulty pacified.

When D'Estaing's fleet lay in Boston harbor, in September, 1778, the British fleet, of twenty sail, hove in sight. It was discovered and the alarm given by Mr. John Cutler from the steeple of the Old South. Admiral D'Estaing, who was on shore, immediately put off for the squadron, and the militia were ordered to the Castle and the works on Noddle's and George's Island, Dorchester Heights, etc., but the enemy made no attempt. The same fleet afterwards made the descent on New Bedford and Martha's Vineyard.

The old church has been considerably changed in its interior. It was one of the last to retain the square pews, elevated pulpit, and sounding-board. The upper gallery was altered, a new organ obtained, and the brush of modern art applied to the

DARING FEAT OF ISAAC HARRIS: THE OLD SOUTH IN FLAMES.

ceilings; otherwise the house remains much the same as when erected. It had a narrow escape from destruction by fire many years ago, but was saved by superhuman efforts on the part of Isaac Harris, the mast-maker, who ascended to the roof while it was on fire, and succeeded in extinguishing the flames. For this brave act he received a silver pitcher.

One of Dr. Sewall's flock was Phillis Wheatley, a woman of color and a slave. She was a pure African, brought to America in 1761, and yet she possessed genius of a high order. She was, in a great measure, self-taught, never having received any school education, yet wrote admirable verses. Her poems were collected in a thin volume and published in London, and have also been reprinted in this country. One of her effusions, addressed to Washington, may be found in Sparks's "Life of Washington"; it brought an acknowledgment from the general, then at Cambridge, also printed therein. She accompanied the son of her master to London in 1773, where she received great notice from the nobility, but soon returned to Boston, where she contracted an unhappy marriage, and died not long after in utter destitution at her house in Court Street. The genuineness of her poems was attested by Governors Hutchinson, Hancock, Bowdoin, her master Wheatley, and almost every clergyman in Boston. The following extract is from her Hymn to the Evening: —

> "Filled with the praise of Him who gives the light,
> And draws the sable curtains of the night,
> Let placid slumbers soothe each weary mind,
> At morn to wake, more heavenly, more refined;
> So shall the labors of the day begin
> More pure, more guarded from the snares of sin.
> Night's leaden sceptre seals my drowsy eyes;
> Then cease my song, till fair Aurora rise."

The church yard was used as a recruiting station in 1862, and the building itself was leased by the government for a Post-Office, after the Great Fire of 1872 compelled its removal from the Exchange.

If you look closely at the masonry of the Old South you will notice that each course is laid with the side and end of the brick alternating. Joshua Blanchard was the mason. The West Church, Old Brattle Street, Park Street, and some others, were built in the same manner. Gawen Brown, of Boston, made the first clock, esteemed the finest in America. The Prince library was deposited in the tower.

Spring Lane recalls the ancient Spring-gate, the natural fountain at which Winthrop and Johnson stooped to quench their thirst, and from which, no doubt, Anne Hutchinson and her neighbors filled their flagons for domestic use. The gentlewomen may have paused here for friendly chat, if the rigor of the governor's opposition to the schismatic Anne did not forbid. The handmaid of Elder Thomas Oliver, another near neighbor on the opposite corner of the Spring-gate, fetched her pitcher, like another Rebecca, from this well; and grim Richard Brackett, the jailer, may have laid down his halberd to quaff a morning draught.

Water Street is also self-explanatory; it descended the incline to the water at Oliver's Dock. We have described elsewhere the primitive aspect of the region from Congress Street to the harbor. A British barrack was in Water Street at the time of the Massacre.

At the north corner of Washington and Water Streets was the sign of the "Heart and Crown." It was the printing-office of Thomas Fleet in 1731. After his death, crowns being unpopular, the sign was changed to the "Bible and Heart." Fleet sold books, household goods, etc. In 1735 he began the publication of the Boston Evening Post, a successor of the Weekly Rehearsal, begun in 1731. Here is one of the Post's advertisements; it would look somewhat strangely in the columns of its modern namesake:—

"To be sold by the printer of this paper, the very best Negro Woman in this Town, who has had the Small-Pox and the measles; is as hearty as a Horse, as brisk as a Bird, and will work like a Beaver. Aug. 23d. 1742."

Having taken in the surroundings of the church to the north, we may now set our faces southward and visit in fancy the official residence of the royal deputies.

The Province House was one of the last relics of the colony to disappear. It has formed the theme of some pleasant fictions by Hawthorne in "Twice-Told Tales," as well as a brief sketch of the edifice not founded in fancy. The liquid which mine host mixed for the novelist before he set about his researches has a smack of reality about it, and may have enlivened his picturesque description.

This ancient abode of the royal governors was situated nearly opposite the head of Milk Street. The place is now shut out

PROVINCE HOUSE.

from the vision of the passer-by by a row of brick structures standing on Washington Street. Before the erection of any buildings to screen it from view, the Province House stood twenty or thirty paces back from old Marlborough Street, with a handsome grass lawn in front, ornamented by two stately oak-trees, which reared their verdant tops on either side the gate separating the grounds from the highway, and cast a grateful shade over the approach to the mansion. At either end of the fence were porters' lodges, and the visitor passed over a paved walk to the building. Ample stables stood in the rear.

The building itself was a three-story brick structure, surmounted by an octagonal cupola. Over all stood the bronze effigy of an Indian, — the chosen emblem of the colony. This figure, which served the purpose of a vane, was of hammered copper; it had glass eyes, and appeared in the act of fitting an arrow to its bow. It was the handiwork of Deacon Shem Drowne. A flight of near twenty massive red freestone steps conducted to the spacious entrance-hall, worthy the vice-regal dwellers within. A portico supported by wooden pillars was surmounted by a curiously wrought iron balustrade, into which was woven the date of erection and initials of the proprietor, Peter Sargeant: —

16. P. S. 79.

From this balcony the viceroys of the province were accustomed to harangue the people or read proclamations. The royal arms, richly carved and gilt, decorated the front; the bricks were of Holland make. The interior was on a scale of princely magnificence, little corresponding to the general belief in the simplicity of the mode of living of the times. The homes of Faneuil, of Hutchinson, and of Frankland have shown that luxury had effected an entrance into the habitations of the rich. The house of Peter Sargeant was a fit companion to the others cited. On the first floor an ample reception-room, panelled with rich wood and hung with tapestry, opened from the hall. This was the hall of audience of Shute, Burnet, Shirley, Pownall, Bernard, Gage, and, last of all, Sir William Howe.

It is probable that the first of the governors who occupied the Province House was Samuel Shute, an old soldier of Marlborough, who had won distinction from his king on the bloody fields of Flanders. His administration of the affairs of the colony, which he governed from 1716 to 1723, was unfortunate. He came into conflict with the Legislature on questions of prerogative. The governor, almost stripped of his authority, was obliged to seek a remedy at court, and though his powers were confirmed, he did not enjoy the fruits of the decision.

It is perhaps not generally known that a paper currency of small denominations was issued in the colony as early as 1722. Specimens are here reproduced. They were printed on parchment, of the size given in the engravings. No other instance is remembered of the emission of such small sums in paper until we come down to the period of the Revolution. The whole amount authorized was only £ 500, and specimens are very rare. The cuts given here are exact fac-similes of the originals now in the possession of the Antiquarian Society. A very full account of early Massachusetts currency may be found in the Proceedings of that society for 1866, from the pen of Nathaniel Paine, Esq. In the first years of the settlement wampum, brass farthings, and even musket-bullets, supplied a circulating medium.

William Burnet was born in 1688, at the Hague. The Prince of Orange, afterwards King William of England, stood godfather for him at the baptismal font. His father was the celebrated Bishop Burnet, author of the "History of the Reformation in England." The elder Burnet, falling under the displeasure of King James, retired to the Continent, entered the service of the Prince of Orange, and accompanied him to England when William obtained the throne of his father-in-law, the fugitive James. He was rewarded with the bishopric of Salisbury, while the son

received subsequently from the House of Hanover the government of New York, and afterwards that of Massachusetts Colony.

The new governor was received with enthusiasm on his arrival. He was met at the George Tavern, on the Neck, by the lieutenant-governor, members of the Council, and Colonel Dudley's regiment. Under this escort, and followed by a vast concourse of gentlemen on horseback, in coaches and chaises, he proceeded to the Court House, where his commission was read. Shouts of joy and salvos of artillery from the forts and Castle welcomed him to Boston. Mather Byles was ready with a laudatory composition : —

"While rising Shouts a general Joy proclaim,
And ev'ry Tongue, O Burnet ! lisps thy name ;
To view thy face while crowding Armies run,
Whose waving Banners blaze against the Sun,
And deep-mouth'd Cannon, with a thund'ring roar,
Sound thy commission stretch'd from Shore to Shore."

Burnet lived but a short time to stem the tide of opposition to kingly authority, and died September 7, 1729. While he lived he maintained in proper state the dignity of his office. His negro valet, Andrew the Trumpeter, stood at the portal of the Province House, or drove his Excellency abroad in his coach. His *ménage* was under the care of a competent housekeeper. Betty, the black laundress, had the care of twenty pair and one of Holland sheets, with damask napkins, and store of linen to match. A goodly array of plate garnished the sideboard, and ancient weapons graced the walls. Hobby, the

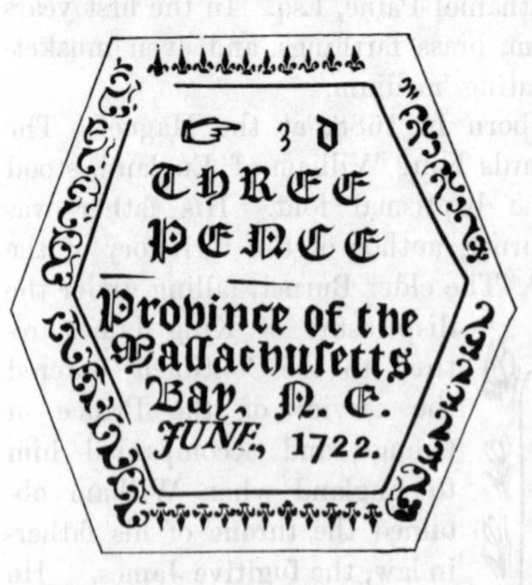

cook, presided over the *cuisine;* and coach, chariot, and chaises stood in the stables. He had a steward and a French tutor.

Notwithstanding the governor directed his funeral to take place in the most private manner, after the form of any Protestant church that might be nearest, the authorities would not have it so, and expended nearly £ 1,100 upon a showy pageant. The governor was a churchman and attended King's Chapel, but showed he had no religious bias in his instructions for his burial. Burnet was probably the first and last governor who died in the Province House.

William Shirley was the admitted chief of the long roll of provincial governors. He lived at one time in King Street, but, after he became governor, built an elegant mansion in Roxbury, afterwards occupied by Governor Eustis, and now, we believe, standing on Eustis Street, metamorphosed by modern improvements. Shirley, no doubt, came to the Province House to transact official business, and at the sitting of the General Court. In the reception-room was, perhaps, matured that celebrated expedition, which resulted in the capture of Louisburg. All the measures relating to the enterprise were conducted with great ability. Profound secrecy was maintained as to its object while under discussion by the General Court; the Governor carried the measure by only a single vote. Volunteers flocked in from all quarters, and the town became a camp. Over two thousand men were raised. Sir William Pepperell, whom an English historian has contemptuously called a "Piscataquay trader," was given the command, and on the 16th of June, 1745, the bulwark of French power in America was in the hands of the provincial forces.

Another measure of Governor Shirley deserves mention. Ten years before the passage of the Stamp Act by the English Parliament, the Legislature of the colony had passed a similar act of their own, laying a tax on vellum, parchment, and public papers for two years; newspapers were included at first, but soon exempted. This shows that it was not the stamp tax to which our ancestors objected, but to its levy without their consent. Specimens are here given from documents of the time to which the stamps were affixed. One of the cuts (the three penny stamp) is engraved from the original die used in the stamp-office. It is a short steel bar attached to the circular part, the impression being made by a blow from a hammer. This interesting souvenir of the times of Shirley was the property of Jeremiah Colburn, Esq., of Boston, a well-known antiquarian.

The expatriation of the unfortunate French from Acadia took place while Shirley was governor, and Massachusetts received about two hundred families. The terrific earthquake of 1755 shook the town to its foundations, and filled the streets with the *débris* of ruined houses, about fifteen hundred sustaining injury. Shirley was a man of letters, and wrote a tragedy, besides the history of the Louisburg expedition. He also held a government in the Bahamas, and was made lieutenant-general. His son, William, was killed at the defeat of Braddock.

Thomas Pownall superseded Governor Shirley, in 1757–58, as governor. He occupied the chair only three years. He made a popular and enlightened chief magistrate, contrasting favorably with the dark, intriguing Lieutenant-Governor Hutchinson. The great and disastrous fire of March 20, 1760, occurred before the departure of the governor to assume the government of South Carolina; also the organization and refitting of the land and naval forces, under General Amherst, for the reduction of Quebec and Montreal.

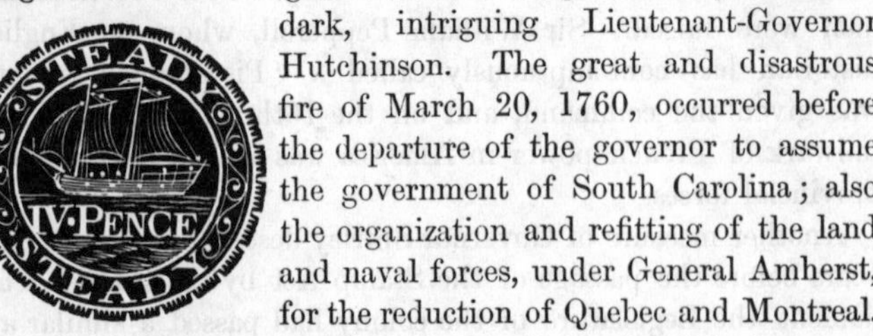

Governor Pownall was a stanch friend of the Colonies, even after hostilities commenced with the mother country. No inmate of the Province House was more respected or more regretted. The governor made an excellent plan or picture of Boston from the Castle in 1757.

Pownall, it is said, was a great ladies' man. He was rather short in stature, and inclined to be corpulent. It was the fashion of that day for a gentleman to salute a lady when introduced to her. The governor was presented to a tall dame whom he requested to stoop to meet the offered courtesy. "No!" says the lady, "I will never stoop to any man, — not even to your Excellency." Pownall sprang upon a chair, exclaiming, "Then I will stoop to you, madam!" and imprinted a loud smack upon the cheek of the haughty one. This, like many good old customs of our forefathers, has fallen into neglect. It was Pownall who induced the Legislature to erect a monument in Westminster Abbey to Lord Howe, who fell at Ticonderoga, and was much esteemed in Boston. Another was ordered to be erected to General Wolfe at the east end of the Town House, but Hutchinson prevented its being carried out.

His successor, Francis Bernard, was received on his arrival from New Jersey with the usual pomp and ceremony, and escorted through the town to his residence at the Province House. During the period of Bernard's administration, from 1760 to 1769, the stormy events which caused the Colonies to throw off the yoke of Great Britain occurred. The Writs of Assistance, the Stamp Act, the introduction of troops, and the removal of the General Court to Cambridge, heaped odium upon his conduct of affairs. Volumes have been written upon the history of those nine years. So Bernard passed out from the shelter of the Province House with none to do him reverence. The king recalled him, and the province spurned him. The last crowned head in this colony was proclaimed by Bernard. He gave a valuable portion of his library to Harvard.

It has been said of Bernard that he was only a facile instrument in the hands of Hutchinson. He was even called Hutchinson's wheelbarrow, carrying the burdens imposed by his wily lieutenant. Bernard's character has been described as arbitrary; he was, however, upright, with correct principles and courteous address. He built him a fine summer residence at Jamaica Plain, afterwards occupied by Martin Brimmer.

After the governor's departure for England, watch and ward was but ill kept at the Province House, or else his Ancient Hutchinson, now his successor, troubled himself but little about the goods and chattels of the baronet. The mansion was broken open, and among other articles stolen were three feather-beds, four pair of blankets, ditto of sheets, all marked with his Excellency's initials. The thief, besides this more bulky booty, stole a crown-piece of James II. and two German rix dollars.

THE COLONY SEAL.

The next inmate of the Province House was Thomas Gage, who was expected to support the kingly prerogative by force of arms. We first found the general in quarters in Brattle Street, and gave there an outline of his career while military governor. He occupied the Province House when appointed to the government in 1774, and the tread and challenge of a British grenadier resounded for the first time in the ancient halls.

Here was held the council between Earl Percy and the governor relative to the expedition to Lexington, so mysteriously noised abroad, and which Gage declared he had imparted the knowledge of to only one other; even Lieutenant-Colonel Smith, who was intrusted with the command, did not know his destination. As Percy was going to his quarters from this interview, he met a number of townspeople conversing near the Common. As he went towards them, one of them remarked, "The British troops have marched, but will miss their aim." "What aim?" asked the Earl. "The cannon at Concord," was the answer. Percy retraced his steps to the Province House, where his chief heard with surprise and mortification the news that the movement was no longer a secret. He declared he had been betrayed.

The following explanation has been given of the manner in which Gage's plans were thwarted. A groom at the Province House dropped into the stables, then opposite the Old South on Milk Street, for a social chat with a stable-boy employed there. The news was asked of the British jockey, who, misconceiving the sentiments of his friend, replied, that he had overheard a conversation between Gage and other officers, and observed, "There will be hell to pay to-morrow." This was immediately carried to Paul Revere, who enjoined silence on his informant, and added, "You are the third person who has brought me the same information."

It was here, too, that the perfidy of Benjamin Church was discovered by Deacon Davis, a visitor to the general. Before this time he had been esteemed an ardent friend of the cause of liberty. His residence was at the south corner of Washington and Avon Streets.

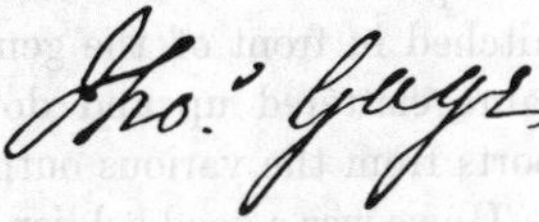

On the morning of the 17th of June, 1775, Gage called his officers together to attend a council of war. Howe, Clinton, Burgoyne, and Grant were present. It was an anxious consultation. Clinton and Grant proposed to land the troops at Charlestown Neck under protection of the ships, and take the American works in reverse. This plan, which would have probably resulted in the capture of the whole provincial force, was disapproved by Gage, who feared to place his men, in case of disaster, between the intrenched Americans and reinforcements from Cambridge. General Gage returned to England in October, 1775. He married an American lady, and a niece of the general by this marriage was the wife of the late General William H. Sumner, of Jamaica Plain. Gage had served at Fontenoy and Culloden, and in Braddock's campaign. He is said to have borne an extraordinary personal resemblance to Samuel Adams, the chief conspirator against his sway, but few can fail to mark in the portrait of the general the absence of that firmness and decision which is so conspicuous in that of the patriot.

Gage's well-known proclamation was thus humorously hit off soon after its appearance : —

"Tom Gage's Proclamation,
Or blustering Denunciation,
(Replete with Defamation,
And speedy Jugulation,
Of the New England Nation),
Who shall his pious ways shun.

"Thus graciously the war I wage,
As witnesseth my hand —
TOM GAGE."

Sir William Howe, as Gage's military successor, took up his quarters at the Province House, and occupied it during the winter of 1775–76. As the siege had now begun, its position was central and well adapted for communication with the works at the Neck, or at Copp's Hill, from which it was about equally distant. The "Governour's House" now presented a busy scene, and so indeed did the neighborhood. The dragoons held possession of the Old South. The orderlies' horses stood hitched in front of the general's quarters, and armed heel and sabre clattered up and down the broad staircase, bringing reports from the various outposts.

Howe was a good soldier, but not an enterprising one. He had fought with Wolfe at Quebec as lieutenant-colonel, receiving the grade of major-general in 1772. During the siege he coolly gave the order to occupy or pull down churches or dwellings as necessity dictated. He has been much execrated for setting fire to Charlestown, but the fire kept up from some of the houses justified the act in a military view. Finally Howe effected the withdrawal of his army without loss from Boston, by making the safety of the town a guaranty of his own. His after career in America was measurably successful; defeating Washington at Long Island and White Plains, he took possession of New York, while the battles of Brandywine and Germantown gave him Philadelphia. He was relieved by his old comrade Sir H. Clinton, and returned home in 1778, when an official inquiry was made into his conduct. Howe's address to his troops before the battle of Bunker Hill is a soldierly document.

"Gentlemen, — I am very happy in having the honor of commanding so fine a body of men; I do not in the least doubt that you will behave like Englishmen, and as becometh good soldiers.

"If the enemy will not come from their intrenchments, we must drive them out, at all events, otherwise the town of Boston will be set on fire by them.

"I shall not desire one of you to go a step further than where I go myself at your head.

"Remember, gentlemen, we have no recourse to any resources if we lose Boston, but to go on board our ships, which will be very disagreeable to us all."

There is every reason to believe Sir William's military duties did not prevent his exercising a generous hospitality. The hall of audience has no doubt resounded with mirth and music when the general received. There were his royalist neighbors, the Mascarenes, Harrison Gray, the Boutineaus and Master Lovell, with many kindred spirits of the court party. There were Clinton, Burgoyne, the noble Percy, and many more of the army and navy to grace the levees of their commander by their presence. The buzz of conversation ceases as Sir William leads out some beautiful tory for the stately minuet, an example speedily followed by his guests. Perhaps amid the strains of the Fusileer's band strikes in the deep diapason of the continental cannon.

The coming of the troops into Boston made formidable innovations in the customs and dress of the old founders. The sad-colored garments and high-crowned hats gave place to velvet coat, ruffles, and cocked hat. Gentlemen of condition wore the small sword in full dress, with a gold-headed cane to set off the lace depending from their sleeves. A gentleman's ball dress was a white coat, trimmed with silver basket buttons, collar and button-holes crossed with silver lace. Or, a coat of blue or scarlet cloth trimmed with gold might serve a gallant of the period. His hair was craped and powdered. A satin embroidered waistcoat reaching below the hips, with small clothes of the same material, gold or silver knee-bands, white silk stockings, and high-heeled morocco shoes, with buckles of some precious metal, completed a truly elegant attire.

The ladies wore a sacque with a long trail petticoat handsomely trimmed. Satin shoes with paste or metal buckle confined delicate feet. The hair was craped and ornamented according to fancy, and profusely sprinkled with white powder. The gown was set off to advantage by two or three tiers of ruffles. Such was court dress, and court etiquette prevailed. The manners were distinguished for stiffness and formality, relaxing a little under the influence of the ballroom. The last queen's ball was held February 22, 1775.

Our reader will care little to know who originally owned the ground whereon stood the Province House. Peter Sargeant built it in the year 1679, and the Provincial Legislature became its purchaser in 1716. After the Revolution it was occupied by the Treasurer and other officers of the Commonwealth. When the building was reconstructed in 1851, old copper coins of the reign of the Georges, and some even of as old date as 1612, were taken from the floors and ceilings, where they had lain *perdu* since dropped by a careless functionary, or perhaps from the breeches pocket of my Lord Howe. Ancient-looking bottles of Holland make were found too, suggestive of Schnapps and Dutch courage. Burnet perchance may have inherited the weakness with his Dutch blood.

After the adoption of the State Constitution it became a "Government House." The easterly half was occupied by the Governor and Council, Secretary of State and Receiver-General. The other half was the dwelling of the Treasurer. The State was inclined to keep up the character of the Province House by making it the governor's official residence, and voted sums of money for the purpose. In 1796 the Commonwealth, being then engaged in building the present State House, sold the Province House to John Peck, but it reverted back to the State in 1799, Peck being unable to fulfil his part of the contract.

Governor Caleb Strong occupied it after his election in 1800. He had been active in promoting the cause of the Revolution, and took part in all the prominent measures of organization of the body politic at its end. He was in the United States Senate in 1789–97. In 1812 he was again elected governor.

Being a strong Federalist, he refused to answer the calls made upon him for troops by the general government, but took measures to protect the State from invasion. The old revolutionary works at South Boston were strengthened and manned, and a new one erected on Noddle's Island in 1814, which bore the governor's name. This conflict between State and Federal authority forms a curious chapter in the political history of the times.

Governor Strong is described as a tall man, of moderate fulness; of rather long visage, dark complexion, and blue eyes. He wore his hair loose combed over his forehead, and slightly powdered. He had nothing of the polish of cities in his demeanor, but a gentle complaisance and kindness.

In 1811 the Massachusetts General Hospital was incorporated and endowed by the State with the Province House. The trustees of the institution leased the estate, in 1817, to David Greenough for ninety-nine years, who, erecting the stores in its front, converted it to the uses of trade. It became a tavern, a hall of negro minstrelsy, and was finally destroyed by fire in October, 1864, to the bare walls.

Some relics of this venerable and historic structure remain. The Indian came into the possession of Henry Greenough, Esq., of Cambridge, and was permitted to remain some time in the hands of the late Dr. J. C. Warren, of Park Street, but at his decease no traces of it could be discovered, much to the regret of its owner. Eventually it came to light, and with the royal arms is in the possession of the Historical Society. Colonel Benjamin Perley Poore became the possessor of much of the cedar wainscot and of the porch. The panelling he made use of for the finish of a pre-Revolutionary suite of rooms, while the porch forms the entrance to his garden at Indian Hill, West Newbury.

The grand staircase down which Hawthorne's ghostly procession descended led to apartments devoted to domestic uses. The massive oaken timbers were memorials of the stanch and solid traits of the builders. Here Shute brooded and fumed; here Burnet wrote and Bernard plotted; and here Gage and Howe planned and schemed in vain. All have passed away.

The Blue Bell and Indian Queen tavern stood on each side of a passage formerly leading from Washington Street to Hawley. Nathaniel Bishop kept it in 1673, which entitles it to be ranked with the old ordinaries. The officers from the Province House and Old South often dropped in to take their cognac neat. The landlady, at this time, a stanch whig, had the repute of an amazon. Some officers one day, exciting her ire by calling for brandy under the name of "Yankee blood," she seized a spit and drove them from her house. Zadock Pomeroy kept the inn in 1800. About 1820 the Washington Coffee House was erected in place of the Indian Queen, but it, too, has vanished. It will be remembered as the starting-place of the old Roxbury Hourlies. The passage-way referred to was about opposite Ordway Place.

Another Indian Queen was in Bromfield's Lane, since Street. Isaac Trask kept it, and after him Nabby, his widow, until 1816. Simeon Boyden was next proprietor; Preston Shepard in 1823, afterwards of the Pearl Street House; and W. Munroe. This was the late Bromfield House, now replaced by a handsome granite block styled the Wesleyan Association Building. It was a great centre for stages while they continued to run. The likeness of an Indian princess gave the name to old and new tavern.

The Bromfield House site becomes important as the birthplace of Thomas Cushing, lieutenant-governor under Hancock and Bowdoin, friend and coworker in the patriot cause with Adams, Otis, and Warren. The British Ministry ascribed great influence to Cushing. He was member both of the Provincial and Continental Congresses, and commissary-general in 1775. Governor Cushing was a member of the Old South. He died in 1788, and was buried in the Granary Burying Ground.

A few paces from the site of the old Indian Queen, in a gambrel-roof house, standing end to the street, was the abode of the gifted Josiah Quincy, Jr., and the birthplace of his son, Josiah, who is best known to Boston as the greatest of her chief magistrates. Uriah Cotting, Charles Bulfinch, and Josiah Quincy are the triumvirate who, by waving their magi-

WASHINGTON STREET, DAY AFTER THE GREAT FIRE: GUARDING THE RUINS.

cian's wand, changed Boston from a straggling provincial town into a metropolis.

Josiah Quincy, Jr., died at the early age of thirty-one, while returning from a voyage to England, undertaken partly for the benefit of his health. He was constitutionally delicate, and his mental strength far exceeded his physical. He was chosen, with John Adams, by Captain Preston, to defend him on his trial for the Massacre in King Street, and did defend him with all his ability, notwithstanding his own father warmly opposed his undertaking it. Mr. Quincy was possessed of high oratorical powers. The phlegmatic John Adams named him the Boston Cicero; his political writings, begun in the Boston Gazette of October, 1767, are full of fire and patriotic fervor. When in England he was, with Franklin, singled out for a brutal allusion by Lord Hillsborough, who declared they "ought to be in Newgate or at Tyburn." His strength proved unequal to the voyage, and he breathed his last within sight of his native land only a few days after the battle of Lexington.

> "Ask ye what thoughts
> Convulsed his soul, when his dear native shores,
> Thronged with the imagery of lost delight,
> Gleamed on his darkening eye, while the hoarse wave
> Uttered his death dirge, and no hand of love
> Might yield its tender trembling ministry?"

Josiah Quincy, Jr. is said to have been the first Boston lawyer who put up a sign-board over his door.

Josiah Quincy succeeded Mr. Phillips as mayor in 1823, over his competitor Otis. We have paid a tribute to his forecast and enterprise already. To him is due the establishment of Houses of Industry and Reformation. Commercial Street completed his transformation of the Town Dock region. Under him the Fire Department was founded in 1827. After a long and useful public service in city, State, and national councils, Mr. Quincy took the presidency of Harvard University in 1829, where he continued in office until 1845.

At the annual festival of the public schools of Boston in Faneuil Hall, August, 1826, and on completion of the granite market-house, Judge Story, being present, volunteered the following sentiment, — "May the fame of our honored mayor prove as durable as the material of which the beautiful market-house is constructed." On which, quick as light, the mayor responded, "That stupendous monument of the wisdom of our forefathers, the Supreme Court of the United States; in the event of a vacancy, may it be raised one story higher." * This pun has also been attributed to Edward Everett.

Benjamin Hichborn, another Revolutionary patriot, next occupied the premises made vacant by the Quincys. He was a graduate of Harvard, and an eminent member of the Suffolk bar. For his zeal in his country's cause he was imprisoned on board a British vessel, the Preston, lying in Boston harbor. Mr. Hichborn was a Jeffersonian Democrat. He was colonel of the Cadets in 1778, and marched at their head into Rhode Island. In the year following he had the misfortune to be connected with an unfortunate accident which caused the death of his friend, Benjamin Andrews. The gentlemen were examining some pistols, Mrs. Andrews being present. One of the weapons, incautiously handled, was discharged, taking effect in Mr. Andrews's head, causing death in a few minutes.

* Quincy's Life.

CHAPTER IX.

FROM THE OLD SOUTH ROUND FORT HILL.

Birthplace of Franklin. — James Boutineau. — Bowdoin Block. — Hawley Street. — Devonshire and Franklin Streets. — Joseph Barrell. — The Tontine. — Boston Library. — Cathedral of the Holy Cross. — Bishop Cheverus. — Federal Street Theatre. — Some Account of Early Theatricals in Boston. — Kean, Finn, Macready, etc. — John Howard Paine. — Federal Street Church. — The Federal Convention. — Madam Scott. — Robert Treat Paine. — Thomas Paine. — Congress Street. — Quaker Church and Burying-Ground. — Sketch of the Society of Friends in Boston. — Merchants' Hall. — Governor Shirley's Funeral. — Fire of 1760. — Pearl Street. — The Ropewalks. — The Grays. — Conflicts between the Rope-Makers and the Regulars. — Pearl Street House. — Spurzheim. — Washington Allston. — Theophilus Parsons. — T. H. Perkins. — Governor Oliver. — Quincy Mansion. — Governor Gore. — Liverpool Wharf. — Tea Party and Incidents of. — The Sconce. — Governor Andros Deposed. — Sun Tavern. — Fort Hill.

WE enter on Milk Street, the ancient Fort Street, conducting from the governor's house to the Sconce, or South Battery, — a route we now propose to follow.

Before we come to Hawley Street we see a granite edifice with "Birthplace of Franklin" standing out in bold relief from the pediment. No new light has been shed upon this interesting question since we left the Blue Ball. It is enough that we honor the philosopher's name in many public places, — no locality may claim him. Apropos of Franklin, when he was at the court of his most Christian Majesty, he soon became the rage, not only of court circles, but of the capital. Presents flowed in upon him, which he, with ready tact, contrived to share with his fellow-commissioners, so as to avoid the appearance of invidious distinction. Among other things, there came to his lodgings a superb gift of fruits, labelled "Le digne Franklin." "This time," said Silas Deane, "you cannot pretend this is not for you alone." "Not so," said Franklin; "the Frenchmen cannot master our American names; it is, plainly, Lee, Deane, Franklin, that is meant."

Arthur Lee, Franklin's fellow-commissioner, composed eight lines of the famous Liberty Song of John Dickinson, which the latter sent James Otis, upon news that the Legislature of Massachusetts refused to rescind the resolve to send a circular letter calling a convention of the sister colonies to oppose taxation without representation. It was printed in the Pennsylvania Chronicle, July 4, 1768, and is the earliest of the Revolutionary lyrics that boldly speaks of independence and union.

FRANKLIN'S BIRTHPLACE.

> "Then join hand in hand, brave Americans all;
> By uniting we stand, by dividing we fall;
> In so righteous a cause let us hope to succeed,
> For Heaven approves of each generous deed.
> Our purses are ready,—
> Steady, friends, steady,—
> Not as slaves, but as freemen, our money we'll give."

The old house here represented is a quaint specimen of the old order of buildings. It was burnt December 29, 1810, shortly after a drawing had been secured. Old Josiah Franklin, the father of Benjamin, was a native of England, and by trade a silk-dyer; he became a respectable soap-boiler and tallow-chandler in Boston. Benjamin was born on the 6th of January, 1706, and is upon the church records as having received baptism the same day. Upon this is founded the claim of the old house to be the place of his nativity. The sign of the statue of Faust, displayed by former occupants of the Birthplace of Franklin, was the same used by Thomas and Andrews in years gone by at the old stand in Newbury Street.

Opposite to us, and just below, is the "Old South Block," built upon the site of the parsonage in 1845. Next below is Sewall Block, which covers the site of the mansion of James Boutineau, a royalist, who departed from Boston in the train of Howe. Boutineau married Peter Faneuil's sister, Susannah, and was, like Faneuil, descended from the French Huguenots. He was a lawyer and managed the case of his son-in-law, Robinson, — the same who assaulted James Otis; his house, a brick mansion, stood a little removed from the street, with the usual flagged walk, shaded by trees, leading up to it.

"Bowdoin Block" has a noteworthy record. It stands at the east corner of Hawley Street, once known as Bishop's Alley, probably from Bishop of the Blue Bell, and also as Boarded Alley, — from its having been boarded over at one time, — a name our readers will see reproduced in a lane leading from Hanover Street to North. On the corner of the alley, Seth Adams once carried on printing; his son was the first post-rider to Hartford, and rode hard to carry the post in four days. In this same Boarded Alley was established the first theatre in Boston, of which more hereafter.

Morton Place was named at the request of Thomas Kilby Jones, whose wife was a Morton, and not for Governor Morton, as has been supposed. It was here Payne, father of John Howard, kept a school, before Morton Place was constructed.

On the site of Bowdoin Block was another old-time mansion, which belonged at one time to James Bowdoin, son of the governor, minister to Madrid in 1808. He was once a merchant in State Street, occupying a row of three stores with John Coffin Jones and Thomas Russell. He was a man of highly cultivated intellectual tastes, but of slender habit. He filled many offices within the State before his appointment to the court of Madrid. James Bowdoin was a munificent patron of Bowdoin College, to which he gave lands, money, and his valuable library and philosophical apparatus collected abroad. His widow, also his cousin, married General Henry Dearborn, and both resided there until their decease. This house was also the birthplace of the Hon. R. C. Winthrop; it became afterwards a hotel called the Mansion House.

Devonshire Street has swallowed up the old Theatre Alley, which conducted by a narrow and by no means straight way to Franklin Street, by the rear of the old Boston Theatre,—hence its name. Besides Pudding Lane, a name borrowed from old London, Devonshire Street, meaning that part lying north of Milk Street, has been known as Jolliffe's Lane. Where the new Post-Office is was once an old inn called the Stackpole House, first the mansion of William Stackpole, and afterwards kept as a tavern by Rouillard of the Julien. It was a large brick building,—end to the street with court-yard in front.

Previous to the year 1792 all the lower part of Franklin Street was a quagmire. No greater change has taken place in Boston than the conversion of this swamp into useful, solid ground. Joseph Barrell, Esq., whose estate was on Summer Street, first drained the slough for a garden, in which he had built a fish-pond, amply stocked with gold-fish. Where the old Boston Theatre stood was a large distillery, and behind it a pasture extending between Summer and Milk Streets as far as Hawley Street.

This Joseph Barrell, whose handsome grounds and mansion became afterwards the property of Benjamin Bussey, was a pioneer in the northwest coast trade, which opened such a magnificent field to American commerce. He with others fitted out the first Boston vessels which doubled Cape Horn. They were the Columbia, Captain Kendrick, and Washington, Captain Gray. The captains exchanged vessels at sea, and the Columbia's was the first keel that passed the bar of the great river, which now bears the name of Captain Gray's vessel, the Columbia.

The improvement was carried out by Charles Bulfinch, William Scollay, and Charles Vaughan. The Legislature refused to incorporate the projectors on the Tontine plan, but the improvement was afterwards carried successfully through, with some modification. A block of sixteen handsome buildings, designed for dwellings, was erected in 1793, and called the "Crescent," or "Tontine." It has been mentioned that this was the first *block* of buildings erected in Boston. The name "Tontine" signified an association for building purposes on the annuity plan, as practised in Europe. A large arch penetrated the block, flanked by buildings on either side, standing a little in advance of the rest; these were ornamented with pilasters and balustrade. The opposite side of the street was called Franklin Place. In the middle of the street was an enclosed grass-plot three hundred feet long, containing a monumental urn to the memory of Franklin, then recently deceased. This central strip, oval in form, has, like the Tontine-Crescent, passed from view; the original conveyance prohibits the erection of buildings upon it.

The rooms over the arch were occupied by the Historical Society and by the Boston Library. This latter was incorporated in 1794, and was designed to be somewhat more popular in its character than either the Athenæum or Historical Society. It grew steadily in public favor, and by the reversion of its shares to the corporation at the death of the shareholder a handsome fund was in time obtained. The Library sold its property, which rested upon no foundation, — the arch excepted, — and removed first to Essex Street, and finally to the building remodelled for them in Boylston Place. These peculiar tenures of houses without land are uncommon in this country, but are said to be quite usual in Scotland, where separate stages or flats of the same building are owned by different proprietors. This arch gave its name to Arch Street.

Looking south across Franklin Street, we see a noble pile with the name of the Rich Buildings on its lofty front. This is, or was, consecrated ground, and supported the weight of the Church of the Holy Cross, until traffic swept it from the street. A brief notice of the origin of the Romish worship in Boston has been given. This church was erected, in 1803, by the efforts of Rev. Father Matignon, who came to Boston in 1792, and of John Cheverus, afterwards Bishop of the diocese, — since of Montauban, France, — who followed him in 1796. The Protestants generously contributed to build an edifice their fathers would not have for a moment tolerated. It was consecrated by Bishop Carroll of Baltimore when completed. The greatly enhanced value of the ground led to its demolition many years ago; a massive and lofty temple has since reared its huge bulk on the Neck, mainly founded on the price of the Franklin Street Cathedral. Beside the church, the Catholics erected a building which was used as a convent of Ursulines. Boston was constituted into a See in 1810 which included all the New England States. A curious parallel might be drawn in the occupation of the house of the French Huguenots, who fled from Catholic persecution, by a congregation of that faith.

Bishop Cheverus, afterwards a Cardinal, was sincerely beloved in Boston by Protestants and Catholics alike. Otis and Quincy were his friends. He took a deep interest in the heated controversy that ensued over the treaty negotiated with Great Britain by Washington, known as Jay's Treaty.

On this question Harrison Gray Otis came before the people of Boston for the first time in a public speech, and the good Bishop was so charmed with the brilliant oratory of the speaker, that he threw his arms around Mr. Otis, and exclaimed, while the tears ran down his face, "Future generations, young man, will rise up and call thee blessed."

The Federal Street was the first regular theatre established in Boston. It was opened February 3, 1794, with the tragedy of Gustavus Vasa. Thomas Paine, the same who afterwards changed his name to Robert Treat, because he wanted a *Christian* name, wrote the prologue, having been adjudged the prize against a number of competitors. Charles Stuart Powell was the first manager. The theatre was also called the Old Drury, after Drury Lane, London. In 1798, while under the management of Barrett and Harper, the house was destroyed by fire, leaving only the brick walls standing. The theatre was soon rebuilt and opened in October, 1798, under the management of Mr. Hodgkinson, with "Wives as they Were." Mr. George L. Barrett conducted the next season, and in the following year, 1800, the celebrated Mrs. Jones appeared. Mr. Dickson was a favorite actor at this house until his retirement from the stage in 1817. In this year the managers were Powell, Dickson, and Duff, and under their auspices Edmund Kean first performed in Boston. He met with a favorable reception, and

BOSTON THEATRE AND FRANKLIN STREET.

departed with a full purse and high opinion of Boston, which he pronounced "the Literary Emporium of the Western World."

In 1825 Kean renewed his visit to America, but the Bostonians, offended at his supercilious conduct on the occasion of his second engagement, when he refused to play to a thin house, would not allow him to utter a word, and he was finally driven from the stage by a shower of projectiles. Henry J. Finn, then one of the managers, vainly endeavored to obtain a hearing for the tragedian, who stood before the audience in the most submissive attitude, while his countenance was a picture of rage and humiliation. A riotous crowd from the outside forced their way into the house and destroyed what they could of the interior. The discomfited Kean sought safety in flight.

Finn was one of the best eccentric comedians Boston has ever known. Besides being an actor, he was a clever miniature painter. He first appeared at the Boston Theatre October 22, 1822, and perished in the ill-fated Lexington lost in Long

Island Sound, January 13, 1840. Finn usually announced his benefits with some witty *morceau* like this:—

> "Like a grate full of coals I burn,
> A great full house to see;
> And if I prove not grateful too,
> A great fool I shall be."

Kean, notwithstanding his *fiasco* in Boston, was possessed of generous impulses, of which many anecdotes are related in illustration. The scene on the night of his retirement from the stage, when he appeared as Othello, at Covent Garden, assisted by his son Charles as Iago, is an ever-memorable event in the annals of the stage. Broken down by emotion and physical infirmity, the actor had to be borne from the theatre by his son to a neighboring house. He survived but a few weeks.

Edmund Kean was noted for the abuse of his powers by indulgence in the social glass. He had a weakness to be thought a classical scholar, and would quote scraps of Latin commonplaces. One evening, while deep in a nocturnal orgie, his secretary, R. Phillips, tired of waiting for him, sent a servant to report the situation at two in the morning.

Phillips. What's Mr. Kean doing now?
Waiter. Making a speech about Shakespeare.
Phillips. He's getting drunk, you had better order the carriage.
(Half past two.)
Phillips. What's he at now?
Waiter. He's talking Latin, sir.
Phillips. Then he *is* drunk. I must get him away.

Mrs. Susanna Rowson, the gifted authoress of "Charlotte Temple," appeared at the Federal Street Theatre in September, 1796. In March of the year following her play of "Americans in England" was brought out at this house, and received with great favor. Mrs. Rowson soon sought a more congenial employment, opening in the early part of 1797 a school for young ladies in Federal Street with a single pupil. Her facile pen was equally ready in prose or verse, the latter covering a wide range from deep pathos to stirring martial odes.

Mrs. Rowson's remarkable force of character enabled her to

rise superior to the deep-seated prejudice against novel-writers and actresses, — she was both, — and to command not only the respect, but the patronage at last of many who would have looked upon an association with her at one time as contaminating.

Macready made his first appearance before a Boston audience at this theatre in the character of Virginius; and Boston was also his place of refuge after the lamentable Astor Place Riot, in New York. John Howard Payne also acted here. About 1833 the house was closed as a theatre, and leased to the society of Free Inquirers. In 1834 the "Academy of Music," an institution for the culture of vocal and instrumental music, obtained possession. Mr. Lowell Mason conducted the Academy, and the name of the theatre was now changed to the "Odeon." Religious services were held on Sundays by Rev. William M. Rogers's society until the building of their church on Winter Street. The stage was again cleared for theatrical performances in 1846–47, under a lease to Mr. C. R. Thorne. Lafayette visited the Boston Theatre on the last evening of his stay in 1824. An entire new front was erected on Federal Street in 1826, and an elegant saloon added with many interior improvements. About 1852 the theatre property was sold. The present business structure is erected on its site at the northeast corner of Franklin and Federal Streets.

Charles Bulfinch was the architect of the Boston Theatre. It was built of brick, was one hundred and forty feet long, sixty-one feet wide, and forty feet high. An arcade projected from the front, serving as a carriage entrance. The house had the appearance of two stories; both the upper and lower were arched, with square windows, those of the second stage being the most lofty. Corinthian pilasters and columns decorated front and rear. Several independent outlets afforded ready egress. The main entrance was in front, where, alighting under cover from their carriages, the company passed through an open saloon to two staircases leading to corridors at the back of the boxes. The pit and gallery were entered from the sides.

The interior was circular in form, the ceiling being composed of elliptic arches resting on Corinthian columns. There were two rows of boxes, the second suspended by invisible means. The stage was flanked by two columns, and across the opening were thrown a cornice and balustrade; over this were painted the arms of the United States and of Massachusetts, blended with histrionic emblems. From the arms depended the motto, "All the World's a Stage." The walls were painted azure, and the columns, front of the boxes, etc., straw and lilac color; the balustrades, mouldings, etc., were gilt, and the second tier of boxes were hung with crimson silk. There was also a beautiful and spacious ballroom at the east end, handsomely decorated, with small retiring-rooms. A *cuisine*, well furnished, was beneath. Such was the first play-house Boston ever had.

Cast on the opening night of the Boston Theatre: —

NEW THEATRE
Will open on Monday next, February 3d,
With the truly Republican Tragedy,
GUSTAVUS VASA,
THE DELIVERER OF HIS COUNTRY.
All the characters (being the first time they were ever performed by the present company) will be personated by Messrs. Baker, Jones, Collins, Nelson, Bartlett, Powell, S. Powell, and Kenny; Miss Harrison, Mrs. Jones, Mrs. Baker, and the Child by Miss Cornelia Powell, being her first appearance on any Stage. To which will be added
an Entertainment called
MODERN ANTIQUES;
or,
THE MERRY MOURNERS.
Mr. and Mrs. Cockletop by Mr. Jones and Miss Baker. The other characters by Messrs. S. Powell, Collins, Nelson, Baker, etc., Mrs. Jones, Mrs. Baker, and Mrs. Collins.

The history of the Boston stage is instructive, as showing the gradual development of a change of feeling in regard to the establishment of theatres. The earliest attempt at such exhibitions was a performance at the British Coffee House of Otway's Orphan, in 1750, followed by a law forbidding them under severe penalties. The British officers had their theatre, in 1775, in Faneuil Hall, where they produced the "Blockade of Boston," by General Burgoyne, "Zara," and other pieces.

In 1792 a company of comedians from London, chief among whom was Charles Powell, fitted up a stable in Board Alley (Hawley Street) into a theatre. Governor Hancock was highly incensed at this infraction of the laws, and made it the subject of special comment in his message to the Legislature. The representations were conducted under the name of "Moral Lectures," but were brought to a summary conclusion by the appearance of Sheriff Allen on the stage, who arrested one of the performers as he stood in the guise of the Crooked Back Tyrant. The audience sympathized with the actors, and amid great excitement, in which Hancock's portrait was torn from the stage-box and trampled under foot, the play ingloriously ended. The law, however, was repealed, before the year was out, mainly through the efforts of John Gardiner, while Samuel Adams and H. G. Otis opposed its abrogation. Mr. Otis, however, defended the captured knight of the buskin, and procured his discharge on technical grounds.

Bill at the opening in Board Alley:—

NEW EXHIBITION ROOM.

BOARD ALLEY.

FEATS OF ACTIVITY.

This Evening, the 10th of August, will be exhibited Dancing on the Tight Rope by Monsieurs Placide and Martin. Mons. Placide will dance a Hornpipe on a Tight Rope, play the Violin in various attitudes, and jump over a cane backwards and forwards.

INTRODUCTORY ADDRESS,

By Mr. Harper.

SINGING,

By Mr. Wools.

Various feats of tumbling by Mons. Placide and Martin, who will make somersetts backwards over a table, chair, &c.

Mons. Martin will exhibit several feats on the Slack Rope.

In the course of the Evening's Entertainments will be delivered

THE GALLERY OF PORTRAITS,

or,

THE WORLD AS IT GOES,

By Mr. Harper.

The whole to conclude with a Dancing Ballet called The Bird Catcher, with the Minuet de la Cour and the Gavot.

John Howard Payne, whose memory is immortalized by "Home, Sweet Home," lived in a little old wooden building at the corner of Channing, formerly Berry and Sister Streets. His father, at one time, kept a school in his dwelling, which he styled the Berry Street Academy. Howard showed an early inclination for theatricals, and was the leader of an amateur company composed of his young companions. He was also possessed of a martial spirit, and organized a band of juvenile soldiers of his own age, with whom he paraded the streets, armed with muskets borrowed of Wallach, the Essex Street Jew. On one occasion, when drawn up on the Common, they were invited into the line and passed in review by General Elliott. The company was called the Federal Band, and their uniform, blue and white, was copied from the Boston Light Infantry. Payne was sent to Union College, Schenectady, through the generosity of a noble-minded New-Yorker. His father's death occurring while he was at college, he resolved to try the stage, and made his first appearance at the Park Theatre in February, 1809, as Young Norval. He astonished everybody, and went the round of American theatres with great success. He went to England in 1813, suffering a brief imprisonment at Liverpool as an American alien. After a time he went to Paris, and devoted himself to adapting successful French plays for the London stage. He witnessed the return of Bonaparte from Elba, and the scenes of the "Hundred Days." His future life was one of trial, vicissitude, and unrequited effort. The plays of "Therese," and "Clari, the Maid of Milan," are from his pen. "Home, Sweet Home," was first sung by Miss Tree, sister of Mrs. Charles Kean, and procured her a wealthy husband, and filled the treasury of Covent Garden. Payne afterwards received an appointment from our government as consul at Tunis. He died in 1852. Who knows that "Sweet Home" was not the plaint of his own heart, sighing for the scenes of his youth?

> "An exile from home, pleasure dazzles in vain,
> Ah, give me my lowly thatched cottage again;
> The birds singing sweetly that came to my call, —
> Give me them, and that peace of mind dearer than all."

Another abandoned church-site is near. The Old Presbyterian Meeting-house stood on the north corner of Federal and Berry Streets. The latter has changed its name to Channing, as it did its ancient orthography, Bury into Berry. The founders of this church were Irish Presbyterians, and their first house of worship was a barn, which sufficed until they were able, in 1744, to build a neat wooden edifice. Governor Hancock presented the bell and vane which had belonged to the Old Brattle Street Meeting-house. The old house was a pattern of many that may still be seen in our older New England villages.

OLD FEDERAL STREET CHURCH.

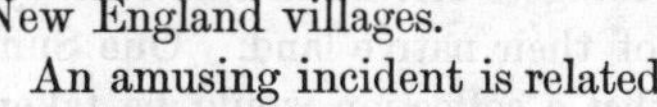

An amusing incident is related of the vane, — Hancock's gift. Colonel Erving, meeting Rev. John Moorhead, directed his attention to the fact that the vane did not move, but remained fixed in its position. "Ay, I must see to it," said the honest parson, who ran immediately to the mechanic who placed the vane on the steeple. A fatiguing climb to the top revealed that the fault was in the wind, which had remained due east for a fortnight.

Mr. Moorhead, the first pastor, was ordained in Ireland, and was installed in Boston in 1730, a hundred years after the settlement. This was also the church of Jeremy Belknap, and of Dr. W. E. Channing, for whom the neighboring street is named.

It was to this church the Convention adjourned from the Old State House, when it met to consider the adoption of the Federal Constitution, January 9, 1788.

> "The 'Vention did in Boston meet,
> But State House could not hold 'em ;
> So then they went to Federal Street,
> And there the truth was told 'em."

Jeremy Belknap was then pastor of the church. John Hancock was president of the Convention, and George R. Minot vice-president. To the efforts of Hancock is largely due the adoption of the instrument. The joy of the people at the ratification was unbounded, and a monster procession celebrated the event, in which the mechanics of Boston, who had taken a lively interest in the proceedings, bore a prominent part. The naval hero, John Foster Williams, then living in Leverett's Lane (Congress Street), lent his aid after the following manner: —

"John Foster Williams, in a ship,
Joined in the social band, sir;
And made the lasses dance and skip
To see him sail on land, sir!"

In 1809 the Federal Street society erected a new and elegant house, designed by Charles Bulfinch. It was, when built, the only specimen of pure Saxon-Gothic architecture in Boston.

In 1834 a number of Polish refugees arrived in this country, after the final dismemberment of their native land. One Sunday Dr. Channing announced that a collection would be taken up for the benefit of these exiles. The call was nobly responded to; among others, Henry Purkett, a member of the Tea Party, and one of the sterling patriots of Revolutionary times, sent his check couched in these words: —

"Pay to Count Pulaski, my commander at the battle of Brandywine, his brethren, or bearer, one hundred dollars."

Anciently Federal Street was known as Long Lane, but from the adoption of the Federal Constitution was known by its present name. What was true of the lower part of Franklin Street is equally so of Federal. There was once a sufficient depth of water near the meeting-house we have just described for smelts to be taken. Shaw cites Dr. Channing as saying he had taken these fish at the corner of Federal and Milk Streets, and another authority as having seen three feet of water in Federal Street.

At the upper end of Federal Street, next the corner of Milton Place, lived Madam Scott, the widow of Governor Hancock. She married Captain James Scott in 1796. He had been long employed by the governor as master of a London packet, and again, after the peace, sailed as master of the Neptune, the first ship of a regular line of London packets. Madam Scott outlived her husband many years, retaining her faculties unimpaired until near the close of her life. She died in 1830, over eighty. She was the daughter of Judge Edmund Quincy, of Braintree, and long celebrated for her wit and beauty.

Dorothy Quincy was at Lexington with her affianced husband (Hancock) when the battle of Lexington occurred, and looked out upon the fearful scenes of that morning. She knew Earl Percy well, and related that she had often heard him drilling his troops of a morning on the Common. Lafayette was a favorite with her, having been entertained by her in 1781. When the Marquis revisited Boston, in 1824, his first call was upon Madam Scott. They regarded each other intently for a few moments without speaking, each contemplating the ravages time and care had made in the features of the other.

As Lafayette rode into town, receiving the private and heartfelt homage of every individual of the immense throng that greeted him, he perceived his ancient hostess of more than forty years before, seated at a balcony on Tremont Street. The General directed his carriage to stop before the house, and, rising to his feet, with his hand upon his heart, made her a graceful salutation, which was as heartily returned. This little episode was loudly applauded by the spectators of the interesting meeting.

The mansion of Robert Treat Paine, the eminent lawyer, judge, and signer of our Magna Charta, was at the west corner of Milk and Federal Streets. The house, a brick one, fronted on Milk Street, and appeared in its latter days guiltless of paint. It was a large, two-story, gambrel-roof structure, with gardens extending back some distance on Federal Street. In the yard was a large jack with a turn-spit, according to the culinary fashion of those days. In this house Judge Paine died May 11, 1814. A Bostonian by birth, pupil and usher of the Latin School, he was a delegate to the Provincial Congress of 1774, which chose him a member of the Continental Congress; he was the first attorney-general of Massachusetts, and member of the State Constitutional Convention; and also judge of the Supreme Court of the State. Judge Paine conducted the prosecution of Captain Preston. He was an able and witty writer; as a man, beloved by his fellow-citizens who honored him with so many high public trusts. He was entertaining in conversation, but subject in his later years to fits of abstraction from which he would rouse himself with a pleasant smile and jest.

The younger Robert Treat Paine was one of those brilliant geniuses which occasionally illuminate a community in which wit combined with sentiment commands a high value. He had a decided *penchant* for the theatre, and married an actress, — Miss Baker. He was first called Thomas, but, strongly disliking the appellation of the great infidel Thomas Paine, he appealed to the Legislature to give him a "Christian" name. He had been a patron of the little theatre in Board Alley, and assisted with his pen at the inauguration of the Boston Theatre. His father, as we know, lived hard by, and young Thomas was scarcely of age when he wrote the successful composition. The greatest of his political lyrics, "Adams and Liberty," was written at the request of the Massachusetts Charitable Fire Society. As first composed, all mention of Washington was — inadvertently, no doubt — omitted. Major Ben Russell, in whose house Paine happened to be, interfered when the poet was about to help himself from the sideboard, humorously insisting that he should not quench his thirst until he had in an additional stanza repaired the oversight. Paine thoughtfully paced the room a few moments, suddenly asked for a pen, and wrote the grand lines: —

"Should the tempest of war overshadow our land,
Its bolts could ne'er rend Freedom's temple asunder;
For unmoved at its portal would Washington stand,
And repulse with his breast the assaults of the thunder.
His sword from the sleep
Of its scabbard would leap,
And conduct with its point every flash to the deep;

For ne'er shall the sons of Columbia be slaves,
While the earth bears a plant, or the sea rolls its waves."

The younger Paine died in 1811, three years before his father. Part of the garden lying on Federal Street became the site of the Fourth Baptist Church. Church and dwelling long ago joined the shadowy procession of vanished landmarks. Father and son were both buried from the family mansion.

Before the occupancy by Judge Paine, this house, it is said, had been the abode of Colonel John Erving, Jr., a merchant of high standing, and colonel of the Boston Regiment. His father, the old Colonel John Erving, was an eminent merchant before him, and lived in Tremont Row. The younger Erving was son in-law of Governor Shirley, and at his death the governor's funeral took place from the house of his relative, Monday, April 1, 1771. A long procession followed the remains to King's Chapel, beneath which they were deposited. The Ancient and Honorable Artillery Company, commanded by Captain Heath; the officers of the Boston Regiment, in full regimentals with the usual mourning of black crape, attended. On the coffin were placed the two swords of the deceased, crossed. The pall was supported by Governor Hutchinson, Lieutenant-Governor Oliver, two judges of the Superior Court, and two of the Honorable Council. Dr. Caner preached the funeral sermon, after which the body was interred, the military firing three volleys, and a detachment of the Train of Artillery as many rounds as the deceased had lived years, namely, sixty-five. The governor will be remembered as a patron of King's Chapel, and it was doubtless his expressed wish to be buried there.

In that part of Congress Street lying north of Water Street were the old Quaker Church and Burying Ground. The latter was situated opposite Exchange Place,* and was the fourth in the town in antiquity, having been established in 1709. The Friends built a brick meeting-house on that part of their lot subsequently occupied by the Transcript, and later by J. E. Farwell & Co. The house was nearly destroyed in the great fire of 1760, but was repaired the same year. Though once numerous, only eleven

* Formerly Lindall Street.

of the sect remained in Boston in 1744; their worship in this house ceased about 1808, and in 1827 the property was sold. The remains were exhumed by the Friends and taken to Lynn, where they again received burial. No interments were made in this cemetery later than about 1815. From time to time the relics of the Quakers have been thrown to the surface by the excavations on and near this site. At a later period the Friends erected a small stone house in Milton Place, Federal Street, still existing in 1872; but in 1848 it was conjectured there was not a single Quaker in Boston; in 1855 none were resident here, — the society, like the French Church, had become extinct. The house in Milton Place was once protected by a fence, and shaded by handsome trees, — all gone, and on the spot a brick warehouse stands to-day.

The Quakers have the distinction of having built the first brick meeting-house in Boston; it was in Brattle Street, and dates back to 1692. This was disused in 1708, and the society removed to Congress Street. The sect seems to have flourished under persecution, dying out when it had ceased. The Quakers suffered every species of cruelty in establishing their faith in Boston. Scourging and imprisonment were the mild means of prevention first employed; banishment and the loss of an ear were subsequently decreed, — at least three persons lost this useful member by the hands of the public executioner about 1658. Even under this severity the Quakers continued to increase and flourish. Selling them into slavery was tried and failed, and the death penalty was applied as a last resort. Four of the persecuted sect were hanged, and but for the fear of intervention by the crown the Puritans would have cut them off root and branch. This occurred in 1660, rather more than two centuries ago. It must be remarked, however, that some of the eccentricities of the early Quakers would not be tolerated even now except among barbarians.

Congress Street has been mentioned as the headquarters of the Anthology Club, the first purely literary society we have an account of since the Revolution.

In Revolutionary times clubs were quite numerous in Boston,

and formed the nuclei around which the patriots gathered. One of the earliest of these was the Whig Club, of which James Otis, Dr. Church, Dr. Warren, Dr. Young, Richard Derby of Salem, Benjamin Kent, Nathaniel Barber, William Mackay, Colonel Bigelow of Worcester, and a few others were members. They corresponded with Wilkes, Colonel Barré, Saville, and other leaders of the opposition in Parliament. Civil Rights and the British Constitution were the standing subjects of discussion.

In 1777–78 there was another club, composed of young men fresh from college, among whom were Rufus King, Christopher Gore, William Eustis, Royal Tyler, Thomas Dawes, Aaron Dexter, etc. They met in Colonel Trumbull's rooms at the corner of Court and Brattle Streets, and discussed politics, literature, and war.

The building on the northeast corner of Water and Congress Streets was formerly called Merchants' Hall, and in it were kept the United States Post-Office, and Merchants' Exchange in 1829. The new edifice occupied for the former is therefore the second location upon the same street. The Post-Office occupied the lower floor. Aaron Hill was the postmaster, with eight clerks, and one penny-postman. Topliff's Reading Room shared the lower apartment with the Post-Office, and contained all mercantile intelligence useful to merchants "where they most do congregate."

Upon this same spot once stood an old gambrel-roofed house with diamond-paned windows, a patriarch among its fellows. On the front was a bull's head and horns, from which the house was known as the Bull's Head. Over opposite was Horn Lane, since Bath Street. This was the habitation of George Robert Twelves Hewes, a member of the Tea Party. His father was a glue-maker, soap-boiler, tanner, tallow-chandler, and perhaps filled up his leisure with other employments. Young Hewes was baptized at the Old South, and had a considerable share in the tumults worked up by the Boston mechanics. He lived to be ninety-eight years old, retaining a clear intellect until near the end of his long life-journey.

Robert Hewes's elder brother, Shubael Hewes, was Butcher-

Master-General in the town while Howe held possession, and at one time during the siege six head of cattle was the entire stock in his hands for troops or inhabitants. His butcher-shop was at the south corner of Washington Street and Harvard Place, opposite the Old South, in an old building with a projecting upper story. A slaughter-house was connected with the establishment. People of wealth and position were glad to obtain the rejected portions of the slaughtered animals during the investment of the town.

JULIEN HOUSE.

The old Julien House must ever remain an object of interest to all gastronomers. It was called "Julien's Restorator," and was the first establishment noticed with this distinctive title; all the rest were taverns or boarding-houses. It was M. Julien who first introduced that agreeable *potage* which bears his name. He came to this country with the celebrated Dubuque, who was a refugee from the French Revolution. Dubuque occupied for a time the Shirley mansion in Roxbury. The old house with its gables, overhanging upper stories, and huge chimney was taken down in 1824, and succeeded by Julien, afterwards Congress, Hall. Its site was once a tanyard. After M. Julien's death in 1805 his widow succeeded him, keeping the house for ten years. It is supposed to have been built about 1760.

That part of Congress Street lying south of Milk was formerly Green Lane, and in 1732 was named Atkinson Street, from an old family whose lands it passed through. The ancient proprietors of the soil, who gave their lands to make our highways, did not stipulate that the original names should remain unchanged, like the far-seeing Chief Justice Sewall. One instance is mentioned of an individual who had lived on eight different streets within fifty years, but had never moved from his original dwelling. Hence the maps of Boston at various periods bear but little resemblance to each other; and he who visits only occasionally distant localities finds himself lost. The happy expedient was hit upon of renewing some of the old names in the new part of the city, and we have Newbury and Marlborough, where they may well baffle some future inquirer. In Green's Barracks in Atkinson Street were quartered part of the 14th Royal Regiment at the time of the Massacre.

As we are now in the route of the Tea Party, we will continue with it through Pearl Street. Before taking leave of Milk Street, however, we must remark that it had some other residents not unknown to fame. Below us is Oliver Street, named for that family. The quarters of General Howe were in a house at the corner of Oliver and Milk Streets. To him, probably, was confided the immediate charge of the troops and works in and around Fort Hill.

In Milk Street was the residence of Thomas Flucker, Secretary of the Province under Hutchinson, whose name is seen appended to the official papers of that interesting period.

Flucker's daughter, Lucy, married General Knox. We have seen her sharing the privations of camp life with her husband wherever his duty called him. She was a lovely and highly accomplished woman, contributing greatly to the little female circle around the American headquarters. Through this marriage Knox became possessed of a large estate at Thomaston, Me., named for General John Thomas.

Admiral Graves, of the fleet, seems to have preferred snug quarters ashore to the cabin of the flagship, for he took up his residence at the southeast corner of Pearl and High Streets, where he might have ready access to his shipping. The admiral, it will be remembered, was exempted, with Gage, from pardon by the Provincial Congress.

The great fire of March 20, 1760, which began at the Brazen Head, in Cornhill, consumed every house on the north side of Milk Street, from Congress Street to the water, and on the opposite side it swept all before it — the dwelling of Secretary Oliver and a few tenements excepted — to Fort Hill. The Battery, or Sconce, took fire and blew up, notwithstanding a large part of the powder was thrown into the harbor, Governor Hutchinson personally assisting in this labor. All the region now known as Liberty Square was burnt over, — shops, warehouses, and the shipyard that has been noted; so that from Devonshire Street to the water's edge, from Milk Street to the north side of State Street, scarcely a house remained standing.

Oliver Street was very badly paved with cobble-stones some time before the Revolution, as far as the Wendell and Oliver Houses, beyond which there was no pavement. High, and all the neighboring Streets, were unpaved, as late as 1808. At this time there was a brick sidewalk on the north side of Pearl Street, but none on the other, and some gentlemen caused a plank walk to be laid from High Street up the hill to their residences at the top. The old Revolutionary fort was levelled and converted into a mall since 1797, the ground lying around it remaining in possession of the town until after 1800.

Kilby Street, noticed at its outlet into State, was named for Christopher Kilby, an eminent Boston merchant, on account of his liberality to the sufferers by the great fire of 1760, when the street was newly laid out and widened. Mr. Charles W. Tuttle says a descendant of Christopher Kilby married the seventh Duke of Argyle, grandfather of the Marquis of Lorne, since married to the Princess Louise of England. Kilby resided in Queen Street.

On the map of 1722 no street is laid down where the present Pearl Street is, but a number of ropewalks extend in its general direction from Cow Lane (High Street) towards Milk. In 1732 the alley along the ropewalks obtained the name of Hutchinson Street, changed in 1800 to Pearl. In 1771 there was but a single house on the east side, — that of Charles Paxton, Esq., an elegant three-story brick, some little distance from Milk Street. Paxton was one of the revenue commissioners, and was not forgotten by the mob which called at Secretary Oliver's. He had, however, made his escape with his valuables, and the owner of the house saved his property by proposing to broach a barrel of punch at the tavern near by. The mob accepted the alternative. Paxton was also a mandamus councillor, and proscribed by the Provincial Congress, with Jonathan Sewall and Benjamin Hallowell.

The west side of the street was occupied in its entire length, at the date mentioned, by seven ropewalks; these were all burnt in 1794, and the street became dotted with the residences of the wealthy and refined.

The first rope-maker in Boston was John Harrison, whose "rope-field" was on Purchase Street, at the foot of Summer; the former street now occupies the ground. From this circumstance arises the name Purchase, part of the way having been thus secured. Harrison first exercised this calling here in 1642, and in 1663 appealed to the selectmen not to license a rival artisan in the town. Isaac P Davis, whose middle name is the capital letter only, was the last rope-maker in Boston.

The Grays were the most celebrated rope-makers of Boston. Edward, the senior, first served an apprenticeship with Barton, at Barton's Point, now West Boston. In 1712 he began making ropes on the Pearl Street tract, purchased of Theodore Atkinson. He was the father of Harrison Gray, treasurer of the province, and of John, who succeeded to the ropewalks, seven hundred and forty-four feet long, warehouse, dwelling, and outhouses, — a snug patrimony.

"In that building long and low,
With its windows all a-row,
Like the port-holes of a hulk,

Human spiders spin and spin,
Backward down their threads so thin,
Dropping each a hempen bulk."

Harrison Gray, treasurer of the colony, and grandfather of Harrison Gray Otis, was proscribed, and had his estates confiscated after his flight from Boston. It is stated, in Sabine's Loyalists, that in August, 1775, inquiry was made in the House of Representatives concerning the horse and chaise, formerly Harrison Gray's, which was used by the late Dr. (General) Warren, and came into the hands of the committee of supplies after Dr. Warren's death. The horse and chaise appears to have been traced to Dr. William Eustis, afterwards governor, as he was directed the next day to deliver it to the committee named. Mr. Gray went first to Halifax, thence to London, where his house was the resort of the Boston refugees. Of him it was written :—

"What Puritan could ever pray
In godlier tones than Treasurer Gray ;
Or at town-meetings, speechifying,
Could utter more melodious whine,
And shut his eyes and vent his moan,
Like owl afflicted in the sun !"

At these ropewalks began the conflicts between the soldiers and rope-makers, which culminated in the 5th of March affair. Among the soldiers were a good many mechanics, who were often employed as journeymen. One of these inquired of a negro workman at Mr. Gray's if his master wished to hire a man. The negro answered that "his master wished to have his vault emptied, and that was a proper work for a *Lobster*." For this insolent remark the soldier gave the negro a severe beating. Mr. Gray came up, parted them, and endeavored to persuade the soldier to return to his barracks, but the latter cursed him, and offered for sixpence to serve him as he had done the negro. Mr. Gray took him at his word, and after a sound thrashing, the soldier rushed off to his barracks at Wheelwright's, now Foster's Wharf, swearing vengeance. But, in the language of Pope, —

"What direful contests rise from trivial things !"

The soldier returned in half an hour with nearly seventy of his comrades of the 14th, armed with pipe-staves which they had obtained at a cooper's shop. They made a furious attack upon the ropewalk men, who stood firm, and finally repulsed their assailants, pursuing them over the hill. The soldiers, reinforced to the number of about three hundred, headed by their sergeant-major, returned with redoubled fury to the conflict, but the rope-makers had been joined by the brawny shipwrights, mast and block makers, from Hallowell's shipyard at the foot of Milk Street, armed with their beetles, wedges, and marlinspikes. The soldiers pulled down the fence in High Street enclosing the field, since Quincy Place, and the ropewalk men levelled that on Pearl Street. A terrific *mêlée* ensued, but the athletic mechanics of Fort Hill were too much for the soldiery, who were again worsted. This occurred on the 3d of March, 1770; the massacre in King Street took place on the 5th.

The northwest corner of Pearl Street is the site of the Pearl Street House, opened in 1836 by Colonel Shepard, formerly of the Indian Queen in Bromfield Street. The house stood until the Great Fire of 1872. It was the first erected on the south side of the street, after the ropewalks, and was built by Mr. Gorham for a residence.

On the opposite corner resided Mr. John Prince, a gentleman of tory proclivities, who, however, did not join the royalist hegira of 1776. His estate, which had a court-yard and gardens, was altered by him in about 1812, when he built a block of five buildings, the centre house twice as large as the others, for his own residence. It had a roof with a pediment raised above the others, giving the whole block somewhat the appearance of a public edifice. After residing there for a few years, he removed to a beautiful residence at Jamaica Plain, and this Pearl Street mansion became the boarding-house of Mrs. Le Kain.

In this house John Gaspard Spurzheim, the gifted Prussian phrenologist, resided during his visit to Boston, and here, also, he died, in the same year of his arrival in this country. He lies buried at Mount Auburn, his tomb being a conspicuous object in that famed cemetery.

Attached to the estate of Mr. Prince was a large barn. This was Washington Allston's studio after his return to Boston, and until his removal to Cambridgeport, in consequence of the conversion of the barn into a livery-stable. Here his large picture of Belshazzar's Feast, now in the Museum of Fine Arts, was rolled up and laid aside, although he worked at it at this time.

Allston was the antipodes of Stuart. He was refined, gentle, and unassuming; a charming companion, and a great favorite in society. Besides being a painter, he wrote verses, and a volume of his poems was published. Coleridge said he was unsurpassed by any man of his age in poetical and artistic genius. For many years after Allston left Rome every American was questioned by the native artists for news of the American Titian; it was generally conceded that for two hundred years no artist's coloring had so closely resembled that of the great master.

His Dead Man won the first prize of two hundred guineas from the British Institution, and the artist could have disposed of it for a large sum on the spot, but he preferred to sell it for less than its value to the Pennsylvania Academy, through Messrs. McMurtie and Sully. Allston employed his leisure hours at Harvard in drawing figures and landscapes. The pictures of Pine, in the Columbian Museum, Boston, were his first masters in coloring; but, most of all, he admired a head of Cardinal Bentivoglio, by Smibert, in the College library, while a student. This was a copy from Vandyke, and seemed perfection to the young artist until he saw works of greater merit.

Allston continued to paint industriously and successfully until his death, which occurred at Cambridge, July 9, 1843. He had painted all day, and during the evening conversed with unusual cheerfulness. His wife left the room for a few moments, and when she returned he was dying. Allston was liberally patronized, and no American painter of his day received such prices. His first wife was a sister of William Ellery Channing; a sister of Richard H. Dana was the Mrs. Allston who survived him. De Tocqueville went to Cambridgeport on purpose to see the artist; and the first inquiry of Lord Morpeth, when he landed in Boston, was, "Where does Allston live?" A number of his pictures are preserved in the Museum of Fine Arts, including several unfinished works. The late S. F. B. Morse was a pupil of Allston.

The house next beyond that of Mr. Prince was that in which Theophilus Parsons, LL. D., lived after his removal to Boston in 1800, and in which he died. Judge Parsons, as chief of the Massachusetts Bench, as one of the framers of the State Constitution, or as a zealous advocate for the adoption of the Federal Constitution, ranks high in the estimation of his countrymen.

An instance of Judge Parsons's address is given in connection with the convention in Federal Street. One of the delegates, Rev. Mr. Perley, of Maine, refused to vote for an instrument which did not acknowledge the Supreme Being. The lawyer undertook to argue him out of his position. "I suppose," said Mr. Parsons, "that in the course of your ministerial labors you have preached from texts in every book of the Old Testament." "Yes," said Mr. Perley, "I probably have." "You have preached from texts in the Book of Esther?" "Doubtless I have," said Mr. Perley. "Do you know that in the Book of Esther," said Mr. Parsons, "there is not a single allusion to the Supreme Being?" "It is not possible," said Mr. Perley. "Look!" said Mr. Parsons. The search was made. "You are right," said Mr. Perley, and the clergyman confessed his scruples removed.

Theophilus Parsons, the younger, is best known by excellent works on commercial law, and for other labors in the literary field. He studied law with Judge Prescott, father of the historian, and son of the Colonel Prescott of Bunker Hill.

Next the house of Judge Parsons was that of Paxton, or Palmer. This house was divided, and became the residence of James Lovell, the naval officer, and of Thomas Handasyd Perkins, so well remembered for his munificent contribution in aid of a blind asylum. Between this mansion and the Quincy estate a field intervened.

Colonel Perkins was one of the most eminent of Boston merchants, and, with his brother James, engaged largely in the

China and Java trade. Amassing great wealth, both brothers contributed freely to benevolent or literary objects. The attention of Colonel T. H. Perkins was probably first drawn to the blind by the partial loss of his own sight. The Quincy Railway, and the Washington and Bunker Hill Monuments were each objects of his interest and efforts. He laid the corner-stone of the Merchants' Exchange in State Street, and liberally aided the Mercantile Library. He was, in common with some of his neighbors, an ardent opponent of the war policy of Mr. Madison.

When Colonel Perkins was in Paris, during a period of apprehended revolution, Lafayette confided his son, George Washington, to his care, and the latter lived for some time in his family in Boston.

Immediately behind the mansion of Mr. Perkins was the residence of Andrew Oliver, lieutenant-governor under Hutchinson's *régime*, distributor of stamps, etc. The house stood near Oliver Street, though it did not appear to have fronted upon it. Its condition was so dilapidated in 1808 as to afford little idea of its former appearance. It was in good repair after the Revolution, and occupied by families of respectability.

Mr. Oliver was visited by the mob who overthrew the stamp-office at the dock, not far distant. Governor Bernard recites in his proclamation that the secretary's house was entered with force and violence, his furniture damaged, windows broken, and fences pulled down, to the great terror of his Majesty's liege subjects. The secretary, apprehensive of a second visit from his fellow-citizens, thought it prudent to resign his office forthwith. Mr. Hutchinson was present at Oliver's house when the mob attacked it; he used his endeavors to suppress the riot with force, but neither the sheriff nor the colonel of the Boston Regiment thought proper to interfere. Peter Oliver, brother of Andrew, was chief justice in 1771, adhered to the royal cause, and left Boston with the king's troops.

Secretary Oliver died in Boston in 1774. He was one of the most affluent of the Old Bostonians, and had a private establishment rivalling that of any in the province. Coaches, chariot, negro slaves, and good sterling plate in abundance attested his wealth. He was a generous patron of Smibert, who painted all the family portraits, including one in which the secretary and his two brothers were represented. Andrew Oliver wished to stand well with his countrymen, and at the same time enjoy the emoluments of an officer of the crown. He soon found the two were incompatible, and passed from the stage soon after the events occurred that have given notoriety to his name. On the opposite side of Oliver Street was the residence of Judge Oliver Wendell. It fronted towards the east, with grounds adjoining.

Until 1872 Quincy Block marked the site of an old estate, which extended to High Street. Here Mr. Quincy passed the earlier years of his married life, until elected to Congress in 1805, when the mansion was occupied by Christopher Gore. It is described by Miss Quincy as

"A handsome edifice of three stories, the front ornamented with Corinthian pilasters; and pillars of the same order supported a porch, from which three flights of red sandstone steps, and a broad walk of the same material, descended to Pearl Street. Honeysuckles were twined around the porch, and high damask rose-bushes grew beneath the windows; at the corner of Pearl and High Streets stood the stable and coach-house. The grounds ascending towards Oliver Street were formed into a glacis, and were adorned with four English elms of full size and beauty, the resort of numerous birds, especially of the oriole, or golden robin."

Christopher Gore was a Bostonian by birth, and an eminent lawyer. It was in his office that Daniel Webster read law, and by his advice that the latter continued steadfast in the profession when beguiled by some offer of place which might have terminated his great career. Mr. Gore was the first district attorney appointed by Washington over the Massachusetts district; he was also a commissioner under Jay's treaty, and a United States senator. In 1809 he was elected governor of Massachusetts. This was the period of the embargo of Mr. Jefferson, and of the stirring scenes preceding the war of 1812. The temper of the Bostonians was decidedly adverse to the measure; the mercantile class, whose interests were most nearly affected, were bitter in their comments upon the administration. Colonel Boyd, commanding at Fort Independence, received orders to fire upon any vessel attempting to violate the embargo, upon which the colors on the shipping were placed at half-mast. The Wasp, afterwards conqueror of the Frolic, lay in the stream watching the idle vessels, and threats were freely made to burn her.

William Sullivan says, Governor Gore was tall, a little inclined to corpulency in middle age, and erect, but began to bend at an earlier age than common. He became bald at an unusually early period. His hair was tied behind and dressed with powder. His face was round and florid, his eyes black; his manners courteous and amiable. Gore Hall, at Harvard, commemorates a magnificent bequest to the University in his will.

On the site of the Athenæum once stood the block of that name; we wish the custom prevailed more generally of thus distinguishing localities. In the hall of the Athenæum the disciples of Baron Swedenborg held their worship; the society had existed in Boston since 1818, receiving legislative sanction in 1823. It has been mentioned that the Athenæum owed their building to the munificence of James Perkins. Quincy Place and Perkins Street were visible memorials of two distinguished families. The Place is now Hartford Street.

High Street has ceased to be high, and, to keep pace with the custom of the times, should receive a more appropriate title. Of yore it mounted the height to the esplanade of Fort Hill; now it has sunk to a monotonous level. Sister Street rejoices in the name as well as the smell of Leather, while Williams Street, named for John Foster Williams, is metamorphosed into Matthews. Pearl Street is the acknowledged shoe and leather mart of the country, and has furnished the State with at least one chief magistrate. The Hutchinsons, Atkinsons, Grays, Perkinses, Quincys, Parsonses, Gridleys, and the rest, have shed a lustre round the ancient hillside, though granite now usurps the terraced gardens, and drays instead of chariots stand at the doors.

The building on the corner of High and Pearl Streets

marks the site of a mammoth structure erected for a private residence, and known as Harris's Folly. Extensive gardens reached up the hill, quite to the enclosure at the top. In 1809 all the land was open to the mall on the summit of the hill. The northwest corner of Pearl and High was for a time the location of the Congress House, altered from a private residence into a hotel.

Proceed we onward to Purchase Street, anciently Belcher's Lane, the birthplace of Thomas Dawes, afterwards a judge of the Supreme Court of the State, and of the Municipal Court of Boston; and of Samuel Adams, the great central figure of the patriot junta. The elder Thomas Dawes was the architect of Brattle Street Church. He was a high patriot, and the caucuses were sometimes held in his garret, where they smoked tobacco, drank flip, and discussed the state of the country. Dawes was also adjutant of the Boston Regiment. The tories gave him the nickname of "Jonathan Smoothing-plane."

A short descent brings us to Liverpool Wharf. Where now Atlantic Avenue winds around the margin of the water, the old footpath under the hill was known as Flounder Lane; Sea Street was its continuation to Windmill Point. Beyond this point the Sea Street of later times was built straight into the harbor, enclosing the South Cove; it is now known as Atlantic Avenue in its entire length, it having been extended round the entire deep-water front of the city.

Liverpool Wharf, then Griffin's, was the destination of the Tea Party of December 16, 1773. It was a cold wintry afternoon, when

> "Just as glorious Sol was setting,
> On the wharf a numerous crew,
> Sons of freedom, fear forgetting,
> Suddenly appeared in view."

The three Indiamen, with their high poops and ornamented sterns, were lying quietly moored at the wharf. They had been for some time under guard of a committee of twenty-five from the grenadier company of the Boston Regiment, of which Henry Knox was one. The hatches were closed, and this vigilance committee took care no attempt was made to land the cargo. The names of the three ships were the Dartmouth, Captain James Hall, The Eleanor, Captain James Bruce, and brig Beaver, Captain Hezekiah Coffin.

The number of persons disguised as Indians was not more than seventeen, but the accessions from the Old South, and of apprentice lads and idlers, swelled the number to more than a hundred; as many as sixty went on board the ships. Each ship had a detachment allotted to it under a recognized leader; Lendall Pitts was one of these chiefs. Everything was orderly, systematic, and doubtless previously concerted. The leaders demanded of those in charge of the ships the keys to the hatches, candles, and matches, which were produced. The Dartmouth was first visited and relieved of her cargo of one hundred and fourteen chests. As the chests were passed on deck, they were smashed, and nervous arms plunged them into the dock. The contents of three hundred and forty-two chests mingled with the waters of the bay, and the work was done.

It was low tide when the ships were boarded, and the apprentice boys, who formed the larger number of those engaged in the affair, jumped upon the flats, and assisted in breaking up and trampling into the mud such of the chests as had escaped the hatchets of those on board the vessels. The tide beginning to flow, the whole mass was soon adrift.

We give the names of the actors in this conversion of Boston harbor into a teapot, as far as known: Dr. Thomas Young, Paul Revere, Thomas Melvill, Henry Purkett, Captain Henry Prentiss, Samuel Gore, George R. T. Hewes, Joseph Shed, John Crane, Josiah Wheeler, Thomas Urann, Adam Colson, Thomas Chase, S. Cooledge, Joseph Payson, James Brewer, Thomas Bolter, Edward Proctor, Samuel Sloper, Thomas Gerrish, Nathaniel Green, Edward C. How, Ebenezer Stevens, Nicholas Campbell, John Russell, Thomas Porter, William Hurdley, Benjamin Rice, Nathaniel Frothingham, Moses Grant, Peter Slater, James Starr, Abraham Tower, Isaac Simpson, Joseph Eayres, Joseph Lee, William Molineux, John Spurr,

Thomas Moore, S. Howard, Matthew Loring, Thomas Spear, Daniel Ingollson, Jonathan Hunnewell, John Hooten, Richard Hunnewell, William Pierce, William Russell, T. Gammell, Mr. McIntosh, Mr. Wyeth, Edward Dolbier, Mr. Martin, Samuel Peck, Lendall Pitts, Samuel Sprague, Benjamin Clarke, John Prince, Richard Hunnewell, Jr., David Kinnison, John Truman, Henry Bass, Joseph Mountfort, William Hurd, Joseph Palmer, Joseph Coolidge, Obadiah Curtis, James Swan, Mr. Kingson, and Isaac Pitman.*

There are authorities who give Dr. Warren as a member of the Mohawk Band. Many incidents are related of this event. It is said that on their return from the wharf the band passed a house where Admiral Montague of the fleet happened to be, and that he raised the window and cried out, "Well, boys, you've had a fine pleasant evening for your Indian caper, have n't you? But mind you have got to pay the fiddler yet!" "O, never mind!" shouted Pitts, the leader; "never mind, Squire! just come out here, if you please, and we 'll settle the bill in two minutes." The populace raised a shout, the fifer struck up a lively air, and the admiral shut the window in a hurry. A powerful fleet lay in the roads; the troops were at the Castle, yet not a move was made to arrest the work of destruction.

Thomas Melvill, in after times a distinguished citizen of Boston, was of the party. On his return home his wife collected a little of the tea from his shoes, which was put into a bottle with a memorandum written on parchment, and kept as a precious relic in the family. Many came to see the famous herb, until at last it was found necessary to seal it, to preserve it from vandal hands. This bottle of tea came into possession of Lemuel Shaw of this city, son of the late Judge Shaw.

John Crane, another of the party, while busily employed in the hold of one of the ships, was knocked down by a chest of tea, falling from the deck upon him. He was taken up for dead, and concealed in a neighboring carpenter's shop under a pile of shavings. After the party had finished they returned, and found Crane living.

* Some of these names are from Lossing's Field-Book.

Several persons who were detected in the act of secreting the fragrant plant were roughly handled.

"One Captain O'Connor," says Hewes, "whom I well knew, came on board for this purpose, and when he supposed he was not noticed, filled his pockets, and also the lining of his coat. But I had detected him, and gave information to the captain of what he was doing. We were ordered to take him into custody, and just as he was stepping from the vessel, I seized him by the skirt of his coat, and in attempting to pull him back, I tore it off; but springing forward by a rapid effort, he made his escape. He had, however, to run the gantlet of the crowd upon the wharf; each one as he passed giving him a kick or a stroke. The next day we nailed the skirt of his coat, which I had pulled off, to the whipping-post in Charlestown, the place of his residence, with a label upon it."

Griffin's Wharf, as well as Wheelwright's, had a number of large warehouses, in which had been quartered the detachment of the 59th, and the train of artillery which landed in October, 1768. A fire caught in one of the stores used as a laboratory in March, 1760, and an explosion occurred, injuring several men and terrifying the neighborhood.

Rowe's Wharf coincides with the old Southern Battery or Sconce, an outwork of Fort Hill, and terminus in this direction of the famous Barricado. As early as 1632 a fort was begun on the eminence then called Corn Hill, but soon changed to the Fort-field, and finally to Fort Hill. The Bostonians were aided by their brethren from Charlestown, Roxbury, and Dorchester; two years after, it was declared in a state of defence.

The Sconce was probably not built until some time after the main work, perhaps at the time of the Dutch war. It was constructed of whole timber, with earth and stone between, and was considered very strong. In time of peace it was in charge of a gunner only, but had its company assigned to it in case of danger. In 1705 it was commanded by Captain Timothy Clark, who was ordered to furnish an account of the ordnance, ammunition, etc., "meete to bee offered hys Grace the Duke of Marlborough Great Master of her Majestye's Ordnance." In 1743 the battery mounted thirty-five guns; at this time no work appears on the summit of the hill. In 1774 Jeremiah

Green was captain with the rank of major. The British continued to hold it with a garrison, and had a laboratory there. Colonel Pomeroy's regiment, the 64th, occupied the hill in November, 1768; the Welsh Fusileers, who had won a splendid name for valor at Minden, were posted there in 1774, and in 1775 the works contained four hundred men. After the evacuation the works were found greatly damaged, but were occupied and strengthened by the Americans. Du Portail, chief engineer of the American army, came to Boston in October, 1778, to make a survey of the works, when this with others was strengthened and put in the best posture of defence. Subsequently, in 1779, when Washington was fortifying the passes of the Hudson on a great scale, the heavy guns were removed from all the works here and sent forward to the army against which Clinton was then advancing.

The battery and fort acquire a celebrity as the theatre of the seizure and deposition of Governor Andros. In April, 1689, the news of the landing of the Prince of Orange at Torbay reached Boston, and threw the town into a ferment. The governor, Randolph, and some others sought the security of the fort; the drums beat to arms, and the inhabitants ran from all quarters to the Town House, where they joined their respective companies. The captain of a frigate which lay before the town was seized on shore, and held as a hostage. Approaching the hill by the rear, the train-bands divided, a part going around by the water to the battery. A few soldiers in this work retreated up the hill to the main body, and the townsmen turned the guns upon them. Andros cursed and fumed, but was forced to yield himself a prisoner, with his companions. Some were imprisoned in the old jail; his Excellency was placed under guard at Mr. Usher's house. The frigate still showed fight, and lay with her ports triced up, and her men at quarters; but after the people had got possession of all the fortifications and pointed the guns at her, the captain was compelled to send down his topmasts, unbend his sails, and send them ashore. The keys of the Castle were next extorted from Andros, and the bloodless revolution was ended. It is said Sir Edmund was handcuffed as he was conducted from the fort; we may well believe he was not allowed to pass through the ranks of the townsmen without some reminders of his fallen state.

Probably Old Boston never knew a day of greater rejoicing than that which brought the news of Burgoyne's surrender. The rumor of the falling back of the American army to Stillwater had been received with deep forebodings for the future, speedily dissipated by the glad tidings of the greatest victory of the war. A thundering salute was fired from Fort Hill and Dorchester Neck. Hope animated every heart anew, and joy was visible in every countenance.

From the Sconce, the lane leading up the hill to the fort was named Sconce Lane, since Hamilton Street, and the walk along the beach the Batterymarch, which has absorbed the street.

A specimen of the small arms in use at the time of the settlement is in the Historical Society's possession. The guns were without locks, match or fuse being used at the rate of two fathoms for every pound of powder and twenty bullets; pikes were still in use for foot-soldiers.

> "Where are those old and feudal clans,
> Their pikes and bills and partisans;
> Their hauberks, jerkins, buffs?
> A battle was a battle then,
> A breathing piece of work; but men
> Fight now with powder puffs."

The building lately occupied by a Glass Company at the corner of Hamilton Street was the residence of Benjamin Hallowell, grandfather of the admiral. It became afterwards a noted inn, known as the "Sun," and kept by Goodrich in 1822.

This old Sun Tavern was demolished many years ago. It was the third or fourth of that name in Boston. One of the same name was in Dock Square in 1724, kept by Samuel Mears; another was in Cornhill in 1755, kept by Captain James Day: we may suppose the conjunction of names did not escape the wits of the day. The sign of the Sun in Batterymarch Street has been compared in shape to a gravestone, with its circular top. There the likeness ended; for underneath the rays of a gilded sun was the legend, —

"The best Ale and Porter
Under the Sun."

By a curious transition the sign was afterwards erected in Moon Street, where it became the proper symbol of Mrs. Milk, whose mixtures were perhaps not as mild as the name indicated. Few of her customers escaped a *coup de soleil*; her neighbors were Waters, Beer, and Legg. Sun Court, near by, reflected the name of the greater luminary.

At the east corner of Milk Street and Liberty Square was the Commercial Coffee House, built on the site of Hallowell's shipyard. It was kept by William Meriam from 1817 until about 1830, and was a house of considerable resort for shipmasters. In 1838 John Low was landlord, and later Colonel Whitney. Its place is now occupied by Thorndike's granite building. Here was in 1798 the principal shipyard in the town, from which was launched the ship Genet fully rigged, and named in honor of the then French minister to this country.

Siste Viator. We were about to invite the reader to ascend Fort Hill. The waters of the harbor have swallowed the eminence, and it is as completely obliterated as if an earthquake had engulfed it. The base indeed is left, but it requires a strong imagination to picture an elevation eighty feet above us, bearing on its top the elegant mansions of a past generation, with the tops of noble elms waving in the cool sea-breezes. Yet this was the peculiar spot to which residents were invited fifty years ago, with the assurance that the green park on its top would afford a perpetual place of recreation.

The streets which struggled up the sides of the hill were once peopled with a highly respectable class, but Broad Street and the outlying works were soon carried by Irish, and the citadel was yielded to them. From the hill radiated the wharves, like the fingers of the hand; the eastern slope was peopled by ship artisans and mechanics pertaining to that craft. The summit of the hill was levelled so as to form a plateau, in the centre of which was the grass-plat encircled with an iron fence and studded with trees. On the south side was built the Boylston

School and gun-house of the Washington Artillery; the space enclosed by the buildings on the other sides was called Washington Place. The school received its name in honor of Thomas and Ward Nicholas Boylston, liberal benefactors of Boston and the neighboring University. A windmill was erected on the hill in the year 1701.

The Washington Artillery Company, on one of its annual visits to East Boston for target-practice, gave a sample of their gunnery by knocking over a cow with a twelve-pounder shot. The owner received the price demanded for the slaughtered animal. The company, with a keen eye to business, had the cow dressed and sold at a considerable advance on the price paid the owner.

The land from the hill-top no doubt furnished the material for filling up the docks east of Kilby and Batterymarch Streets. The old fort had disappeared long before the Revolution, and it was not until then that the hill was again fortified. In 1869 the levelling of the hill was ordered, and fully completed within three years. Then came the Great Fire of 1872 to transform the region we have been traversing into a heap of blackened rubbish, with the rectification of some street lines, the widening of others, and the inconsiderate changing of street names, consequent upon the rebuilding, still further to confuse the nomenclature already sufficiently perplexing in all conscience.

CHAPTER X.

A TOUR ROUND THE COMMON.

Long Acre. — Tremont House. — Mr. Clay. — President Jackson. — Charles Dickens. — Little House-lot. — Tremont Theatre. — The Cadets. — Adino Paddock. — Paddock's Mall. — Granary Burying-Ground. — The Granary. — Almshouse. — Workhouse. — Bridewell. — Park Street Church. — Manufactory House. — Linen-Spinning Introduced. — Elisha Brown. — Massachusetts Bank. — Incident of the Lexington Expedition. — The Common. — Its Origin. — The Great Mall. — Fences. — Winter Street. — Governor Bernard. — John McLean. — Samuel Adams. — St. Paul's. — Masonic Temple. — Margaret Fuller. — Washington Gardens. — The Haymarket. — West Street. — The Gun-House. — Colonnade Row. — Massachusetts Medical College. — Haymarket Theatre. — Boylston Street. — John Quincy Adams. — General Moreau. — Charles Francis Adams.

UPON the pavement of Tremont Street once more, we renew our wanderings in the vicinity of the Old Granary Burying-Ground. Common Street was the first distinctive appellation received by that part of Tremont from School Street to Boylston, or, to copy the language of the record, "from Melyne's corner, near Colonel Townsend's, passing through the Common, along by Mr. Sheef's into Frog Lane." It did not become Tremont Street until 1829. The name of Long Acre was given to that part of the street between School and Winter by Adino Paddock, of whom something anon. It came from that part of London in which the great plague originated, and which was noted for its mughouses. In London Long Acre is the scene of Matt Prior's amours, when, after an evening with Swift, Oxford, Bolingbroke, and Pope, he would go and smoke a pipe and drink a bottle of beer with a common soldier. This name of Paddock's was generally accepted, though we do not learn that it ever had any official sanction.

The Tremont House, so long a marked feature of this locality, is no more. The corner-stone was laid on the 4th of July, 1828, and it was opened to the public October 16, 1829. Isaiah

Rogers was the architect. It was thought to be, and was at this time, a model of luxury and elegance. It had seen some notable guests. Henry Clay, or, more familiarly, Harry of the West, tarried here. So did his antagonist, then President, Jackson, on his visit to Boston in June, 1833. These two men gave rise to two party watchwords which have been perpetuated in a singular manner. Two rival political bands of Kentuckians went to settle on the banks of the Missouri. One party came from the Blue-Grass region, and were Clay men. The other was from the Big Sandy, and were Jackson men. The battle-cry of the parties was, "Clay and Liberty," "Jackson and Independence." Each little band of settlers named their villages for their war-cry, and eventually the counties for their political chiefs. So they now remain.

Brave Hull came also to see the docking of his old ship, the Constitution. Charles Dickens, on his first visit to America, came to the Tremont House. It took him eighteen days to come over in the Britannia. It is said the first person he asked for on his arrival was Bryant; but, as the steamer reached her dock after dark, we may conclude the comforts of his hotel engrossed the novelist's mind. He gives a somewhat humorous account of his initiation into American hotel customs:—

"'Dinner, if you please,' said I to the waiter.

"'When?' said the waiter.

"'As quick as possible,' said I.

"'Right away?' said the waiter.

"After a moment's hesitation, I answered 'No,' at hazard.

"'*Not* right away?' cried the waiter, with an amount of surprise that made me start.

"I looked at him doubtfully, and returned, 'No; I would rather have it in this private room. I like it very much.'

"At this, I really thought the waiter must have gone out of his mind; as I believe he would have done, but for the interposition of another man who whispered in his ear, 'Directly.'

"'Well! and that's a fact!' said the waiter, looking helplessly at me. 'Right away.'

"I now saw that 'right away' and 'directly' were one and the same thing. So I reversed my previous answer, and sat down to dinner in ten minutes afterwards, and a capital dinner it was.

"The hotel (a very excellent one) is called the Tremont House. It has more galleries, colonnades, piazzas, and passages than I can remember, or the reader would believe."

Lieutenant Derby, better known as John Phœnix, humorously reviews the prospect of the burial-ground from the windows, which he considered, not without some degree of plausibility, part and parcel of all Boston hotels. Derby was a very clever artist, and used to draw comic caricatures on the blackboard of Jones's in San Francisco. This was before the merchants had an exchange there, and Phœnix was accustomed to put himself under the head of ship arrivals, instead of registering his name at the office.

Before the hotel was taken down, and next the cemetery, there was a vacant lot, on which once stood a modest little brick dwelling, built by a Mr. Newman. The hotel displaced three ante-Revolutionary houses: one, fronting Beacon Street, was the residence of John Parker; the corner of Tremont was an open lot, with handsome horse-chestnut trees, belonging to an old-fashioned house with the end to the street, the mansion of the Hubbard family. Next was a house built by Thomas Perkins, whose wife was a Mascarene. It fronted on the street, and had a garden.

The old Tremont Theatre stood on the spot now covered by the Tremont Temple. The corner-stone was laid on the morning of July 4, 1827. The theatre was built so rapidly that a performance took place on the 24th of September. "Wives as they Were, and Maids as they Are," was the piece chosen by Mr. Pelby. Ostinelli, the father of the since famous Eliza Biscaccianti, led the orchestra. W. R. Blake read the prize address, — the same eminent comedian so long connected with the New York theatres.

Mr. Pelby was the prime mover in the project to erect another theatre, which had professedly for its object the elevation of the character of the Boston stage. But little opposition was encountered from the Boston Theatre proprietors. A company was organized in February, and the work pressed to early completion.

TREMONT HOUSE AND THEATRE.

The elder Booth succeeded Pelby in the management of the second season, but withdrew before it ended. Wilson and Russell successively conducted, the latter bringing out the celebrated Master Burke, who produced an unparalleled excitement. For twenty-five nights he filled the house with fashionable audiences. Messrs. Barrett and Barry were subsequent managers.

The Tremont always maintained a high standing, though its patronage fell off in later years. It is noticeable as the first Boston house in which operas were produced. Many sterling actors have appeared here, among whom the veteran John Gilbert and wife long held a high place in general esteem. Finn played here, investing his parts with a quaint fine humor that seldom failed to set the house in a roar. In 1842 the Tremont ceased to be a theatre, having been sold to the Baptist Society of Rev. Dr. Colver. The interior was remodelled, and received the name of the Tremont Temple. The present building is the third, the first having been destroyed by fire on Wednesday, March 31, 1852. The falling walls crushed and bruised a number of persons.

The Theatre was a plain substantial edifice with granite front, in imitation of the Ionic, with pillars supporting an entablature and pediment. The entrance doors were arched, opening into a wide hall from which ascended a staircase to the boxes of the dress circle. There were lobbies for promenade, withdrawing-rooms, and a pretty saloon in the centre. Isaiah Rogers was the architect. The house had a third tier and pit. It was sold for about $ 55,000.

Elihu Burritt, the learned blacksmith, lectured in the theatre before its alteration, for the benefit of the Church Society. Under the auspices of the Mercantile Library Association, Webster, Choate, and Everett have delivered addresses in the Temple, while Jenny Lind and Catherine Hays have here poured forth their golden notes to enraptured audiences. Here, too, Gliddon unrolled his mummy in presence of astonished spectators, and set the medical fraternity in a fever of excitement. Last, but not least, came Charles Dickens, to interpret his own incomparable works.

In the building adjoining the Temple were the quarters of the Independent Cadets, the oldest military organization, next to the Ancient and Honorable Artillery Company, in Boston. This corps was instituted in 1786, but existed prior to that time. It was first styled the Governor's Foot Guards. The commanders have the rank of lieutenant-colonel. Leonard Jarvis was the commander in 1768, and John Hancock was elected in 1772, receiving his commission from Governor Hutchinson. The Boston Gazette of May 12, 1772, contains the following advertisement :—

"WANTED, *Immediately*, For His Excellency's Company of Cadets, Two Fifers that understand Playing. Those that are Masters of Musick, and are inclined to engage with the Company, are desired to apply to Col. John Hancock."

The company received General Gage when he landed at Long Wharf, in May, 1774, and escorted him to the Court House and thence to the Province House, his residence. The general had caused a beautiful silk standard with his arms embroidered thereon to be made in London, and presented to the Cadets. Becoming, however, jealous and suspicious of Hancock, the governor revoked his commission through Thomas Flucker, his secretary, upon which the corps disbanded, and through a committee returned the standard to Gage at Danvers.

In 1778 the Cadets were *redivivi*, being then commanded by Colonel Hichborn. In that year they took part in the expedition to Rhode Island, as did also the Light Infantry Company. Hancock, their old commander, was now major-general, and accompanied them. The first parade of the Cadets after the peace was in 1785. Colonel T. H. Perkins commanded in 1789. In 1795 the corps was reorganized.

Bromfield Street was named, in 1796, for Honorable Edward Bromfield, a distinguished merchant, whose mansion stood on the site of the Bromfield House. Previously it was Rawson's Lane; it continued to be called Bromfield's Lane until 1829.

The Horticultural Building stands on the site of the old Museum. Montgomery Place is Bosworth Street. Bumstead Place, once the abode of Adino Paddock, coach and chariot builder for the gentry of Boston and the country round, has been sealed by a solid wall of buildings, closing up the old entrance to Music Hall. Paddock was a hot tory, and left Boston with the royal party. His estate, it is said, fell into the hands of Bumstead, a coach-maker like himself, from whom the place took its name.

Paddock is entitled to grateful remembrance for the noble English elms he planted opposite his habitation, known as Paddock's Mall. The year 1762 has been assigned as the probable period of their setting out, consequently they had stood considerably more than a hundred years, before being destroyed root and branch. The trees came from England. They were kept for a time in a nursery at Milton, until placed here by Paddock, assisted by John Ballard and John Crane; the latter a member of Paddock's train of artillery. "Paddock's Walk" and "Row" are other names by which the mall has been called.

These well-remembered trees were practically a continuation of the Tremont Street Mall, which, at first, extended no farther than West Street, and, with Paddock's Mall, made the only shaded walk in this part of the town. As long as he remained in Boston, Paddock gave these elms his personal care, for in 1771 we find him offering a guinea reward for information of the "person or persons" who had "cut and hacked one of the trees opposite his house in Long Acre." Until 1874 they remained a marked feature of this locality, but some of the trees having then suffered from neglect, they were declared to be an obstruction to travel, and cut down in haste, notwithstanding public sentiment strongly expressed itself against the act. With the aid of axes and derricks, fifty laborers quickly undid the work of a hundred years, and vain was the appeal:

> "Woodman, spare that tree!
> Touch not a single bough!
> In youth it sheltered me,
> And I 'll protect it now.
> 'T was my forefather's hand
> That placed it near his cot;
> There, woodman, let it stand,
> Thy axe shall harm it not."

Paddock was, in 1774, captain of the train of artillery belonging to the Boston Regiment, of which John Erving was colonel. This company was particularly distinguished for its superior discipline and the excellence of its material. In this school were raised two artillery officers of high repute in the Revolutionary army, namely, Colonel John Crane and General Ebenezer Stevens. Both were housewrights, and the company was itself composed of mechanics. The two officers named are not the only ones who gained distinction in the battle-fields of the old war. Paddock, on his return to England, was frequently consulted by the ministry about American affairs, and received the military command of the island of Jersey. In 1769 Paddock was one of the firewards of the town of Boston, associated with John Hancock, Samuel Adams, Thomas Dawes, and others.

George Cabot, a prominent leader of the Massachusetts Federalists, lived in the first house in Bumstead Place in 1810. He was in early life like the old navigators, his namesakes, a sailor, and became a very successful merchant; was president of the United States Branch Bank in the year mentioned, having a conceded reputation as a financier. While in the United States Senate in 1791–96, Hamilton, the founder of our financial system, often conferred with him. Mr. Cabot incurred great odium for his connection with the Hartford Convention in 1814, of which body he was president. Aaron Burr said of him when in the Senate, that "he never spoke but light followed him."

Granary Burial-Ground is notable for the honored ashes it contains. It dates back to 1660, and was first called the "South Burying-Ground"; the subsequent name of "Granary" was from the town granary, which stood within the enclosure. It is necessary to say here that the Common originally extended in this direction to the Tremont House, and the cemetery is formed from its ancient territory. The eastern margin reached to Mason Street, and Tremont Street therefore runs *through* the Common, as it originally was. After the creation of the Common Burying-Ground, the Granary was sometimes styled the "Middle" Ground.

> "I like that ancient Saxon phrase which calls
> The burial-ground God's Acre! It is just;
> It consecrates each grave within its walls,
> And breathes a benison o'er the sleeping dust."

The Checkleys, Byfields, Lydes, Faneuils, Wendells, and a host of the old Bostonians, Governors Bellingham, Dummer, Hancock, Adams, Bowdoin, Cushing, Sullivan, Eustis, and Sumner lie beneath the sod in this cemetery. The celebrated surgeon, Dr. John Jeffries, Uriah Cotting, Rev. Messrs. Eckley, Belknap, Stillman, Lathrop, and Baldwin, and Judge Sewall and John Hull, were also entombed here.

The Bellingham family becoming extinct, his tomb was given to the family of Governor James Sullivan. It lies on the west side of the enclosure. The Faneuil inscription was chiselled Funal by some awkward hand, who thus clipped the old Huguenot patronymic of its due proportions. Governor Hancock's tomb is on the Park Street side. His remains, after lying eight days in state, were brought to their last resting-place by an immense concourse of people. The venerable

Samuel Adams followed the bier until fatigue compelled him to retire. It was one of the greatest funeral pageants Boston had seen. The ranks of the procession were swelled by the

GRANARY BURYING-GROUND.

militia of town and country. The Judges of the Supreme Court on this occasion made their last appearance in their big wigs and black silk gowns. They were followed by the barristers in black gowns and club wigs.

General Warren's remains were placed in the tomb of the Minots, next to that of Hancock, and immediately in rear of the residence of Dr. J. C. Warren, after they were exhumed at Bunker Hill.

The cemetery acquires an even greater interest from being the place where the victims of the Boston Massacre were buried. Their funeral was conducted with great pomp; but although their martyrdom has been heralded as the foundation-stone of American Liberty, the remains of the slaughtered Bostonians have received no fitting testimonial from their countrymen. The spot is in the extreme northeast corner of the yard, identified by two bronze markers.

The Franklin cenotaph stands out in bold relief in the midst of the field of the dead. Under it repose the dust of both of Franklin's parents. The monument was erected through the exertions of a few citizens in 1827, and the ceremony of laying the corner-stone was attended by the governor, lieutenant-governor, and many other officials. General H. A. S. Dearborn delivered an address; some Franklin School medals were appropriately placed underneath.

By the year 1738 both this and King's Chapel ground became so filled with the dead that the grave-diggers were obliged to bury them four deep. In this year the brick wall and tombs were erected on the front of the old, or Chapel, burying-place. The Granary ground was enlarged in 1716 – 17 by taking in part of the highway on the easterly side, but in about twenty years it became overcrowded, as we have seen, and the town began to cast about for a new location. It was not until after the date last mentioned that any tombs were erected here.

Where was there ever a graveyard without its attendant horrors? Tradition is responsible for the statement that the hand of Hancock was severed from the arm the night after his interment; but this proved a cruel invention. An instance is given of an empty tomb being taken possession of by some wandering vagrants, from which they terrified the neighborhood by the sound of midnight revelry. Human jackals have practised here their hateful calling, robbing the graves of their peaceful inhabitants.

The stone wall and fence were erected under the administration of Mayor Armstrong. When, in 1897, the new Congregational House was being erected, on Beacon Street, it became necessary to demolish a row of tombs on that side, which was done, and the remains removed to suburban cemeteries.

> "Imperial Cæsar, dead, and turned to clay,
> Might stop a hole to keep the wind away."

Next the burial-ground stood the Old Granary. It was a

long wooden building, erected first at the upper side of the Common, but removed about 1737 to the present site of the church. It was established so as to have a supply of grain, especially in cases of scarcity, where the poor might purchase the smallest quantities at a small advance on the cost. The building contained, when full, twelve thousand bushels, and was the largest in the town. The selectmen appointed a keeper at their March meeting, also a committee for the purchase of grain. John Fenno, a noted wit, was keeper before the Revolution. It was not used as a granary after the American war, but was occupied by various minor town officials. In 1795 the town voted to sell the building, on condition of an early removal. Still it remained tenanted by various tradesmen, refreshment stands, etc., until 1809, when it was removed to Commercial Point, Dorchester, and altered into a hotel. There it may now be seen. We have noticed that the Constitution's sails were made in the Granary.

All the land upon which Park Street is built belonged to the Common, and was at an early day appropriated to uses of the town for various institutions. The street was first called Centry Street, from its leading up to Centry Hill, as the summit of Beacon Hill was called.

The Almshouse was first erected on Beacon Street, in 1662. It was burnt in 1682, measures being then taken to rebuild it. The reconstructed building was a two-story brick, with a gable roof, fronting on Beacon Street; it was of an L shape. This was designed as a home for the poor, aged, or infirm. It was soon found that the mingling under the same roof of persons deserving charity with those confined for offences against the laws was an evil demanding a remedy, and measures were taken, in 1712, to build a Bridewell, or House of Correction. This was erected in Park Street, in what year does not appear, but it is shown on the map of 1722. A part of this house was applied to the use of the insane.

A Workhouse was erected in 1738, contiguous to the Bridewell. It was a large, handsome brick building, facing the Common, of two stories, gable roof, and was a hundred and twenty feet in length. This building was devoted to the confinement of minor offenders, such as the province law styled "rogues and vagabonds."

The Almshouse became, in the lapse of years, totally inadequate to its purposes. It had no proper ventilation, nor separate hospital for the treatment of the sick; bad air, filth, and overcrowding told fearfully upon the inmates. No remedy was applied to these evils until 1801, when a new building was erected in Leverett Street. During the Revolutionary War the inmates frequently suffered for the necessaries of life, and appear to have been at all times largely dependent on the charity of the townspeople. In 1795 the town sold all its property on Park and Beacon Streets, except the Granary or church lot.

Both Almshouse and Workhouse were under the government of the overseers of the poor, represented by keepers. The inmates of the former, whatever may have been their temporal needs, were cared for spiritually, a sermon being preached to them every Sunday in summer. Captain Keayne, in 1656, left a legacy of £120, and Mr. Webb, in 1660, one of £100, for the founding of the Almshouse, which was received and applied by the town in 1662. The former also left a sum to be used in building a granary. Both Workhouse and Almshouse were occupied by the British wounded after Bunker Hill.

Adjoining the Bridewell was the Pound, situated where No. 5 Park Street now is. Such were the antecedents of Park and Beacon Streets.

For a long time the handsome spire of Park Street Church was the highest object seen on approaching the city. It, however, succumbed to its neighbor in Somerset Street, placed at a greater altitude. As one of the monuments of the Common it is inseparable from the landscape, the slender, graceful steeple rising majestically above the tree-tops from any point of observation. The little monitor of the weather on its pinnacle recalls the lines of Albert G. Greene: —

> "The dawn has broke, the morn is up,
> Another day begun;
> And there thy poised and gilded spear
> Is flashing in the sun,

Upon that steep and lofty tower,
Where thou thy watch hast kept,
A true and faithful sentinel,
While all around thee slept."

The church was erected in 1809, and was the first Congregational Society constituted since 1748. From the fervor of the doctrines preached within its walls, its site has been known as "Brimstone Corner," — a name too suggestive to be agreeable.

PARK STREET CHURCH.

Edward D. Griffin, D. D., was the first pastor. Dwight, Beecher, Stone, and other gifted preachers have occupied its pulpit. Underneath were vaults — long since removed — for the dead. Peter Banner, an English architect, the same who made the plan for the fine old mansion-house of Eben Crafts in Roxbury, designed this church.

The Manufactory House of the old colony times stood on the east side of what is Hamilton Place. The west end fronted Long Acre, or Tremont Street, and had delineated upon the wall a female figure, distaff in hand, symbolic of the industry it was intended to promote.

The establishment of spinning-schools is an interesting incident in the history of Boston. The manufacture of cotton had begun as early as 1643, the raw material being obtained from the West Indies. In 1665, owing to the scarcity of cloth, the court ordered spinning to be employed in private families, some abatement from the rates being made as compensation.

LINEN SPINNING-WHEEL.

About 1718 a number of colonists arrived from Londonderry, bringing with them the manufacture of linen and the implements used in Ireland. The matter was earnestly taken up by the Bostonians, and a vote passed to establish a spinning-school on the waste land in front of Captain Southack's, — about where Scollay's buildings were. These emigrants likewise introduced the general use of their favorite vegetable, the potato.

From these beginnings dates the establishment of the Manufactory House by the province. William Phillips, Molineux, and others carried the measure through the General Court. An excise was laid on carriages and articles of luxury to erect the building. Spinning now became the order of the day. Young and old, rich and poor, repaired to the Common with their spinning-wheels, great and small, stimulated by a premium offered to the most skilful. Many were clad in garments of their own manufacture as evidence of their industry, and on the appointed days the mall resounded with the hum of busy wheels. The novelty soon wore off, and after three or four years the manufacture wholly ceased. For a short

WOOLLEN SPINNING-WHEEL.

time after the building was used for the manufacture of worsted hose, metal buttons, etc., but in 1768 was rented by the province and occupied by private families.

At this time it acquired celebrity from the attempt made by Colonel Dalrymple, of the 14th royal regulars, to obtain it for quarters for his regiment; but the tenants, with Mr. Elisha Brown at their head, flatly refused them admission. Governor Bernard issued his mandate, which was served by the sheriff, ordering the surrender of the premises; but the doors were securely closed, and Brown boldly denied the right of Bernard to dispossess him. The wily lieutenant-governor tried next to induce the tenants to open, but with no greater success, and at last a stratagem was tried. The sheriff and his deputies obtained an entrance to the cellar, but instead of securing the obstinate tenant, were by him made close prisoners in the cellar, where they remained until a file of soldiers from the Common came and released them.

Thus did Elisha Brown make good his resistance against the combined civil and military authority of the province, after enduring a state of siege for several weeks. A gravestone in the Granary commemorates his gallant vindication of private rights. Dalrymple's men were quartered in Faneuil Hall.

The Massachusetts Bank was first located in this building. It was instituted in 1784, in which year the bank became a purchaser of the building, sold by order of the General Court. Banking was a very different affair in those days from what it is at present. Articles of merchandise were received as security for loans, and an entertaining picture might be drawn of the procession drawn up before the doors on discount days. One half per cent per month was the rate demanded, and no credit could exceed sixty days. Governor Bowdoin was the first president.

The building was of two stories, of brick, with an entrance on Hamilton Place by a flight of double stone steps protected by an iron railing. It was used by the British during the occupation, and received its quota of the wounded from Bunker Hill. Various families occupied it in after years; also P. A. von

Hagen, a pioneer in the manufacture of pianofortes. In 1806 it was pulled down, and Hamilton Place then built. The Manufactory House was one hundred and forty feet long, with an unobstructed southerly view in 1784. It had a large hall in the centre, with wings fifty feet long extending upon either side; underneath was an excellent cellar, the same in which Sheriff Greenleaf sojourned. The central part was occupied by the bank, giving twenty other apartments for tenants. The land belonging to it covered the whole place.

"The corner of Hamilton Place has interesting literary associations, having been occupied by the publishers of the Atlantic Monthly and the North American Review. The originator of the Review was William Tudor, son of Hon. Judge Tudor, and one of the founders of the Anthology Club. The first four volumes of the Review, which was first published in 1811, are said to be almost entirely from his hand; the first number, even to the literary notices, was, as Mr. Tudor himself stated, wholly written by him. Mr. Tudor, as the agent of his brother Frederick, established in 1805 the traffic in ice with the West Indies, which has grown to such prodigious proportions. He was also the first to draw public attention to the erection of a monument on Bunker Hill, but did not live to see its completion.

As we are trenching on the limits of Long Acre, a Revolutionary incident rises into view. Here, on the morning of the 19th of April, Earl Percy ranged his columns for the march to Lexington. Colonel Smith had sent a courier requesting reinforcements, and Percy was to command them. His brigade, made up of eight companies of three regiments of infantry, the 4th, 23d, and 49th, detachments of Pitcairn's marines, and two pieces of artillery, extended from the head of the mall to Court Street, opposite the school-house of Master Carter. Percy, mounted on a white horse, galloped up and down his ranks. The school, thrown into a ferment by the unusual spectacle, was dismissed by the master with the speech,—"Boys, war has begun; the school is broken up."

The column took up its march over the Neck to the tune of Yankee Doodle. Percy seems to have stood high in the confidence of his general, and, in fact, he appears to have been a universal favorite. The return from the march in which the provincials

> "Taught Percy fashionable races,
> And modern modes of Chevy-chaces,"

is celebrated in the Revolutionary ballad in this wise: —

> "Lord *Piercy* seemed to snore, — but may the muse
> This ill-timed snoring to the peer excuse.
> Tired was the long boy of his toilsome day;
> Full fifteen miles he fled, — a tedious way;
> How should he then the dews of Somnus shun,
> Perhaps not used to walk, much less to run."

The Common is now, as under the government of John Winthrop, the common land of the inhabitants of Boston. Its original purpose was for pasturage and military parade. From the earliest times until after Boston became a city, the tinkling of bells and lowing of cattle might be heard across its hills and dales. It was, after its purchase from Blackstone, preserved from encroachment by a vote passed March 30, 1640: —

"Ordered, that no more land be granted in the Town out of the open ground or common field, which is between Centry Hill and Mr. Colbron's end, except 3 or 4 lots to make vp the street from Bro. Robt. Walker's to the Round Marsh."

Colbron's field was at the lower end of the Common, lying along Pleasant Street and the water, to Washington Street. It was Boylston Street that the selectmen had in view.

No other city in America has fifty acres of green turf and noble forest trees in its very midst. Its central position renders it accessible from every quarter of the town, and, although it is not dignified with the name of a park, it is at once the glory and beauty of the ancient peninsula. We shall take up its features as we pass along under the green arches of the Great Mall.

Upon the earliest map you will see but three trees on the Common. These were the monarch, then and long known as the "great tree," and two of respectable size standing near the middle of Park Street. The first trees planted were the outer row on Tremont Street, between 1722 and 1729. A second row was placed there in 1734, and the third was added fifty years later, — some authorities say before the Revolution. This walk was long known as "The Mall," there being no other within the Common, until that next Beacon Street was laid out in 1815 – 16. Charles Street was the next laid out, in 1823; and Park Street Mall, in 1826, under the elder Quincy's mayoralty.

It has been stated, on the authority of the son of one of those employed, that the first trees of the Great Mall, set out near the Park Street Church, were planted by the apprentices of Adam Colson the elder, then one of the selectmen of the town. One of the apprentices was named Hurd. Colson was a leather-dresser, and lived in Frog Lane, now Boylston Street.

But the Great Mall was not at the beginning of this century, as now, a grove of near a third of a mile in length. The large trees scarcely extended below West Street, those beyond being merely saplings. That part of the Common forming the southeast corner, comprising a little more than two acres, and lying east of the burying-ground, was not acquired until 1787, when it was purchased of William Foster, whose mansion stood where now the Hotel Pelham is. The tract acquired was known as Foster's Pasture.

The British soldiers, with a truly vandal spirit, cut down several of the largest trees in the mall the morning they evacuated the town. A large number had before been sacrificed to provide fuel, but this was the act of malice alone. The surface of the Common was greatly disfigured by cellars and ditches dug throughout the camps, traces of which long remained visible, even to the circles made by the tents. General Howe stayed the destruction of the trees of the mall at the solicitation of the selectmen.

Before the Revolution there was a wooden fence, but this, too, was used for fuel, and the Common lay open until after the peace, when it was rebuilt by a subscription set on foot by Dr. Oliver Smith. The iron fence was erected in 1836, at a cost of $82,500. Its length was 1,932 yards, — rather more than a mile. In 1733, when the town voted to plant a second row of trees at a suitable distance from those already set out, the selectmen were directed to set up a row of posts with a rail on the top of them, extending from the Granary Burying-Ground to Colonel Fitche's, leaving openings at the several streets and lanes. In 1739 a similar fence was ordered from Common Street to Beacon.

The Common appears to have been first called "Centry Field," taking this name from the hill on whose slope it lay, which later received the name of Beacon Hill. Century Field is another instance of the quaint orthography, of which the records furnish abundant specimens. It appears to have been indifferently called the "Training Field" and "Centry Field" for a long time.

The building of the Subway has effected a marked transformation in the Tremont Street Mall, compelling, as it did, the removal of many of the noble elms that overarched it, and leading to the removal of the iron fence by which it was enclosed, so practically resulting in a widening of Tremont Street.

On the corner of Winter Street once stood an old ante-Revolutionary house, with a fine garden, in which, it is said, Governor Bernard at one time made his town residence. It became a famous boarding-house under the successive auspices of Mrs. Hatch and Mrs. Dexter. Governor Strong, when in town during his second term, resided with Mrs. Hatch.

The following toast was published in 1817, as having been given at the celebration by the blacks in Boston of the anniversary of the abolition of the slave-trade: —

"Governur Brouks, may the mantelpiece of Caleb Strong fall upon the hed of his distinguished predecessor."

John McLean, the eminent merchant, founder of the McLean Asylum, boarded with Mrs. Dexter. His financial reverses are well known. It is related of him that he one day assembled his creditors at a dinner, where each found under his plate a check for the full amount due him. This was after he had been legally released from his obligations.

Among the names bestowed upon this busy mart of fashion was Blott's Lane, from Robert Blott; also Bannister's and Willis's Lane.

Winter Street once boasted a resident so influential in the cause of liberty as to receive the distinction of outlawry from George III. The offences of Samuel Adams and John Hancock were too flagitious to admit of pardon. The house of Samuel Adams stood on the south side of Winter Street, on the corner of Winter Place. It was a two-story wooden house, fronting on the street; at the back was an L, and in the rear a small garden. The building was standing as late as 1820, and, while it remained, was not the least interesting object to be seen in Boston.

Samuel Adams was a Boston boy. Born in 1722, he had seen the administrations of the royal governors from Burnet to Gage. He took his degree at eighteen at Harvard, and after trying unsuccessfully a merchant's career, devoted himself to literature, until called to a political life. First a tax-gatherer, then a representative, his influence begins to appear at the commencement of the Stamp Act difficulties. After the Massacre, he overbore the flimsy objections of Hutchinson to a removal of the troops from the town by a manly, bold, and unanswerable argument.

In later times, in all the movements of the people of Boston preceding actual hostilities, Samuel Adams was the admitted power behind the throne. Warren was brave, Hancock rich, and Adams sagacious. It was remarked of Hancock that he paid the postage, while Adams did the writing. Lord North, when informed that Hutchinson had yielded to the demand of the chairman of the town committee, called the regulars "Sam Adams's two regiments," in contempt. The Ministry styled him "Chief of the Revolution."

Mr. Jefferson's opinion of Samuel Adams is a concise and deserved tribute to the patriot. Says the sage of Monticello, "I can say that he was truly a great man, — wise in council, fertile in resources, immovable in his purposes, — and had, I think, a greater share than any other member in advising and directing our measures in the Northern war."

When Adams, a fugitive with Hancock, heard the firing on Lexington Common, he exulted, knowing that the day of humiliation was passing forever away. The sword was now to decide the contest, and Adams labored without intermission in the councils of the incipient nation. He was an active member of the Congress of 1774; and he drew up, with John Adams, the draft of the State Constitution. A member of the convention to consider the Federal Constitution, he was not at first in favor of its adoption, but acceded to the plan of Hancock to ratify the instrument and propose amendments to it in accord with the views of Massachusetts statesmen. He was lieutenant-governor under Hancock, and followed him to his last resting-place. From 1794 to 1797 the venerable Samuel Adams governed the State. He died in 1803, an octogenarian.

It is related by Waterhouse that the two Adamses, John and Samuel, were one day walking in the mall we have just been describing. As they came opposite the noble mansion of Hancock the latter remarked, with emphasis, "I have done a very good thing for our cause, in the course of the past week, by enlisting the master of that house into it. He is well disposed, and has great riches, and we can give him consequence to enjoy them."

Samuel Adams was of ordinary height, muscular form, and had light complexion and light blue eyes. He wore a red cloak, a gray tie-wig, and cocked hat. In person he was very erect. His father was a brewer, and his son Samuel succeeded to his business. Admiral Coffin used to relate that he had carried malt on his back from Adams's brewery.

The old estate on Purchase Street, where Adams was born, was only about sixty feet north of Summer. It faced the harbor, commanding a fine view, and was conspicuous among the few buildings contemporary with it. On the roof was an observatory and a railing, with steps leading up from the outside. It was improved in 1730, and the grounds were still adorned with trees and shrubbery as late as 1800.* This was the estate

* Wells's Life of Samuel Adams.

preserved by Samuel Adams after his father's unsuccessful speculation in the Land Bank scheme.

Other statesmen and soldiers famous in the pages of history have walked in the old mall. We have no doubt that Washington and Winslow, Loudon, Amherst, and Hood, Gage, Clinton, Burgoyne, and Howe, have all sought its leafy shades. Talleyrand, Moreau, Louis Philippe, and Lafayette have doubtless paced within its cool retreats, and meditated upon the fate of empires they were to build or overthrow. Silas Deane, Pulaski, Gates, and Greene have certainly trod this famous walk.

St. Paul's, overshadowed and overtopped as it is by its feudal-looking neighbor, has yet some points of attraction. It was

ST. PAUL'S CHURCH AND MASONIC TEMPLE.

designed by Captain Alexander Parris, though, it is said, Willard drew some of the working plans, and superintended the stone-work, cutting some of the capitals with his own hand in the adjoining gardens. The front is unfinished, and the general aspect of the building did not satisfy the expectation for a model of ancient art. The pediment was intended to be ornamented with *bas-reliefs* representing Paul before Agrippa, which would have added to the beauty of the front, but want of funds compelled the abandonment of this design. The main building is of gray granite, once white, but now blackened by the action of the elements. The portico is of sandstone from Acquia Creek, the columns of which have been compared, not inaptly, to a collection of grindstones, they being composed of many separate sections. Taken as a whole, the appearance of St. Paul's may be styled "dark, gloomy, and peculiar."

The erection of St. Paul's marked an era in the architecture of Boston churches. Hitherto the houses of worship were of the same general character, King's Chapel and Brattle Street alone excepted. The latter were the only departures from the stiff, and, we may add, ugly structures introduced by the Puritans. St. Paul's was the first specimen of the pure Ionic in the town.

This was the fourth Episcopal church erected in Boston; consecrated June 30, 1820. Dr. Samuel F. Jarvis was the first rector. The interior is chaste and beautiful. The ceiling is a cylindrical vault, with panels spanning the whole width of the church. Underneath the floor are tombs. The remains of General Warren were deposited under St. Paul's in the tomb of his nephew, Dr. John C. Warren, until removed in August, 1855, to the family vault at Forest Hills.

Solomon Willard came to Boston in 1804, and first worked at his trade of carpenter. He was employed on the famous Exchange Coffee House, the conflagration of which, in 1818, was seen a hundred miles from Boston. He very soon applied himself to the study of architecture and carving in wood. The capitals for the Brighton Meeting-house, and those for Park Street Church steeple, are by his hand. He also carved a bust of Washington for the seventy-four-gun ship of that name, and executed a model of the public buildings in Washington for Mr. Bulfinch. The eagle now on the apex of the pediment of the Old Custom House was carved by Mr. Willard; it is five feet high, and measures the same distance from wing to wing. His great work was the Bunker Hill Monument, of which he was the architect, and he was also the discoverer of the Bunker Hill Quarry at Quincy. The Court House, in Court Square, was designed by Mr. Willard.

The old Masonic Temple, now occupied by R. H. Stearns & Co., is built upon a part of the Washington Gardens. The corner-stone was laid in 1830, and two years elapsed before it was dedicated. The basement and belt is of hammered granite. Two lofty Gothic towers, with battlements surmounted by pinnacles, flank the entrance, and are a picturesque feature of the environs of the Great Mall. Busy trade now usurps the high places of Masonry, to which a newer and more magnificent temple has been dedicated.

In the upper story of the Masonic Temple was the school of A. Bronson Alcott, the philosopher, and father of the popular authoress, Louisa May Alcott. In Mr. Alcott's school Sarah Margaret Fuller, afterwards Countess d'Ossoli, was an assistant teacher before she went to Providence, R. I., to teach. Miss Fuller, "the best talker since De Staël," lived with her uncle, Henry H. Fuller, on the north side of Avon Place (Street), where she held for several seasons her "Conversations" for young ladies. She was afterwards invited to New York, by Horace Greeley, as a contributor to the New York Tribune. The memory of her remarkable talents and literary successes is still fresh, and recalls the painful impression caused by her sad fate from shipwreck on Fire Island, when returning from Europe in 1850 with her husband and child.

It is said she could compose Latin verse when only eight years old. Her writings, much as they were admired, were not equal to her conversation, in which her wonderful brilliancy and force of expression came forth with full power, until the best talkers preferred to become listeners in her society. The story of her life has often been told, and constitutes one of the brightest as well as one of the saddest pages of our history.

The Washington Gardens extended to the corner of West Street. They were surrounded by a brick wall, a part of which

The Great Mall, Haymarket, and Theatre.

is seen in the foreground of the view of the Haymarket in the illustration. A concert was announced here as early as 1815, by J. H. Shaffer. In 1819 an amphitheatre was erected within the grounds, which afterwards took the name of the Washington Theatre. The managers of Federal Street were at first interested in this establishment, until it passed from their control and became a rival. The house was adapted to the uses of a circus as well as for a theatre, equestrian performances having been given in it a number of times. As such it appears to have been the first in Boston. Following the Old Drury and Haymarket, it had an English name, being called Vauxhall. A battalion of British troops is said to have been quartered in the grounds at the time of the occupation, when they were known as Greenleaf's Gardens.

The site of these gardens was the residence of Stephen Greenleaf, the old sheriff of Suffolk under the stormy administration of Governor Bernard. He was the same whose exploits at the Manufactory House have been chronicled. The sheriff was a confirmed royalist, but did not join in the hegira of that party from Boston. He died at the great age of ninety-one. After him it became the mansion of James Swan, who long lived in Paris, and was imprisoned in St. Pelagie for many years.

The reader will obtain from the illustration an excellent idea of what the district embraced between West and Boylston Streets was in 1798. At the lower corner of West Street was the Haymarket. Beyond, at the south corner of Mason Street, was Hatch's Tavern, with Frothingham's carriage factory in the rear; farther on is seen the Old Haymarket Theatre, and, at the corner of Boylston Street, the residence of William Foster, where now the Hotel Pelham stands. In the right foreground is the West Street entrance to the Common; the trees receding along the mall disclose the river beyond, whose breezes then fanned and invigorated the *habitués* of the spot. The picture is from a water-color by Robertson, once the property of John Howard Payne, now in possession of the Public Library. The Whipping-Post and Pillory were situated near the West Street gate after their removal from State Street.

Long before the Revolution, as early as 1722, a free school was established in what is now Mason Street, near the corner of West. It was then on the boundary of the Common, the land now lying between having been sold off from it. The school was called the South Writing, was the fourth in the town, and has, in later times, been known as the Adams School. The Common extended to Mason Street since 1800.

A gun-house stood at the corner of West Street at the beginning of the Revolution, separated by a yard from the school-house. In this gun-house were kept two brass three-pounders belonging to Captain Adino Paddock's train. These pieces had been recast from two old guns sent by the town to London for that purpose, and had the arms of the province engraved upon them. They arrived in Boston in 1768, and were first used at the celebration of the King's birthday, June 4, when a salute was fired in King Street. Both school and gun-house are connected with a celebrated event.

Major Paddock had expressed an intention of surrendering these guns to Governor Gage. The mechanics, who composed this company, resolved that it should not be so. The British general had begun to seize the military stores of the province and disarm the inhabitants. Accordingly, the persons engaged in the plot met in the school-room; and when the attention of the sentinel stationed at the door of the gun-house was taken off by roll-call, they crossed the yard, entered the building, and, removing the guns from their carriages, carried them to the school-room, where they were concealed in a box in which fuel was kept.

The loss of the guns was soon discovered, and search made, in which the school did not escape. The master placed his lame foot upon the box, and it was not disturbed. Several of the boys were privy to the affair, but made no sign. Besides the schoolmaster, Abraham Holbrook, Nathaniel Balch, Samuel Gore, Moses Grant, Jeremiah Gridley, —— Whiston, and some others executed this *coup de main.*

Loring's account says the guns remained a fortnight in the school-room. At the end of that time they were taken in a wheelbarrow at night and carried to Whiston's blacksmith's shop at the South End, and deposited under the coal. From here they were taken to the American lines in a boat. The guns were in actual service during the whole war. After the peace the State of Massachusetts applied to Congress for their restoration, which was granted by a resolve passed May 19, 1788, in which General Knox, Secretary at War, was directed to place a suitable inscription upon them. The two guns were called the "Hancock" and "Adams," and were in charge of the Ancient and Honorable Artillery Company, until presented, in 1825, by the State to the Bunker Hill Monument Association. They are now to be seen in the chamber at the top of Bunker Hill Monument. The inscription. except the name, is the same on each:—

The Hancock:
Sacred to Liberty.
This is one of four cannon,
which constituted the whole train
of Field Artillery
possessed by the British Colonies of
North America
at the commencement of the war,
on the 19th of April, 1775.
This cannon
and its fellow,
belonging to a number of citizens of
Boston,
were used in many engagements
during the war.
The other two, the property of the
Government of Massachusetts,
were taken by the enemy.
By order of the United States
in Congress assembled,
May 19, 1788.

The two guns referred to as captured by the enemy were concealed in a stable belonging to a house on the south side of Court Street, near the Court House. They were taken out over the Neck in a cart loaded with manure, driven by a negro servant of George Minot, a Dorchester farmer. Thus the four guns belonging to the province escaped the clutches of Gage. The two last referred to were some time in possession of the Dorchester Artillery.

Colonnade Row, a uniform range of twenty-four brick buildings, was constructed in 1811, and occupied by the *élite* of Boston society. Each house had, or was intended to have, a row of freestone columns in front supporting a piazza, — hence the name. In 1824, after the visit of Lafayette, Amos Lawrence and other occupants of the row petitioned to have Colonnade Row called Fayette Place, but it failed to receive official sanction, though it continued to be so called by the residents. At the same time the name of South Allen Street was changed to Fayette Street. But few of the buildings in the row retain their original appearance, inexorable trade having demanded and obtained admittance into this stronghold of Boston aristocracy. A more plebeian appellation of the block was "Cape Cod Row," either from the antecedents of some of the dwellers, or their traffic in the staple of the Commonwealth.

The Lowells have been a distinguished family in Massachusetts, from Revolutionary times to the present day. Judge Lowell was a delegate to the Congress of 1782–83, and was appointed by Washington Judge of the United States District Court at its organization. The judge will ever be remembered as the member of the convention which framed the State Constitution, where, as one of the committee to draft that instrument, he inserted in the "Bill of Rights" the clause declaring that "all men are born free and equal," with the avowed purpose of abolishing slavery in the Commonwealth.

Rev. Charles Lowell, of the West Church, was a son of Judge Lowell, who first studied law in Boston before he took up theology. Our distinguished contemporary poet, James Russell Lowell, was a son of the clergyman. Another of the sons of the Revolutionary judge was Francis Cabot Lowell, to whom, more than any other, belongs the credit of establishing the Waltham cotton factory, the precursor of the Lowell works. The city of Lowell was named for him. It was his son, John Lowell, Jr., who founded by his will the Lowell Institute.

At No. 19 of the Colonnade resided John Lowell, son of the

judge of Revolutionary antecedents. Mr. Lowell acquired fame as a political writer, wielding a trenchant pen. As an opponent of the "Last War," — as that of 1812 was long called, — he obtained considerable celebrity under his *nom de plume* of the "Boston Rebel," from the boldness and severity with which he attacked the administration. He refused office, deeming the post of honor the private station, but is remembered as a founder of the Massachusetts General Hospital, the Athenæum, Savings Bank, and the Hospital Life Insurance Company. He built a brick house in School Street, occupied for lawyers' offices, on the ground now open in front of the City Hall.

The Massachusetts Medical College, an appendage of Harvard University, was at one time situated in Mason Street, immediately behind Colonnade Row. It was a brick edifice, with a pediment raised above the central portion. A dome, with balustrade, surmounted the whole. The double tier of windows were enclosed in arches rising the whole height of the building. Taken altogether, its external aspect might be called ugly. Within, the central building was occupied by an anatomical museum, with a laboratory underneath; the lecture-room was in the south wing.

Untold horrors were associated with this building in the minds of the urchins who frequented the adjoining school-house. Its contiguity to the Common Burying-Ground, too, seemed to savor of a strong union between demand and supply. The professors were regarded in the neighborhood as so many ogres, and the students as no better than vampires. They ate their oysters or passed the jest over the dissecting-table with a *sang-froid* simply horrible to the uninitiated. An instance is remembered of a student, who went to pass the evening at a friend's house, taking a dead woman's arm, which he coolly unwrapped from a newspaper to the affright of his hostess. The college was removed to the West End, where it has acquired a fearful notoriety in connection with a well-remembered tragedy enacted there.

The Haymarket Theatre stood next south of Colonnade Row. This was an immense structure of wood, erected in 1796, and opened December 26, of that year, by Powell, of the Federal Street. Powell had fallen out with the proprietors of the latter house, and the Haymarket was built by his friends. It was designed to accommodate the middling interest, but the town could not support two theatres. The property proved a poor speculation, and was taken down after standing six years only. The huge structure was said to have been the largest and best-arranged theatre in America; while it stood it was a source of terror to the neighborhood from its liability to take fire. No other theatrical enterprise was started in Boston until the Washington Garden entertainments, in 1819 began.

The Haymarket opened with the "Belle's Stratagem." Mr. J. A. Dickson, afterwards of the Federal Street, appeared on the boards here for the first time. He became, after his retirement from the stage, a well-known merchant in Cornhill, and accumulated a handsome fortune. Dickson was the first agent in this country of Day and Martin's blacking. Mrs. Darley made her *début* at this theatre as Narcissa in "Inkle and Yarico." There were a pit, gallery, and three tiers of boxes, with a handsome saloon and minor conveniences for the audience. Mr. and Mrs. G. L. Barrett also appeared at this house, the latter making her *début* as Mrs. Beverly in the "Gamester." The following was the bill on the opening night at the Haymarket: —

BELLE'S STRATAGEM.

Doricourt,	S. Powell.
Sir George Touchwood,	Marriott.
Flutter,	C. Powell.
Saville,	J. H. Dickson.
Courtall,	Taylor.
Villars,	A Young American.
Hardy,	Simson.
Letitia Hardy,	Mrs. S. Powell.
Lady Frances,	Mrs. Hughes.
Miss Ogle,	Miss Harrison.
Mrs. Racket,	Mrs. Simpson.

The Winthrop House and the adjoining Freemason's Hall, which made the corner of Boylston Street, were destroyed by fire in April, 1864, which left nothing but the walls standing. The present grand temple of Masonry succeeds to both the former. It is a magnificent monument of this angle of the Common.

The Masonic Temple is not unworthily supported on the opposite corner by the Hotel Touraine, — a site which will never lose interest as the home of John Quincy Adams, sixth President of the United States. In the old mansion-house was born Charles Francis Adams, who erected the Hotel Boylston on this site.

Boylston Street was the ancient Frog Lane of the South End. Its route was the same as now, except that the sea washed the southerly end at the foot of the Common. We have remarked that the fathers of Boston were not particular about names. The future was veiled from them, and any peculiarity served their purpose. The amphibious croaker may have rendered the air of the neighborhood vocal with his evening song in the day of Adams or his neighbor Foster. Sloughs and mud-holes were common to the vicinity. It is recorded that one, both wide and deep, lay in front of Mather Byles's house. The selectmen were importuned to see to it without avail, until one morning a pair of them got their chaise stuck fast in the midst, when the parson accosted them with, — "Well, gentlemen, I am glad to see you stirring in this matter at last."

The "Old Man eloquent" is one of the honored names on the roll of the Boston Bar. The Athenæum was enriched by his private library at a merely nominal sum. He studied law with Theophilus Parsons, and wrote powerful political articles under the signature of Publicola, in 1791, advocating neutrality with France. Minister to Holland, England, and Prussia, he was intimate with Burke, Fox, Sheridan, Pitt, and their contemporaries of the period of the French Revolution. A member of the United States Senate from 1803 to 1808, his views on the measures of Mr. Jefferson were in conflict with those of Massachusetts, and he resigned. He was minister to Russia in 1809, and a commissioner at Ghent in 1815. Again minister to England in 1817, he became subsequently Mr. Monroe's Secretary of State, and his successor in 1825. In 1831 he was returned to Congress, where he continued until his sudden decease in the Capitol in 1848. "This is the last of earth; I am content," were the last words he spoke.

Mr. Adams was minister to Russia during the invasion of Bonaparte. When questioned as to the burning of Moscow, he stated that both the Emperor and Rostopchin, the governor, denied having ordered it. Had the government assumed the responsibility, they would have been obliged to indemnify the sufferers.

In Miss Quincy's Memoir are some interesting personal recollections of Mr. Adams while at the court of St. Petersburg. Said he: —

"I never saw Alexander on the throne. He was a man who cared little about thrones, and was one of the most complete republicans, in character and manners, I have ever known. He used to walk the streets of St. Petersburg every day, and stop and talk to every one he met. He was extremely popular, and I do not believe he was carried off by treachery. Alexander, during the whole of the war with Bonaparte, exposed himself as much as any of his officers. At the close of that war he was undoubtedly one of the first generals in Europe. Moreau was killed at his side by a cannon-ball from the walls of Dresden."

Speaking of Moreau's death, Mr. Adams observed: —

"He was fighting against his country, which no man can ever be justified in doing. A man, if he disapproves a government or a war, may remain quiet and neutral; but nothing should ever induce him to take up arms *against his country*. I saw Moreau's funeral at St. Petersburg, which was attended with great pomp."

The victor of Hohenlinden was excluded by decree from the ranks of the French army, July 6, 1804, and under the surveillance of a colonel of gendarmes went to Cadiz, where he embarked for the United States. Moreau was in America eight years, during which he travelled extensively, visiting Boston among other places. The venerable William Minot, of this city, once stated, in an interview, that he remembered seeing the general in a passing carriage while he was in Boston. He went to Niagara Falls, and descended the Ohio and Mississippi. A small affluent of the Missouri is named for him.

He lived for some time at Morrisville, in Pennsylvania, in a house purchased by him on the banks of the Delaware, — the most conspicuous in the place. The general was very affable and hospitable. He also resided in New York, where he was much consulted by American politicians, though he sedulously abstained from party intrigue himself. After a residence of about eight years in the United States he returned to Europe, to engage in the strife then raging there. The American vessel which carried Moreau — this was in 1813 — was permitted to pass the blockade by Admiral Cockburn, at the request of the Russian minister.

His death-bed was attended by the King of Prussia, the Emperor of Austria, and Emperor Alexander, who manifested the deepest grief at his loss. Metternich, Schwartzenburg, and the allied generals visited him, and Alexander, who had a great friendship for the dying general, held him a long time in his arms. The following is an extract of a letter to Madame Moreau, written by him, with a steady hand, while sinking under the amputation of his limbs: —

"My dear friend, at the battle of Dresden, three days ago, I had both legs carried away by a cannot shot. That scoundrel, Bonaparte, is always lucky."

Charles Francis Adams passed his boyhood with his father at St. Petersburg, and while the elder Adams was minister at the court of St. James, the son went to an English school. He studied law in Webster's office, and was admitted to the bar, but never practised. Mr. Adams, after having edited a Boston newspaper, and served in the legislature, was the candidate of the Free Soil party for the Vice-presidency in 1848. But Mr. Adams is best known by his diplomatic services at the same court where his father served so long. His conduct of delicate negotiations during the great civil war was such as to place him at the head of American *diplomats*. His services were further required by our government in the negotiations at Geneva, arising from the Alabama and other claims. Mr. Adams married a daughter of Peter C. Brooks, a wealthy citizen of Boston.

In this corner of the Common, and adjoining the Burying-

Ground on the east, were situated the hay-scales, after their removal from the corner of West Street, and also a gun-house; the latter was transferred, in 1826, to a location near the former Providence depot. It contained a laboratory, well furnished with warlike material. There was also a laboratory on Pleasant Street, between the corner of Boylston and Pfaff's Hotel, during the Revolution, on what is now called Park Square, and another, subsequently used by Frothingham, Wheeler, and Jacobs as a carriage factory, as shown in the illustration.

The first manufacture of duck was begun by an incorporated company in Boston, about 1790. They erected buildings on a large lot in Boylston Street, at the corner of Tremont. In 1792 they were in the full tide of success, employing four hundred operatives, and turning out fifty pieces a week of excellent canvas. Here were manufactured the Constitution's sails, so that she was an American ship throughout, except in her armament. The manufacture of cotton began in New England as early as 1643, and calico printing was undertaken in Boston before 1794.

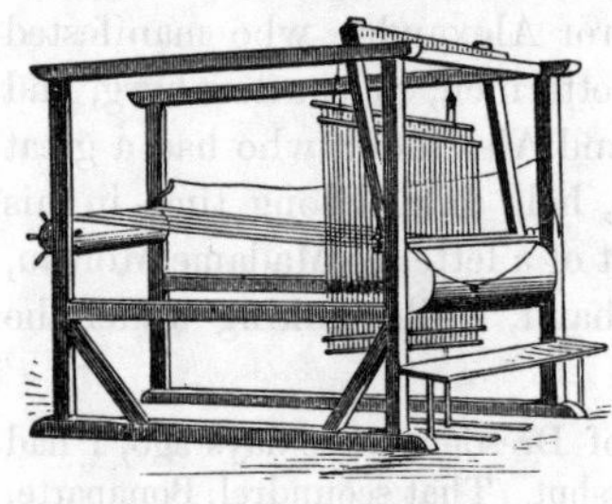

OLD LOOM.

During the war of 1812 a number of field-pieces belonging to the government were collected in this corner of the Common, and the city military took turns mounting guard over the park. The New England Guards, which were organized in 1812, performed their share of this duty, and several of the members, among whom was Abbott Lawrence, got their one hundred and sixty acres of land from the general government in requital for a certain term of service here, at the Charlestown Navy Yard, and at Noddle's Island. There were sixty-seven names on the muster-roll in 1814, and in 1859, after the lapse of nearly half a century, forty-three of the sixty-seven were still living, of whom it is doubtful if any now survive.

CHAPTER XI.

A TOUR ROUND THE COMMON CONTINUED.

Common Burying-Ground. — Joshua Bates. — Public Garden. — Ropewalks. — Topography of the Common. — British Troops on. — Description of their Camps. — The Light Horse. — Powder House. — Old Elm. — Witchcraft and Quaker Executions. — The Duel in 1728. — Mill-Dam. — Mexican Volunteers. — Beacon Street. — Prescott. — Copley. — John Phillips. — Wendell Phillips. — Robert C. Winthrop. — Hancock Mansion. — Governor Hancock. — General Clinton. — State House. — Public Statues, etc. — The Beacon. — The Monument. — Lafayette's Residence. — George Ticknor. — Malbone. — Samuel Dexter. — Incidents of Lafayette's Visit in 1824. — Josiah Quincy, Jr. — Historical Résumé. — Repeal of the Stamp Act.

THE Common Burying-Ground has but little antiquity compared with the Chapel, Copp's Hill, or Granary Cemeteries. It was opened after these in 1756, and has, according to its changing relations with others, been called at various times the South and Central Ground.

Under Mayor Armstrong, the Boylston Street Mall was carried across the foot of the Common, cutting off some of the tombs on that side of the graveyard. The owners of the vaults resisted the invasion of the sacred dust, but the improvement was accomplished by which Beacon and Tremont Street Malls were connected.

Unsupported tradition has given to the Common Ground the credit of being first used for negro burials, but we find no better evidence of this than that some very thick skulls were dug up at a considerable depth from the surface. It is known, however, that this was the sepulchre of such of the common soldiers as died from disease during the British occupation, and of those who died from their wounds received at Bunker Hill. They were buried in a common trench, according to military custom, and many of the remains were exhumed when the excavations were proceeding at the northwest corner of the yard.

The officers who died of their hurts at Bunker Hill were interred in the churches and cemeteries, hastily, but with greater decency. Many of these have been forwarded to their far-away homes.

We cannot pass the Old Public Library site without an allusion to its great benefactor, Joshua Bates. This eminent Bostonian, who became a member of the great house of the Barings in London, was a poor boy, almost as humble as the least among those who daily benefit by his generosity. He attracted the attention of his patron, William Gray, while driving a load of stones on his father's team. His quick, ready replies interested the merchant, who gave him a place in his counting-house, whence graduated a financier second to none in the Old or New World.

In the Public Library is a Revolutionary relic of interest, which acquired an even greater importance in connection with the Sanitary Commission in the war of Rebellion. It is the original capitulation of Burgoyne at Saratoga, with the signatures of the king's commander, Riedesel, and the lesser officers, English and Hessian, in order of rank.

> "In vain they fought, in vain they fled;
> Their chief, humane and tender,
> To save the rest, soon thought it best
> His forces to surrender."

Where now the Public Garden is teeming with beauty, nearly the whole extent of the ground was occupied by ropewalks, five in number. As you pass along Charles Street going in the direction of Beacon, these ropewalks stretched about three fourths of the distance, there meeting the water which washed Charles Street. On the other hand, they continued nearly to Eliot Street. Charles Street was divided from the Common about 1804.

These ropewalks were the successors of those in Pearl and Atkinson Streets, destroyed by fire in 1794. The town granted the tract in order to prevent the erection of new buildings in a district they endangered, as well as to render substantial aid to the unfortunate rope-makers; they were again consumed in their new location in 1806. The land whereon these rope-walks were situated was marsh, or flats, which indeed was the prior condition of nearly all that low ground now known as the parade of the Common. At high tides most of this tract was probably overflowed. On the verge of it was a little elevation known as Fox Hill, long ago levelled to contribute to the filling of the marsh. As long ago as 1750 the town voted to lease these marsh-lands; but if they were used, the purpose has not transpired.

To continue the topography of this region of the Common, from the bottom of Beacon Street to Cambridge Bridge was a high bluff, similar to the headlands of the harbor islands; the base washed by the river. Excellent springs, covered at high water, trickled along the beach. This eminence, known as West Hill, was occupied by the British as a mortar-battery; it has been reduced to a convenient grade, and employed in making Charles Street. It seems clear that the shore or beach once left this headland with an inward sweep, southerly to the higher ground at the foot of Boylston Street.

After the era of improvement was begun by the Mount Vernon proprietors, the hill was reduced by them. In this labor they employed the first railway used in New England, by an inclined plane, over which box cars conveyed their loads to the water at the foot of the hill. About this time a sea wall was built along Charles Street from Beacon to Boylston.

To return to the ropewalks. The town, in its generosity, invested the proprietors with a title which might have forever prevented the existence of the Public Garden, now properly a part and parcel of the Common. The rights of the proprietors were finally purchased by the city. The question whether the city should sell these lands lying west of Charles Street, was, in 1824, negatived by the citizens, who thus decided to preserve the beautiful view of the river and its shores beyond, now obstructed by the newly erected city of the Back Bay. In this manner has been secured the Public Garden, —

> "Where opening roses breathing sweets diffuse,
> And soft carnations shower their balmy dews;

Where lilies smile in virgin robes of white,
The thin undress of superficial light,
And varied tulips show so dazzling gay,
Blushing in bright diversities of day,
Each painted floweret in the lake below
Surveys its beauties, whence its beauties grow."

From the bottom of the Common the troops were embarked in silence for Lexington, at about ten o'clock on the night preceding the memorable 19th of April. On the Common were arrayed the forces engaged at Bunker Hill before they marched to the points of embarkation. Many a tall fellow heard the drums beat the rappel for the last time as he shouldered his firelock, and fell in the ranks on that eventful morning.

Of the first troops which the Ministry despatched to Boston, the 29th went into camp on the Common for a short time, until they were quartered in various parts of the town. The 14th and the Train marched with the 29th to the Common from Long Wharf, but were assigned to other localities. On the 31st of October, 1768, took place the first military execution ever witnessed in Boston. The doomed man was Richard Ames, a private of the 14th; his crime, desertion. He was shot on the Common, both regiments being present under arms. Intercession was made with General Gage to spare the man's life without avail.

These were not the first troops to use the town training-field by many, but their coming marked an epoch in history. The provincial forces of Shirley and Pepperell enlivened the green sward in 1745; and in 1758, on the 13th January, General Amherst and his army, 4,500 strong, disembarked from their ships, and pitched their tents on the Common. This was the force destined to operate against Canada. At this time, and long afterwards, the British officers wore bayonets. A portrait of General Wolfe is extant with a firelock slung at his back and the bayonet by his side. Burgoyne's officers also wore them when they came to Boston in 1777.

The Highland Regiment, commanded by Colonel Fraser, excited the admiration of the town, which had seen nothing like it before. Their colonel was the same who displayed such conspicuous bravery at the battle of Stillwater in 1777, under Burgoyne's command. In the crisis of the second day's battle General Morgan called some of his trusty riflemen, and, pointing out the gallant Briton, said to them: "That gallant officer is General Fraser. I admire and honor him, but it is necessary he should die; victory for the enemy depends upon him. Take your stations in that clump of bushes, and do your duty." In a few minutes Fraser fell, mortally wounded. He requested to be buried in a redoubt he had erected, which was accordingly done, under the fire of the American guns. The object of the burial-party being discovered, the firing ceased, except the occasional booming of a minute-gun in honor of the valor of the deceased soldier. Fraser's regiment was with Wolfe at the memorable ascent of the Heights of Abraham in 1759, and, under Murray, was engaged at the battle of Quebec in 1760.

On the 2d July, 1774, the train of artillery from the Castle landed, and marched to the Common. On the 4th of October there were two regiments stationed here, and it continued thereafter a permanent camp until the evacuation. Two companies were stationed in the mortar redoubt, and also held a small three-gun battery higher up on the slope of the hill. When the British departed, the thirteen-inch mortar from the battery was found lying on the beach, where it had been overturned, uninjured. Another of the same calibre, found sunk at the end of Long Wharf, was placed by the Americans in the South Battery. One of these Revolutionary relics was taken to Charlestown Navy Yard; the other was mounted on the battery at New York, the same year it was captured. Two twelve-pounders from the battery on Beacon Hill were also secured by the Americans. There were a few shot thrown into the British camp during the siege by an American floating battery, but no harm was done.

The positions of the British defences and encampments on the Common during the winter of 1775–76 were as follows: A small earthwork was thrown up at the northwest corner, a little higher up than the present entrance on Charles Street; this was designed for infantry, and held by a single company.

The little elevation mentioned by the name of Fox Hill was nearly or quite surrounded by water at times, and was hence called the island ; on this was a small redoubt. At the south-west corner, at a point at high-water mark, — now intersected by Boylston Street extension, — was another breastwork for infantry. South of this was a strong redoubt, which would be bisected by Hollis Street, were it extended to the shore as it then existed ; one front faced Pleasant Street, while the other was along the then beach. This formed the first line, the Pleasant Street redoubt and the battery at the foot of Beacon Street being on the flanks.

On the westerly slope of the hill overlooking the parade, and on which the monument is now situated, was a square redoubt, behind which lay encamped a battalion of infantry ; to the east, and on a line with the easternmost point of the hill, were two half-moons for small arms, with a second battalion in its rear. About opposite Carver Street, resting on the southwest corner of the burial-ground, was a bastioned work, directly across Boylston Street. This was the second line. On the hill formerly known as Flagstaff Hill, but now dedicated to the soldiers' monument, the artillery was parked, protected by intrenchments. Immediately behind this hill, stretching from the burial-ground across to Beacon Street Mall, were the camps of three battalions of infantry. Such were the dispositions to prevent a landing by the American forces under Washington. None of the works were formidable except the most southern, which was connected with the lines on the Neck. The Common was an intrenched camp, with a regular garrison of 1,750 men.

The remains of the British works were visible until the beginning of the century. I have talked with those who have seen the holes made by the soldiers for their kitchens, and the ditches on the hill where the monument now stands.

The strength of the British position may be inferred from the fact that Du Coudray, an experienced French officer of artillery, engaged by our commissioners to command that arm in our service, laughed long and heartily on viewing from Beacon Hill the works which the British had erected, and which they had so precipitately abandoned.

Boston Common as a Cow Pasture, with the Great Elm.

Behind the three-gun battery situated on Beacon Hill were a number of ropewalks, bounding north on Myrtle Street, and occupied in Revolutionary times by Henderson Inches. This was the camp of the British Light Horse, who used the rope-walks as their stables, and the Old South as a riding-school. Joy Street now passes through the site of these ropewalks. The spur of Beacon Hill known as Mt. Vernon, and for which that street takes its name, was called Mt. Hoardam, and Mt. Whoredom, a difference merely of orthography. We shall see that the military positions in and around the Common were presided over by some distinguished personages.

In May, 1706, an act was passed erecting a Powder House in the town, and one was built on the hill near the Frog Pond. There was another pond on the Common in early times called the Horse Pond, a stagnant pool of water long since filled up. It was situated a little to the southeast of old Flagstaff Hill, and was connected by a ditch with the river ; across the ditch a little foot-bridge was thrown. A third pond, to the westward, was called Sheehan's, from a man of that name hanged there. The Powder House referred to must not be confounded with the one at West Boston, — a much larger and better-built magazine.

The superficial features of the Common, except in the instances pointed out, remain unchanged. It is true that the Mighty Elm, once undisputed monarch of all it surveyed, no longer rears its hoary front, or puts forth its scanty verdure as of old. Long had increasing decrepitude presaged its downfall, for it had battled with the gales of many a winter, and had been shorn of its strength of limb by the stroke of many an icy blast. Yet like a giant it stood, majestic in decay, until laid low by the great gale of February 15, 1876. Thousands flocked to the spot, eager to secure some relic of this brave old tree, now only a memory and a regret.

The branches of the Old Elm, if we may believe tradition, had been adorned with strange fruit, such as Tristan L'Hermite delighted to suspend from his master's forests. We know that

William Robinson and Marmaduke Stevenson, convicted Quakers, were hung upon the Common. Mary Dyar was reprieved after her foot was on the fatal ladder, through the intercession of her son, and escaped to meet a similar fate the next year. The lifeless forms of Margaret Jones, of Anne Hibbins, and perhaps

THE OLD ELM.

other victims of judicial murder, may have depended from these same limbs during the reign of the witchcraft horrors. The remains of those who suffered at this time were treated with studied cruelty. Their bodies were refused their friends, and even the privilege of protecting their place of sepulture was denied.

The best judges considered the age of this tree to have been considerably more than two hundred and fifty years. It appears to have exceeded the usual term of maturity allotted to its species; but artificial means, with great care for its preservation, had no doubt eked out its existence. A terse biography of the tree is found on the entrance to the enclosure, placed there by Mayor Smith, under whose direction the fence was erected : —

THE OLD ELM.

This tree has been standing here for an unknown period. It is believed to have existed before the settlement of Boston being full grown in 1722. Exhibited marks of old age in 1792, and was nearly destroyed by a storm in 1832. Protected by an Iron Enclosure in 1854.

J. V. C. Smith, Mayor.

It should be mentioned, however, that a tradition has been current which assigns to Captain Daniel Henchman — the same who commanded a company of foot from Boston, in King Philip's war, and was also captain of the Ancient and Honorable Artillery Company in 1676 — the honor of planting the Great Elm, six years earlier. This, if true, would make the elm more than two hundred years old. But the tree could hardly have attained, in fifty-two years, to the size represented on the earliest plan of the town. It is also worthy of remark that the age of Liberty Tree, planted only sixteen years after the settlement, was definitely known and established by the Sons of Liberty, while we nowhere meet with any contemporary account of the planting of the Great Elm.

The shooting of Matoonas, one of King Philip's sagamores, is chronicled in 1656. He was tied to a tree, — perhaps this very elm, — and met death with the stoical indifference of his race.

There was, formerly, on the northerly side of the Great Elm, a cavity large enough to serve as a hiding-place for boys. This being filled with clay and covered with canvas, in process of time was closed up by the natural action of the tree. Known a hundred years ago as The Great Tree, and appearing full-grown a century and a half gone by, this venerable tree might, without dispute, have claimed to be the oldest inhabitant.

Among the events with which the history of the Common is connected is the duel fought near the Powder House, July 3,

1728, at between seven and eight o'clock in the evening. Both the combatants were young men of the first respectability; their names, Benjamin Woodbridge and Henry Phillips. They fought with swords, the former being thrust through the body, while his adversary received some slight wounds. Phillips was hurried away on board the Sheerness man-of-war, then lying in the harbor, by his brother Gillam Phillips, Peter Faneuil, and some others. The body of the unfortunate Woodbridge was found the next morning lying near the scene of the affray. Mr. Sargent, better known as the "Sexton of the Old School," has given some interesting details of this affair. The Faneuils and Phillipses were connected by marriage, which accounts for the agency of Peter Faneuil in Henry Phillips's escape. Young Woodbridge lies in the Granary Burying-Ground.

This duel gave rise to a new law, which decreed that the offender, upon conviction, should "be carried publicly in a cart to the gallows, with a rope about his neck, and set on the gallows an hour, then to be imprisoned twelve months without bail." Any person killed in a duel was denied "Christian Burial," and interred "near the usual place of public execution with a stake drove through the body." Death was the penalty meted out to the survivor with the same vindictive pursuit of the senseless remains.

When the British troops were first stationed in the town, they had a hospital at the bottom of the Common; it took fire and was nearly consumed in May, 1769. There was also, at a later period, a guard-house in the same locality.

Public executions have occurred at the bottom of the Common, at or near the foot of Beacon Street, the criminals being hastily buried in the loose gravel of the beach. So carelessly was this performed that an eyewitness relates that he has seen the corpse of one victim disinterred by the sea, with the mark of the hangman's noose still visible.

The Mill-Dam, or Western Avenue, now Beacon Street, shows hardly a trace of its old character or purpose, it being bordered in its whole extent by residences. It was the greatest undertaking in its day Boston had witnessed; we may even doubt whether the far-seeing Mr. Cotting perceived it to be the first step towards converting the Back Bay into *terra firma*.

The work was begun in 1818 by the Boston and Roxbury Mill Corporation, but Mr. Cotting did not live to see its completion, Colonel Loammi Baldwin succeeding him as engineer. In our Introduction we have given a very brief account of this thoroughfare. Laborers were brought from Ireland specially to be employed on it, and it was opened with due ceremony. A cavalcade of citizens crossed from the Brookline shore, and were received by the inhabitants on the Boston side.

Many recollect the entrance into the city of the Massachusetts Volunteers after the Mexican war. They were almost literally in rags, and it was not until the charitable hands of Boston ladies had supplied needful clothing that the regiment was able to march into town. Their appearance indicated little of the "pomp and circumstance," but much of the hard usage and bad rations, of glorious war.

We may now pursue our way up the ascent of Beacon Street and its neighboring mall. The expense of this mall was defrayed from a fund raised by subscription to erect fortifications during the war of 1812, then remaining in the hands of the town officers.

> "Here aged trees cathedral walks compose,
> And mount the hill in venerable rows."

The name of Beacon Street was applied very early to that portion north and east of the State House, and to the westerly part before the Revolution. At this time there were not more than three houses between Charles Street and the upper end of the Common, the Joy house, when built, making the fourth. The rest of the hill was covered with small cedars and native shrubbery, with here and there a cow-path, through which the herds ranged unmolested.

The home of Prescott, the eminent historian, was at 55 Beacon Street. A deeper interest attaches to the labors of the gifted author on account of his partial blindness, caused by an injury to his eye while at Harvard. All efforts both at home and abroad failed to improve his sight, and his literary work had to be performed with the aid of an amanuensis, though he occasionally wrote with a stylus on a writing-frame prepared expressly for him. No library can be called complete that does not contain "Ferdinand and Isabella," "The Conquest of Mexico," "Peru," and "Charles the Fifth." He died before completing his Philip II., which he had intended to make his greatest work. Mr. Prescott was the grandson of the old soldier of Louisburg and Bunker Hill, and by a coincidence married a granddaughter of that Captain Linzee who commanded the Falcon at the battle just named. He was a D. C. L. of Old Oxford, and member of many of the learned societies of Europe and America.

The mansion of the late David Sears, now a club-house, is rendered interesting as the site of the home of John S. Copley, the distinguished American painter. Copley owned the greatest estate in Boston, embracing eleven acres, in which were included the reserved six acres of Blackstone. Walnut Street was the eastern boundary, Pinckney Street its northern, and the bay its westerly limit. On the northwest corner of the tract stood the old Powder House to which we have referred. It was built in 1774, remote from the position of the former magazine near the Great Tree, where it had been exposed to accidents on days of public rejoicing. The walls were of Braintree granite, seven feet thick, with bomb-proof arch. It was surrounded by palisades, and was estimated to contain, when full, a thousand barrels of powder. Near it was a watch-house.

Copley was in a certain sense a pupil of Smibert, the works of that artist having been his first studies. He married a daughter of Richard Clarke, a rich merchant, and one of the obnoxious tea-consignees. The painter acted for the consignees in one of the conferences with the town committee. The Clarkes had a store in King Street, and lived in the Cooke mansion, previously described, in School Street. The house was visited by a mob, and the Clarkes with the other consignees retired for safety to the Castle.

In the old two-story house which formerly stood here Copley painted some of his best pictures, probably those of Hancock and Adams among the number. Here also Charles W. Peale, father of Rembrandt Peale, studied with Copley in 1768. In 1774, leaving his family in Boston, Copley went to England, where he at once gained an advanced rank among the

THE SEARS ESTATE.

British painters. His Death of Lord Chatham established his fame, and his large picture of the Siege and Relief of Gibraltar was hung in Guildhall, London. He died suddenly in 1813.

Dunlap relates that Copley's death was thought to have been hastened by the following circumstance: —

"Some American speculator who was acquainted with the superb situation of Copley's house in Boston, overlooking the beautiful green and parade called the Common, made an offer to the painter for the purchase, which, in comparison to the value of property in former days in Boston, seemed enormous. Copley eagerly closed with him, and sold the property for a song compared with its real value. Shortly after, he, learning it was worth twenty times the money he had sold it for, tried to undo the bargain, and sent his lawyer son to Boston for the purpose, but it was too late."

The following is the true history of this transaction. When Colonel William Hull was in England, he bought of Copley all his tract of land west of the Beacon Hill. About the same time Gardiner Greene, Copley's son-in-law and agent, sold the same property to Harrison Gray Otis and Jonathan Mason. The other claimants at length compromised with Colonel Hull, and the conveyance was made by the younger Copley in 1796, when he came to the United States. The society of the future Chancellor of Great Britain was much courted during his visit to Boston and New York. The elder Copley never returned to his native city.

Trumbull describes Copley as an elegant-looking man, dressed in fine maroon cloth coat with gilt buttons. Besides being a painter, Copley was an engraver, having executed a portrait of Rev. William Welsteed of Boston. This knowledge served him in good stead in London. Copley, with West, was one of Trumbull's sureties when the latter was thrown into prison in London.

Lord Lyndhurst said his father was his own master, and entirely devoted to his art to the last year of his life, and that he never saw a decent picture, except his own, until he was thirty. Sully's opinion of Copley was that he was equal "in all respects but one to West; he had not so great despatch, but then he was more correct, and did not so often repeat himself."

The adverse criticism upon Copley's pictures was that they were crude in coloring, and wanted ease and naturalness. His historical paintings were a collection of portraits without action, but his draperies were considered exquisite. Dr. Dibdin considered his portraits admirable, but too stiff and stately. A catalogue of the existing works of this eminent native artist was prepared by Mr. Augustus T. Perkins of Boston.

General Knox lived in the Copley House, after the war, for

Residence of Hon. John Phillips, First Mayor of Boston, Beacon Street

a short time. The old mansion fronted Beacon Street, and had fine grounds and a stable attached.

David Sears inherited a large fortune from his father, and, go where you will in Boston, you will find monuments of his wealth and enterprise. He commanded the Cadets previous to the war of 1812, as well as since that time. His mansion was long the admiration of the town. Some beautiful panels in the front were executed by Willard.

Harrison Gray Otis erected a handsome residence next west of the Sears estate; Judge Cushing's adjoined it on the east, and was the second of the three houses mentioned as constituting Beacon Street.

The house standing at the corner of Walnut Street was the first built of brick on Beacon Street. It was erected in 1804 by Hon. John Phillips, first Mayor of Boston, and father of Wendell Phillips, the celebrated antislavery orator of Boston. His maiden speech on this question was made in Faneuil Hall in 1837, twenty-four years before the antagonism between the North and South culminated in civil war. Unlike most reformers, he lived to see the triumph of the great principles to which he devoted the best years of his life. He also outlived the social ostracism to which his undeviating advocacy of those principles subjected him for years.

This mansion, now considerably altered in its exterior appearance, was next the residence of Thomas L. Winthrop, lieutenant-governor of Massachusetts from 1826–32, who died in 1841. He was father of the Hon. Robert C. Winthrop, who has been prominently connected with most of the societies for the advancement of science, art, and literature, and whose services in many fields of usefulness are fully acknowledged by his fellow-citizens. Mr. Winthrop's mother was a daughter of Sir John Temple, and he was, therefore, by this marriage, a great-grandson of Governor Bowdoin. The statue to Franklin, in School Street, is the product of his suggestion; and, at its inauguration, he delivered an address on the life and character of the great Bostonian worthy of the occasion.

On the opposite corner of Walnut Street was the residence of B. P. Homer, a highly respected merchant. In the rear of Mr. Homer's, on Walnut Street, was the house in which Dr. George Parkman lived at the time of his murder by Webster in 1849.

Joy Street recalls the name and estate of Dr. John Joy, extending between this thoroughfare and Walnut Street, and Beacon and Mt. Vernon Streets. Dr. Joy was an apothecary in Washington Street, at the corner of Spring Lane. It is related that his wife was much averse to a removal so far out of town as Beacon Street then was, and exacted a promise from the Doctor to return into the town at no distant day. In that day a residence in Williams Court was considered far more eligible. The doctor built a wooden house on the hill back from Beacon Street, which was ultimately removed to South Boston Point.

Next to the corner of Joy Street lived Samuel T. Armstrong, another of Boston's chief magistrates, of whose improvement of the Common we have recited several instances. He was the son of the Revolutionary soldier, John Armstrong. Mr. Armstrong was lieutenant-governor of Massachusetts in 1836. He had in former years been a bookseller in State Street, at the corner of Flagg Alley, — the firm being Belcher and Armstrong, — and then at No. 50 in Old Cornhill, the site of Paul Revere's shop. This vicinity took the name of Booksellers' Row, from the number of that trade there congregated.

Before you come to the grounds of the State House, two freestone residences attract your notice. These showy edifices have displaced one of the noblest private mansions of the Colonial period, built by Thomas Hancock in 1737, and given to his nephew, the governor, by his aunt, Lydia Hancock. The house long remained a unique feature of the surroundings of the Common, until it became too antiquated for modern ideas, and too valuable. The front of the estate embraced from Mt. Vernon Street, given to the town by the governor, to Joy Street, formerly Clapboard, and since Belknap Street. All of the original State House and part of the new, including Hancock Avenue, Mt. Vernon Place, and a part of Hancock Street, in which was situated the nursery, belonged to the Hancocks. The site of the State House was Hancock's pasture; and gardens and orchards surrounded this truly princely mansion.

HANCOCK MANSION.

The building was of stone, built in the substantial manner favored by the wealthier Bostonians. The walls were massive. A balcony projected over the entrance-door, upon which opened a large window of the second story. The corners and window-openings were ornamented with Braintree stone, and the tiled roof was surmounted by a balustrade. Dormer windows jutted out from the roof, from which might be obtained a view as beautiful as extensive. A low stone wall protected the grounds from the street, on which was placed a light wooden fence, with gate-posts of the same material. A paved walk and a dozen stone steps conducted to the mansion, situated on rising ground at a little distance back from the street. Before the door was a wide stone slab, worn by the feet of the distinguished inhabitant and his illustrious guests. A wooden hall, designed for festive occasions, sixty feet in length, was joined to the northern wing; it was afterwards removed to Allen Street.

"As you entered the governor's mansion, to the right was the drawing or reception room, with furniture of bird's-eye maple covered with rich damask. Out of this opened the dining-hall referred to, in which Hancock gave the famous breakfast to Admiral D'Estaing and his officers. Opposite this was a smaller apartment, the usual dining-hall of the family; next adjoining were the china-room and offices, with coach-house and barn behind.

"At the left of the entrance was a second saloon, or family drawing-room, the walls covered with crimson paper. The upper and lower halls were hung with pictures of game, hunting-scenes, and other subjects. Passing through this hall, another flight of steps led through the garden to a small summer-house close to Mt. Vernon Street. The grounds were laid out in ornamental flower-beds bordered with box; box-trees of large size, with a great variety of fruit, among which were several immense mulberry-trees, dotted the garden."

Such is the description given by Miss Eliza G. Gardner, many years an inmate of the Hancock House.

This was the house pillaged by the soldiers about the time of the battle of Lexington, who also broke down and mutilated the fences, until, on complaint of the selectmen, General Gage sent Percy to occupy it. It is also stated that in the previous month of March British officers had set an example to the men by hacking the fences with their swords, breaking windows, etc. A few days afterwards Hancock was again intruded upon by his red-coated neighbors, who refused to retire from his premises at his request, and mockingly told him his possessions would soon be theirs.

At this time Gage had an order from the king for Hancock's apprehension, but he feared to meet the issue; a second order directed him to hang the patriot. The wrath against Hancock escaped in a variety of ways more harmless. One of the effusions indited to the patriot reads thus: —

"As for their king, John Hancock,
And Adams, if they 're taken,
Their heads for signs shall hang up high
Upon that hill called Beacon."

The Hancock House became the quarters of General Clinton while he remained in Boston; he took command at Charlestown, September, 1775. Both house and stables were in part occupied by the wounded from Bunker Hill. The house, however, received no important injury during the occupation, the furniture showing but little signs of ill-usage, and the pictures remaining untouched.

In this house Hancock had entertained D'Estaing in 1778,

Lafayette in 1781, Washington in 1789, Brissot, chief of the Girondists, and, in later times, Lords Stanley and Wortley, and Labouchière and Bougainville.

D'Estaing rested under a cloud for his desertion of our forces in Rhode Island, but was, nevertheless, hospitably entertained by Hancock. About forty of the French officers dined every day at the governor's table, for he was a generous host. On one occasion an unusual number assembled to partake of the governor's viands, when, in the language of Madam Hancock, "the Common was bedizened with lace." The cooks were driven to despair, and the exigency was only met by milking the cows on the Common. We do not learn whether this was acceptable to the owners of the cows. The Count requited the governor's entertainments by a grand dinner on board his ship. The governor's lady, seated near her host, was requested to pull a cord, which was the signal for a discharge of all the guns of the squadron. The good dame confessed herself surprised at this *coup de théâtre*.

Brissot was astonished to find the governor in friendly converse with "a hatter" (Nathaniel Balch). Balch was a great favorite of the governor's. He was a "fellow of infinite jest," majestic in appearance, benevolent, and of sterling worth. His witticisms never failed "to set the table in a roar." Loring relates that when Hancock had occasion to go into the district of Maine on an official visit, he was attended by Hon. Azor Orne of his council, and his old friend Balch. Their arrival at Portsmouth, N. H., was thus humorously announced: —

"On Thursday last, arrived in this town, Nathaniel Balch, Esq., accompanied by His Excellency John Hancock, and the Hon. Azor Orne."

When Hancock was dying he called his old friend Balch to his bedside, and dictated to him the minutes of his will, in which he expressly gave his mansion-house to the Commonwealth. Death intervened before this intention could be carried out.

A strong effort was made to save this old New England monument, but without avail. It was proposed by Governor Banks, in 1859, that the Commonwealth should purchase it, and the heirs offered it at a low valuation. A joint committee of the Legislature reported favorably upon the measure, but it met with strong opposition from the rural districts, and was defeated. Suggestions were offered to make it the residence of the governors, or a museum for the collection of Revolutionary relics. The house was in excellent preservation, the interior wood-work being sound as when the halls echoed to the tread of the old governor. The chamber of Lafayette remained as when he slept in it; the apartment in which Hancock died was intact; the audience-hall was the same in which Washington, D'Estaing, Brissot, the Percy, and many more had stood; and, finally, the entrance-hall, in which for eight days the dead patriot lay in state, opened upon the broad staircase as in the time of old Thomas and Lydia Hancock.

State action failing, some efforts were made by the city, in 1863, to secure the relics of the building itself. The heirs offered the mansion, with the pictures and some other objects of historical interest, as a free gift, with the design of preserving it as a memento of Colonial and Revolutionary history. It was proposed to take it down and erect it anew on some other site. Few will regret that such an historical anachronism was not committed. The building was pulled down, and with it disappeared the only monument to the memory of John Hancock, until one was recently erected in the Granary Ground.

Governor Hancock entered the Latin School in 1745. He went to England when quite young, where he witnessed the coronation of the monarch who afterwards set a price upon his head. President of the Provincial Congress in 1774, of the Continental Congress in 1776, he first affixed his bold autograph to the Declaration of Independence, and it thus circulated upon the floor of Congress. We find him acting as moderator at a town-meeting in 1778, the same year he was appointed major-general of the Massachusetts militia. We have seen him presiding over and directing the action of the convention which ratified the Federal Constitution, and at the peace, the choice of the people of his native State as their chief

Hancock House, Beacon Street

magistrate. Hancock died sincerely regretted. If he had some conspicuous faults, they were more than counterbalanced by his many noble qualities.

Hancock was tall, nearly six feet, and thin. In later years he stooped a little, and was a martyr to the gout. In his attire he was a type of the fine gentleman of his day, — a scarlet coat, richly embroidered, with ruffles of the finest linen, being his ordinary dress.

We give herewith a fac-simile of the much-admired autograph of Governor Hancock appended to a ticket of the lottery authorized by law for the rebuilding of Faneuil Hall after the fire of 1761. The engraving is of the exact size of the original.

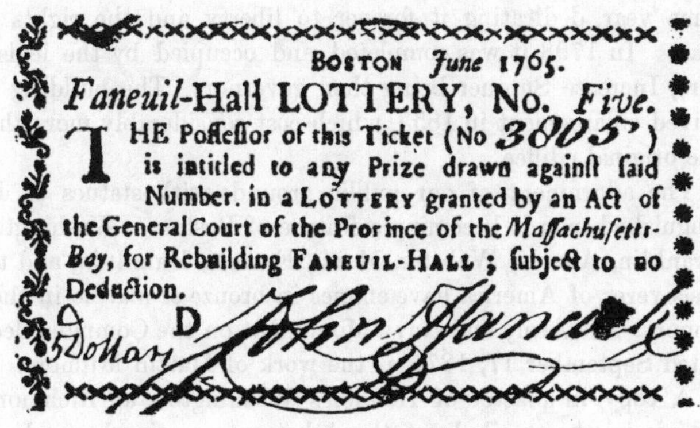

BOSTON *June* 1765.

Faneuil-Hall LOTTERY, No. *Five*.

THE Poſſeſſor of this Ticket (No *3805*) is intitled to any Prize drawn againſt ſaid Number. in a LOTTERY granted by an Act of the General Court of the Province of the *Maſſachuſetts-Bay*, for Rebuilding FANEUIL-HALL; ſubject to no Deduction.

D

5 Dollars

John Hancock

FANEUIL HALL LOTTERY TICKET.

We have reached the highest point of the city, and can leisurely contemplate the immense pile of the State House, with its glistening dome, which fitly crowns the view of Boston as you approach by land or water. It is another monument to the genius of Charles Bulfinch, by whom it was designed. Were we to ascend to the cupola we should see a panorama spread before us which even the famed Neapolitan seaport can hardly surpass. But of Old Boston, as it stood when the first Legislature assembled in the Capitol, we should find but little left. Even the Capitol itself is much changed.

Dr. Holmes has said in his "Autocrat,"—

"Boston State House is the hub of the solar system. You could n't pry that out of a Boston man if you had the tire of all creation straightened for a crowbar."

This expression thus applied only to the State House, but since modified into the "Hub of the Universe," is now generally used in connection with Boston itself, until the Bostonian abroad has become familiar and even content with hearing his native or adopted city styled the "Hub" from Maine to California.

The State House tract was passed by the town to the Commonwealth in 1795; the nominal consideration was five shillings. Samuel Adams laid the corner-stone July 4 of the same year, dedicating it forever to liberty and the rights of man. In 1798 it was completed, and occupied by the legislature, Increase Sumner being then governor. The building received enlargement in 1855, which cost considerably more than the original edifice.

The adornment of our public grounds with statues of distinguished men is becoming a feature of Boston. Washington, Franklin, Adams, Webster, Mann, Everett, Hamilton, and the discoverer of America have effigies in bronze or marble in their honor. The Army and Navy Monument on the Common, dedicated September 17, 1877, is the work of Martin Milmore.

A copy in plaster of Houdon's Washington, at Richmond, Va., is in the vestibule of the Athenæum, as is also a plaster model of the statue of Bowditch by Ball Hughes. The figure of the Saviour on the apex of the pediment of the Church of the Immaculate Conception is a copy from Thorwaldsen. The Aristides and Columbus in Louisburg Square are specimens of Italian art, and were imported by Mr. Iasigi. The statue of Hamilton in granite in Commonwealth Avenue is by Dr. Rimmer, and is believed to have been the first in the country cut from that material. There are also three typical figures in granite on the front of Horticultural Hall, representing Flora, Ceres, and Pomona. These are by Milmore.

The bronze statue of Webster in the State House grounds is

by Powers. It was the second executed by the artist, the first being lost at sea while *en route* from Leghorn. The work hardly fulfilled the expectations of Mr. Webster's admirers, or the hopes founded on the high reputation of the sculptor. It was first placed in the vestibule of the Athenæum, until removed to its present position by consent of the Legislature.

The statue of Horace Mann was cast in Munich, and is the work of Miss Stebbins. The fund was raised by the contributions of school-children and teachers throughout the State. The State paid for the pedestal.

In the vestibule are the statues of Governor Andrew and of Washington. The latter was placed in the State House in 1827, and is by Sir F. Chantrey. The idea originated with gentlemen of Boston who had been associated with Washington in public life. They organized under the name of the Washington Monument Association, and first intended to erect an equestrian statue,—a purpose which want of sufficient funds obliged them to abandon.

We give the interior arrangement of the old halls, as they existed before the remodelling of this building, a hundred years after its erection, and so fortunately preserved from threatened demolition when the palatial addition was built on the Reservoir site.

The torn and battle-stained colors of the Massachusetts regiments are here gathered in the keeping of the Commonwealth. In life, Governor Andrew presented most of these flags; his statue is their appropriate guardian.

In the lower halls were also placed the tablets from the monument formerly on the summit of Beacon Hill. They are four feet four inches long, and three feet three inches wide. The gilt eagle which perched upon the top of the column found a place over the Speaker's chair, in the Hall of Representatives. A reputed bust of Samuel Adams stood in a niche in the wall; and the alcove in which stands the Chantrey statue was flanked by two brass cannon consecrated to the valor of Isaac Davis and John Buttrick, two heroes of the battle of Lexington.

On the 26th of August, 1824, Lafayette received the citizens of Boston in the lower hall; and on the next day a second reception was given by the distinguished Frenchman. No greater crowds ever thronged to do homage to any visitor in the halls of the Capitol. On this occasion the national standard was displayed for the first time from the cupola.

When the General was again in Boston in 1825, to assist at the laying of the corner-stone of Bunker Hill Monument, the Legislature resolved to invite him to meet it in the Hall of Representatives, and requested ex-Governor Lincoln to address him on the occasion. The General was received by both houses in joint convention on the 16th of June, Governor Lincoln in the Speaker's chair. Among the distinguished guests was Mr. Barbour, United States Secretary of War.

In the old Senate Chamber are portraits of the old Colonial governors Endicott, Winthrop, Leverett, Bradstreet, and Burnet. A fine portrait of Governor Sumner, presented by General W. H. Sumner, hung above the President's chair. There are also portraits of Francis Higginson, first minister of Salem, and of Lieutenant-Governor Bill.

On the front of the gallery are some interesting relics of the battle of Bennington, presented by General John Stark. They are a musket, drum, a heavy trooper's sword, and grenadier's cap with the curious conical brass plate, on which, as well as the brass plate of the drum, is embossed the emblematic horse of the Duchy of Westphalia.

Underneath is the letter of acceptance written by order of the General Assembly, and signed by Jeremiah Powell, President of the Council.

Besides these are two old firelocks, bequeathed to the State by Rev. Theodore Parker. One of them has the maker's name on the lock-plate, "Grice, 1762," and an inscription on the butt as follows: —

> "The First Fire Arm,
> Captured in the
> War for Independence."

The other is more antiquated in appearance. It has the donor's name on the lock-plate, and an inscription on the breech which reads, —

"This Firearm was used by
Capt John Parker
in the Battle of Lexington
April 19th
1775."

In connection with the State House we present an engraving of the desk, long used in the Old State House by successive speakers of the House of Representatives. On the removal of the Legislature from their time-honored place of meeting, this desk was deemed too antiquated for further service. It is now one of the interesting memorials of the colony in the keeping of the Historical Society. The chair is a relic of Plymouth Colony, having belonged to Governor Edward Winslow, and is also deposited with the same society.

SPEAKER'S DESK, AND WINSLOW'S CHAIR.

Let us contrast for a moment the spacious halls of legislation and conveniences of the New State House with the confined limits of the Old, and let John Adams describe the famous Council Chamber of the latter as he saw it in 1768.

"The same glorious portraits of King Charles II. and King James II., to which might be added, and should be added, little miserable likenesses of Governor Winthrop, Governor Bradstreet, Governor Endicott, and Governor Belcher, hung up in obscure corners of the room. Lieutenant-Governor Hutchinson, Commander-in-Chief in the absence of the Governor, must be placed at the head of the council table. Lieutenant-Colonel Dalrymple, Commander-in-Chief of his Majesty's military forces, taking rank of all his Majesty's counsellors, must be seated by the side of the Lieutenant-Governor and Commander-in-Chief of the province. Eight-and-twenty counsellors must be painted, all seated at the council-board. Let me see, what costume? What was the fashion of that day in the month of March? Large white wigs, English scarlet cloth cloaks, some of them with gold-laced hats, not on their heads, indeed, in so august a presence, but on a table before them. Before these illustrious personages appeared Samuel Adams, a member of the House of Representatives, and their clerk, now at the head of the great assembly at the Old South Church. Thucydides, Livy, or Sallust would make a speech for him, or perhaps the Italian Botta, if he had known anything of this transaction, one of the most important of the Revolution; but I am wholly incapable of it; and if I had vanity enough to think myself capable of it, should not dare to attempt it."

The portraits referred to by the venerable writer were full lengths, attributed to Vandyke, but evidently erroneously, as these monarchs were minors when Vandyke died. Governor Pownall, in whose time they were sent over, placed them in some obscure corner, where they remained until Governor Bernard discovered and mounted them in elegant frames, and hung them in the Council Chamber.

In the State Library was a fine original portrait of General Gage, presented to the State by General W. H. Sumner, between whom and the British general's wife it will be remembered a relationship existed. The last of the royal governors is now restored to fellowship with his illustrious predecessors.

Suspended from the ceiling of the Representatives' Chamber is the ancient symbol of Massachusetts, the codfish, which has been a greater source of wealth than the mines of California. The same fish, which the reader may see upon one of the colony stamps we have represented in a previous chapter, hung in the old hall in State Street, but was taken down, and was not restored until after the peace, when, on the motion of John Rowe, it was again displayed before the assembled wisdom of the Commonwealth.

Other evidence that the much maligned codfish was the accepted official emblem of Massachusetts, in bygone days, is found in the fact stated by Colden that, at a conference held with the Five Nations at The Oneida Castle, in 1690, "New England, which the Indians call Kinshon, a fish," sent the wooden model of a codfish, as a token of its adherence to the general covenant. "This fish was handed round among the sachems, and then laid aside to be put up." On another occasion "3000 of codfish" was sent to England as a present to the king from the General Court, hoping thus to win a monarch's favor by hook or by crook.

The summit of Beacon Hill, on which stood the ancient Pharos of Boston, is intersected by Temple Street, named for Sir John Temple, who married a daughter of Governor Bowdoin. A portion of the elevation comes within the Reservoir site, and the houses south of it. The tract owned by the town was only six rods square, with a way of thirty feet leading to it. This was sold to John Hancock and Samuel Spear in 1811, when the action of the abutters in digging down the hill rendered it untenable. On the top of this grassy mound was erected the Beacon, shown in all the early plans of the town. It was a tall mast standing on cross timbers placed upon a stone foundation, and supported by braces. Treenails were driven through the mast by which it was ascended; and near the top projected a crane of iron sixty-five feet from the base, upon which was suspended an iron skeleton frame, designed to receive a barrel of tar, or other combustibles. This receptacle was placed at an altitude of more than two hundred feet from the sea level, and could be seen, when fired, for a great distance inland. Its object was to alarm the country in case of invasion. This beacon was erected about 1634–35, the town having ordered it set up on Centry Hill in this year, with a watch of one person, to give the signal on the approach of danger. It was newly erected in 1768, having fallen from some cause unknown. In November, 1789, the beacon was blown down.

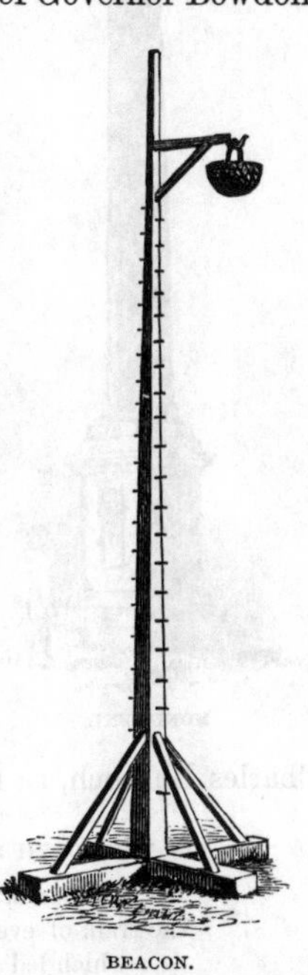
BEACON.

Following the primitive signal spar, a monument of brick, sixty feet in height and four in diameter, was erected, in 1790, commemorating the events of the Revolution. Charles Bulfinch was the designer. It was a plain Doric shaft, raised on a pedestal of stone and brick, eight feet high. The outside was encrusted with cement; and on the top was a large gilded eagle of wood, supporting the American Arms. After the fall of the old beacon, Governor Hancock offered to erect another at his own cost, but the movement for an obelisk being already on foot, the proposal was withdrawn, and the selectmen proceeded to lay out the hill for the monument. The monument was taken down and the hill levelled in 1811. It stood very near the southeast corner of the Reservoir, Temple Street passing directly over its position. The earth which formed the cone was deposited in the Millpond, making a future foundation for the Lowell and Eastern Railroad stations. The tablets of slate bear inscriptions written by the architect, Charles Bulfinch, as follows:—

MONUMENT.

ON THE SOUTH SIDE.

To Commemorate
the train of events
which led
to the American Revolution
and finally secured
Liberty and Independence
to the United States,
this column is erected
by the voluntary contributions
of the citizens
of Boston
M.D.CCXC.

ON THE EAST SIDE.

Americans
While from this eminence
Scenes of luxuriant fertility
of flourishing commerce
and the abodes of social happiness
meet your view,
Forget not those
who by their exertions
Have secured to you
these blessings.

ON THE WEST SIDE.

Stamp Act passed 1765. Repealed 1766.
Board of Customs established, 1767
British troops fired on the inhabitants of Boston,
March 5, 1770
Tea Act passed 1773. Tea destroyed in Boston, December 16.
Port of Boston shut and guarded June 1, 1774.
General Congress at Philadelphia Sept. 5
Battle at Lexington, April 19, 1775.
Battle at Bunker Hill, June 17.
Washington took command of the army July 2.
Boston evacuated, March 17, 1776.
Independence declared by Congress,
Hancock President, July 4.

ON THE NORTH SIDE.

Capture of the Hessians at Trenton, Dec. 26, 1776
Capture of the Hessians at Bennington, Aug. 16, 1777
Capture of the British army at Saratoga, Oct. 17.
Alliance with France Feb. 6, 1778.
Confederation of the United States formed,
Bowdoin President of Convention, 1780.
Capture of the British army at York, Oct. 19, 1781
Preliminaries of Peace Nov. 30, 1782
Definitive Treaty of Peace Sept. 10, 1783
Federal Constitution formed, Sept. 17, 1787
And Ratified by the United States, 1787 to 1790.
New Congress assembled at New York, April 6, 1790.
Washington inaugurated President, April 30.
Public Debt funded, August 4, 1790.

The base of the monument was enclosed by a railing, with benches for the use of pilgrims to the spot. A view, equalled only by that now to be obtained from the lantern of the State House, well repaid a breathless scramble up the steep acclivity. On the Derne Street side a flight of wooden steps conducted part way up the eminence, but, after that, the explorer had to avail himself of the foot-holes worn by other visitors, until he reached a space fifty feet square on the summit. On all sides, except the north, the contour of the ground was perfect; there it had been encroached upon, in 1764, to a degree endangering the elevation, by one Thomas Hodson. The town, by a committee, remonstrated with Hodson, but to no purpose, although Thomas Hancock and James Otis, Esqrs., were of the delegation.

The contumacious Hodson persisted in digging gravel on his lot, and the committee were obliged to content themselves with a recommendation to employ the intervention of the General Court.

No account appears that the original beacon was ever used, but when the troops were momentarily expected in 1768, the Bostonians prepared it for firing, to give the intelligence to the country. Governor Bernard waxed very wroth at this presumption, and sent Sheriff Greenleaf to remove the tar-barrel which the Sons of Liberty had placed in the skillet. "Matters now," wrote the governor, "exceeded all former exceedings."

In 1865 the Legislature authorized the rebuilding of Beacon Hill Monument by the Bunker Hill Monument Association, they to receive the tablets now in the custody of the Commonwealth. To Mr. R. C. Winthrop is said to belong the credit of the suggestion, since carried out to completion.

Mt. Vernon Street was formerly called Sumner Street as far as Belknap; beyond this it was Olive Street. The whole was then called Sumner, and, in 1833, by its present name. Hancock was George Street; Bowdoin, like Hancock, named for the governor, was first Middlecott Street. As early as 1722 only a narrow pathway prolonged Beacon Street across the Hancock pasture, around the base of Beacon Hill. To this the name of Davie's Lane was given. Beacon Street then terminated at the Almshouse.

Besides the ropewalks mentioned west of Hancock Street, there was one east of it, which became the property of the State by purchase. This ropewalk-site now forms the westerly side of the State House. A long ropewalk, coinciding nearly with the line of Joy Street, is upon the earliest map; ropemaking was an important industry of Old Boston, especially of the westerly portion of it.

Succeeding to the old gambrel-roofed Almshouse came the stately edifice at the corner of Park and Beacon Streets, chiefly remarkable as having been the house in which Lafayette sojourned during his visit to Boston in 1824. It was erected by Thomas Amory, before 1800, for his residence, its site commanding a beautiful view of the Common, but was later divided into four dwellings. In part of this mansion resided Christopher Gore, during the year he was governor of Massachusetts. Fisher Ames, who died July 4, 1808, was buried from this house. The funeral services took place at King's Chapel. Hon. Samuel Dexter pronounced his eulogy. It was later tenanted by George Ticknor, the distinguished scholar, one of the founders of the Public Library, and author of the History of Spanish Literature.

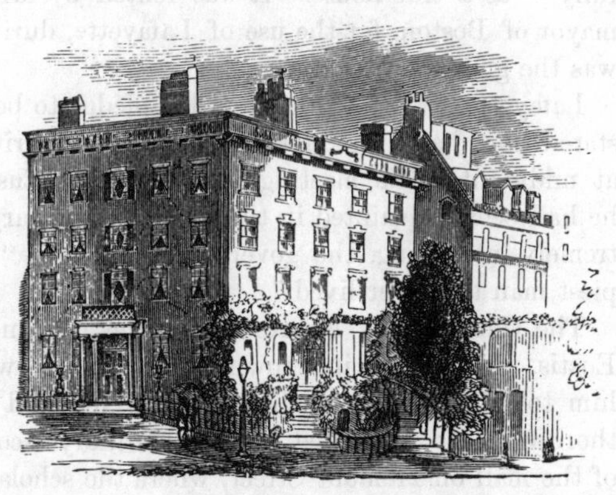

LAFAYETTE'S RESIDENCE.

Before the division of the building, it was kept as a fashionable boarding-house by Mrs. Carter, until she removed to the present Howard Street. These boarding-houses were, before the erection of the Tremont House, the resort of strangers visiting Boston.

Edward G. Malbone, the celebrated portrait-painter, had his studio there. He accompanied Allston to Europe, and was urged by West to remain, but preferred returning to the United States. Malbone excelled in miniature-painting.

Samuel Dexter was a resident in that part of the house fronting on Beacon Street. A Bostonian and a Harvard man, Mr. Dexter was one of the greatest lawyers Massachusetts ever had. Judge Story said of him that he never descended to *finesse* or cunning before a jury; Webster, that his statements were arguments. He served in both houses of Congress; in the upper branch during the exciting times of the troubles with the French Republic. He was successively Secretary of War and of the Treasury, under Mr. Adams, and for a time acting Secretary of State. In politics Mr. Dexter was a stanch Federalist, but supported the war of 1812. He was first president of the first temperance society formed in Massachusetts. The accomplished scholar, Lucius M. Sargent, studied law with Mr. Dexter.

After Mr. Dexter, the building was used — not too successfully — as a club-house. It was rented by Mr. Quincy, when mayor of Boston, for the use of Lafayette, during the week he was the guest of the city.

Lafayette, in order to redeem his pledge to be in Boston at a stated time, had to ride forty miles at night, arriving at Dedham at midnight. His meeting with Governor Eustis, with whom he had been acquainted in the old Revolutionary army, was extremely interesting, the governor exclaiming, "I am the happiest man that ever lived."

The General was escorted from the residence of Governor Eustis, in Roxbury, into town, by a cavalcade which conducted him to the city limits, where he was received by the city authorities. He proceeded, under a military escort, to the head of the mall on Tremont Street, where the scholars of the public schools were drawn up to receive him. All accounts agree that on no occasion were there ever so many people in Boston before. After paying his respects to the governor and Council in the Senate Chamber, the General was conveyed to his lodgings. A handsome arch was thrown over Washington Street, at the site of the old fortifications, with this inscription written on the spur of the moment the day previous by the poet Sprague : —

"Welcome, Lafayette !
The fathers in glory shall sleep,
That gathered with thee to the fight,
But the sons will eternally keep
The tablet of gratitude bright.
We bow not the neck, and we bend not the knee ;
But our hearts, Lafayette, we surrender to thee."

Another arch was erected on the site of the Old Liberty Stump, opposite Boylston Market. Lafayette rode, uncovered, in the barouche with Mr. Quincy, bowing incessantly to the multitudes that pressed around him. A scene of great interest occurred when the General appeared on the balcony of the mansion he was to occupy. On either side of him were Governor

Eustis and ex-Governor Brooks, clad in their old Continental uniforms. These two, brothers in arms, had buried an old animosity to greet the noble Frenchman,—a circumstance known to and applauded by many. The Boston Regiment, which had escorted the General, passed in review; and, amid the cheers of thousands of spectators, the General and his distinguished companions withdrew.

A dinner was given to Lafayette at the Exchange Coffee House on the 27th, at which, after the company had partaken of an elegant repast provided by Colonel Hamilton, the General gave the following toast: —

"The city of Boston, the cradle of Liberty; may Faneuil Hall ever stand a monument to teach the world that resistance to oppression is a duty, and will, under true republican institutions, become a blessing."

The General made a visit to the battle-ground of Bunker Hill, also to the Navy Yard, where he was welcomed by Commodore Bainbridge. He passed an evening at Mrs. Lloyd's, lady of Senator Lloyd, at their residence in Somerset Street. He also visited Governor Eustis at Roxbury, and Governor Brooks at Medford, where, in allusion to the ex-governor, an arch was erected near the meeting-house with the inscription: —

"General Lafayette,
Welcome to our hills and Brooks."

He attended divine service on Sunday at Brattle Street, where he heard Dr. Palfrey, and in the afternoon went to Quincy to dine with the venerable John Adams. "That was not the John Adams I remember," said the General, sadly, afterwards. "That was not the Lafayette I remember," said the patriarch after the meeting.* Both had changed, the ex-President was verging on ninety, and the General sixty-seven; Mr. Adams died in 1826, Lafayette in 1834.

On Monday, August 30, a grand military review took place on the Common. The troops were under the command of Major-General Crane. The Cadets escorted General Lafayette from his lodgings to the State House, thence to the Common,

* Life of Quincy.

where the governor and other officers of the Commonwealth were assembled. About six thousand troops took part in the review, Generals Lyman and Appleton commanding brigades. Dinner was served in an immense marquee, to which more than twelve hundred guests sat down. In the evening the General gave a levee at his residence which was thronged by all classes, the Marquis bestowing particular attention on every individual of humble appearance or advanced age.

Lafayette enjoyed his visit to Boston highly. He was cheered to the echo whenever he went abroad, and the corner of Park Street was seldom deserted. One day, when he returned from some excursion with the mayor, there was a great crowd to see him alight. He turned to the mayor and said, "Mr. Quincy, were you ever in Europe?" "No, General." "Then," said Lafayette, "you cannot understand the difference between a crowd in Europe and here in Boston; why, I should imagine the people of your city were a picked population out of the whole human race."

General Lafayette's first visit to Boston was in 1778, with D'Estaing. He was next here in 1780, when he returned from a trip to France, where he had been to transact some business. He remembered perfectly the persons who had received him on that occasion, — when he landed from the frigate Hermione at Hancock's wharf, — and whom he had visited. On his second visit he was accompanied by his son and by M. Levasseur. The people of America will not soon forget their generous and gallant ally, who asked permission to serve as a volunteer in the American army. Brandywine, where he was wounded, and the trenches of Yorktown, alike attest his valor. He has no monument; but paper, even more durable than marble, furnishes us with records like this: —

"Head-quarters Oct. 15th, 1781.

For to-morrow.

M. G. M. La Fayette,

B. G. Muhlenburg and

Haynes' brigade.

Maj. gen. La Fayette's division will mount the trenches to-morrow."

It was at Yorktown that the Marquis, with his American Light Division, stormed the enemy's river-battery, while Baron Vioménil, with the French grenadiers and chasseurs, assaulted another important work on the extreme left. The Americans, with the Marquis at their head, succeeded in capturing their redoubt first, when Lafayette sent his aid, Major Barbour, to the Baron with the message, "I am in my redoubt; where are you?" The Baron, who was waiting for his men to clear away the abattis, returned answer, "I am not in mine, but will be in five minutes." A touching incident of his visit connected with this exploit is related by Mr. Quincy:—

"On the day of his arrival an old soldier would press through the crowd in the State House, and cried out, 'You don't remember me, General; but I was close to you when we stormed our redoubt at Yorktown. I was just behind Captain Smith. You remember Captain Smith? He was shot through the head as he mounted the redoubt.' 'Ah yes, yes! I remember,' returned Lafayette. 'Poor Captain Smith! *But we beat the French! we beat the French!*'"

Next below the residence of Mr. Ticknor on Park Street was that of Hon. Abbott Lawrence. Farther down was that of Josiah Quincy, Jr., the second mayor of that name. His administration will be remembered for the introduction of the Cochituate water,—a measure strenuously urged by his father twenty years before its accomplishment. The event was celebrated with military and civic displays, and an immense multitude thronged the Common to see the water let on for the first time.

At the corner of Beacon and Mt. Vernon Streets was the residence of William Molineux, one of the early patriots and a prominent merchant. He built a splendid mansion for his day, but died in 1774. Mr. Molineux was one of the famous committee that demanded of Governor Hutchinson the immediate removal of the troops after the Massacre. His colleagues were Adams (Samuel), Hancock, Warren, Phillips, Henshaw, and Pemberton. John Adams relates, as an amusing incident, that Molineux was obliged to march side by side with the commander of some of the troops, to protect them from the indignation of the people, in their progress to the wharf, from which they were to embark for the Castle.

As the agent of Charles Ward Apthorp, Mr. Molineux rented the stores belonging to the former, on Wheelwright's wharf, for barracks. The estate of Molineux seems to have passed to Mr. Apthorp, for we find it confiscated as such by the Commonwealth. In 1782 it became the residence of Daniel Denison Rogers.

Having completed our circuit of the Common, we may venture the remark that its beauty, as a park, is surpassed by the value of its historical associations.

We have seen that part of the forces which captured Louisburg were assembled and organized here; that the troops which conquered Quebec were recruited and probably brigaded here by Amherst; that it was the mustering-place for the conflicts which ushered in the American Revolution; and the fortified camp which held the beleaguered town in subjection.

It is associated with the deep horrors of Quaker executions; with the eloquence of Whitefield, which paved the way for many eminent divines after him to address the people under the "Cathedral trees." It has in all times been a place for public rejoicings, for the celebration of our republican calendar days, or for martial displays.

The repeal of the Stamp Act was celebrated in Boston on the 19th May, 1766, as no event was ever observed before. Daybreak was ushered in with music, the beating of drums, and firing of small-arms. The guns of the Castle proclaimed the joyful intelligence, which was taken up and echoed by the town batteries. In the evening an obelisk, which had been erected on the Common, was illuminated with two hundred and eighty lamps. There was a general illumination. Hancock's mansion was brilliant with lights, and in front of the house a stage was built from which fireworks were exhib-

REPEAL OBELISK.

ited. The Sons of Liberty had erected a similar stage in front of the Workhouse, from which they answered the display at the Hancock House. Under this hospitable roof were entertained "the genteel part of the Town," while the crowd outside were treated with a pipe of wine.

The obelisk was intended to be placed under Liberty Tree, but was consumed the night of the celebration. Next above the pedestal were allegorical figures on each of the sides, symbolizing the condition of the colony from the enactment to the repeal of the Stamp Act. We give a copy of an engraving, by Paul Revere, reproducing one of the sides.

AMERICA IN DISTRESS.

Accident alone prevented the Common being the scene of a sanguinary struggle between the royal and American forces. When Washington occupied Dorchester Heights, he confidently expected an attack from Howe, and had prepared a counterstroke. Two divisions, under Putnam, were to attack the town. Sullivan, with one, was to assault the works on Beacon Hill, Greene, with the other, was to carry the post at Barton's Point, and make his way to a junction with Sullivan. Greene was well qualified for the task assigned him, having been in Boston two years before, and seen the lines on the Common. Providence arrested the purpose of Howe, and the town was entered without a shot being fired.

Hancock has the credit of first introducing music upon the Common for the benefit of the people. He caused a band to play in front of his dwelling, paid for by himself. In former times booths and stands for the sale of refreshments were erected along Paddock's and the Great Mall, ultimately embracing all four sides of the Common.

Lord Harris, who was captain of the grenadier company of the Fifth Foot, Percy's regiment, wrote home, in 1774, "Our camp is pitched in an exceedingly pleasant situation on the gentle descent of a large common, hitherto the property of the Bostonians, and used for the purpose of grazing their cows, which now, poor creatures, often attempt to force their way into their old pastures, where the richest herbage I ever saw abounds."

Lord Harris relates an instance of a cow impaling herself on a range of firelocks with the bayonets on, going off with one sticking in her side. Harris's company was at Lexington. At Bunker Hill he received a wound in the head, falling senseless into the arms of his lieutenant, Lord Rawdon.

Public executions occurred occasionally on the Common until 1812, when the park was rescued from these legalized exhibitions. It ceased to be a common grazing-field under the elder Quincy in 1830, dangerous accidents having occurred to promenaders. If a mere handful of settlers more than two centuries ago allotted fifty acres for the common benefit, a quarter of a million people can well afford to preserve it.

CHAPTER XII.

VALLEY ACRE, THE BOWLING GREEN, AND WEST BOSTON.

Governor Bowdoin. — General Burgoyne. — Boston Society in 1782. — David Hinckley's Stone Houses. — James Lloyd. — Lafayette. — Daniel Davis. — Admiral Davis. — Historic Genealogical Society. — Valley Acre. — Uriah Cotting. — Governor Eustis. — Anecdote of Governor Brooks. — Millerite Tabernacle. — Howard Athenæum. — Bowling Green. — Old Boston Physicians. — Charles Bulfinch. — New Fields. — Peter Chardon. — Mrs. Pelham. — Peter Pelham. — Thomas Melvill. — Dr. William Jenks. — Captain Gooch. — West Church. — Leverett Street Jail. — Poor Debtors. — Almshouse. — Massachusetts General Hospital. — Medical College. — National and Eagle Theatres.

GOVERNOR JAMES BOWDOIN lived on Beacon Street, near the corner of the street named for him, the house being situated at some distance back from the street, with a high flight of stone steps leading up to it. The family name of the governor was Baudoin. Frequent mention is made in these pages of prominent events or institutions with which the name of Governor Bowdoin is connected. He was chief magistrate of Massachusetts from 1785 – 87, and Shays's Rebellion occurred under his administration. It was vigorously suppressed by Bowdoin, to whose aid the officers of the old army quickly rallied. This was the dark period of our history. The old Articles of Confederation were entirely inadequate to carry on the government. No taxes could be levied without the consent of all the States, and the central government was likely to fall to pieces for want of the means to carry it on. Public and private credit shared the general wreck.

At this crisis the rebellion of Shays broke out. General Lincoln commanded the State forces, with Generals Brooks and Cobb to support him. The outbreak was crushed with little bloodshed, and the authority of the laws restored. Bowdoin's popularity was impaired by this affair, and he lost his election in

1787. He was a sufferer from consumption, and finally succumbed to its attacks.

General Burgoyne occupied the Bowdoin mansion in 1775; at the same time Clinton resided in that of Governor Hancock. These two chiefs overlooked the forces on the Common, and had particular charge of the defences of West Boston. The mansion in after times became the boarding-house of Mrs. Delano.

Next, to the eastward, was the residence of William Phillips, Senior, — a fine old pre-Revolutionary mansion, approached by several flights of stone steps. It stood on the hill, at a higher elevation than the Bowdoin or Sears houses on either side of it, the summit being considerably higher than the house-tops now in Ashburton Place. Some noble trees standing on the estate formed a landmark for approaching vessels, — they were cut down for fuel by the British. This estate belonged successively to Samuel Sewall and Edward Bromfield. Freeman Place Chapel was erected on the site.

What the society of Beacon Street and its vicinity was in the last century may be gathered from the testimony of a keen observer of that period.

Count Segur says that "Boston affords a proof that democracy and luxury are not incompatible, for in no part of the United States is so much comfort or a more agreeable society to be found. Europe does not offer, to our admiration, women adorned with greater beauty, elegance, education, or more brilliant accomplishments than the ladies of Boston, such as Mesdames Smith, Tudor, Jervis, and Morton." M. de Chastellux also pays suitable acknowledgments to the Boston ladies, like a gallant Frenchman; while both unite in eulogy of Adams, Hancock, Dr. Cooper, and other leading spirits it was their fortune to meet.

The two stone houses at the easterly corner of Beacon and Somerset Streets, sometime the home of the American Congregational Association, were erected soon after the war of 1812 by David Hinckley. They were, at that time, the handsomest private residences in Boston, and were occupied successively by citizens distinguished in financial or commercial pursuits, until they became the Somerset Club House. They have lately passed into the hands of Houghton and Dutton.

Connected with one house is a domestic tragedy, which can now affect no one by repetition. An Italian, named Perodi, who was the French teacher of a daughter of Mr. Hinckley, availed himself of the opportunity to secure the young lady's affections. This, coming to the knowledge of her friends, resulted in an interview, at which Perodi advanced pretensions to rank and position in the old country by documents afterwards alleged to be forged. The *dénouement* occasioned the absence of Perodi for a time; but he returned, and, ascertaining that the object of his pursuit was then living in Somerset Place (Allston Street), repaired thither, entered the house unperceived, ascended the stairs to the lady's apartment, and, being discovered, stabbed himself with a poniard.

Mr. Hinckley took down an old stone house situated on his lot, considered the oldest, of stone, in Boston. It was built by Rev. James Allen of the First Church, and was occupied by his descendants until about 1806, one of whom, Jeremiah Allen, was high sheriff of Suffolk.

Proceeding onward through Somerset Street, *modo pedestri*, we pass the site of the First Baptist Church, Ashburton Place, formerly Somerset Court, to Pemberton Square, and its new Court House, where before stood a double brick mansion, with arched doorway, under the sign of the "Somerset House."

This house was built by Hon. James Lloyd after Somerset Street was laid out, and opened at the back upon the gardens of his father's estate, which extended up the hill beside that of Gardiner Greene. The elder Lloyd was a very distinguished physician; Drs. Joseph Warren, John Jeffries, Isaac Rand, and John Clarke were students with him. He was for some time surgeon at the Castle, and had a fine old residence on Tremont Row.

His son was in the United States Senate in 1808–13, during a most exciting period. A Bostonian by birth, he had been active in mercantile affairs before engaging in political life. Lafayette became his guest in this house in 1825. During this sojourn the Marquis paid visits to Daniel Webster, John Adams, at Quincy, General Hull, at the residence of Mr. McLellan in Winthrop Place, where he met his old companions in arms, Generals Cobb, Huntington, Colonel Putnam, and others. He also visited General Dearborn and Hon. T. L. Winthrop, Mrs. Ticknor, in Tremont Street, Madam Humphries, widow of his old comrade General Humphries, in Mt. Vernon Street, and attended a party given in his honor by Mayor Quincy.

A public dinner was given to Lafayette at the Marlborough Hotel, at which were present the Secretary of War, Governor, and Lieutenant-Governor, Hons. Messrs. Phillips, Lloyd, and Webster, the veteran Colonel McLane, and others. Odes were delivered on this occasion by Charles Sprague and Colonel Everett. The General went afterwards to the Boston Theatre, where he listened to a complimentary address from Miss Powell, and witnessed the play of Charles II., with Finn, Kilner, etc., in the cast.

The two buildings on the opposite side of the street, one of which is used by the Historic Genealogical Society, were built by Daniel Davis, a lawyer of some prominence in the District of Maine, who removed to Boston in 1804. As a barrister, his talents were not, perhaps, conspicuous at a bar where Otis, Morton, and their peers practised, but he had the faculty of grasping the points of a case in the court-room, and constructing his argument as the trial progressed. He was appointed Solicitor-General by Governor Strong, — an office created expressly for him, as, in 1767, it had been for Jonathan Sewall. Perez Morton was at the same time Attorney-General.

Rear-Admiral Charles H. Davis was the son of Daniel Davis, and was born in the most southerly of the two houses. Admiral Davis is best known as victor in the engagement with the rebel fleet before Memphis, Tenn., in June, 1862. His scientific labors in connection with the naval service have been of great value. He was with Dupont in the expedition which captured Port Royal, with Farragut below Vicksburg, and in the expedition up the Yazoo. While engaged in the coast survey he discovered several dangerous shoals off Nantucket, in the track of vessels bound into New York.

The New England Historic Genealogical Society occupies the northerly house, — a handsome and well-arranged building. The local histories and family genealogies of New England are the objects upon which the society has been founded. For an antiquarian association it is eminently progressive, — a circumstance that accounts for its rise and progress among older institutions of its kind. Its collections, open to every student, are made available through the exertions and interest of its officers in every department of historical research. The collections and publications of the society have stimulated the writing of town histories, so that what was once a hopeless labor may be investigated in a brief period and with system.

The society had its beginning in 1844, with five gentlemen well known in antiquarian circles, namely, Charles Ewer, Samuel G. Drake, W. H. Montague, J. Wingate Thornton, and Lemuel Shattuck. Mr. Ewer, an old Boston bookseller, was the first president. He deserves honorable mention as the projector of the South Cove improvement and the opening of Avon Street. In 1845 the society was incorporated.

This elegant building, which was dedicated in 1871, cost about $40,000, and was entirely paid for by subscriptions among members and others, raised chiefly through the instrumentality of its president, Hon. Marshall P. Wilder. It contains 30,000 volumes, 25,000 pamphlets, and a large collection of manuscripts and curiosities, which, being wholly germane to the field in which the society labors, form a unique and valuable library.

Valley Acre was a name anciently applied to the valley lying between Pemberton and Beacon Hills, now intersected by Somerset and Bulfinch Streets, and reaching to the low ground below. The name was retained until about the present century, or until the disappearance of the hills upon either side deprived it of significance.

Farther down Somerset Street we miss the substantial, comfortable-looking residences of Messrs. Webster and Cotting, and of Dr. Jackson, whose name is associated with the ether discovery. The Sultan sent a decoration to Dr. Jackson, whose claims to be the discoverer of the great anæsthetic were disputed by Dr. Morton, the weight of public opinion favoring the latter. We have in the Public Garden a monument dedicated to the discovery, whereon one may seek in vain for the name of him who has conferred such incalculable benefit upon the human race.

It will scarcely be credited that a discovery fraught with such important consequences as was that of applying ether in surgical operations could not be announced in a Boston newspaper until the discoverer sent to the office of publication a paid advertisement. Yet this actually happened less than sixty years ago. Ether was first administered by Dr. W. T. G. Morton, at his office, 19 Tremont Row, now Street, about opposite the northerly end of the Museum, September 30, 1846. The value of the discovery was at first more readily appreciated abroad than at home.

Mr. Cotting, notwithstanding the gigantic enterprises he conducted, in consequence of reverses during the war of 1812, died in straitened circumstances. To his genius Boston owes the inauguration of an era of improvement begun against the traditional and conservative policy of the citizens generally. By dint of indomitable energy and perseverance he succeeded in realizing most of his designs, and, had he lived, would have worthily continued what he had so well begun. Besides the distinguished occupants of the Webster mansion mentioned was William Ropes, an eminent merchant connected with the Russian trade.

Dr. William Eustis, who succeeded John Brooks as governor of Massachusetts in 1824, found his residence in Roxbury — he lived in the old Shirley mansion — too distant from the State House, during sessions of the General Court, and, in the winter of 1825, took lodgings with Mrs. Miles, the successor of Mrs. Carter, in Howard Street. The house stood where the Howard Athenæum is. Here he soon fell ill and died, being buried from this house on the 12th of February with military honors. The funeral services took place at the Old South, and the remains were placed in the Granary Burying Ground. Governor Eustis studied medicine under Joseph Warren; he served as surgeon in the Revolutionary army, and, at its conclusion, took a residence in Sudbury Street, and commenced a practice. He served two terms as member of Congress, and held other offices under the State.

General Sumner relates of him some interesting reminiscences. He says: —

"I remember one occasion particularly, when I was invited to the governor's table to a dinner given in compliment to Lord Stanley, Lord Wortley, and M. Labouchière. The latter gentleman, in his visit to Boston, was so impressed with the beauty and execution of Allston's picture of Elijah in the Wilderness, that he purchased it of the painter at the price of a thousand dollars.

"Brooks and Eustis, two old cronies of the Revolution, about the time of Lafayette's reception, in 1824, were on unfriendly terms. The difference was caused by the election of Brooks as President of the Society of the Cincinnati, a vacancy having occurred while Eustis was vice-president and absent from the country. The friends of both exerted themselves to bring about a reconciliation, and, an interview being arranged, the old friends did not embrace each other merely as old friends, but they shook hands so heartily, and the intercourse was so familiar, — the one calling the other 'John,' and the other calling Eustis 'Doctor,' and sometimes 'Bill,' — that they parted with as friendly feelings as had existed between them at any period.'"

Upon the spot where stands the Howard Athenæum was built, during the excitement of 1843–44, a huge wooden structure, dignified with the name of "Tabernacle." Here the disciples of the prophet Miller awaited the day of ascension, amid scenes that beggar description. The interior was hung with pictures representing the monsters of the Book of Revelation, in which the artist had drawn freely upon imagination to depict the grotesque and horrible. Frenzy seemed to hold possession of the worshippers at this temple; many disposed of all their worldly goods, the reason of others was affected, and the whole city was agitated almost beyond belief, until the day fixed for the end of all things human came and went like other days. An error of calculation had been made by the prophet, but his deluded congregation dissolved silently and ingloriously.

It is related that in building the front wall on Howard Street due regard was not had to safety, and that it had a decided leaning outwards. The mayor's attention being called to the fact, he expostulated with the builders, who replied, "that it made but little difference as the world itself would last but a few days at the most." The mayor, Martin Brimmer, compelled them to rebuild the wall in question, observing that they might incline it so as to fall inward, but not outwardly. Miller, the apostle of the sect, had been a soldier of 1812, serving with distinction on the northern frontier with the rank of captain.

The Tabernacle was next leased for theatrical performances, and under the hands of carpenters and painters underwent a speedy transformation. A new front, painted in imitation of freestone was erected, and the house received the name of the Howard Athenæum.

The first performance was on the night of October 13, 1845, when the "School for Scandal" was given. Messrs. Johnson, Ayling, Ford, and Brayley were the managers. Mr. James H. Hackett, since so famous for his impersonations of the "fat knight," made his first appearance in Boston at this house. In February, 1846, a few minutes after the closing of the theatre, fire was discovered issuing from it, and the theatre-tabernacle was speedily consumed.

The present theatre was built in 1846, and was opened in October of that year under the control of Mr. Hackett. Isaiah Rogers was the architect. At this theatre Mr. William Warren made his *début* before a Boston audience as Sir Lucius O'Trigger, in the "Rivals." The Viennoise Children also appeared at the Howard, creating an unexampled *furor*. The house is further celebrated for the first representations of Italian opera in Boston by a company from Havana, who opened in April, 1847, with "Ernani," when the golden notes of Fortunata Tedesco first enraptured Bostonians. Blangy, the Ravels, Madame Anna Bishop, and other celebrities brought the theatre into high repute. Eliza Ostinelli made her first appearance on the stage at the Howard in "La Sonnambula."

This estate is further noted as the old-time habitation of Hon. James Pitts, a counsellor and mover of the address to General Gage.

Valley Acre is not more obsolete than the old Bowling Green, upon which we have entered to find it changed to Bowdoin Square. Cambridge Street began in early times at Sudbury Street, extending along the green, and thence to the river. What is now the square fell away in a natural slope to the Mill Pond. The rest of the quarter known as West Boston was very sparsely peopled. On a small eminence in the present neighborhood of the West Church was a windmill; rope-walks covered most of the neck known as Barton's Point, on one extremity of which were situated the copper-works, which gave their name to Copper, now Brighton Street. Across the point earthworks were thrown up in 1775. The greater part of the area west of Bowdoin Square was in its primitive condition of fields or pastures, and so remote was it considered from the centre of population, that the Province Hospital and Pest House was located near West Boston Bridge, on what is now Grove Street, from which the point was called "Pest House Point."

A hundred years ago there were but three-and-twenty physicians and surgeons in all Boston. Besides the honored names of Lloyd, Rand, Danforth, Eustis, Jarvis, Hayward, Homans, and Warren, there was Dr. Thomas Bulfinch in Bowdoin Square, father of Charles Bulfinch, the distinguished architect.

The impress of Mr. Bulfinch's genius is seen not only in his native city, but in the Capitol of the nation, which was planned by him after the destruction of the original by the British General Ross. Mr. Bulfinch's early taste for this branch of art was cultivated by travel in the Old World amid the works of Inigo Jones, Sir Christopher Wren, and the old masters of the Continent. Returning, he at once applied himself to the beautifying of his birthplace. Before his day there were but few public buildings that would attract the notice of a stranger. Architectural beauty was but little considered, mere adaptation to the purposes of the structure being all that the builder attempted. The Beacon Hill Monument, the Franklin Street Crescent, the new State House, introduced a new era, which Rogers and Willard, Bryant and Billings, have perpetuated.

Of Mr. Bulfinch's public works the State House was indeed considered somewhat faulty in its proportion of length to height; but it is stated that the original plan contemplated greater length to the wings, — departed from on economical grounds. Mr. Bulfinch was a Harvard man, graduating in the same class with Samuel Dexter and Judge John Davis. He was closely identified with the interests of the town, serving on the Board of Selectmen a period of twenty-two years, during nineteen of which he was Chairman of the Board.

Besides other works of which mention has been made, Mr. Bulfinch was architect of the State Prison, the Old City Hall, the Cathedral in Franklin Street, Federal Street Church and Theatre, the New South Church in Summer Street, the Massachusetts General Hospital, Haymarket Theatre, and of the enlargement of Faneuil Hall. University Hall, at Cambridge, and numerous private residences, attest his industry and the general estimation in which his services were held.

The names of the early dwellers in the "New Fields," as the pastures of West Boston were called, have or had their names reproduced in Allen, Buttolph, Middlecott, Bulfinch, Lynde, and Southack Streets. Garden and Grove were descriptive of points of rural beauty in Allen's pasture, as was Centre Street, of its equal division. Leverett is from the famous old Governor John, and Staniford and Chambers (part of which was called Wiltshire) and Belknap left their patronymics to those avenues. Cambridge Street terminated in a marsh, from which arose the northwest slope of Centinel Hill, the shore receding a considerable distance from the line of Charles Street. The ropewalks referred to were situated upon and in the vicinity of Poplar Street. John Steel made bolt-rope, lines, and other cordage there in 1719.

Before the work of demolition began in Bowdoin Square, it was the seat of many elegant old-time estates, with broad acres, gardens, and noble trees, of which but a solitary specimen here and there is left. The Revere House, from which Webster harangued the citizens, is on the grounds and residence of Kirk Boott, whose son Kirk Boott was connected many years with the Lowell manufactures. The hotel is named for Paul Revere, first president of the Mechanic Charitable Association, by which it was built. It has enjoyed the distinction of entertaining President Fillmore, Jenny Lind, the Prince of Wales, and the Grand Duke Alexis of Russia.

On the site of the Baptist Church, erected in 1840, was the dwelling of Theodore Lyman, Sr. The space in front of the church, once ornamented with trees and separated from the street by an iron fence, is at present utilized by a row of unsightly shops, between which one must pass to reach the church. The Coolidge and Parkman estates are covered with modern structures, as is also that of Lieutenant-Governor Armstrong, on the corner opposite the Revere House. The two stone houses fronting the square were built by Samuel Parkman, father of Dr. George Parkman. The range of brick buildings, from Howard Street in the direction of Bulfinch, was the second built in the town, in 1800, and obtained the name of West Row, as distinguished from South Row, near the Old South, and North Row in Anne Street.

Peter Chardon, another of the Huguenot descendants, built a house on the corner of the street bearing his name. It was hit several times during the bombardment of March 2, 1776. A school-house was erected in 1804, at the corner of Chardon and Hawkins Streets, the eighth in the town. In 1800 Hawkins was commonly known by the name of Tattle Street. A portion of the latter street was occupied by the distil-houses which gave the name of Distil-House Square to the neighboring space.

Mrs. Mary Pelham, mother of Copley the painter, lived in a house between the estate of Governor Sullivan, where the Bowdoin Square Theatre is, and Alden Court. She was the widow of Richard Copley, tobacconist, and continued to follow the business after her second marriage. The following advertisement may be found in the Boston News Letter of July 11, 1748 :—

"Mrs. Mary Pelham (formerly the widow of Copley, on Long Wharf, tobacconist) is removed to Lindel's Row, against the Quaker Meeting House, near the upper end of King Street, Boston, where she continues to sell the best Virginia Tobacco, Cut, Pigtail, and Spun, of all sorts, by Wholesale and Retail, at the cheapest rates."

At this time the Pelhams lived over the tobacco shop. Pelham possessed a versatile genius. He kept a writing and arithmetic school in 1748, and was one of the earliest teachers of dancing to the Bostonians, having had a school at the house of Philip Dumaresq, in Summer Street, as early as 1738.

He is still more noted as the earliest Boston engraver we have an account of, having, in 1727, engraved a portrait of Cotton Mather. He also engraved a number of Smibert's paintings, chiefly of the leading Boston divines of that day. Mr. Pelham also used the pencil with considerable skill.

Retracing our steps to Green Street, we find a resident who brought the old and new Boston into juxtaposition, until his decease, in 1832, at the advanced age of eighty-one. We allude to Major Thomas Melvill, who lived in an old wooden house on the south side of Green Street, between Staniford and the building formerly the Church of the Advent. Thomas Melvill's father was a cadet of the Scottish family of the Earls of Melvill and Leven. He came to this country quite young, and at his death left Thomas, his only son, an orphan at the age of ten years. The latter was educated at New Jersey College, whence he graduated in 1769 ; he took the degree of A. M. at Harvard in 1773. He was a democrat, and a firm friend of Samuel Adams, of whom he had a small portrait by Copley, now at Harvard. Herman Melville, the well-known author, is his grandson.

Major Melvill's long and honorable connection with the Boston Fire Department continued for forty years, and his death was finally caused by over-fatigue at a fire near his house. This connection commenced as fireward in 1779, in the good old times when those officers carried staves tipped at the end with a brass flame, and marshalled the bystanders into lines for passing buckets of water to the scene of conflagration. One of the town engines was named Melvill, in honor of the major.

Major Melvill was a member of the Cadets, one of the memorable Tea-Party, and captain in Craft's regiment of artillery in the Revolutionary War. He commanded a detachment sent to Nantasket to watch the movements of the British fleet. In the expedition into Rhode Island, in 1778, he took the rank of major. On the organization of the Custom House, under State authority, he was appointed surveyor, which office he held until the death of James Lovell, when he was commissioned naval officer by Washington, remaining in office more than forty years, until superseded by President Jackson in 1829.

The brick church mentioned in Green Street was consecrated in 1826, at which time Rev. Dr. William Jenks was installed as pastor. He was the first to found a Seamen's Bethel in Boston; and was the author of a valuable Commentary on the Bible, and many other useful works. The Doctor was a valued member of a number of learned societies, a pure and much-beloved member of society, and died sincerely regretted. His residence was in Crescent Place.

Gouch Street, which we think should be spelled Gooch, is connected with an incident of American history fitly perpetuated by the name.

When Sir William Howe attacked Fort Washington, on the Hudson, and had summoned the garrison to surrender, Washington, who from the opposite shore had witnessed the assault, wished to send a note to Colonel Magaw, acquainting him that if he could hold out till evening, he (Washington) would endeavor to bring off the garrison during the night. The brave Captain Gooch offered to be the bearer of the note. "He ran down to the river, jumped into a small boat, pushed over the river, landed under the bank, ran up to the fort, and delivered the message; came out, ran and jumped over the broken ground, dodging the Hessians, some of whom struck at him with their pieces, and others attempted to thrust him with their bayonets;

escaping through them, he got to his boat and returned to Fort Lee."

Gouch Street is further noted for its sugar-houses, of which there were seven in the town in 1794, each capable of manufacturing 100,000 pounds annually.

The West Church, on Lynde, fronting Cambridge Street, was organized in 1736. Rev. William Hooper, father of a signer of the Declaration of Independence, was the first pastor, but after nine years' service he became attached to the Church of England, and crossed the ocean to take orders. He became afterwards pastor of Trinity.

WEST CHURCH.*

Jonathan Mayhew, one of the greatest lights of the Boston pulpit, whose eloquence stimulated and upheld the cause of liberty, succeeded Mr. Hooper. His usefulness was terminated by his decease in July, 1766, two months after the Stamp Act repeal, on which he preached a memorable discourse. Simeon Howard, Charles Lowell, and C. A. Bartol have been the successive pastors.

The frame of the original Church was set up in September, 1736, but it was not until the following spring that it was completed. It shared the fate of other Boston churches in 1775, being used for barracks, and also suffered the loss of its steeple, taken down by the British to prevent signals being made to the Provincials at Cambridge. The old house was taken down and the present one built in 1806. The first Sunday school established in New England is said to have originated in the West Church, in 1812.

The charitable and corrective institutions of the town, after their removal from Park, Beacon, and Court Streets, were located at West Boston. The jail remained in Leverett Street until 1851, when it was removed to its present location on the north-

* Now a branch of the Public Library.

erly extension of Charles Street, situated on land reclaimed from the sea. This was not effected until after twelve years' agitation had demonstrated the necessity for the change. There were two separate prisons within the same enclosure in Leverett Street, one of which was converted into a House of Correction in 1823, and was so used until some time after the completion of the House of Correction at South Boston. The Leverett Street jail was considered very secure, walls and floors being composed of large blocks of hewn stone clamped together with iron, while between the courses loose cannon-balls were laid in cavities hollowed out for the purpose. Such a building necessarily occupied some time in construction, and upon its completion, in 1822, the old stone jail in Court Street was taken down, the materials going in part to build the gun-house in Thacher Street.

In the Leverett Street jail debtors were confined, and even when under bail could not go out of the narrow limits of the ward in which it was situated, without forfeiture of their bonds, and subjecting their bondsmen to payment of the entire claim against them. The law which gave the creditor this power over the person of his unfortunate debtor was not repealed until a comparatively recent period, although mitigated in some of its more rigorous provisions.

Charles Dickens animadverted severely upon our prison system, which he examined when in this country, and pronounced barbarous. The "American Notes" may have wounded our self-love, but they told some unpleasant though wholesome truths.

Among the executions which have taken place in the enclosure of Leverett Street jail, that of Professor Webster is prominent. His demeanor at the gallows was dignified and self-possessed. Before he suffered the penalty of the law he addressed a letter to a relative of the family he had so terribly wronged, in which he eloquently implored that his punishment might fully expiate his crime.

The streets Barton, Vernon, and Minot are of comparatively recent origin. They occupy the site of the Almshouse built in 1800, after its demolition in Beacon Street. At the time of its erection here it was situated on the bank of the river, from which a wharf, now forming the site of the old Lowell depot, extended.

The New Almshouse, as it was called, was a brick building of three stories, with a central structure, from which wings extended. This central building was considerably higher than the rest, and had lofty, arched windows, with a raised pediment relieved by ornamental work; on either gable stood a carved emblematic figure. The whole edifice was two hundred and seventy feet in length by fifty-six in depth. It stood until May, 1825, when it was superseded by the House of Industry at South Boston, and the land sold to private individuals. A brick wall, with iron gates, surrounded the Almshouse enclosure. No building having been erected to take the place of the Workhouse, or Bridewell, the inmates were obliged to be received into the Almshouse; but a small brick building was subsequently erected, adjacent to the latter, for a Bridewell.

It has always been the fate of some who have known better days to become dependants upon the public charity. One notable instance is mentioned of the daughter of a clergyman of the French Protestant Church having sought and obtained an asylum in the old Almshouse. She continued to visit and be received into the houses of her former friends, who, with intuitive delicacy, forebore to question her on the subject of her residence.

The tract bounded by Cambridge Street, North Russell Street, and the Hospital grounds was once under water. Bridge, Blossom, and Vine Streets have all been built since 1800.

At the west end of McLean Street (formerly South Allen), with the front towards Cambridge Street, stands the Massachusetts General Hospital. It is built of Chelmsford granite, and was considered in 1821, when completed, the finest public or private edifice in New England. It stands on what was formerly Prince's pasture, four acres of which constitute the Hospital domain. In 1846 it was enlarged by the addition of two wings. Charles Bulfinch was the architect of the original. In this hospital ether was first applied in a surgical operation of magnitude, by request of Dr. J. C. Warren.

Some of the sources from which the Hospital drew its being have been adverted to. A bequest of $5,000, at the close of the last century, was the beginning. Nothing further was effected until 1811, when fifty-six gentlemen were incorporated under the name of the Massachusetts General Hospital. The

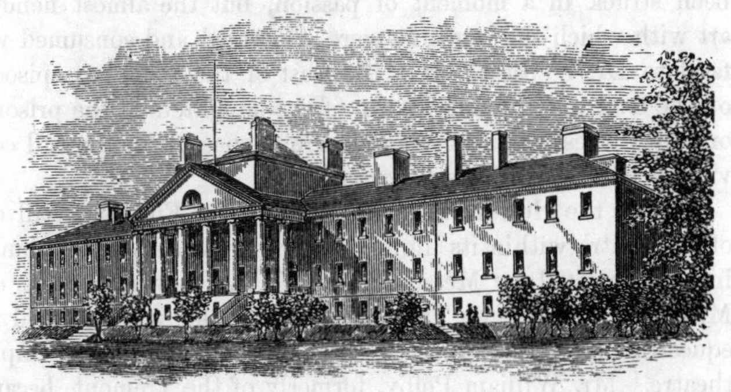

MASSACHUSETTS GENERAL HOSPITAL.

charter likewise granted the Province House, under condition that $100,000 should be raised from other sources within ten years. The Hospital Life Insurance Company was required to pay tribute to its namesake by its act of incorporation.

No eleemosynary institution in the country ever accumulated the means of carrying out its humane objects with greater rapidity. John McLean bequeathed $100,000 to the Hospital, and $50,000 more to be divided between that institution and Harvard. By the year 1816 the trustees were able to purchase the estate at Charlestown, now Somerville, and build two brick houses, which were ready for the reception of the insane in 1818. This is the asylum so long known by the name of its noble benefactor, McLean. His name was justly conferred upon the street without loss to its ancient possessor, as there was also North Allen Street, now known simply as Allen.

In Grove Street we have the new location of the Massachusetts Medical College, after its removal from Mason Street. The building derives a horrible interest as the scene of the murder of Dr. Parkman, the details of which long dwelt in the memories of many. The unsuspecting victim repaired to the College, where he had an appointment with his murderer, from which he never departed alive. No similar event ever produced so great a sensation in Boston. Both the parties were of the first standing in society. The deadly blow might have been struck in a moment of passion, but the almost fiendish art with which the remains were concealed and consumed was fatal to Dr. Webster. Not the least of the touching episodes of the trial was the appearance of the daughters of the prisoner on the witness stand, giving their evidence under the full conviction of their father's innocence.

Besides the Howard Athenæum the West End had still another theatre within its limits. In 1831 a small wooden building was erected by Messrs. W. and T. L. Stewart on the old Mill Pond, fronting on Traverse Street. This was designed for equestrian performances, and was called the American Amphitheatre. Mr. William Pelby, formerly of the Tremont, became the lessee, and remodelled the interior so as to adapt it to dramatic performances, opening it on the 3d of July, under the name of the Warren Theatre. The enterprise proving successful, Mr. Pelby was enabled to build a new house in the summer of 1836, which was inaugurated on the 15th of August as the National Theatre. At this house Miss Jean Margaret Davenport made her first appearance before a Boston audience, as did also Julia Dean, a favorite Western actress. In April, 1852, the theatre was destroyed by fire, but was rebuilt and reopened in November of the same year by Mr. Leonard.

There was a little theatre erected in 1841, at the corner of Haverhill and Traverse Streets, opened by Mr. Wyzeman Marshall under the name of the Eagle Theatre. Mr. W. H. Smith officiated a short time here as manager, but the concern proving a serious rival to the National, Mr. Pelby obtained an interest, and closed the house in a manner not altogether creditable to him.*

Several of the companies of the regiment of Massachusetts volunteers, raised for service in the Mexican war, were quartered at

* Clapp's Boston Stage.

the West End. Companies "A" and "B" had quarters in Pitts Street. Lieutenant-Colonel Abbott's company was located in the old wooden building on the east side of Leverett Street, which was afterwards used as a police station. Captain Edward Webster's company was enlisted in the famous building on the corner of Court and Tremont Streets, and in the office of his father, Daniel Webster. Captain Webster afterwards became major of the regiment, and died in Mexico. Isaac Hull Wright was the colonel.

The Mexican war was unpopular in Boston. The regiment was neglected by the State officials, and greeted with opprobrious epithets, and even pelted with mud, when it paraded in the streets. Meetings were called in Faneuil Hall, at which the war and the soldiers were denounced by the antislavery leaders, Theodore Parker, Wendell Phillips, W. Lloyd Garrison, and others. As soon as the regiment was mustered into the United States service, the State refused to have anything further to do with it.

NATIONAL THEATRE.

CHAPTER XIII.

FROM CHURCH GREEN TO LIBERTY TREE.

Church Green. — New South Church. — Dr. Kirkland. — American Headquarters. — General Heath. — Anecdote of General Gates. — Jerome Bonaparte. — Sir William Pepperell. — Nathaniel Bowditch. — George Bancroft. — Trinity Church. — Seven Star Inn and Lane. — Peter Faneuil. — Governor Sullivan. — Small-Pox Parties. — Duke of Kent. — Sir Edmund Andros. — Lamb Tavern. — White Horse Tavern. — Colonel Daniel Messinger. — Lion Tavern. — Handel and Haydn Society. — Lion Theatre. — Curious Statement about Rats.

THE name of Church Green was applied very early to the vacant space lying at the intersection of Bedford and Summer Streets, from which we may infer that it was looked upon as a proper site for a meeting-house by the earliest settlers of Boston. The land was granted by the town to a number of petitioners in 1715, of whom Samuel Adams, father of the patriot, was one.

There was not a more beautiful site for a church in Boston. The ground was high and level, the old church having an unobstructed outlook over the harbor. Samuel Checkley was the first pastor, ordained in 1718. Our engraving represents the church as rebuilt in 1814. The originators of the movement for the new church held their first meetings at the old Bull Tavern, at the corner of Summer and Sea Streets, of which we find mention in 1708.

NEW SOUTH CHURCH.

The church spire towered to a height of one hundred and ninety feet from the foundation. The building was of Chelmsford granite, and designed by Bulfinch; a portico projected from the front, supported by four Doric columns. In 1868 it was demolished, and the temples of traffic have arisen in its stead.

Fifty years gone by Summer Street was, beyond dispute, the most beautiful avenue in Boston. Magnificent trees then skirted its entire length, overarching the driveway with interlacing branches, so that you walked or rode as within a grove in a light softened by the leafy screen, and over the shadows of the big elms lying across the pavement. The palaces of trade now rear their splendid fronts where stood the gardens or mansions of the old merchants or statesmen of Boston.

The old wooden house — quite respectable for its day — in which Dr. John T. Kirkland resided was at the corner of Summer and Lincoln Streets. He was the son of the celebrated Indian missionary, Samuel Kirkland, founder of Hamilton College, who was instrumental in attaching the Oneidas to the American cause during the Revolution, and acted as chaplain to our forces under General Sullivan in 1799. The younger Dr. Kirkland, who possessed abilities of a high order, became, in 1810, president of Harvard. Another eminent clergyman, Jeremy Belknap, was also a resident of Summer Street.

Bedford Street was in former times known as Pond Lane, from the Town Watering-Place situated on the east side. A line drawn due south from Hawley Street would pass through the pond. Blind Lane was a name applied to the lower part of the street in 1800. Summer Street was called "Y^e^ Mylne Street," from its conducting towards Windmill Point, where a mill was erected, it appears, as early as 1636, the highway to it being ordered laid out in 1644.

As late as 1815 there was a pasture of two acres in Summer Street, and the tinkling of cow-bells was by no means an unusual sound there. The fine old estates of the Geyers, Coffins, Russells, Barrells, Lydes, Prebles, etc. were covered with orchards and gardens, and these hospitable residents could set before their guests cider of their own manufacture, or butter from their own dairies. Chauncy Place, named for the distinguished pastor of the First Church, was laid out in 1807, over a part of the estate of Ebenezer Preble, brother of Commodore Edward, a leading merchant of Boston, and at one time a partner of William Gray. Mr. Preble's house was on the lower corner of what is now Chauncy Street. The estate of the First Church adjoined on the west.

We have noticed the residence in this street of Daniel Webster, which the stranger may find without trouble, and will not pass without rendering silent homage to the matchless abilities of that great man. Mr. Webster cared little for money, and was sometimes pressed by his creditors. On one occasion he was dunned by a needy tradesman for a trifling sum, and, after emptying his pockets in vain, he bade his visitor wait until he could call on a friend near at hand for the money. The loan was no sooner asked than obtained; but at his own door Mr. Webster was met by an application from another friend for a deserving charity, to whom he gave the money he had borrowed, and returned empty-handed to his creditor.

When Mr. Webster received Lafayette after the ceremonies at Bunker Hill, to give *éclat* to the occasion and accommodate the numerous and distinguished company, a door was made connecting with the adjoining house of Mr. Israel Thorndike.

The bullet which the Marquis received in his leg at Brandywine was the occasion of a graceful compliment by President John Quincy Adams. A new frigate was ready to launch at Washington, in which it was intended Lafayette should take passage for France, and, when all was ready, the President, who had kept his purpose a secret from every one, himself christened her the Brandywine, to the surprise of Commodore Tingey and the naval constructor, who supposed she would be called the Susquehanna.

The impression has obtained that Boston ceased to be a garrisoned town after the evacuation by Sir William Howe, and the departure of the great body of our own troops for New York. This is very far from being the case. The command of the town was first assumed by Putnam, was transferred to Greene, and finally remained with General Ward, whose age and infirmity prevented his taking the field actively. The camps at Cambridge and Roxbury continued to be the rendezvous of the new levies. The town of Boston was the headquarters of the Eastern District, with a regular garrison. James Urquhart, the British town-major, was succeeded by an American officer, Major Swasey, with the same title. Colonel Keith was deputy adjutant-general under Heath.

General Ward was relieved by General Heath in 1777, and retired from the army. General Heath established his headquarters at the mansion-house of Hon. Thomas Russell, which stood some distance back from Summer Street, about where Otis Street now is. Here the General entertained D'Estaing, Pulaski, Silas Deane, Burgoyne, Phillips, and Riedesel. It was the fortune of General Heath to command in Boston while the prisoners from Saratoga and Bennington remained at Cambridge, and he was soon engaged in a *petit guerre* with Burgoyne. Soon after the arrival of the convention troops, Phillips proposed to General Heath that all orders affecting the prisoners should be transmitted through their own generals, but the American commander was not disposed to thus delegate his authority.

Heath was succeeded by General Gates in October, 1778, who arrived with his wife and suite on the 6th of that month and assumed the command. Gates, like Washington and Gage, had served in the campaign of Braddock, where he was severely wounded, and brought off the field by a soldier for whom he ever after entertained an affectionate regard. Gates was then a captain in the British army, and his preserver was a private in the royal artillery, named Penfold. The old soldier, having been invalided, desired to remain in America, and applied to Gates for his advice. We give a part of the reply, which does honor to the heart and memory of Gates : —

"Come and rest your firelock in my chimney-corner, and partake with me ; while I have, my savior Penfold shall not want ; and it is my wish, as well as Mrs. Gates's, to see you spend the evening of your life comfortably. Mrs. Gates desires to be affectionately remembered to you."

Boston can thus boast of having been commanded by the ablest generals on either side of the Revolutionary struggle.

General Gates was said to have lived at one time with his father in the service of Charles, Duke of Bolton. It was his fortune to have achieved the greatest victory of the Revolution at Saratoga, and sustained the most complete defeat at Camden, of any officer commanding in that war.

The Russell mansion was afterwards occupied as a public house by Leon Chappotin. Jerome Bonaparte, after his marriage with Miss Patterson at Baltimore, made a visit to Boston, and lodged here for a time. It will be recollected that this marriage was never sanctioned by the Emperor. Otis Place, now Street, was laid out through the estate of Sir William Pepperell.

The Sir William Pepperell of our notice was the grandson of the captor of Louisburg, and son of Colonel Nathaniel Sparhawk. By the tenor of his grandfather's will, which made him the residuary legatee of the baronet's possessions, he was required to change his name to Pepperell. This was done by an act of the Massachusetts Legislature. The baronetcy became extinct with the decease of the elder Sir William, and was re-created by the king for the benefit of his grandson in 1774. The younger Sir William was a stanch friend of the mother country, and was one of the King's Mandamus Councillors in 1774. He left America with the Royalists in 1775, and his large estates in Boston and in Maine were confiscated.

At No. 8 Otis Place lived Nathaniel Bowditch, so long Actuary of the Massachusetts Hospital Life Insurance Company in Boston. Born in poverty, after serving an apprenticeship to a ship-chandler until he was twenty-one, and following the sea for a number of years, he published in 1800, before he was thirty, his work on navigation. His commentary on the celebrated *Mécanique Céleste* of Laplace established his fame as one of the leading scientific minds of either the Old or New World. His son, Nathaniel Ingersoll, had improved an antiquarian taste by exhaustive researches among the records of the town and colony, and the articles from his pen under the signature of "Gleaner" were of the greatest interest to all students of our local history. His contemporary "Sigma" (L. M. Sargent), wielded in the same cause a brilliant and caustic pen, investing the characters of the dead past with life and action.

At the corner of Winthrop and Otis Place was the residence of George Bancroft in 1840, at which time he was Collector of the port of Boston. Emerson, Margaret Fuller, Channing, and Samuel Osgood were members of the literary coterie who met in that house, to discuss the new philosophy of Transcendentalism, which for a season turned the heads of all educated Boston. While Secretary of the Navy, in Polk's cabinet, Mr. Bancroft has the credit of establishing the Naval Academy at Annapolis.

The estate at the southwest corner of Summer and Chauncy Streets was the property of the First Church, having been conveyed to it in 1680. The greater part of the original place was laid out over the church estate to gain access to the church, which was placed upon that part of the ground in the rear of Summer Street formerly the garden of the parsonage. Four brick dwellings were built on the Summer Street front by Benjamin Joy in 1808. Before this took place the ground was occupied by the parsonage. One of the pastors who filled the pulpit after the removal to this locality was William Emerson, father of Ralph Waldo Emerson, the essayist and poet. His ministrations continued from 1799 to 1811, and he had the distinction of preaching the first sermon here.

After sixty years' service, the house in Chauncy Place was deserted by the society for the new and elegant temple at the corner of Marlborough and Berkeley Streets, which was occupied December, 1868. An enduring relic of the "Old Brick" church remains in a slab of slate taken from beneath a window in the second story, south side, on which is inscribed, —

> "Burned to ashes October 3, 1711.
> Rebuilding June 25th. 1712. July 20, 1713."

The Post-Office occupied this corner in 1859, at which time Nahum Capen was postmaster; but remained only until the next year, the site not being considered an eligible one.

By the year 1728 King's Chapel could not accommodate its numerous parishioners at the south part of the town, and steps were taken to build an Episcopal church at the corner of Hawley and Summer Streets. The corner-stone was not laid, however, until 1734, when Mr. Commissary Price of King's Chapel officiated at this ceremony. The next year it was opened for worship. Among the first officers we find the familiar names of Charles Apthorp, Benjamin Faneuil, Philip Dumaresq, William Coffin, and Thomas Aston. Rev. Addington Davenport, a brother-in-law of Peter Faneuil, who had been an assistant at King's Chapel in 1737, was the first rector of Trinity.

The first building was of wood. It was ninety feet long, and sixty broad, without any external adornment. It had neither tower nor steeple, nor windows in the lower story of the front. There were three entrances in front unprotected by porches. The interior was composed of an arch resting upon Corinthian pillars with handsomely carved and gilded capitals. In the chancel were some paintings, considered very beautiful in their day. Taken altogether, Trinity might boast the handsomest interior of any church in Boston of its time. In 1828 it was supplanted by the granite edifice seen in our view on the opposite page, Rev. John S. J. Gardiner laying the corner-stone. Trinity, like the other Episcopal churches, had tombs underneath it.

OLD TRINITY CHURCH.

We do not learn that Trinity received any special marks of royal favor, such as were shown to its predecessors, King's Chapel and Christ Church. To the former the king and queen (William and Mary) gave, besides the communion plate, a pulpit-cloth, a cushion, and a painting which reached from the top to the bottom of the east end of the church, containing the Decalogue, the Lord's Prayer, and the Apostles' Creed. But Governor Shirley, who had so liberally aided the Chapel, gave Trinity a service for communion, table-cloths, and books. Peter Faneuil had in 1741 offered £100 towards an organ, but one was not procured until 1744.

When General Washington was in Boston in 1789 he passed the Sabbath here, and went to hear Dr. (afterwards Bishop) Parker in the forenoon, and to Brattle Street in the afternoon, where he sat in Governor Bowdoin's pew.

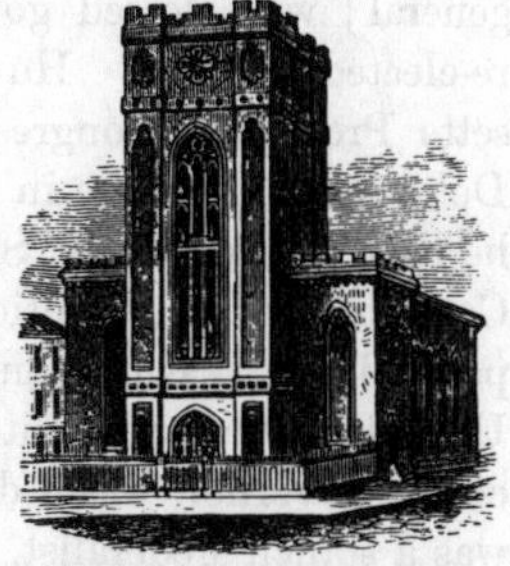
TRINITY CHURCH IN 1872.

Curiously enough, Trinity Church occupied the site of the old "Pleiades" or "Seven Star Inn," from which Summer Street took the name of Seven Star Lane. Trinity was completely destroyed by the Great Fire of 1872, to rise again, in greater beauty, on Copley Square.

Peter Faneuil occupied pew No. 40 in Old Trinity. We may easily picture him descending from his chariot on a Sunday morning while his negro coachman assists him to alight. We doubt not the heads of the young Boston belles were turned towards the wealthy bachelor as he advanced up the aisle to his devotions. His good brother Davenport no doubt enjoyed those perquisites so pleasantly referred to by Pope when he says, —

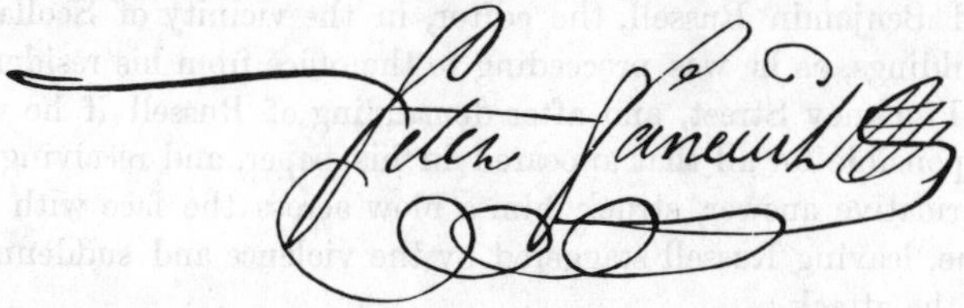

> "He that hath these may pass his life,
> Drink with the 'squire, and kiss his wife;
> On Sundays preach, and eat his fill;
> And fast on Fridays, — if he will;

Toast Church and Queen, explain the news,
Talk with church-wardens about pews,
Pray heartily for some new gift,
And shake his head at Dr. Swift."

The corner of Hawley Street, next below Trinity, will be remembered as the estate of Governor James Sullivan and of Lieutenant-Governor Gray.

Governor Sullivan was the brother of the Revolutionary general; was elected governor of Massachusetts in 1807, and re-elected in 1808. He had been a member of the Massachusetts Provincial Congress; Judge of the Superior Court; and Delegate to Congress in 1784, from the District of Maine where he then resided. Mr. Sullivan was also a member of the State Constitutional Convention, and one of the Commissioners appointed by Washington to settle the boundary between the United States and British Provinces. William Sullivan, son of the governor, was a distinguished lawyer and scholar. He was a stanch Federalist, and wrote an able vindication of that party.

When Governor Sullivan was before the people as a candidate, it is said a caricature appeared in the Centinel reflecting severely upon his integrity. His son, Richard Sullivan, waylaid Benjamin Russell, the editor, in the vicinity of Scollay's Buildings, as he was proceeding to the office from his residence in Pinckney Street, and after demanding of Russell if he was responsible for all that appeared in his paper, and receiving an affirmative answer, struck him a blow across the face with his cane, leaving Russell staggered by the violence and suddenness of the attack.

The elder Levi Lincoln was lieutenant-governor with Governor Sullivan, and on his decease became acting governor. His son Levi was lieutenant-governor in 1823, and governor in 1825–34. Another son, Enoch, was governor of Maine in 1827–29. On the decease of their mother, Martha Lincoln, her remains were followed to the grave by her two sons, then chief magistrates of two States.

Joseph Barrell, whom we have mentioned in our view of Franklin Street, was one of the foremost of the old merchants of Boston. His name stands first on the list of directors of the Old United States Bank, in company with John Codman, Caleb Davis, Christopher Gore, John Coffin Jones, John Lowell, Theodore Lyman, Jonathan Mason, Jr., Joseph Russell, Jr., David Sears, Israel Thorndike, and William Wetmore.

It is related that a person carried to a bank in Pennsylvania some bills which that bank had issued, and demanded gold and silver for them. He was answered that the bank did not pay gold or silver. "Give me, then," said he, "bills of the United States Bank." "We have none." "Then give me bills on any bank in New England." "We have none of these." "Pay me, then, in the best *counterfeit* bills you have."

The reader will perhaps experience some incredulity when he is told that, before the discovery of the present mode of vaccination, small-pox parties were among the fashionable gatherings of Old Boston. The guests were inoculated, and withdrew for a time from the world. An invitation of this kind appears in the following extract from a letter of Joseph Barrell, dated July 8, 1776 : —

"Mr. Storer has invited Mrs. Martin to take the small-pox at his house : if Mrs. Wentworth desires to get rid of her fears in the same way, we will accommodate her in the best way we can. I 've several friends that I 've invited, and none of them will be more welcome than Mrs. W." *

Joseph Barrell occupied store No. 3, south side of the Town Dock, where he advertised brown sugar, double and treble refined, looking-glasses, wine, oil, etc.

He was the owner of the triangular estate at the junction of Washington with Brattle Street, of which he gave a portion to the town for the widening of the latter.

The fine granite structure of the Messrs. Hovey stands on the site of the old-time mansion of the Vassalls, erected by Leonard Vassall, whose son William built the house on Pemberton Hill, afterwards the residence of Gardiner Greene. Thomas Hubbard, who preceded Hancock as Treasurer of Harvard College, and Frederick Geyer, who left Boston with the

* Brewster's Portsmouth.

adherents of the crown, were subsequent proprietors; as the estate of the latter it was confiscated, but was subsequently restored.

When the Duke of Kent, son of George III., and father of Victoria, the reigning Queen of England, was in Boston, he was present at the wedding of Nancy W. Geyer, who married Rufus G. Amory. Prince Edward, as he was then styled, did not incline to visit Lieutenant-Governor Samuel Adams.

South of the Vassall-Geyer property was the estate of John Rowe, whose house — subsequently that of Judge Prescott, father of the historian — stood upon the spot formerly occupied by Dr. Robbins's Church in Bedford Street, opposite the building of R. H. White and Co. A wharf and street once handed down the name of Rowe, — as true a friend to his country as any whose names have reached a greater renown, — but the wharf alone retains this title. Rowe Street, which was given to and accepted by the city on condition that it should be so called, has become since 1856 absorbed in Chauncy Street, that part lying between Bedford and Summer Streets having been previous to this divided by an iron fence, the southerly portion being known as Bedford and the northerly as Chauncy Place.

Bidding adieu to Summer Street, we pause for a moment at what was formerly Bethune's Corner, where now are the glittering shop-windows of Shuman and Company, and where a ceaseless human tide, crossing the narrow street, struggles with the passing vehicles. From the old mansion-house of Thomas English, which stood here, was buried Benjamin Faneuil.

Looking in the direction of the Old South, a little north of Summer Street, was the reputed residence of Sir Edmund Andros, who dwelt, it is said, in an old house which disappeared about 1790, and which stood nearly on the spot now occupied by number 422 Washington Street. This tradition existed early in the present century, and may have been true, though it could not have been the habitation of the knight when Lady Andros, to whose funeral we have referred in a former chapter, died. Andros was governor of New England only three years. We know that his country-seat was at

Dorchester, — it was still standing in 1825, — and there is abundant evidence that he lived in Boston, but none that we are aware of, that he owned an estate here. Though a change of residence was less common among the old inhabitants of Boston than at the present day, it was no anomaly.

Earl Bellomont, writing to the Lords of Trade from Boston, in 1698, says he paid £100 a year for a house, besides his charge for a stable, and continues in the following strain: —

"It is for the King's honour that his Governour have a house; there is a very good house plot where Sir Edmund Andros lived in the best part of the town. 'T is the least of their thoughts I doubt to build a house for the King's Governour."

This refers without doubt to Cotton Hill or the vicinity, which was then the best part of the town, and Andros only followed the example of Endicott, Bellingham, and Vane, when he located there. The region lying around Summer Street was then considered remote. Even as late as when Boston became a city, it was thought too far out of town by small shopkeepers, business not having then encroached so far upon the residence quarter.

FAUST'S STATUE, 1790.

Threading our way through old Newbury Street with our face towards the south, we pass the old stand of Thomas and Andrews at number 45. Thomas printed the Spy in "Union Street, near the market," "at the south corner of Marshall's Lane, leading from the Mill Bridge into Union Street," and "at the bottom of Royal Exchange Lane near the Market, Dock Square," besides Back Street, where the first number was probably printed.

We cannot pass by the neighborhood of Avon Street without thinking of old Bartholomew Green and his News Letter, of Benjamin Church and his treachery, of Margaret Fuller and her untimely fate, any more than we can pass the Old South without thinking of the riding-school, or Bunker Hill Monument without thinking of Prescott and Warren.

A group of taverns next claims our attention. The inns of Old London rendered up their names freely to their colonial imitators, and our older residents might drink their punch under the same signs they were used to frequent beneath the shadow of Old Saint Paul's. We have had no Johnson with his corner at the Mitre, no Dryden with his snug retreat at Will's Coffee-house, nor can we show any as famous as Button's, where Pope, Steele, Swift, Arbuthnot, and Addison were wont to assemble at "the best head in England"; but we have visited some where matters more serious than wit and sentiment were discussed, and where measures were digested more important to mankind.

We commend to our modern hotel-keepers the following extract from a law enacted about 1649: —

"Nor shall any take *tobacco* in any inne, or common victual house, except in a private room there, so as the master of said house nor any guest there shall take offence thereat; which if any do, then such persons shall forbear, upon pain of two shillings and sixpence for every such offence."

We come first to the Adams House, which stands on the ground formerly occupied by the Lamb Tavern, sometimes styled the White Lamb. The "Lamb" was an unpretending building of two stories, but of good repute in Old Boston. The sign is noticed as early as 1746. Colonel Doty kept at the sign of the Lamb in 1760; Edward Kingman kept it in 1826; after which it was conducted successively by Laban Adams, for whom the house was named, father of "Oliver Optic" (W. T. Adams), and by A. S. Allen. The first stage-coach to Providence, advertised July 20, 1767, by Thomas Sabin, put up at the sign of the Lamb.

The White Horse Tavern was a few rods south of the Lamb, situated nearly opposite the mansion-house of Dr. Lemuel Hayward, physician and surgeon, from whose estate Hayward Place

LAMB TAVERN, NEWBURY (NOW WASHINGTON) STREET.

is named. It had a large square sign projecting over the footway, on which was delineated a white charger. We find this tavern mentioned in 1794, and infer that it was the rendezvous of one of the companies of the Boston Regiment, as young Woodbridge came here for his sword before meeting Phillips on the Common. It was kept by Joseph Morton, father of Perez Morton, in 1760, and for a long time thereafter. In 1787 Israel Hatch became mine host ; we append his advertisement entire : —

TAKE NOTICE !

Entertainment for

Gentlemen and Ladies

At the White Horse Tavern,

Newbury-Street.

My friends and travellers, you 'll meet
With kindly welcome and good cheer,
And what it is you now shall hear :
A spacious house and liquors good,
A man who gets his livelihood
By favours granted ; hence he 'll be
Always smiling, always free :
A good large house for chaise or chair,
A stable well expos'd to air :
To finish all, and make you blest,
You 'll have the breezes from the west.
And — ye, who flee th' approaching Sol,
My doors are open to your call ;
Walk in — and it shall be my care
T' oblige the weary traveller.
From Attleborough, Sirs, I came,
Where once I did you entertain,
And now shall here as there before
Attend you at my open door,
Obey all orders with despatch,
— Am, Sirs, your servant,

ISRAEL HATCH.

BOSTON, May 14, 1787.

Colonel Daniel Messinger, who was always in request to sing the odes on public occasions, commenced business near the Lamb Tavern in 1789. He was by trade a hatter, and had served an apprenticeship with Nathaniel Balch (Governor Hancock's favorite) at 72 Old Cornhill. Colonel Messinger had a voice of great strength and purity, and had sung in presence of Washington, Lafayette, Jerome Bonaparte, and other distinguished personages.

Another neighbor of the Lamb was the Lion Tavern, on the site of the former Melodeon. Its sign was the traditional British Lion, but it seems to have lived on terms of amity with its peaceful neighbor. The tavern at length passed into the possession of the Handel and Haydn Society, and was devoted to the performance of oratorios. This society organized 30th March, 1815, and first met at Graupner's Hall, Franklin Street. The original number of members was thirty-one, and their first public performance was given in King's Chapel, Christmas evening, 1815, when selections from the Creation, Messiah, etc. were given in presence of an audience of upwards of a thousand persons. The Lion was, in 1789, called the Turk's Head.

The Lion Tavern estate was called the Melodeon by the Handel and Haydn Society, in place of which we now have the annex to Keith's fine theatre. The first Melodeon was occupied by Rev. Theodore Parker's society on Sundays. Both societies removed later to Music Hall in Winter Street.

In 1835 the Lion Tavern became the property of Mr. James Raymond, and was immediately transformed into an amphitheatre, under the name of the Lion Theatre. It opened in January, 1836, with a comedy by Buckstone, supplemented by equestrian performances. Mr. J. B. Booth appeared at this theatre in May, 1836. It passed through varying fortunes until 1844, when, after it had been rechristened the Melodeon, Mr. Macready and Miss Cushman appeared here for a short season. Jenny Lind, Sontag, and Alboni, all gave concerts at the Melodeon.

There seems to have been a time in the history of Boston when the settlers were called upon to wage a war of extermination against a domestic enemy, one which they had undoubtedly brought among themselves. Our readers have heard of a bounty for the scalps of savages, wolves' ears, and bears' claws, but never perhaps of a price being set upon rats, as the following extract from the town records, selected from a number of the same description, will show was once the case : —

"On the first day of January, 1743, the Selectmen gave a certificate to the Province Treasurer, that they had paid out of the Town Stock to sundry persons for 9280 Rats killed in or near the Town, since the last day of August, £154. 13^s 4^d old tenor — and desired him to pay the same to Joseph Wadsworth Esqr., Town Treasurer."

CHAPTER XIV.

LIBERTY TREE AND THE NEIGHBORHOOD.

Liberty Tree. — Its History. — Hanover Square. — Liberty Hall. — Hanging in Effigy. — Auchmuty's Lane. — The Old Suffolk Bench and Bar. — Boylston Market. — Charles Matthews. — James E. Murdoch. — Peggy Moore's. — Washington Bank. — Beach Street Museum. — Essex Street. — Rainsford's Lane. — Harrison Avenue. — Admiral Sir Isaac Coffin. — General John Coffin. — Anecdote of Admiral Coffin. — Sir Thomas Aston Coffin. — Henry Bass. — Old Distill-houses. — Manufacture of Rum. — Gilbert Stuart, — Anecdotes of. — First Glass Works. — Disappearance of Trees. — Early Planting of Trees. — Sir Roger Hale Sheaffe. — South Cove. — Hollis Street. — Colonel John Crane. — General Ebenezer Stevens. — Mather Byles, — Anecdotes of. — Hollis Street Church. — Fire of 1787.

LAFAYETTE said, when in Boston, "The world should never forget the spot where once stood Liberty Tree, so famous in your annals." It has been the care of David Sears that this injunction should not fall to the ground unheeded.

In the wall of the building at the southeast corner of Essex Street, at its junction with Washington, we see a handsome freestone bas-relief, representing a tree with wide-spreading branches. This memorial is placed directly over the spot where stood the famed Liberty Tree. An inscription informs us that it commemorates : —

Liberty 1776
Law and Order
Sons of Liberty 1766
Independence of their country 1776.

The open space at the four corners of Washington, Essex, and Boylston Streets was once known as Hanover Square, from the royal house of Hanover, and sometimes as the Elm Neighborhood, from the magnificent elms with which it was environed. It was one of the finest of these that obtained the name of Liberty Tree, from its being used on the first occasion of resistance to the obnoxious Stamp Act. In 1774 this tree, with another, stood in the enclosure of an old-fashioned dwelling at the historic corner; in 1766, when the repeal of the Stamp Act took place, a large copper plate was fastened to the tree inscribed in golden characters: —

"This tree was planted in the year 1646, and pruned by order of the Sons of Liberty, Feb. 14th, 1766."

In August, 1775, the name of Liberty having become offensive to the tories and their British allies, the tree was cut down by a party led by one Job Williams. "Armed with axes, they made a furious attack upon it. After a long spell of laughing and grinning, sweating, swearing, and foaming, with malice diabolical, they cut down a tree because it bore the name of Liberty." * Some idea of the size of the tree may be formed from the fact that it made fourteen cords of wood. The jesting at the expense of the Sons of Liberty had a sorry conclusion; one of the soldiers, in attempting to remove a limb, fell to the pavement and was killed.

LIBERTY TREE.

The ground immediately about Liberty Tree was popularly known as Liberty Hall. In August, 1767, a flagstaff had been erected, which went through and extended above its highest branches. A flag hoisted upon this staff was the signal for the assembling of the Sons of Liberty for action. Captain Mackintosh, the last captain of the Popes, was the first captain-general of Liberty Tree, and had charge of the illuminations, hanging of effigies, etc.

* Essex Gazette, 1775.

After the old war was over a liberty-pole was erected on the stump of the tree, the latter long serving as a point of direction known as Liberty Stump. A second pole was placed in position on the 2d July, 1826. It was intended to have been raised during the visit of Lafayette in 1825, and the following lines were written by Judge Dawes: —

"Of high renown, here grew the Tree,
The Elm so dear to Liberty;
Your sires, beneath its sacred shade,
To Freedom early homage paid.
This day with filial awe surround
Its root, that sanctifies the ground,
And by your fathers' spirits swear,
The rights they left you 'll not impair."

Governor Bernard, writing to Lord Hillsborough under date of June 18, 1768, gives the following account of Liberty Tree: —

"Your Lordship must know that Liberty tree is a large old Elm in the High Street, upon which the effigies were hung in the time of the Stamp Act, and from whence the mobs at that time made their parades. It has since been adorned with an inscription, and has obtained the name of Liberty Tree, as the ground under it has that of Liberty Hall. In August last, just before the commencement of the present troubles, they erected a flagstaff, which went through the tree, and a good deal above the top of the tree. Upon this they hoist a flag as a signal for the Sons of Liberty, as they are called. I gave my Lord Shelburne an account of this erection at the time it was made. This tree has often put me in mind of Jack Cade's Oak of Reformation."

Liberty Tree Tavern in 1833 occupied the spot where once Liberty Tree stood. It was kept by G. Cummings. In its immediate vicinity and opposite the Boylston Market was Lafayette Hotel, built in 1824, and kept by S. Haskell in the year above mentioned.

The Sons of Liberty adopted the name given them by Colonel Barré in a speech in Parliament, in which he took occasion thus to characterize those who evinced a disposition to resist the oppressive measures of the Ministry. Under the branches of Liberty Tree that resistance first showed itself by public acts.

At daybreak on the 14th August, 1765, nearly ten years before active hostilities broke out, an effigy of Mr. Oliver, the Stamp officer, and a boot, with the Devil peeping out of it, — an allusion to Lord Bute, — were discovered hanging from Liberty Tree. The images remained hanging all day, and were visited by great numbers of people, both from the town and the neighboring country. Business was almost suspended. Lieutenant-Governor Hutchinson ordered the sheriff to take the figures down, but he was obliged to admit that he dared not do so.

As the day closed in the effigies were taken down, placed upon a bier, and, followed by several thousand people of every class and condition, proceeded first to the Town House, and from thence to the supposed office of the Stamp Master, as has been detailed in that connection. With materials obtained from the ruins of the building, the procession moved to Fort Hill, where a bonfire was lighted and the effigies consumed in full view of Mr. Oliver's house. Governor Bernard and council were in session in the Town House when the procession passed through it, as the lower floor of the building left open for public promenade permitted them to do. In the attacks which followed upon the houses of the secretary, lieutenant-governor, and officers of the admiralty, Mackintosh appears to have been the leader. In these proceedings the records of the court of vice-admiralty were destroyed, — an irreparable loss to the province and to history. Mackintosh was arrested, but immediately released on the demand of a number of persons of character and property.

Mr. Oliver now publicly declared his intention of resigning, and when the stamps arrived in Boston in September they were sent to Castle William. In November there was another hanging in effigy of two of the king's advisers. The anniversary of Pope Day was celebrated by a union of the rival factions, who met in amity and refreshed themselves under Liberty Tree before proceeding to Copp's Hill, as was customary. But the greatest act which occurred under this famous tree was the public declaration of Secretary Oliver that he would not in any way, by himself or by deputy, perform the duties of stamp master. The Secretary, desirous of less publicity, had requested that the ceremony might take place at the Town House, but the "Sons" had determined that the "Tree" was the proper place, and Mr. Oliver presented himself there. Besides this declaration, subscribed to before Richard Dana, justice of the peace, Mr. Oliver fully recanted his sentiments in favor of the Stamp Act, and desired the people no longer to look upon him as an enemy, but as a friend, — a piece of duplicity fully exposed by the discovery of his correspondence on the subject.

On the 14th February, 1766, the tree was pruned under the direction of skillful persons, and on the 20th the plate was attached. On this day the ceremony of burning stamped papers, and the effigies of Bute and Grenville, took place at the gallows on the Neck, the Sons returning to Hanover Square, where they drank his Majesty's health and other toasts expressive of their *loyalty* to the throne.

From this time all measures of public concern were discussed by the Sons of Liberty under the umbrageous shelter of their adored tree. The affair of Hancock's sloop, the arrival of the troops, the Non-importation Act, each received the attention they merited. On the 14th August, 1769, anniversary of the first Stamp Act proceedings, and "the day of the Union and firmly combined Association of the Sons of Liberty in this Province," there was a great assembly under Liberty Tree. Many came from great distances. Reed and Dickinson (a brother of John Dickinson) were present from Philadelphia. Peyton Randolph was expected, but did not come. The British flag was hoisted over the tree, and, after drinking fourteen toasts, the meeting adjourned to Robinson's Tavern, Dorchester, known also as the sign of the Liberty Tree, where the day was passed in festivity and mirth. John Adams was present, and has left an account of the gathering, into which we should not have to look in vain for Samuel Adams, Otis, and their compatriots.

After the establishment of the troops in Boston the necessity for secrecy in their movements compelled the patriots to resort to the clubs for conference. The tree, however, had borne its part in the acts preliminary to the great conflict which ensued, and to pilgrims to the shrines of American history the spot where it once stood must ever possess an interest second to no other in this historic city.

"The tree their own hands had to liberty reared
They lived to behold growing strong and revered;
With transport then cried, 'Now our wishes we gain,
For our children shall gather the fruits of our pain.'
In freedom we 're born, and in freedom we 'll live;
Our purses are ready, —
Steady, friends, steady; —
Not as slaves, but as freemen, our money we 'll give."

Samuel Adams, a namesake of the Revolutionary patriot and an old resident of North End, had in his possession until his death, in 1855, a flag which was used on the liberty-pole prior to the Revolution, and which he displayed on public occasions with great satisfaction. Some services which he performed on the patriots' side, in which he sustained losses, procured him a small appropriation from the State.

The hanging of effigies appears to have originated in England in 1763. This was at Honiton, in Devonshire, famous for its lace manufacture, two years before the exhibitions in Boston from the limbs of Liberty Tree. A tax having been levied upon cider, the effigy of the minister concerned in it was suspended from an apple-tree that grew over the road, with the following lines affixed to it: —

"Behold the man who made the yoke
Which doth Old England's sons provoke,
And now he hangs upon a tree,
An emblem of our liberty."

Essex Street was the line of division between old Newbury and Orange Streets. Newbury reached to Winter Street, while Orange conducted from the fortifications on the Neck into town; its name was no doubt given in honor of the Prince of Orange. Essex Street, which was named in 1708, was also called Auchmuty's Lane, for the family so distinguished in the history of the old Suffolk Bar.

The elder Robert Auchmuty was a barrister during the administration of Belcher and Shirley, and in his latter years judge-advocate of the Court of Admiralty.

The younger Auchmuty was judge of the same court when the Revolution began. His associates at the bar were Read, Pratt, Gridley, Trowbridge, Adams, Otis, the gifted Thacher, and the brilliant Quincy. He was born in Boston, and assisted Adams and Quincy in the defence of Captain Preston, for his participation in the massacre in King Street. His residence was in School Street, next the old Extinguisher Engine-house. A nephew, Sir Samuel Auchmuty, born in New York, fought against his countrymen in the service of King George.

Benjamin Pratt, afterwards chief justice of New York, married a daughter of the old Judge Auchmuty. He was a small, thin man, and from the loss of a limb was obliged to use crutches. It was of him that John Adams said "that he had looked with wonder to see such a little body hung upon two sticks send forth such eloquence and displays of mind." Pratt's office was in the second house north of the corner of Court Street in old Cornhill, where Gould and Lincoln's bookstore was formerly kept; his country-seat was on Milton Hill.

Oxenbridge Thacher's office was opposite the south door of the Old State House. Sampson Salter Blowers, eminent at the same bar, lived in Southack's Court (Howard Street). Gridley, with whom James Otis studied, lived in a house next north of Cornhill Square. John Adams's office was in a house next above William Minot's; which was on Court Street, opposite the Court House, where now stands Minot's Building. Read built and lived in the house described as Mr. Minot's. Cazneau lived in a house next east of the Court House. Chief Justice Dana's father lived at the corner of Wilson's Lane. John Quincy Adams's office was in Court Street.

Before the Revolution eight dollars was the fee in an important cause, five dollars was the limit for a jury argument, two dollars for a continuance. Then the lawyers went the circuits with the judges. The courtesy and dignity which distinguished the intercourse between bench and bar did not continue under the new order of things, if we may credit Fisher Ames, who, in allusion to the austerity of the court, supposed to be Judge Paine, and the manners of the attorneys, remarked, that a lawyer should go into court with a club in one hand and a speaking-trumpet in the other. Chief Justice Parsons and Judge Sedgwick were the last barristers who sat upon the bench. Perez Morton and Judge Wetmore were the last survivors who had attained the degree.

Boylston Market, when opened to the public in 1810, was considered far out of town. It was named to honor the benevolent and philanthropic Ward Nicholas Boylston, a descendant of that Dr. Zabdiel Boylston so famous in the history of inoculation. The parties interested in the movement met at the Exchange Coffee House on the 17th of January, 1809, when their arrangements were perfected. John Quincy Adams, who then lived in Boylston Street, was much interested in the new market, and made a brief address at the laying of the corner-stone. The building was designed by Bulfinch, and Mr. Boylston presented the clock. In 1870 the solid brick structure was moved back from the street eleven feet without disturbing the occupants. Before the erection of this market-house, Faneuil Hall Market was the principal source of supply for the inhabitants of this remote quarter.

Boylston Hall, over the market — which has also been known as Pantheon Hall and Adams Hall — is associated with a variety of musical, theatrical, and miscellaneous entertainments. It was occupied by the Handel and Haydn Society in 1817, the year after their incorporation, and used by them for their musical exhibitions. In 1818 Incledon and Phillips, the celebrated vocalists, assisted at their performances. The celebrated Charles Matthews gave his "Trip to Paris" here in 1822, after the close of his engagement at the old theatre, as Mr. Clapp says, "to meet the wants of those holy puritans who would not visit the theatre to see an entertainment which they patronized in a hall." Mr. Buckingham, editor of the Galaxy, characterized the performance as low and vulgar, for which and other strong expressions Matthews commenced an action for damages; the suit never came to trial. A theatre was also established here by Wyzeman Marshall, and the since much-admired and successful actor Murdoch conducted at one time a gymnasium and school of elocution in Boylston Hall. Added to these, it was used by several religious societies and as an armory, prior to its being replaced by the Continental Clothing House.

Upon this spot once stood the tavern of "Peggy" Moore. The vicinity was the usual halting-place for the country people coming into town with their garden produce. Then ox-teams were the rule, few farmers having horses, and the neighborhood of Peggy Moore's was usually a scene of plenty and of jollity. From the shrewdness with which barter was carried on, the place was dubbed "shaving corner," and among the keen blades who trafficked on this exchange, none, it was said, excelled William Foster of the neighboring lane. Even the future President may have cheapened his joint here, or turned the scale in his favor by a call at Peggy Moore's.

The Washington Bank was long located at the corner of Washington and Beach Streets, where its imposing granite front remained until the erection of the present buildings. The bank was incorporated in 1825, with a capital of half a million. For a long time previous to its demolition the building was occupied as a furniture warehouse. In Beach Street was established the short-lived Dramatic Museum in 1848, in a building known as the Beach Street Market.

We will enter upon Essex Street. A short walk brings us to Harrison Avenue, one of the new streets risen from the sea-shore. The beginning of this now handsome street, shaded for a considerable distance by trees, was in the portion from Essex Street to Beach, where it was arrested by the water. This was called Rainsford's Lane, until included in Front Street (Harrison Avenue) in 1825. The name was from Deacon Edward Rainsford, who took the oath of freeman in 1637, and was one of those disarmed in the Anne Hutchinson controversy. His tract was on the westerly side of Essex Street extending to the sea, and separated from Garrett Bourne on the west by his lane.

Harrison Avenue, which was built in 1806–07, and first named Front Street, extended from Beach Street to South Boston bridge. Up to 1830 the docks and flats on the west side of this street were not all filled up. Its present name was given, in 1841, in honor of General Harrison. A straight avenue, three fourths of a mile in length and seventy feet wide, was something unknown in Boston before this street was laid out.

On the east side of Rainsford's Lane was the house in which were born Admiral Sir Isaac Coffin and his brother John, a major-general in the British army. Both were sons of Nathaniel Coffin, Collector of his Majesty's Customs, and a firm loyalist. Sir Isaac was educated in the Boston schools, and entered the royal navy in 1773, just before the Revolution.

John Coffin volunteered to accompany the royal army in the battle of Bunker Hill, and soon after obtained a commission. He rose to the rank of captain, and went with the New York Volunteers to Georgia, in 1778. At the battle of Savannah, at Hobkirk's Hill, and at Cross Creek near Charleston, his conduct won the admiration of his superiors. At the battle of Eutaw his gallantry attracted the notice of General Greene. He was made colonel, 1797; major-general, 1803; general 1819.

The old mansion of the Coffins was afterwards removed farther up Harrison Avenue. It was of wood, three stories high, with gambrel roof, and was still to be seen by the curious on the east side of the street, standing at a little distance back with the end towards it, not many years ago.

The following anecdote of Sir Isaac is authentic. While in Boston once, the admiral stopped at the Tremont House, and, being very gouty, was confined to his room. At King's Chapel prayers were offered for his recovery, and after service was over a gentleman paid his respects to the distinguished visitor at his room, where he found him with his leg swathed in bandages, and in no conciliatory mood. His footman having accidentally run against his gouty foot, the admiral discharged a volley of oaths at his devoted head, following them with his crutch. The efficacy of the prayers may be doubted.

Still another of this famous royalist family was destined to acquire rank and distinction in the British service. Sir Thomas Aston Coffin, Bart., was a son of William Coffin of Boston, and cousin of Admiral Sir Isaac. All three of the distinguished Coffins were born in Boston, and bred in her public schools. Thomas was at one period private secretary to Sir Guy Carleton, and attained the rank of commissary-general in the British army. He was a graduate of Harvard.

The admiral ever retained an affectionate regard for his native country. His family were descended from that tight little isle of Nantucket, where the name of the Coffins has been made famous in story for their exploits in the whale fishery. He gave evidence of his attachment by investing a large sum in the English funds for the benefit of the Coffin school on the island, of which fund the mayor and aldermen of Boston were made trustees for the distribution of the annual interest among five of the most deserving boys and as many girls of that school.

Next south of the little alley that divides Harrison Avenue lived Henry Bass, one of the Tea Party, at whose house Samuel Adams and Major Melvill often passed a convivial evening and ate a Sunday dinner.

By the extension of Harrison Avenue north to Bedford Street, the residence of Wendell Phillips was demolished. A handsome tablet affixed to the wall of the adjoining building acquaints us with this fact. There is still another. It was the expressed wish of Mr. Phillips to the writer to be remembered as a resident of Essex Street, where forty years "all his life" had been passed among the plain people, whose lifelong champion he was.

The manufacture of rum in Boston has been referred to elsewhere. Prior to 1793 the neighborhood of Essex and South Streets was largely occupied by distilleries. In 1794 the town contained no less than thirty. The oldest in this vicinity, long in possession of the French family, is found as early as 1714, operated by Henry Hill, and later by Thomas Hill. Besides this, there were also Child's on Essex Street, and Avery's and Haskins' distilleries, between Essex and Beach Streets.

Gilbert Stuart lived and painted in 1828 in a modern three-story brick house, standing alone in Essex Street, numbered 59, near the opening of Edinboro. The latter is a modern thoroughfare. Before removing to Essex Street, Stuart resided in Washington Place, Fort Hill, where he had a painting-room. He took up his permanent residence in Boston in 1806, and died here July 9, 1828. His two daughters, Mrs. Stebbins and Miss Jane Stuart, pursued their father's profession in Boston; the latter long followed her art at Newport, R. I. Stuart, it is said, did not instruct his daughters as he might have done.

Stuart was not particularly prepossessing in appearance, and was very careless in dress, but a man of great genius. His eye was very piercing, and photographed a subject or a sitter at a glance. He was easily offended, and would then destroy his works of great value.

Having exhausted the patronage of Newport, Stuart went over to London, where he began to paint in 1781. He soon found himself without money and without friends in the great capital, and for some time played the organ at a church to secure the means of living. In this the knowledge of music cultivated in America stood him in good stead. He was a capital performer on the flute, and it is related by Trumbull that he passed his last night at Newport serenading the girls. His passion for music led him to neglect his art at this time, and some of his friends thought it necessary to advise him to go to work. To his musical genius he owed his bread in the swarming wilderness of London.

Among the first patrons of Stuart were Lord St. Vincent, the Duke of Northumberland (Percy), and Colonel Barré, who, learning of his embarrassments, came into his room one morning soon after he had set up an independent easel, locked the door, and made friendly offers of assistance. This the painter declined. They then said they would sit for their portraits, and insisted on paying half price in advance. This is Stuart's own relation.

Stuart became a pupil of West at twenty-four, the latter having lent him a small sum and invited him to his studio.

He afterwards painted a full length of his old master. While with West, Stuart often indulged of a morning in a bout with the foils with his master's son Rafe (Raphael West). He was surprised one morning by the old gentleman just as he had driven Rafe to the wall, with his back to one of his father's best pictures. "There, you dog," says Stuart, "there I have you, and nothing but your background *relieves* you." Stuart painted in London at John Palmer's, York Buildings.

Stuart, while in Paris, painted Louis XVI. But his greatest work was the head of Washington, now in the Museum of Fine Arts. This portrait he offered to the State of Massachusetts for one thousand dollars, but it was refused. It would now be a matter of difficulty to fix a price upon it. The head remained in Stuart's room until his widow found a purchaser for it. The first picture of Washington painted by Stuart was a failure, and he destroyed it, but he produced at the second trial a canvas that never can be surpassed. Of the works of the older painters there are said to be eleven of Smibert's and eighteen of Blackburn's now in Boston.

The first glass-works in Boston were located in what is now Edinboro Street; the company was established in 1787. The Legislature granted an exclusive right to the company to manufacture for fifteen years, and exemption from all taxes for five years; the workmen were relieved from military duty. The company first erected a brick building, conical in form, but this proving too small, it was taken down and replaced by a wooden one a hundred feet long by sixty in breadth. After many embarrassments the company began the manufacture of window-glass in November, 1793. Samuel Gore was one of the originators of the enterprise, but the company failed to make the manufacture remunerative. In 1797 the works were controlled by Charles F. Kupfer, who continued to make window-glass. They were blown down in the great gale of 1815, and subsequently taking fire, were consumed.

The manufacture of glass in Massachusetts was begun some time before the Revolution in a part of Braintree called Germantown. Nothing but bottles, however, were produced here, and the works failed before the commencement of the war. The house was burnt down and never rebuilt.

Opposite Oliver Place were two magnificent specimens of the American elm, standing in the pavement before two old-time brick houses. They were as large as those of the Tremont Street mall, and were pleasant to look at.

Time was when the trees were everywhere; now they are indeed rare, and the places that once knew them "now know them no more." Formerly there were few, if any, situations in the town in which trees were not seen, but they are now fast following the old Bostonians who planted them or dwelt beneath their grateful shade. Fifty were removed at one time from Charles Street when the roadway was widened; these were replanted on the Common. There were two noble elms at the corner of Congress and Water Streets fifty years ago, scarcely exceeded in size by those of the malls. Bowdoin Square, the Coolidge, Bulfinch, and Parkman estates, were adorned with shade and fruit trees. Occasionally, during our pilgrimage, we have discovered some solitary tree in an unexpected place, but it only stands because its time has not yet come.

> "But rising from the dust of busy streets,
> These forest children gladden many hearts;
> As some old friend their welcome presence greets
> The toil-worn soul, and fresher life imparts.
> Their shade is doubly grateful where it lies
> Above the glare which stifling walls throw back;
> Through quivering leaves we see the soft blue skies,
> Then happier tread the dull, unvaried track."

We have remarked that the old peninsula was but thinly wooded, and the settlers soon began to plant trees, supplying themselves with wood from the islands for a time. We find by the records that the town took order as early as 1655 "to prevent the trees planted on the Neck from being spoiled." In March, 1695, it appears that several attempts had been made by Captain Samuel Sewall "to plant trees at the south end of the town for the shading of Wheeler's Point," and all others were prohibited from meddling with them. The trees on the Common and Liberty Tree were planted early. There was an

English elm on the Storer estate, Sudbury Street, which had few horizontal limbs, but which attained a very great height, the trunk being larger than those of Paddock's Mall. We have pointed to its fellow on West Street. Three English elms, thought to have been planted by some of the Oliver family early in the last century, stood on the edge of High Street, in what was Quincy Place, on the building of which they were levelled. They were of the size of those in Paddock's Mall. A fourth of the same species stood in solitary grandeur at the upper part of the lot on Fort Hill, for years denominated as Phillips's Pasture, which was the finest specimen of the English elm in the town. Having "ample room and verge enough," it extended its branches horizontally in every direction. This must have corresponded nearly in age with those mentioned in High Street.

In Essex Street was the cooper-shop of Samuel Peck, one of the Tea Party, whose two apprentices, Henry Purkett and Edward Dolbier, followed him to the scene of action at Griffin's Wharf.

The visitor to this quarter once saw, at the corner of Essex and Columbia Streets, an old wooden house, to which is ascribed the honor of being the residence for a time of the ubiquitous Earl Percy. It stood at a little distance back from Essex Street, on which it fronted. Built of wood, with gambrel roof, it belonged, at an earlier date, to Thomas Child the distiller previously mentioned.

According to Mr. Sabine, this was the residence of Mrs. Sheaffe, whose son, Roger Hale, became the *protégé* of Percy, who took a great liking to him while lodging with his mother in this house. Under the protection of the Earl the young Bostonian advanced to the rank of lieutenant-general in the British army, and became a baronet. His principal military service seems to have been in Canada, though it was his wish not to have been employed against his native country. He took command at Queenstown after the fall of General Brock, and defended Little York (Toronto) from the attack of our forces under General Dearborn. He was also in the attack on

Passenger Train and Station of the Boston and Worcester Railroad, with Trinity Church in the Distance.

Copenhagen under Nelson in 1801, and saw service in Holland. Sir Roger made several visits to his native town, and is represented as a man of generous impulses, high-minded, and well worthy the interest of his noble friend and patron. Mrs. Sheaffe was a daughter of Thomas Child.

The lower part of Essex Street brings us to the limit of the South Cove improvement in this direction, by which the ancient sea-border was obliterated, and a territory nearly twice as large as the Common added to the area of Boston. Charles Ewer has been named as the projector of this enterprise, which reclaimed from tide-water that part of the South Cove from Essex Street to South Boston Bridge, and lying east of Harrison Avenue. Work was begun in 1833, a bonus of $75,000 being paid to the Boston and Worcester Railroad Company to locate its depot within the cove forever. The railway purchased 138,000 feet of land for its purposes, and 48,000 were sold for the City, now the United States, Hotel. Another parcel of land was sold to the Seekonk Branch Railroad Company. By 1857 the agent had acquired seventy-three acres of land and flats; seventy-seven acres in all were proposed to be reclaimed.

The locomotives, cars, rails, etc. first used on the Worcester railroad were all of English make. The passenger carriages were shaped like an old-fashioned stage-coach, contained a dozen persons, and ran on single trucks. They bore little comparison, either in size, comfort, or adornment, to the luxurious vehicles now used on the same road. The freight cars, or vans, had frames, over which was drawn a canvas covering similar to those in use on the army baggage-wagon, so that when seen at a little distance a freight train did not look unlike a number of haystacks in motion across the fields. The first locomotive used on this road was brought over from England on the deck of a ship, and was with great difficulty landed and moved across the city from Long Wharf. It was called the Meteor.

We will now transfer our readers to the vicinity of Hollis Street. Opposite the entrance to that avenue on Tremont Street is a remnant of old wooden buildings, whose antiquity is vouched for by their extreme dilapidation. Patches of the roof seem returning to their native earth, and the crazy structures appear to have outlived their day and generation.

Here was the dwelling and carpenter-shop of Colonel John Crane, who came so near meeting his death in the hold of the tea-ship. The shop is still used by mechanics of the same craft. Crane, after the construction of the fortifications on the Neck, commanded that post, being then major of a regiment of artillery, of which the Boston company formed the nucleus. He became an expert marksman, and was considered the most skilful in the regiment. It is related that one day, as he sighted a gun bearing upon Boston, he intended to hit the house of Dr. Byles, a tory neighbor of his, who lived next door. The shot, however, passed over the doctor's house, and tore away his own ridgepole.

Crane was wounded in New York in 1776; he was in Sullivan's expedition to Rhode Island in 1778, and succeeded Knox in the command of the Massachusetts artillery. His services were highly valued by the commander-in-chief, who retained him near his headquarters. Colonel Crane was a Bostonian by birth.

Mather Byles lived in an old two-story wooden house, with gambrel roof, situated just at the commencement of the bend or turn of Tremont Street; so that when that street was extended, it cut off a part of the southeast side of the house. What is now called Common Street is a part of old Nassau Street, which commenced at Boylston and ended at Orange, now Washington Street. Tremont Street was opened through to Roxbury line in 1832. At one time that part from Boylston to Common was called Holyoke Street.

Rev. Mather Byles, the first pastor of Hollis Street Church, came on his mother's side from the stock of those old Puritan divines, John Cotton and Richard Mather. He was by birth a Bostonian, having first seen the light in 1706, and died, an octogenarian, in his native town in 1788. He was evidently popular with his parish, as he continued his ministrations for more than forty years, until his tory proclivities caused a separation from his flock. After the name of tory came to have a peculiar significance, Mather Byles's associations seem to have been almost altogether with that side. He was a warm friend of Hutchinson and other of the crown officers, but remained in Boston after the adherents of the royal cause had generally left the town.

"In 1777 he was denounced in town-meeting, and, having been by a subsequent trial pronounced guilty of attachment to the Royal cause, was sentenced to confinement, and to be sent with his family to England. This doom of banishment was never enforced, and he was permitted to remain in Boston. He died in 1788, aged eighty-two years. He was a scholar, and Pope, Lansdowne, and Watts were his correspondents."*

Many anecdotes are recorded of this witty divine. On one occasion, when a sentinel was placed before his door, he persuaded him to go an errand for him, and gravely mounted guard over his own house, with a musket on his shoulder, to the amusement of the passers-by. Dr. Byles paid his addresses unsuccessfully to a lady who afterwards married a Mr. Quincy. "So, madam," said the Doctor on meeting her, "you prefer a Quincy to Byles, it seems." The reply was, "Yes; for if there had been anything worse than biles, God would have afflicted Job with them." His two daughters, whose peculiarities were scarcely less marked than those of their father, continued to reside in the old homestead. They remained violent tories until their death, though they were very poor and somewhat dependent upon the benevolence of Trinity Church parish.

The following anecdotes of Rev. Mather Byles illustrate his peculiar propensity. Just before the Revolution, Isaiah Thomas, author of the History of Printing, paid a visit to the Rev. Dr. B., and was taken by him to an upper window, or observatory as the Doctor called it, from which there was a fine prospect. "Now," said Dr. Byles to his companion, "you can *observe-a-tory*." At another time, when Dr. Byles was bowed with the infirmities of years, Dr. Harris, of Dorchester, called upon him, and found him sitting in an arm-chair. "Doctor," said the aged punster, "you will excuse my rising; I am not one of the rising gener-

* Sabine's Loyalists.

ation." In his last illness he was visited by Rev. William Montague, rector of Christ Church, and Rev. Dr. Parker, rector of Trinity. Dr. Parker approached the sick man's bedside, and asked him how he felt. "I feel," said the inveterate joker, "that I am going where there are no bishops."

The two following verses, addressed to Dr. Byles, are from a poetical description of the Boston clergy, which appeared about 1774. It contained thirty-seven stanzas, and was the rage of the town. Green, Trumbull, Dr. Church, and Dexter of Dedham were all charged with the authorship.

"There 's punning Byles, provokes our smiles,
A man of stately parts;
Who visits folks to crack his jokes,
That never mend their hearts.

"With strutting gait and wig so great,
He walks along the streets,
And throws out wit, or what 's like it,
To every one he meets."

The original name of Hollis Street was Harvard. Street and church were named for Thomas Hollis, an eminent London merchant, and benefactor of Harvard College. Hollis Street appears on a map of 1775, continued in a straight line to Cambridge (Back) Bay. The growth of this part of Boston had, by 1730, called for a place of worship nearer than Summer Street. Governor Belcher, who was then a resident in the vicinity, gave the land for a site, and a small wooden meeting-house, thirty by forty feet, was erected in 1732. The first minister was Rev. Mather Byles. A bell weighing 800 pounds was given by a nephew of the Thomas Hollis for whom the church was named, and was placed in the steeple on its arrival. This bell began the joyful peal at one o'clock on the morning of the 19th of May, 1766, as nearest to Liberty Tree, and was answered by Christ Church from the other extremity of the town, announcing the Stamp Act Repeal. The steeples were hung with flags, and Liberty Tree decorated with banners.

The church was destroyed by the great fire of 1787, but the society, nothing daunted, reared another wooden edifice in the year following, of which we present an engraving. It was erected upon the same spot as the former church, but had, unlike it, two towers instead of a steeple. Charles Bulfinch was the architect, and Josiah Wheeler the builder. This building was removed in 1810, to give place to the present edifice, and was floated on a raft down the harbor to East Braintree, where Rev. Jonas Perkins preached in it forty-seven years. Though now turned into a theatre, and denuded of its fine steeple, the main building remains substantially as before.

HOLLIS STREET CHURCH.

The steeple of Hollis Street reached to an altitude of nearly two hundred feet, and was one of the most prominent objects seen from the harbor. This was the church of West, Holley, Pierpont, and Starr King. Singularly enough, the church had lost by death, while in the service of the church, but a single one of its pastors (Dr. Samuel West) since its organization. Rev. John Pierpont, one of our native poets, was first a lawyer, and then a merchant. In the late civil war, though past his "threescore and ten," he joined a Massachusetts regiment as chaplain. He died at Medford, in 1866, while holding a clerkship in the Treasury Department at Washington. Thomas Starr King was but twenty-four when he assumed the pastorate of Hollis Street, and after twelve years of service removed to San Francisco, where he bore a prominent part in arraying California in active sympathy with the North during the civil war. A number of works have emanated from the pen of this gifted and lamented author and divine, of which the White Hills is perhaps the best known, and most enjoyable.

It is a singular fact that in only two instances the (Hanover Street Methodist and Hollis Street) have three churches been erected on the same spot in Boston. The New North, Old South, Brattle Square, Bromfield Street, Bulfinch Street,

West, Baldwin Place, Phillips, Maverick, and Trinity churches, Baptist Bethel, and King's Chapel, are or were the second edifices on the same site.

Zachariah Whitman, in his History of the Ancient and Honorable Artillery, says, —

"The erection of pews on the ground-floor of meeting-houses was a New England invention. Some of the first meeting-houses in Boston that had pews had no broad or other aisle, but were entered from without by a door, the owner keeping the key."

The tablets in Hollis Street Church bearing the Ten Commandments were the gift of Benjamin Bussey.

The terrible fire of 1787 laid waste the whole of the region around Hollis Street. It commenced in William Patten's malt-house in Beach Street, extending with great rapidity in a southerly direction. The spire of Hollis Street Church soon took fire from the burning flakes carried through the air, and the church was burnt to the ground. Both sides of Washington Street, from Eliot to Common on the west, and from Beach to a point opposite Common Street on the east, were laid in ruins. This fire cost the town a hundred houses, of which sixty were dwellings. Subscriptions were set on foot for the sufferers, and the Marquis Lafayette, with characteristic generosity, gave £ 350 sterling towards the relief of the sufferers.

The British, it is said, on their retreat from the works on the Neck left a rear-guard at Hollis Street, who had orders, if the Americans broke through the tacit convention between Washington and Howe, to fire a train laid to Hollis Street Church, which had served them as a barrack. This guard, after remaining a short time at their post, took to their heels, and scampered off under the impression that the Yankees were close upon them.

We conclude our chapter with a visit to another poet, Charles Sprague, who resided in the evening of his life, and died in his eighty-fifth year, at No. 636 on the east side of Washington Street, in a substantial old-fashioned house.

It has been stated that the oration which Mr. Sprague delivered July 4, 1825, before the city authorities was afterwards effectively used on a similar occasion as an original production by a Western Cicero, who might have worn his laurels undiscovered had he not in an unguarded moment furnished a copy for the press.

Mr. Sprague went to the Franklin School when Lemuel Shaw, the late Chief Justice, was usher there. He became connected with the State Bank in 1820, and subsequently cashier of the Globe when that bank was organized. His first poetical essay, by which his name came before the public, was a prize prologue, delivered at the opening of the Park Theatre, New York, of which the following is an extract: —

"The Stage! where Fancy sits, creative queen,
And waves her sceptre o'er life's mimic scene;
Where young-eyed Wonder comes to feast his sight,
And quaff instruction while he drinks delight.
The Stage! that threads each labyrinth of the soul,
Wakes laughter's peal, and bids the tear-drop roll;
That shoots at Folly, mocks proud Fashion's slave,
Uncloaks the hypocrite, and brands the knave."

CHAPTER XV.

THE NECK AND THE FORTIFICATIONS.

The Neck described. — Measures to protect the Road. — Paving the Neck. — Henry T. Tuckerman. — Old Houses *vs.* Modern. — Massachusetts Mint. — The Gallows. — Anecdote of Warren. — Executions. — Early Fortifications. — The British Works and Armament. — American Works. — George Tavern. — Washington's Staff. — His Personal Traits. — Washington House. — Washington Hotel. — Anecdotes of George Tavern. — Scarcity of Powder. — Continental Flags. — Entry of Washington's Army. — Entry of Rochambeau's Army. — Paul Jones.

WE have conducted the reader through all of Colonial Boston embraced within the peninsula, and are now to survey the barrier which the colonists raised against the power of the mighty British Empire. The more we examine the resources and state of preparation of the people, the more we are astonished at the hardihood with which a mere collection of the yeomanry of the country, without any pretension to the name of an army, sat down before the gates of the town of Boston, and compelled the haughty Britons to retire from her profaned temples and ruined hearthstones.

A strip of territory lying along the great avenue to the mainland still retains the appellation of "The Neck." Long may the only battle-ground within our ancient limits preserve the name by which it was known to Winthrop and to Washington. All Boston proper was once styled "The Neck," in distinction from Noddle's Island, Brookline, and other territory included within the jurisdiction. The peninsula outgrowing her dependencies, the name attached itself to the narrow isthmus connecting with the mainland.

The Neck may be said to have begun at Beach Street, where was its greatest breadth, diminishing to its narrowest point at Dover Street, increasing gradually in width to the neighborhood

Winter Scene on Boston Neck, Fifty Years Ago.

of Dedham Street, thence expanding in greater proportion to the line at the present car stables nearly opposite Arnold Street. The Neck, according to its designation in Revolutionary times, was that part lying south of Dover Street.

Captain Nathaniel Uring, in his account of his visit to Boston in 1710, printed in London in 1726, says: —

"The Neck of Land betwixt the city and country is about forty yards broad, and so low that the spring tides sometimes wash the road, which might, with little charge, be made so strong as not to be forced, there being no way of coming at it by land but over that Neck."

Whether what constituted old Boston was at one time an island, or was becoming one by the wasting forces of the elements, is an interesting question for geologists. We know that for nearly a hundred and fifty years scarcely any change had taken place in the appearance of the Neck; but the action of the town authorities seems to indicate a fear that its existence was seriously threatened.

Within the recollection of persons now living the water has been known to stand up to the knees of horses in the season of full tides at some places in the road, on the Neck. The narrowest part was naturally the most exposed, as it was the most eligible also for fortifying. At some points along the beach there was a good depth of water, and Gibben's shipyard was located on the easterly side a short distance north of Dover Street as early as 1722, and as late as 1777. Other portions, on both sides of the Neck, were bordered by marshes, more or less extensive, covered at high tides.

Wharves were built at intervals along the eastern shore, from Beach to Dover Street. In front of these wharves dwellings and stores were erected, facing what is now Washington Street. Josiah Knapp's dwelling, formerly standing at the corner of Kneeland Street, was one of these, his wharf being so near the street that the passers-by complained that the bowsprits of his vessels unlading there obstructed the highway.

In the spring the road upon the Neck was almost impassable, especially before the centre was paved, which was from necessity done at last, but with such large stones that the pavement was always avoided by vehicles as long as the old road was practicable.

Measures began to be very early considered to protect the Neck from the violence of the sea. In 1708 the town granted a number of individuals all the tract included within Castle and a point a little north of Dover Street, conditioned upon the completion of a highway and erection of certain barriers to "secure and keep off the sea." A second grant was made nearly eighty years later for a like purpose, extending from the limits of the first grant to a point a little beyond the former estate of John D. Williams, Esq., where the Cathedral now stands. From this beginning dates the reclamation of that extensive area now covered in every direction with superb public edifices or private mansions.

A dike was built on the exposed eastward side, crossing the marshes to the firm ground on the Roxbury shore, before the Revolution, which traversed both the British and American works on the Neck. This followed in general direction the extension of Harrison Avenue. A sea-wall was built about the same time on the west side, for some distance south from the bridge at Dover Street, nearly as far as Waltham Street. In a word, the general appearance of the Neck eighty years ago, to a spectator placed at the Old Fortifications, was similar to the turnpikes crossing the Lynn marshes to-day, and was desolate and forbidding in the extreme, especially to a nocturnal traveller.

From the old fortifications, northwardly, the highway was called Orange Street as early as 1708. Washington Street was named after the memorable visit of the General in 1789, and at first extended only from near Dover Street to Roxbury line; the name was not applied to the whole extent of the present thoroughfare until 1824, when Cornhill, Marlborough, Newbury, and Orange became one in name as well as in fact.

Few of the thousands who daily traverse the Neck, with its elevated road, street-cars and private equipages following each other in rapid succession, can realize that travellers were once in great danger of losing their way along the narrow natural causeway and its adjacent marshes. Yet so frequent had such accidents become that not only the town but the General Court took action in 1723 to have the dangerous road fenced in.

The Neck marshes were a favorite resort for birds, and were much frequented by sportsmen. It is related that Sir Charles and Lady Frankland one day narrowly escaped being shot as they were passing over the highway. In 1785 the town of Roxbury was obliged to place sentinels here to prevent the desecration of the Sabbath. The meadows continued in much later times to be a resort for this purpose.

The Neck was paved quite early in the last century, according to the fashion we have described elsewhere. In 1757 the General Court authorized a lottery to raise funds for paving and repairing the highway. The forty-two rods of Orange Street, mentioned as having been ordered paved in 1715, were probably the portion nearest the town, but it was paved in 1775 as far as the British works. The whole Neck was paved under the mayoralty of Josiah Quincy.

In colonial times the fortification which was raised a little south of Dover Street was the limit of the town, — all beyond was nearly in its primitive condition. In 1794 there were but eighteen buildings between Dover Street and the line. In 1800 there were not more than one or two houses from the site of the new Catholic Cathedral to Roxbury. The few buildings standing between the American and British lines were burnt during the siege, and only two barns and three small houses were then left on what was properly termed the Neck.

A few doors north of Dover Street, on the easterly side of what was then old Orange Street, was the home of the favorite author and poet, Henry T. Tuckerman. The house was struck during the siege by a shot from the American lines. Mr. Tuckerman has contributed largely to our literature both in verse and prose, as an essayist, critic, biographer, and accomplished traveller. He was also well known through his articles in our leading magazines. As a poet, his "Rome" gives a good sample of his style.

"A terrace lifts above the People's Square
Its colonnade;
About it lies the warm and crystal air,
And fir-trees' shade."

This house, like most of those on our main avenue in the beginning of the century, stood end to the street, which gave a singular impression to a stranger, and recalls the following quaint description of Albany by old Jedediah Morse, which has given rise to a witticism on the peculiarity of the inhabitants of that town: —

"This city and suburbs, by enumeration in 1797, contained 1,263 buildings, of which 863 were dwelling-houses, and 6,021 inhabitants. Many of them are in the Gothic style, with the gable end to the street, which custom the first settlers brought from Holland; the new houses are built in the modern style."

The only purpose of utility for which the Neck was formerly used, except perhaps the grazing afforded by the marshes along the causeway, was for brick-making. There were brickyards north of Dover Street, as well as south, before the Revolution. These gave employment to many poor people during the continuance of the Port Act. In this connection we may mention the total absence of building-stone of any kind on the site of original Boston. The principal elevations have been either wholly or partially removed without encountering a ledge of any description.

In October, 1786, the State of Massachusetts, being greatly in want of a specie currency, passed an act to establish a mint for the coinage of copper, silver, and gold. This was one of the powers of sovereignty which the States continued to exercise under the old "Articles of Confederation." Joshua Wetherle was appointed master of the mint

MASSACHUSETTS CENT OF 1787.

in May, 1787, and authorized to erect the necessary works and machinery. $70,000 in cents and half-cents were ordered to be struck as soon as practicable.

Wetherle established his works on the Neck, in the rear of what is now Rollins Street, and at Dedham, the copper being first carted to Dedham to be rolled, and then brought back to Boston to be coined. In July, 1787, the national government established the devices of its copper coin.

Early in 1788 the copper coin ordered by the State began to be issued, but only a few thousand dollars of the large amount ordered were put in circulation before the work was suspended by the State in consequence of the adoption of the Federal Constitution, which reserved the right to coin money to the general government. The emblems on the Massachusetts cent and half-cent were the same. One side bore the American eagle with a bundle of arrows in the right talon and an olive-branch in the left, with a shield on the breast, on which is the word "cent"; the word "Massachusetts" encircling the border. The reverse represents a full-length Indian grasping his bow and arrow, but, as Mr. Felt remarks, considerably improved in appearance since he appeared on the colony seal. A star appears near the head, as in the State seal, emblematic of one of the United States, and the word "Commonwealth" completes the device.

The first object which arrested the attention of the traveller as he journeyed towards Old Boston was the gallows, standing as a monument of civilization at the gates. It was at first situated near the old fortification on the easterly side of the Neck, but stood at a later period not far from the site of the New England Conservatory of Music.

A characteristic anecdote is related of Dr. Warren in connection with the gallows. It is said that as he was one day passing the spot he met some British officers, one of whom exclaimed, "Go on, Warren, you will soon come to the gallows." Warren immediately turned back and demanded to know which of them had thus accosted him, but neither of the warriors had the courage to avow it.

Here were hanged the pirates John Williams, Francis Frederick, John P. Rog, and Niles Peterson, in 1819; and in the following year Michael Powers was also executed for the murder of Timothy Kennedy. Perez Morton was then district-attorney. Powers was defended by Daniel Webster, but was convicted, on an unbroken chain of circumstantial evidence, of having murdered and then buried his victim in a cellar.

The defences of Boston very early engaged the attention of the settlers. Fort Hill was fortified as early as 1634, and steps were taken to build a work on Castle Island in the same year. It is reasonable to conclude that the protection of the land side received even earlier attention, the danger being more imminent. The Indians in the neighborhood were, as a general thing, friendly, but were not trusted, and a guard of an officer and six men was placed on the Neck, by order of the court, in April, 1631. We cannot, however, fix the date with precision, though a barrier was certainly erected prior to 1640. The gates of the old fortification were constantly guarded, and were shut by a certain hour in the evening, after which none were allowed to pass in or out.

The primitive barrier had disappeared before 1710, the broken power of the Indians leaving nothing to apprehend from that quarter. In this year the town voted that a line of defence be forthwith made across the Neck, between Boston and Roxbury. A suitable number of great guns were ordered to be mounted, and a gate erected across the road. The foundation of this work was of stone and brick, with parapet of earth; part of what was considered to be the remains of the old fort was uncovered in 1860, when excavations were making in the street, just south of the corner of Dover Street.

In September, 1774, when matters were approaching a crisis between the people and the King's troops, Gage began to fortify the Neck. The remains of the old works were strengthened, guns mounted, and earthworks thrown up some distance in advance of these on both sides of the highway. The armament at first consisted of two twenty-four and eight nine pounders. The first troops stationed by Gage in this quarter were the

59th regiment, which arrived from Salem September 2, and encamped on the Neck. On the 4th four pieces of field artillery were taken from the Common and placed in front of the troops, fatigue parties from which went to work upon the intrenchments. By midwinter the ordinary garrison was one hundred and fifty men, with a field-officer in command. This force was increased before the battle of Lexington to three hundred and forty men. A deep fosse, into which the tide flowed at high water, was dug in front of the Dover Street fort, converting Boston for the time into two islands.

In July, 1775, when the siege had fairly begun, the work nearest the town mounted eight twenty-four, six twelve, two nine, and seven six pounder guns, and was called during the siege "The Green Store Battery," from the warehouse of Deacon Brown, painted that color, which stood on the site of the New Grand Theatre. The advanced work, which was much the stronger, mounted eight twenty-four, four twelve, one nine, and seven six pounders, with six eight-inch howitzers, and a mortar battery. The road passed directly through the centre of both lines, the first being closed by a gate and drawbridge. The redan was flanked by a bastion on each side of the highway, from which the lines were continued across the intervening marshes to the sea. Floating batteries, abattis, *trous-de-loup*, and other appliances known to military science, were not wanting. Two guard-houses were on either side of the road immediately in the rear of the advanced post, while a third and smaller work, lying between the others on the eastern sea-margin, bore on Dorchester Neck, and took the left curtain and bastion of the main work in reverse. Above all waved the standard of England.

BRITISH LINES ON BOSTON NECK IN 1775.

The position of the main British work, vestiges of which were distinctly visible as late as 1822, particularly on the west side of the Neck, was between Dedham and Canton Streets. Mounds, ramparts, and wide ditches yet attested the strength of the defences which Washington deemed too formidable to be carried by assault. Remains of planks and poles used to support the embankment of what may have been one of the bastions were discovered many years since in digging the cellar of Edward D. Peters's house on the north corner of Canton and Washington Streets. Mr. John Griggs, whose recollections of the Neck went back more than half a century, remembered traces of the intrenchments on the east side, where we have located them. The visitor to the spot will not fail to observe that from this point the first unobstructed view is obtained in front as far as Washington Market.

By Washington's order Colonel Gridley rendered these works useless as soon as the Continental army moved to New York, so that if the enemy, whose fleet was still on the coast, should suddenly repossess themselves of Boston, they might not find the old defences available. From this stronghold Gage, Howe, Clinton, and Burgoyne grimly marked the rising intrenchments of the Americans three quarters of a mile away, or listened to the roll of the drums that greeted the approach of their chieftain as he made his daily tour of the hostile lines. Gage at one time appears to have intrusted the defence of his lines on the Neck to Lord Percy.

Colonel Trumbull, afterwards one of Washington's military family, but then belonging to a Connecticut regiment, first brought himself to the notice of the general by a daring exploit. Learning that a plan of the enemy's works was greatly desired at headquarters, he crept near enough to them to make a drawing, with which he returned to camp. For this act he was appointed aide-de-camp. A British soldier of artillery soon after came into the American lines with a plan of the hostile forts. From the time of the investment until the siege was raised, rigid martial law prevailed in Boston, with sentinels posted at all important points, patrols traversing the streets, and a town major at the head of police affairs.

Here Gage remained ignobly shut up, attempting nothing

after the battle of Bunker Hill but a few marauding excursions along the coast in search of fresh provisions. His extremities are ludicrously set forth by that inimitable Revolutionary poet, Philip Freneau. The scene is a midnight consultation at the general's quarters.

"The clock strikes *two* ! — Gage smote upon his breast,
And cry'd, — 'What fate determines must be best —
But now attend — a counsel I impart
That long has laid the heaviest at my heart —
Three weeks — ye gods ! nay, three long years it seems —
Since *roast-beef* I have touch'd, except in dreams.
In sleep, choice dishes to my view repair ;
Waking, I gape and champ the empty air. —
Say, is it just that I, who rule these bands,
Should live on husks, like rakes in foreign lands ?"

The space between the opposing works became a battle-ground for the skirmishing parties of the two armies, each of which had pickets in their front, covered by slight intrenchments. A short distance in advance of the British works on the west side of the highway were the house and barns of Enoch Brown, which served the British admirably as a post from which to annoy our men. This was the house at which Burgoyne proposed to meet Charles Lee, to discuss the differences between the colonies and the mother country. Congress, however, put a veto on a proceeding neither military nor diplomatic. On the 8th of July (1775) Majors Tupper and Crane surprised the guard and destroyed the house and out-buildings. The bare chimneys remained standing, and to some extent afforded a protection to the enemy.

After the battle of Lexington the Americans at first merely guarded the passage of the Neck with a small force under Colonel Robinson, or until the Provincial Congress took measures to organize an army, and regular military operations were undertaken.

No intrenchments appear to have been thrown up on the Neck by the Continental forces until after the battle of Bunker Hill, when the famous Roxbury lines were laid out by Colonel Richard Gridley, the veteran of Louisburg, Quebec, and Bunker Hill, now chief-engineer of the army.

From the best evidence to be obtained these lines were situated on the rising ground a little north of the old monument on the line of division between Boston and Roxbury, and near Clifton Place. An abattis was formed of trees felled with the tops pointed towards Boston, as an obstacle to the much-dreaded Light Horse, — a needless precaution, for this choice band of heroes never appeared outside their defences. The embankments were strengthened with planks filled between with earth. The works were bastioned, and rested with either flank on arms of the sea.

The American advanced post was first at the George Tavern, which stood a little south of the site of the present Washington Market, and was burnt by a British sally on the night of Sunday, July 30, 1775.

The George Tavern, sometimes called the St. George, which we have had occasion to mention in connection with the receptions of some of the royal governors, was included in an estate of more than eighteen acres, extending nearly or quite to Roxbury line on the south and across the marshes to the great creek, which formed its boundary on the west. It had orchards, gardens, and a site which commanded a view of the town of Boston and the harbor on one hand, and Cambridge Bay with the shores of the mainland on the other. While it remained, but few travellers might venture over the gloomy Neck, over which the cold winds swept with violence, without a pause under its hospitable roof.

The George is noted in the history of the Colony as the place of meeting of the General Court in 1721, perhaps on account of the prevalence of the small-pox in Boston in that year, when it raged with frightful violence. In 1730, while it was kept by Simon Rogers, the Probate Court was held there. Rogers continued to be landlord until 1734. It was kept at different times by Gideon Gardner and Samuel Mears, and in 1769 by Edward Bardin, who changed the name to the King's Arms, a title it retained but a short time. In 1788 a tavern was reopened on or near the site of the George, but was not of long continuance.

Before the destruction of the tavern the Americans threw up a work a little below where it had stood, and within musket-range of the British outpost. To this point it was Washington's daily custom to proceed, accompanied by his personal staff, composed of men subsequently famous in Revolutionary annals. There was Mifflin, first aide-de-camp, afterwards governor of Pennsylvania, who, as president of the Congress in 1783, received the resignation of his old chief; Joseph Reed of Philadelphia, his trusted friend and secretary; and Horatio Gates, whose military experience enabled him to fill acceptably the arduous post of adjutant-general, and bring a little order out of the chaos that prevailed in the American camp.

General Washington's uniform at this time was "a blue coat with buff-colored facings, a rich epaulet on each shoulder, buff under-dress, and an elegant small-sword; a black cockade in his hat." * It was at this point, from which he had, in 1775, daily viewed the inactivity of his enemy with a surprise he has not concealed in his letters, that the general, in 1789, then become President, mounted his famous white charger, a present from Charles IV. of Spain, and, attended by his secretaries, Colonel Lear and Major Jackson, made his last entry into Boston.

Probably no great personage has ever lived whose career has afforded fewer anecdotes to his biographer then General Washington. The calm dignity of his manner repelled every attempt at familiarity, but this dignity was in no way associated with hauteur. It is related that Gouverneur Morris, having undertaken once the hazardous experiment of accosting the President unceremoniously, declared that nothing would induce him to repeat the attempt. The French officers who served with Rochambeau were at once captivated by Washington's noble presence and gracious manner.

The Washington Market stands on the site of the Washington House, in which Mrs. Rowson once kept her school for young ladies, and which, under the control of the Cooleys, father and son, became a much-frequented resort for sleighing·

* Thacher's Military Journal.

parties, when the Neck was the course to which, in winter, the beauty and fashion of the town repaired.

Next south of the market is a three-story brick building, kept as a tavern as far back as 1820, and known first as Washington Hall, and subsequently as the Washington Hotel. It was kept in 1837, and for some time subsequently, by Amherst Eaton of Concert Hall. Both of these houses were on the George Tavern estate.

In 1737 the following petition was presented by Stephen Minot to be allowed a license to sell liquors at his tavern on the Neck (supposed to be the George Tavern). It was allowed.

"That your petitioner lately met with very heavy losses by the way of the sea it stands him in stead to put his estate on the land to the best improvement he possibly can in a way of Trade &c. And as he designs to keep for sale a variety of goods suitable for the country, So he apprehends it will but little avail him unless he may be permitted to supply his customers with Rum also, because they usually chuse to take up all they want at one place."

Thacher, who was a surgeon of Colonel Jackson's regiment in the old war, relates an amusing incident of the arrival of that regiment at Boston after a forced march from Providence, R. I. : —

"A severe rain all night did not much impede our march, but the troops were broken down with fatigue. We reached Boston at sunrising, and near the entrance of the Neck is a tavern, having for its sign a representation of a globe, with a man in the act of struggling to get through it ; his head and shoulders were out, his arms extended, and the rest of his body enclosed in the globe. On a label from his mouth was written, 'Oh ! how shall I get through this world ?' This was read by the soldiers, and one of them exclaimed, 'List, d—n you, list, and you will soon get through this world ; our regiment will be through it in an hour or two if we don't halt by the way.'"

The scarcity of powder within the American lines during the siege of Boston is connected with an incident not without interest. At first, a few country people were allowed to pass into town with provisions, after undergoing a search at the British post at the Green Store. Market-wagons were but little used, the farmers riding on horseback with panniers containing their marketing. George Minot, of Dorchester, from his frequent visits was well known to the guard, who allowed him to pass without examination. Had they looked into the honest man's panniers, they would have found them well filled with "villanous saltpetre," which he was, at great personal risk, conveying to his friends. The money to buy the powder was furnished by Minot's father, John Minot, a selectman of Dorchester. The government afterwards acknowledged and paid the claim, with which Minot purchased a part of Thompson's Island.

It is a matter of history that, within musket-shot of twenty British regiments, Washington's whole army was disbanded and reorganized; it is no less true that in August, 1775, the entire supply of powder was only nine rounds per man. Washington's letters at this time are full of anxiety.

The flags used by the Americans during the siege of Boston have always been a subject of much interest. The flag of thirteen stripes was first raised on the heights near Boston, probably at or near the commander-in-chief's headquarters, January 2, 1776. Letters from Boston at this time say that the regulars did not understand it; and, as the king's speech had just been sent to the Americans, they thought the new flag was a token of submission. The British Annual Register of 1776 says, more correctly, that the provincials burnt the king's speech, and changed their colors from the plain red ground they had hitherto used to a flag with thirteen stripes, as a symbol of the number and union of the colonies. This was, without doubt, the flag that, on the 17th March, 1776, waved over the Old State House and Province House, and was borne in the van of the American troops.

The Pine Tree, Rattlesnake, and striped flag were used indiscriminately until July, 1777, when the blue union, with the stars, was added to the stripes, and the flag established by law. The private arms of Washington, bearing three stars in the upper portion, and three bars across the escutcheon, were thought to have had some connection with the flag, but this does not appear probable.

"Forever float that standard sheet!
Where breathes the foe but falls before us?
With freedom's soil beneath our feet,
And freedom's banner streaming o'er us!"

The first troops to enter the town after the evacuation were five hundred men, under command of Colonel Ebenezer Learned, who unbarred and opened the gates of the British works. General Ward accompanied this detachment. They found the Neck thickly scattered with "crows'-feet" to impede their advance. At the same time a detachment under General Putnam, with whom was Colonel John Stark, landed at the foot of the Common, and to the old wolf-hunter belongs the honor of first commanding in Boston as the successor of Sir William Howe. On the 20th the main army marched in, and on the 22d such of the inhabitants as had been separated from their friends during the ten months' siege thronged into the town. Putnam took possession of, and garrisoned all the posts.

Washington himself entered Boston the day after the evacuation, but, as the small-pox prevailed in town, the army did not march in until the 20th, as stated. By Washington's order, works were thrown up on Fort Hill, and those defending from the country were demolished. The general remained ten days in Boston. He attended the meetings of the Legislature, and on the 28th, accompanied by the other general officers and their suites, marched in procession from the Council Chamber to the Old Brick Church, where appropriate services were held, after which a dinner was provided for the general and his officers at the Bunch of Grapes, in King Street. During his stay Washington reviewed the Continental troops on the Common.

The first national medal voted by Congress was presented to General Washington for his successful conduct of the siege of Boston, by a resolution passed March 25, 1776. It was struck in Paris from a die by Duvivier.

Wilkes, in a speech delivered in Parliament on the evacuation, said: "All the military men of this country now confess that the retreat of General Howe from Boston was an absolute flight; as much so, sir, as that of Mahomet from Mecca."

One other grand martial pageant of the Revolutionary period

Boston in 1775, from Roxbury, near Shirley House.

remains to be chronicled. This was the entry of Rochambeau's forces into Boston in December, 1782. The army was commanded by the brave General Baron de Vioménil, Rochambeau having taken leave of his troops at Providence, returning with a part of his staff to France.

The French army was divided into four grand divisions, to which was added the field artillery. The second division was the first to arrive in the neighborhood of Boston, on the 4th, the first and third on the 5th, and the fourth on the 6th. The artillery did not arrive until the 18th. A few desertions occurred on the march, and the officers were obliged to exercise the greatest vigilance, as many of the poor fellows preferred remaining in the country to embarking for an unknown destination.

Notwithstanding it was midwinter, the troops, before entering the town on the 7th, changed their dress in the open air, and appeared in such splendid array as gave but little hint of their long, weary march from Yorktown. Their welcome was enthusiastic and heartfelt. At a town-meeting held Saturday, December 7, of which Samuel Adams was moderator, James Sullivan and Samuel Barret, with the selectmen, were appointed a committee to wait on General Vioménil with an address of welcome, to which the Baron returned a courteous reply.

What shall be said of the editorial and reportorial enterprise of that day? Beyond the brief notice we have given of the action in town-meeting, — and that appears as an advertisement, — there is not a single line referring to the entry in the columns of the Independent Chronicle, then published in Boston, nor any clew to a sojourn of seventeen days in the news department; the other two papers dismiss the affair each with half a dozen lines. Such an event would now occupy the greater part of one of our mammoth journals; not the smallest scrap of information would be too trivial, not a button would escape scrutiny. To the greater enterprise of Isaiah Thomas's Massachusetts Spy, and particularly to its Boston correspondent, regular or special, who writes under date of December 12, 1782, we are indebted for the following: —

"Last week arrived in town from the southward, in four divisions, the troops of our generous ally, the King of France. A finer corps of men never paraded the streets of Boston in the infamous administrations of *Bernard, Hutchinson, and Gage.* The quiet, peaceable, and orderly behavior of these troops during their long march sufficiently contradicts the *infamous falsehoods* and *misrepresentations* usually imposed on the world by *perfidious Britons,* who have often led us to entertain an unfavorable opinion of the French troops. We are happily convinced that such a character belongs *wholly and only* to the troops employed by the Royal Despot of Britain."

The day was favorable, and the sunbeams danced and glittered on the bayonets of these veterans of two continents as they proudly marched over the Neck and through the modest streets of Old Boston. At their head rode Vioménil, who achieved such renown at Yorktown, and afterwards lost his life heroically defending his king at the attack on the Tuileries. At his side rode the Chevalier Alexander de Lameth, severely wounded at Yorktown, and afterwards a soldier of Napoleon; the Marquis de Champcenetz; Count Mathieu Dumas; Alexander Berthier, afterwards the adjutant-general and confidant of Napoleon, but deserting him in the hour of adversity; Lynch, the intrepid Englishman, who served in the ranks of France, and many others who gained renown in the wars into which that nation was shortly after plunged. The officers wore singular-looking, two-cornered cocked hats with the white cockade, the uniform being white broadcloth, with facings of red, blue, or green, according to the corps to which they belonged; the general alone wore a blue overdress faced with red. All the officers wore high military boots, were splendidly mounted, and their equipments and side-arms were elegant and costly.

A complete band of music accompanied the troops, whose martial strains were the first the Bostonians had heard since the evacuation by the British forces; our own army yet marched to the music of the fife and drum.

After these marched the regiment Royal Deux-Ponts, the largest in the army, in four battalions, with its colonel, Count

Christian de Deux-Ponts, from whom the regiment took its name, at its head. Count Christian afterwards commanded the Bavarian corps at the battle of Hohenlinden with distinguished valor. Count William, second colonel of the same regiment, who was wounded in the assault on the redoubt at Yorktown, where he won the order of Saint Louis, was on his way to France with the news of Cornwallis's surrender. The dress of this regiment was white. The men wore cocked hats, with pompons instead of cockades, woollen epaulets, white cross-belts, from which was suspended a short hanger and cartouche-box, and spatterdashes; the hair was worn *en queue;* — so far the description will apply to the whole army, the colors varied in all the regiments.

Next came the Soissonnais, with Count Segur, son of the Minister at War, and afterwards a peer of France, in their front. Segur was *colonel en second* of the regiment, but his senior, Count de Saint Maime, had come into Boston in advance of the army. Segur is also known as a historian, and author of his own memoirs.

The regiment Saint-Onge, in white and green, follows, with Colonel Count de Custines, who became a general, and the Prince de Broglie, second in command. Both fell under the axe of the guillotine during the French Revolution.

The Bourbonnais in black and red, the infantry of Lauzun, all with arms and accoutrements in complete order, crowned with the laurels of victory and bearing the white standard and golden lilies in their serried ranks, close the brilliant procession. Pichegru, afterwards general, was a soldier of the Bourbonnais.

An episode of this famous entry deserves mention. Young Talleyrand Périgord, brother of Prince Talleyrand, was on the staff of the Marquis Chastellux, who wished to take him back to France; but the young warrior of eighteen was determined to remain with the army, and, having obtained a grenadier's uniform, marched in the ranks of the Soissonnais, with his haversack on his back and his gun on his shoulder. Talleyrand was well known to the superior officers, who pretended not to recognize him, and his warlike ardor became the town talk

He was christened *Va-de-bon-cœur* (go willingly), and was the subject of many attentions.

The cavalry of the Duke de Lauzun, which had crossed steel with Tarleton's famous troopers and held him at bay at Gloucester, Virginia, were left behind with Washington's army on the Hudson. They carried lances, and were styled *Uhlans*, — a name rendered formidable by the Prussians in the late Franco-German war. The uniform of this famous corps was a blue hussar jacket, with high-crowned round hat. Their leader, the beau-ideal of a dashing cavalier, carried the news of the capitulation of Cornwallis to the king. When condemned afterwards by the tribunal of Fouquier Tinville, a moment before his execution he turned to those who were to suffer with him and said, "It is finished, gentlemen: I depart on the great journey." To the executioner he offered a glass of wine, saying, "Take it, you have need of courage to perform your duty."

The artillery, although it did not join in the display, must not be forgotten. This arm was attired in blue, faced with red, with white spatterdashes and red pompons. The men wore the short Roman sword, and carried their firelocks by the slings. The heavy artillery train remained with the American forces, to assist, if necessary, in the reduction of New York.

A great concourse of people came out to the Neck to welcome the gallant Frenchmen, and as the brilliant column moved along it was met with the liveliest demonstrations of joy and affection. Ladies waved their handkerchiefs from the windows, and the old streets echoed again with the plaudits of the people. Our readers will doubtless agree that, of the many pageants of which the Neck has been the theatre, none were so well worth witnessing as the one on the day when the superb host of our ally, Louis XVI., with closed ranks and firm tread passed into the town; or that other day when,

> "In their ragged regimentals,
> Stood the Old Continentals,"

with little of the pomp of war in their appearance, but with the light of victory in every countenance, as they marched in triumph through the abandoned works of the enemy, inaugurating by their valor and constancy the hope of a successful issue to the conflict just begun.

The stay of the French was taken up by a round of reviews, balls, dinners, and receptions. The officers found quarters and genuine hospitality among the inhabitants, and the men were well cared for. Both officers and men parted with keen regret from the friends they had found, — a regret sincerely shared by the inhabitants. At a fire which occurred in the town the French displayed such good-will and gallantry in assisting to extinguish it that they were publicly thanked. On the 11th, Governor Hancock and the council gave one of their solemn feasts to the general and field officers, the Marquis de Vaudreuil, and principal officers of the fleet.

The fleet of the Marquis lay in the roads, consisting of the eighty gun-ships Le Triomphant, Le Couronne, and Le Duc de Bourgogne ; the seventy-fours L'Hercule, Le Souverain, Le Neptune, La Bourgogne, Northumberland, Le Bravo, Le Citoyen, and the two frigates L'Amazone and La Néréide.

At this time the squadron was joined by a most notable volunteer in John Paul Jones, who was, at his own solicitation, permitted to accompany M. de Vaudreuil. He was received with distinction by the Marquis on board his own vessel, Le Triomphant, and lodged with the Baron Vioménil. The destination of the squadron — a secret which was well kept — was Jamaica. On the 24th of December the fleet set sail from Boston for the rendezvous at Porto Cabello, which after numerous disasters it reached in February. While lying there, Paul Jones fell dangerously ill of the fever. Peace ensued before the fleet of D'Estaing, which was to co-operate, arrived from Cadiz. It will be remembered that Jones was compelled, by a resolution of Congress, to surrender the America, the building of which he had for sixteen months superintended, to M. de Vaudreuil, to replace Le Magnifique, which had belonged to the fleet of the Marquis.

The reader, who has patiently followed us in the attempt to reconstruct to some extent the Boston of our fathers, to rebuild in imagination their habitations, and to revive their venerable customs, may, in a measure, realize those changes which have swept over the ancient peninsula, and wellnigh totally effaced its landmarks ; and while he feels a just pride in that growth which is the expression of power, he may yet render due tribute to the solid traits and heroic deeds of those antique characters who laid the foundations deep and permanent on which have risen the Metropolis of New England.

INDEX.

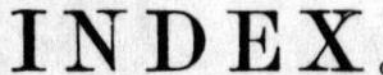

INDEX.

B.

C.

D.

H.

I.

J.

O.

P.

Q.

R.

U.

THE END.

Other TUT BOOKS available:

BACHELOR'S HAWAII *by Boye de Mente*

BACHELOR'S JAPAN *by Boye de Mente*

BACHELOR'S MEXICO *by Boye de Mente*

CALABASHES AND KINGS: An Introduction to Hawaii *by Stanley D. Porteus*

CHINA COLLECTING IN AMERICA *by Alice Morse Earle*

CHOI OI!: The Lighter Side of Vietnam *by Tony Zidek*

CONFUCIUS SAY *by Leo Shaw*

THE COUNTERFEITER and Other Stories *by Yasushi Inoue; translated by Leon Picon*

CURIOUS PUNISHMENTS OF BYGONE DAYS *by Alice Morse Earle*

CUSTOMS AND FASHIONS IN OLD NEW ENGLAND *by Alice Morse Earle*

DINING IN SPAIN *by Gerrie Beene and Lourdes Miranda King*

EXOTICS AND RETROSPECTIVES *by Lafcadio Hearn*

FIRST YOU TAKE A LEEK: A Guide to Elegant Eating Spiced with Culinary Capers *by Maxine J. Saltonstall*

FIVE WOMEN WHO LOVED LOVE *by Saikaku Ihara; translated by William Theodore de Bary*

A FLOWER DOES NOT TALK: Zen Essays *by Abbot Zenkei Shibayama of the Nanzenji*

FOLK LEGENDS OF JAPAN *by Richard M. Dorson*

GOING NATIVE IN HAWAII: A Poor Man's Guide to Paradise *by Timothy Head*

HAIKU IN ENGLISH *by Harold G. Henderson*

HARP OF BURMA *by Michio Takeyama; translated by Howard Hibbett*

THE HAWAIIAN GUIDE BOOK for Travelers *by Henry M. Whitney*

HAWAIIAN PHRASE BOOK

HAWAII: End of the Rainbow *by Kazuo Miyamoto*

HOMEMADE ICE CREAM AND SHERBERT *by Sheila MacNiven Cameron*

HOW TO READ CHARACTER: A New Illustrated Handbook of Phrenology and Physiognomy, for Students and Examiners *by Samuel R. Wells*

INDIAN RIBALDRY *by Randor Guy*

IN GHOSTLY JAPAN *by Lafcadio Hearn*

JAPAN: An Attempt at Interpretation *by Lafcadio Hearn*

THE JAPANESE ABACUS *by Takashi Kojima*

THE JAPANESE ARE LIKE THAT *by Ichiro Kawasaki*

JAPANESE ETIQUETTE: An Introduction *by the World Fellowship Committee of the Tokyo Y.W.C.A.*

THE JAPANESE FAIRY BOOK *compiled by Yei Theodora Ozaki*

JAPANESE FOLK-PLAYS: The Ink-Smeared Lady and Other Kyogen *translated by Shio Sakanishi*

JAPANESE FOOD AND COOKING *by Stuart Griffin*

A JAPANESE MISCELLANY *by Lafcadio Hearn*

JAPANESE RECIPES *by Tatsuji Tada*

JAPANESE TALES OF MYSTERY & IMAGINATION *by Edogawa Rampo; translated by James B. Harris*

JAPANESE THINGS: Being Notes on Various Subjects Connected with Japan *by Basil Hall Chamberlain*

THE JOKE'S ON JUDO *by Donn Draeger and Ken Tremayne*

THE KABUKI HANDBOOK *by Aubrey S. Halford and Giovanna M. Halford*

KOREAN FOLK TALES *by Im Bang and Yi Ryuk; translated by James S. Gale*

KWAIDAN: Stories and Studies of Strange Things *by Lafcadio Hearn*

LET'S STUDY JAPANESE *by Jun Maeda*

THE LIFE OF BUDDHA *by A. Ferdinand Herold*

MODERN JAPANESE PRINTS: A Contemporary Selection *edited by Yuji Abe*

MORE ZILCH: The Marine Corps' Most Guarded Secret *by Roy Delgado*

PHYSICAL FITNESS: A Practical Program *by Clark Hatch*

POO POO MAKE PRANT GLOW *by Harvey Ward*

PROFILES OF MODERN AMERICAN AUTHORS *by Bernard Dekle*

READ JAPANESE TODAY *by Len Walsh*

SALMAGUNDI VIETNAM *by Don Pratt and Lee Blair*

SELF DEFENSE SIMPLIFIED IN PICTURES *by Don Hepler*

SHADOWINGS *by Lafcadio Hearn*

A SHORT SYNOPSIS OF THE MOST ESSENTIAL POINTS IN HAWAIIAN GRAMMAR *by W. D. Alexander*

THE STORY BAG: A Collection of Korean Folk Tales *by Kim So-un; translated by Setsu Higashi*

SUMI-E: An Introduction to Ink Painting *by Nanae Momiyama*

SUN-DIALS AND ROSES OF YESTERDAY *by Alice Morse Earle*

THE TEN FOOT SQUARE HUT AND TALES OF THE HEIKE: Being Two Thirteenth-century Japanese classics, the "Hojoki" and selections from the "Heike Monogatari" *translated by A. L. Sadler*

THIS SCORCHING EARTH *by Donald Richie*

TIMES-SQUARE SAMURAI or the Improbable Japanese Occupation of New York *by Robert B. Johnson and Billie Niles Chadbourne*

TO LIVE IN JAPAN *by Mary Lee O'Neal and Virginia Woodruff*

THE TOURIST AND THE REAL JAPAN *by Boye de Mente*